STAY COOL BABY! CAXTON CLUB, 1969

SCORCHA!
SKINS, SUEDES AND STYLE
FROM THE STREETS
1967 - 1973

OMNIBUS PRESS

London • New York • Paris • Sydney • Copenhagen • Berlin • Madrid • Tokyo

OMNIBUS PRESS

London • New York • Paris • Sydney • Copenhagen • Berlin • Madrid • Tokyo

Copyright © 2021 Omnibus Press
(A division of the Wise Music Group
14–15 Berners Street, London, W1T 3LJ)

Cover design and book artwork by Paul McEvoy Art Dept. Picture research by Paul Anderson.

ISBN 9781785584930

A catalogue record for this book is available from the British Library.

Printed in Slovenia.

www.omnibuspress.com

THE NEW RELIGION CONTINUES...

JIMMY JAMES & THE VAGABONDS, BIRDCAGE, PORTSMOUTH, 1966

SCORCHA!
CONTENTS

ACKNOWLEDGEMENTS

The authors would like to thank the following for their time, knowledge and insight. In no particular order…

Willy Deasy, Dave Foley, Jimmy West, Mickey Tenner, Carmen Gimenez, Cathy Roberts, Graham 'Cartz' Cartwright, John 'Pears' Perry, John 'Woody' Wood, Lesley Gould, Peter Gage, Mick Eve, Jeff Dexter, Brian Crane, Grahame Joyce, Chris Farlowe, Terry Smith, Dan Meaden, Barry Thane, Sandra Smith, Patricia Yilal, Damian Jones, Bill Sullivan, Paul Newman, Chris Casey, Roy Emberson, Charlie Taylor, Kenny Moran, The Junction Boys, Tony Ellis, Barry Quinnell, Tony Rounce, Raymond Potter, Becky Potter, Bill Fordham, Brian Wright, Tony Haddow, Bob Wheeler, Coleen Wheeler, John 'Bomber' Wild, Michael Holland, Ian Hingle, Clive Banks, Colin Staplehurst, Bonny Staplehurst, Laurence Cane-Honeysett, Caeisha St. Paul, Trojan Records, Mark Powell, Andrew Vaughan, Geoff Deane, Paul McEvoy, Nick Lowe, Greg Farmer, Norman Jay MBE, David Rosen, Stephen Dench, Jonathan Freedman, The lovely Sue and Big John at Brutus, Terry Reader, Douglas Hadgraft, Michael Mulligan, Big Steve Ellison, Bradley Hall, Jacky Abramovich, Alec the Cloth Man, Sharon Williams, Robert Elms, Barry Cain, John Brazil, Dean Coubrough, Gary Malby, Phillip Ellisdon, The Watford Skinheads, Lin Davidson (nee Howarth), Ray Butters, Penny Reel, Pete Schaffert, Austin Myers, Bob Brooks, Jean Brooks, Geraldine Choules, Bernard Jennings, Clive Knight, Lester Owers, Paul Owers, Lorraine Le-Bas, Mauro Antoniazzi, Chris Difford, Dave Edwards, Steve Ellis, Emperor Rosko, Frank Pitter, Jim Cameron, Alan Daly, Bryan Duffy, Dave Coleman, Sarah Coleman, Chris Burstin, Colin Brown, Lee Davies, David 'Dicky' Rogers, Gareth 'Gary' Ivins, Gary Horwell, Chris Bethell, Smut Smithson, Robert Russell, Matthew Wright. Kevin Johansen and Maggie Brown.

Special thanks to Paul Weller for inspiration and ideas, John Simons for the great clobber, and Suggs for the passion.

AUTHORS' PREFACE

It was probably around 1970 or 1971, I would have only been 5 or 6 years old and I was playing in the park just outside my parents' back gate. There was a whole group of us, of all ages. An older boy, Paul Harris, who was probably about 10 or 11, bent down and said to me, "Ask your Mum for some braces."
"Why?" I responded.
"Because Skinheads wear braces," he replied.
So, off I ran to see my mum, who was busy in the kitchen.
"Mum, can I have some braces please?"
"What an earth for?" she questioned.
"Because," I said knowingly, "Skinheads wear braces."
Her face looked puzzled. "What's a Skinhead?"
"Er… hold on, I'll just ask…"

I WOULD LIKE TO DEDICATE THIS BOOK TO THREE PEOPLE.

Keith Matthews

When I met Keith, I'd been DJing for nearly seven years and we just clicked. Together, we went on a musical journey that saw us side by side, behind a pair of record decks, on and off for the next twenty-eight years. I like to think we both educated each other in our love of black music, but in truth he influenced me far more than I did him. For that, as well as his love, laughs and friendship, I am forever thankful.

Martin Weller

I can still see the Cheshire cat smile of this big friendly bear. Martin's passion for reggae always dominated his conversations with me. His enthusiasm and knowledge for the music bordered on obsession. Constantly cheery and laughing, Martin would do anything for anyone, and was always offering to help when needed. Sadly, he leaves another vacant space behind a record deck which will never be filled.

Penny Reel

Born Peter Simons, Reel was an absolute champion of black music from R&B to Roots. He wrote and co-published, with Nick Kimberley, *Pressure Drop*, the first reggae fanzine. He contributed to many magazines, mainly on reggae, including *International Times*, *Black Echoes*, *NME*, *Sounds* and *Small Axe*, and they all benefitted from his knowledge. He also wrote a number of books, like *Deep Down With Dennis Brown*, using different pseudonyms. I was lucky enough to meet Peter and interview him a few times, the last occasion being for this book.

All three are no longer with us and the world is an emptier place without them.

PAUL 'SMILER' ANDERSON READING, BERKSHIRE, SPRING 2021

I can see them now. Three of the sharpest looking 'dressers' I have ever seen.

Ok, I was only 8 or 9, but boy, did they make an impression on my young impressionable mind.

Bright coloured mohair shone from them like the colours you'd see on a rainbow trout.

Shimmering.

One second there was green, the next blue.

They were simply cutting though my council estate in Peckham, southeast London on the way to who knows where. Around them were tens of kids playing football, run outs or British Bulldog.

But these three stopped all that. Just by walking and looking like that.

We stood and stared; admiring what was in front of us.

They were Suedeheads. Sharp and crisp and clean and hard.

When we were first kicking the idea of this book around a few years ago, I kept seeing these three in my mind's eye. They had simply never left the head space I had parked them in.

I still thank them daily for teaching me the importance of good clothes. It was a lesson I learnt that day. If they are going to stare, give them something to stare at.

I dedicate my work on this book to them, whoever they are/were. Cheers chaps.

MARK BAXTER CAMBERWELL, LONDON, SPRING 2021

FOREWORD BY SUGGS

Times... them

John Peel
God rest his soul, said he didn't hear
reggae till 1975
Because people like Eric Clapton,
String Driven Thing and co. said
it was simplistic, repetitive shit
(Until Clapton did that shit version of
'I Shot The Sheriff').
But the proper working class have
always gone under the radar
Singing and dancing to black music
from the word go.

Hippies don't dance.
I always remember my first contact
with puff.
People sitting 'round
listening to Pink Floyd
When I saw others saying let's get
charged, go out and dance.

June 1971
11 years old
I was deposited halfway through the
first term of secondary school at
Quintin Kynaston in Finchley Road.
A social experiment.
1,600 boys
Mostly second-generation Irish and
Jamaican
A swagger in their stride
Pride in their appearance.

I'd been living with my aunt in Wales
Due to the social services
And in Haverfordwest
Skinheads had just caught on.

Upon my return
I'd seen Suedehead.
A mere dot in social history
They say
But for me
Mind-blowing.
For possibly only one summer
A brief window between
Mod/Skin/Bootboy.

The last of the dedicated
working class aesthetic
Side-parting
Crombie
Red handkerchief
With ruby stud
Powder blue Sta-Prest
Tight fit
Tighten up
Smooths/Solatios/Gibsons
The occasional bowler hat
Sharpened umbrella
The last click of Blakeys
Rock Steady and then gone...

SUGGS, WINTER 2019

CHAPTER 1: WHEN WILLY MET JOHNNY

Beads of sweat formed on Johnny's forehead and ran down the side of his face as he waited anxiously to see if he'd reached his target. The sun continued to beat down, and the old man looked up and glared at Johnny, but soon returned his concentration to weighing another huge bundle of cigarette coupons.

Back in the 1960s, cigarette brands such as Kensitas and Embassy would give away coupons in each packet and, when saved in large amounts, they could be exchanged for items, in a similar manner to Green Shield Stamps. Johnny had his heart set on their top prize but it wasn't going to be easy, for two very simple reasons. The first was that the top prize needed 195,000 of the cards, and the second was that Johnny didn't even smoke. Never one to let a minor detail like that ruin an East End boy's ambition, he set about acquiring bundles of the coupons by buying them from people selling them in *Exchange & Mart* magazine and small ads. After a year collecting them, he prayed he'd got his figures right.

One afternoon he found himself, with his best friend Willy Deasy, in a van loaded down with bundle upon bundle of cigarette cards. As they stood by, watching the ageing official strictly weighing them, a sense of devilment overcame Deasy. He had noticed that every so often the elderly man would turn his back to stack the accounted-for bundles. What harm could it do, if timed right, to nip around, take a few of these and add them to the piles at the front waiting to be counted?

Willy worked his magic well. The old boy finally gave Johnny the good news that he had got the top prize he was craving: a brand new Mini Moke car. They'd even got enough for a new kettle and an electric alarm clock as well.

Soon Johnny could be seen zooming around the capital in his yellow open-topped jeep with bright red bumpers that looked like some mad Noddy car. From that day forth, John Joseph Rowley became known simply as Johnny Moke.

The two of them were partners in crime. 'Mokey', as he was affectionately known, was the quiet and sensible guvnor, and Willy was his faithful wingman who would arrange things and get them done. They'd come a long way from the night that they'd first met.

Willy Deasy was an Islington boy who had grown up never knowing his dad. He lived with his mum and sister and in truth was a bit of a loner. At the age of 16 he was working as a printer's apprentice on £6 10s a week. He'd started going out with a girl called Vivienne, and together they'd do the Sunday and Tuesday evening sessions at the Lyceum. When he and Vivienne parted company in 1962, he found himself accompanying an old school friend, Roy Stubbs, to a night out at the Tottenham Royal.

News went around fast that night, and the word was that Johnny Rowley was having a party back at his parents' house in Blackhorse Road, Walthamstow. Roy Stubbs was invited and asked if Willy could come too. At first the idea didn't go down well but Johnny relented. That evening he and Deasy just gelled and the pair became inseparable.

The Royal was at 415–419 High Road in Tottenham. It had originally opened as a roller-skating rink but quickly converted to an ice-skating rink. In 1925 it had become the Tottenham Palais De Dance. It was acquired by Mecca, who also owed the Lyceum and the Streatham Locarno, and renamed the Royal. Throughout the 1950s and 1960s, the Royal was definitely the place to be seen on a Thursday night.

At the Tottenham Royal, all the top faces stood on the right-hand side of the club. The left-hand side was where Ronnie and Reggie Kray drank, plus the usual club-goers, and the kids who fawned over the resident group. From January 1964, it was The Dave Clark Five. The bands, though, meant nothing to Willy and Johnny and their little firm, which included Kenny Hurst, Gypo, Billy Lampy, Frankie North, Ray Gaunt, Reggie Vincent, Terry Charles, Roy Stubbs and Mickey Butler. They were there to dance, have a laugh, check out clothes and more importantly, meet girls. "The Dave Clark Five may have been the resident band, and yeah, that Dave Clark was clever about money, but fuck off, we never listened to them," says Willy. None of the firm cared about drinking or

> "The Dave Clark Five may have been the resident band, and yeah, that Dave Clark was clever about money, but fuck off, we never listened to them."
> WILLY DEASY

mono

RLOPHONE

JEREMY GEIDT / JOHN FORTUNE / JOHN BIRD / ELEANOR BRON

THE ESTABLISHMENT
THE ESTABLISHMENT
THE ESTABLISHMENT
THE ESTABLISHMENT
THE ESTABLISHMENT
THE ESTABLISHMENT

> "Ralph, Jimmy and David took it all very seriously. They made a pact to have a wank before going out at night so they could remain aloof amongst birds, so they could stay cool."
> WILLY DEASY

smoking, although if you could score purple hearts or black bombers that would do very nicely, thank you. Willy didn't even realise that there was a bar on the other side of the dancehall until a long time later.

All the members of the firm were into clothes and they'd look up to the older and established faces at the Royal.

"Ralph Berenson, Jimmy West and David Foley. They were the top Mods at the Tottenham Royal and all in to tailoring," remembers Willy. "We loved their style of clothing. They were top dressers and really French-orientated. We went down Brick Lane one day and saw one of their firm dressed in a striped jumper, beret and a bike [probably John Llewellyn]. They used to go and watch French films in the West End but that just didn't turn me on. I loved the French clothes though. Newman's clothes were very expensive and Westaway & Westaway did really nice French jumpers. Ralph, Jimmy and David took it all very seriously. They made a pact to have a wank before going out at night so they could remain aloof amongst birds, so they could stay cool."

Although both Jimmy and Dave deny this, it does lend a bit of legend to their story. Willy and Johnny were now the new emerging faces on the scene. They were doing the rounds – the Royal, the Lyceum, Finsbury Park Majestic and, of course, later, the Scene.

Willy Deasy: "Clothes were important, but not everybody had loads of money. There was a guy called Lee Tribe from Grays in Essex. He always had pretty girlfriends and was always dead smart. He was the first guy I knew who came to the Tottenham Royal in a roll-neck cotton jumper. He wore different colours each week, pink, green, brown, etc. Later, we found out that he'd just bought a load of white ones and dyed them."

Willy was sporting a haircut courtesy of Bruno of Tottenham and a button-down shirt from Flash Harry's of Dalston Way, and of course was always on the lookout for new clobber.

"We used to go shoplifting on a Friday. French clothes shops mainly because the clothes were well made and they never suspected shoplifters," says Willy. "Westaway & Westaway in Holborn. I've gone in there one day, gone into the changing room, put on four jumpers and walked straight out. There was this little shop in Church Street, I've done the same type of thing in there, and the owner came over to me and asked, 'Why are you wearing three pairs of trousers?' I just told him that it's really cold out, and he just said, 'Yeah, it is a bit.'"

Then of course there was Cecil Gee's in Shaftesbury Avenue, which was easy pickings. "They used to do pork pie hats and macs. In the window they had this lovely suede trench coat, they had a male one and a female one. I noticed this window was open. There was this lift inside, and they had an old boy who operated it, so when his back was turned I got in the window and nicked them both. That coat was lovely, until somebody else stole it off me at a party!"

Clothes and music were the obsessions that mattered. Authenticity was key too.

Willy Deasy: "We went to Klooks Kleek and saw Howlin' Wolf.

There were seats behind us, five of 'em, all empty. So, we're sitting there and the lights go down and he's started singing. Suddenly, there's scuffling behind us and it was The Beatles and Brian Epstein coming in late. Five of the biggest stars around but I never rated them then. I hated The Rolling Stones and I hated The Beatles too, until they did 'Paperback Writer'. I saw the Stones at Eel Pie Island too. Crap! They were singing stuff like Arthur Alexander. Now, he was fucking brilliant!"

One of the clubs that most faces aspired to be seen in was the Establishment, which had opened at 18 Greek Street, Soho, in October 1961. It was founded by the comedian, Peter Cook and the writer and politician, Nicholas Luard. The venue was known for live jazz acts, and also allowed budding comedians and satirists to perform new material in a nightclub setting.

In his September 1962 *Town* article Michael Simmonds had written, "We've been to the Establishment a few times. You hang around outside and join on the end when a crowd's going in."

"Then you stand in the bar," said Peter Sugar, "among all the faces, as if you own the place and everyone looks at you and wonders who you are."

"They wonder if you're a playboy or something," added Mark Feld (later known as Marc Bolan).

The Establishment was very exclusive and it was hard to gain entry. One way to gain access to a club was to be known by the doorman, to be a face. But even when you did manage to get in, it was expensive, both to enter and to drink there. Dave Foley went in with a friend, bought a round of drinks and found all his money for that evening gone.

Willy Deasy had his own way of gaining entry to these types of club: "Me and Billy Lampy got in to the Establishment, great club. I used to like the 'walking backwards' trick, which is when you want to get in somewhere that you may not have money to get in to, or you wouldn't be allowed entry to anyway. First you check that the doorman is facing the other way, then you turn around and walk backwards up the stairs to the top. When the bouncer looks around, you are facing the wrong way, as if going out. They think you are going back down the stairs. You then look puzzled and enquire, 'Sorry, got lost. Which way to the toilets please?' We used to do all these little things, but that was one of my favourites."

What has all this got to do with Skinheads or Suedeheads? You may ask.

The answer is: EVERYTHING. The holy trinity for both Skinheads and Suedeheads was music, fashion and football. But the roots of those cultures lie in three other important elements:

1. the West Indian migration to the UK after the Second World War;

2. the emergence of the Soho faces that would lead to what are better known as 'Mods'; and

3. the interest in and spread of black American music, including rhythm & blues and soul throughout the UK, the chief pioneer being Guy Stevens.

There are lessons to be learnt. Let us begin...

On June 22nd, 1948, the HMT *Empire Windrush,* a former troopship, docked in Tilbury, Essex with around 800 passengers on board. The majority had made the journey from Jamaica, hoping to start a new life in Britain. The arrival of the ship marked the beginning of the mass immigration of West Indians to Britain that continued until the early 1970s.

As they walked down the gangplank, dressed in their finest clothes of wide-lapelled single- and double-breasted suits, colourful ties and wide-brimmed trilby hats, carrying battered suitcases with their names on, many were slightly taken aback by the appearance of normal working-class ticket collectors. This new land wasn't all top hats and tiaras after all.

From the mid-1950s, the number of arrivals jumped dramatically. The majority of migrants from the West Indies had been adult males to begin with, but gradually more women and children made the journey too as husbands longed to be reunited with their families.

On arrival, they would be asked their journey's end and whether they had an address to go to. Some would produce an air-mail letter from a relative or friend, where they could at least stay temporarily. Others arrived with just hope, and would have to be found rooms in Salvation Army hostels. Welfare officers from the London County Council, the Colonial Office or the Red Cross would quiz them, and they might be told that their destination was 'Sloobucks' (Slough, Buckinghamshire, even though it is actually in Berkshire) or 'Baldockerts' (Baldock, Hertfordshire).

The migrants came from the British West Indies, from various territories that belonged to the West Indies Federation, British Guiana and British Honduras. The main reason for the increase in migration to post-war Britain was the rapid growth in the population of Jamaica and other territories such as Trinidad, Tobago and British Guiana. Barbados was the most densely populated territory of the West Indies Federation, and the Barbados government granted loans to prospective migrants and helped with finding them employment and accommodation in Britain. The majority, though, came from Jamaica, the largest of the Caribbean islands. Natural disasters in these regions, such as flooding and hurricanes, caused mass unemployment. Poor wages and lack of opportunity had already caused many to seek work away from the islands to improve their lives.

America may have been seen as the Promised Land but it was not easily accessible owing to the 1952 McCarran–Walter Act governing immigration to the USA, which reduced the flow of West Indians there. So, Britain became the next obvious destination, especially as people were aware of the

country's need for post-war development. Stories had filtered back to the islands from some of the 8,000 West Indians who had helped defend Britain during the Second World War by serving in the Royal Air Force.

By their very upbringing they were British, and as such had a legal right to enter the United Kingdom freely, therefore West Indians were migrants and not immigrants. Most of these people, unlike other coloured migrants, spoke English as their main language. Their chosen religion was, in the main, Christian, and so Britain seemed an ideal destination.

The main employers of these island castaways, especially in London, were public transport, the post office and local authorities. It was commonplace to see them working in factories, on building sites and in the catering industry, in cafés, canteens and restaurants. Many men found jobs as porters and cleaners in London hospitals, while women took on nursing roles or became clerks or typists.

They settled in Kensington, Islington, Paddington, Hammersmith, Shepherd's Bush, Fulham, Lambeth, Wandsworth, Camberwell, Battersea, Hackney and Stepney; on the outskirts of London such as Willesden; and in areas of Essex, Surrey and Kent. Brixton, Stockwell, Maida Vale, Notting Hill and North Kensington all had a reasonably large population of West Indians.

In fact, Brixton had gained favour from the very first arrival, way back in 1948. The day after the arrival of the *Windrush*, on Wednesday, June 23rd, a representative group of forty Jamaicans were invited to take tea with the Mayor, in a room over the Astoria Cinema in Brixton. They had cake and refreshments with the Mayor, local officials and two MPs, and were treated to a free cinema show.

At the time, 242 West Indians were being temporarily housed in Clapham Junction Underground station. That evening, the lucky forty representatives told the others of their welcoming, and word went around that Brixton would be a good place to settle.

Middle-class and upper-class areas such as Chelsea, Mayfair and Westminster were out of reach for the newcomers. Instead, they had to find refuge in unfashionable, neglected areas of inner London that were near to their places of work. They lived in tall four- and five-storey houses built on main roads or near railways, often with damp basements, that had fallen into disrepair. The houses had broken roofs, plaster falling away, overgrown gardens and smashed windows; there would be a single toilet, kitchen and bathroom shared by everybody lodging there. Sometimes there was not even a gas supply. These were the types of accommodation on offer in places like Paddington and Notting Dale.

FACE THE FACTS

IF YOU DESIRE A **COLOURED** FOR YOUR NEIGHBOUR **VOTE LABOUR**

IF YOU ARE ALREADY BURDENED WITH ONE **VOTE TORY**

The Conservatives once in Office, will bring up to date the **Ministry of Repatriation,** to Speed up the return of home-going and expelled immigrants.

NO IRISH NO BLACKS NO DOGS.

They were usually subdivided for multiple occupation and owned by unscrupulous landlords such as Peter Rachman. The standard rate migrants paid for a room was £2 10s to £3 a week. Of course, if you could get five people to share a room, you could charge one pound a head, thus doubling the income for a single room. Thugs threatened violence to anybody daring to mention a visit to the Rent Tribunal.

In fact, because the West Indians regarded themselves as British they took more effort to understand the British than the British did to understand them. People took a dislike to their clothes and voices, especially as both were loud. They didn't like their music, their dancing, and their love of outdoor life. Some British white women found these qualities attractive, and because of this the West Indians were

OSWALD MOSLEY ATTACKED, AUGUST 1962

deemed competitive intruders by the men. It was the same mentality that the Americans had encountered here during the Second World War.

In 1948 there was trouble between whites and Indians in both Birmingham and Liverpool, and then a year later in Deptford Broadway. In the summer of 1954 there was trouble in Camden Town, involving bottles, axes and eventually petrol bombs.

The biggest incidents, however, came four years later. In August 1958 there were race riots in Nottingham which had come from a build-up of growing tension. Teddy Boys had been highlighted among the white offenders. It made the national newspapers, and in a press conference, the local Chief Constable was quoted as saying that "the coloured people behaved in an exemplary way by keeping out of the way". The blame was focused on "Teddy Boys and persons who had had a lot to drink".

Of course, all of this was only relevant if they could actually find somewhere to stay. In recent years there have been doubts as to whether the infamous 'No Irish, No blacks, No dogs' signs ever actually existed. What is definite is the fact that a certain number of people were prejudiced against the newcomers. While some were more than bold enough to write 'No coloured' on their advertisements offering rooms, others found ways to deliver the message indirectly. 'Europeans only' was a euphemism for white people. 'English only' was another, but was also used as a synonym for 'No Jews', and lines like 'Suit English Business lady' helped to cover a whole heap of racial prejudice.

At the same time there were even more violent outbursts in London. They had started in Shepherd's Bush and Notting Dale, then moved to Notting Hill, Kensal New Town, Maida Vale and Paddington. Again, Teddy Boys were in the frame, but this time there was also a wide variety of people, some motivated by local fascist groups. The far-right White Defence League and the Union Movement had held meetings and handed out leaflets. This was rioting on a large scale, which continued into September with sporadic incidents. Cries of "Keep Britain white!" and "Lynch him!" were among the cries echoing around these London streets. Weapons included bicycle chains, iron bars, leather belts, flick knives, choppers and petrol bombs.

The main days of the disturbances stretched from August 30th to September 4th, 1958. By the time they had stopped, around 140 people had been arrested. The majority were white; one in four were black. Of the white people, around 60 per cent were under 20 years of age.

Young hooligans, often referred to as Teddy Boys, were held responsible, although sections of the press were also accused of contributing to the situation by the sensationalist way they reported events, thus attracting even more troublemakers.

In September 1958, the Labour Party issued a statement on racial discrimination, condemning the recent occurrences. But it would take the murder of a 32-year-old West Indian carpenter named Kelso Cochrane, stabbed in Kensal New Town on May 17th, 1959, to change things. He was walking alone, when he was attacked by five or six white youths.

The newspapers, which had previously been heavily criticised for incitement, issued headlines such as 'Knives in Notting Hill' and 'Smash White Gangs'. This helped to put a spotlight on the organisations intent on stirring up colour prejudice, which included the National Labour Party, the White Defence League and Oswald Mosley's Union Movement.

Mosley prepared for the forthcoming General Election being held on October 8th, 1959. One of his first rally meetings was held in July on the corner of Southam Street and Golborne Road – the site on which Kelso Cochrane had been murdered. In North Kensington, the Labour Party candidate was re-elected with 43 per cent of the votes. Mosley's Union Movement gained 8 per cent. On a national scale, the Conservative Party, led by Harold Macmillan, entered their third consecutive term.

On July 31st, 1962, Mosley and members of his anti-Semitic blackshirt group arrived at Ridley Road, Dalston, to speak from the back of a lorry. As he walked through the crowd, the cries of "Down with Mosley!" were followed by action, and he was brought to the ground by a protester.

He was helped up, and two lines of policemen with linked arms kept the crowd at bay as Mosley climbed on the lorry to make his speech. His voice was drowned out by jeering, and he was met with a hail of missiles including stones, pennies and rotten fruit. Police stopped the meeting within three minutes and it was abandoned. The protesters, including members of the emerging Mod culture, had won the day.

Many of the West Indians still felt rejected by their adopted country. They found their own hangouts and their own clubs scattered around places like North Kensington, Paddington and the East End, members-only clubs with booming jukeboxes filled with calypso and ska. They sought refuge in each other's houses, cellars and basements, making a small

charge for the cost of the liquor and curried goat, with records fresh from Jamaica providing the soundtrack.

The white allies of these people were the young 'Modernists' (or Mods), who thought the whole Jamaican 'Rude Boy' style of stingy brim trilbies and narrow 'ankle swinger' socks looked cool, compared to the drab British demob look. Visiting black US servicemen also had a profound effect, as they brought goods from their stores to sell in the West End clubs, such as the Roaring Twenties in Carnaby Street, the Limbo in D'Arblay Mews or the Flamingo in Wardour Street. Records and items of clothing, along with pills, would influence some of the British kids who would make the style their own.

The whole essence of the beginnings of Mod may seem familiar, but many involved would not consider themselves as 'Mods'. As dear Carmen Gimenez stated while talking of her past: "All this 'Mod' shit. I've said this to Mickey Tenner before, 'What's all that about?' I don't get it, this insistence on a Mod thing. I've never got my head around it… Two people's version of the same thing can be so completely different from each other. I always say I was there, and I used to go to the Scene, Ronnie Scott's and so on, but what I read is such crap. I wasn't involved in any of that beach riot stuff. I thought it was a load of hooligans and I had no interest or sympathy for them… To me, it was clothes, food, music and dancing. All that other stuff, I didn't even notice it."

"I wasn't involved in any of that beach riot stuff. I thought it was a load of hooligans and I had no interest or sympathy for them… To me, it was clothes, food, music and dancing. All that other stuff, I didn't even notice it."
CARMEN GIMENEZ

CHAPTER 3 : SOHO FACES

> "Monk was featured in an edition of *Vogue* magazine before that *Town* article came out about 'faces' in '62. It was Brian who used Bilgorri of Bishopsgate. He was way ahead of Sugar and his mob. As for relating to Mark Feld et al. … it is like comparing Peter Crouch to Ronaldo."
>
> JIMMY WEST

Between 1945 and 1950 the average real wage of teenagers had increased at twice the adult rate, and so despite having mostly unskilled jobs, the Teddy Boys of the early 1950s were relatively affluent.

The Daily Sketch printed a piece on the origins of the Teddy Boy look on 14th November, 1953 which had originally appeared in *Tailor and Cutter*.

"Originally, the Edwardian suit was introduced in 1950 by a group of Savile Row tailors who were attempting to initiate a new style. It was addressed, primarily, to the young aristocratic men about town. Essentially the dress consisted of a long, narrow-lapelled, waisted jacket, narrow trouser (but without being 'drainpipes'), ordinary toe-capped shoes, and a fancy waistcoat. Shirts were white with cutaway collars and ties were tied with a 'Windsor' knot. Headwear, if worn, was a trilby. The essential changes from conventional dress were the cut of the jacket and the dandy waistcoat."

This style was being taken up by working-class youths by 1952. Later, additional modifications included 'beetle-crusher' crepe shoes, bootlace ties, drainpipe trousers, and less waisted jackets with bright satin collars. Soon more and more of the Edwardian style suits were turning up at second-hand markets because they were being discarded by the upper-class dandies, who distanced themselves from what they saw as the yob element.

In 1956, a 13-year-old Dave Foley joined Burley Secondary Modern in Tufnell Park, north London. At the time he was trying to find his own identity by denying his Irish roots and trying to be a proper Londoner. It was a time of rock 'n' roll, and when Dave was put in Class 2A he immediately noticed a classmate, Jimmy West. Jimmy was rock 'n' roll. He wore open-necked checked shirts so that the collars sat outside his jacket. Dave was impressed, as his own home life was very Irish and even television was frowned upon. He begged his parents for a radiogram, and was soon buying records by Elvis Presley, Little Richard and Fats Domino.

Jimmy's family life was different. His sister, Jean, adored Elvis. His dad, Bert, had a jazz collection in the front room, which he kept locked. Eventually, he let the two boys in the room, and through this they discovered Leadbelly, and there was the sudden realisation that Lonnie Donegan wasn't the real deal. The hunger for authentic blues began. Elvis was still adored, but the recognition that his influences were gospel and black music made him seem slightly phony. Once that all clicked, it would put them on the path to modern jazz.

By now Jimmy was sporting a black square-front jacket with one button and a white checked shirt with the collar out. Dave had a blue sports jacket with a white fleck in it. They were 14 years old, and in love with fashion.

1950s Soho was happening. From New Bond Street to New Oxford Street, from the Strand to Piccadilly Circus, everything was there for the taking. Old Compton Street, Wardour Street, Greek Street, Dean Street, Berwick Street, Shaftesbury Avenue, Charing Cross Road and St Martin's Lane were full of vibrant cafés, clubs, clothes shops, at least a dozen record shops and a whole world of sleaze in the form of porn shops, strip clubs and 'near beer' joints enticing naive young things into their bosom.

Soho's community foundations had been built in the 1930s by various bohemians of the art and literary worlds. But in the 1950s, the emphasis moved away from literature to music.

The decade would see a massive boost in the popularity of coffee houses, with the Moka at 29 Frith Street being the first espresso bar to open in London, in 1953. Soon they became the late-night meeting places for young people as they didn't need alcohol licensing laws.

There was the House of Sam Widges on the corner of Berwick Street and D'Arblay Street, which had originally started out life as a pub. Le Macabre at 23 Meard Street used coffins as tables; it had white painted skeletons on the black walls, skull ashtrays and a Wurlitzer jukebox, where, for 6d, you could play a funeral march.

The 2i's Coffee Bar was at 59 Old Compton Street. The name of the 2i's derived from earlier owners, Freddie and Sammy Irani, who ran the venue until 1955. It was then taken over by Paul Lincoln and Ray Hunter. They opened it as a coffee bar on 22nd April, 1956. In July 1956, a skiffle band called Wally Whyton & The Vipers popped into the bar for a coffee during the Soho Fair and decided to play a few numbers. The Vipers soon gained a residency there, and one evening a guest vocalist, Tommy Hicks (later to be known as Tommy Steele), was spotted; he became the first British rock star. Soon afterwards it became a focal point for rock 'n' roll enthusiasts and the most famous music venue in England at that time.

Next to the 2i's at 57 Old Compton Street was the Heaven & Hell Coffee Lounge, which opened in early 1956, run by Eric Lindsay and Ray Jackson. 'Heaven' was the brightly lit, white-painted ground-floor coffee bar and 'Hell' was a darker, atmospheric basement room sparsely lit by red-eyed devil masks along the walls.

There were of course many more, including the Freight Train, the Zodiac, Act One Scene 1 and Bar Italia.

Soho had become Dave and Jimmy's playground. There was a musical melting pot: rock 'n' roll, skiffle, trad jazz, blues, modern jazz and pop music, but mainly American pop music.

Jimmy West: "We loved all music, but we were more into jazz. Anything that was watered down didn't cut it. I've been a member of Ronnie Scott's club since I was 18. We were definitely into the British stuff too though, like Tubby Hayes." There were record-shopping trips to Dobell's at 77 Charing

Cross Road, or Collett's, Imhof's, and a stall at The Cut in Waterloo on Saturday mornings. These were the places for the 'platters that matter'. They checked out the names, such as Gigi Bryce, Shirley Scott, Eddie 'Lockjaw' Davis, Richard Groove Holmes, then on to Charlie Mingus, Duke Ellington, Miles Davis and Oliver Nelson, and studied Blue Note jazz album covers.

In the 1957 autumn edition of *Man About Town* magazine it was noted that: "Basis for the fashion trend among the lads at the end of the street is the Italianate influences of extremely short, top-heavy jackets, wide widely draped shoulders, very rounded jacket fronts, at least three buttons probably fastened on the top one, and a narrow turn-up-less trouser which uses an interior stiffening inside the lower part of the trouser and gives the effect of a plain deep cuff. The effect is of a peg top jacket – heavy across the shoulders and gathered in fittingly around the hips."

Then it goes on to mention "those sharply pointed, apparently weltless slippers which the retail shoe shops assure us are 'Made in Italy', and which it seems like you'd have to have a toe amputated to get into."

In 1959 Jimmy West and Peter Brown started to learn tailoring by working for three Polish Jewish brothers in Kingly Court, Carnaby Street. Dave Foley worked for a couple of months as a messenger for the *Daily Sketch*, until he joined Jimmy as an apprentice tailor. There were about twenty tailors working at the industrial unit. The first thing Dave noticed was that his wages had gone from £4 a week working as a messenger, to £3 10s. Luckily Dave fell in love with tailoring straight away.

Dave reflects: "All the apprentices with the black cloth bags under their arms, all crossing the road from that side of Regent Street to the other side, where all the shops were. All the workers and makers were on the opposite side and all the top shops that would be buying sat across from them. We'd be making for Thresher and Glenny, Hope Brothers, Horne Brothers, Burberry's and Aquascutum. We did theatre stuff for Burman's and Nathan Williams. We'd have to go in the back entrance of Burberry's in Orange Street, go through the bowels of the building and come up into the shop with the jackets that the Brown Brothers had made. They used to make fifty jackets a week, fifty-five coats a week."

As 1960 dawned in Britain, Emile Ford was at number one with 'What Do You Want To Make Those Eyes At Me For?' Sharing the top twenty with him were Americans such as Neil Sedaka with 'Oh Carol' and Bobby Darin with 'Mack The Knife'. British entries were Adam Faith with 'What Do You Want?', 'Little White Bull' by Tommy Steele and 'Bad Boy' by Marty Wilde.

Around this time, the boys hooked up with a guy called Laurie Allan who was a budding jazz drummer, known as 'Lol'.

It wasn't only formal attire that interested the boys. Casual American wear was another big factor in clothes to be seen in. Jimmy West discloses: "Levi 501s were unheard of. We knew a guy who was a merchant seaman. He looked like a dream. He had a white T-shirt on and these jeans that we'd never seen before, original 1937 501s. The next trip he goes on, he gets me, Dave and Laurie Allan these Levis."

Earning a living at Brown Brothers influenced them in other ways. "Working amongst the Brown Brothers tailors, we found they were communists," says Dave. "For me, that was another education. I learnt more there, hearing stories of the East End, Mosley and the blackshirts, rolling the marbles under the feet of police horses, and all that. By then I'd got in to communism. We never had any problems with gay or black people. A bit later on, we'd go over to parties in Kilburn, and there would be Africans with all their tribal gear on. We'd take all our little firm with us, crates of beer, and never had any trouble. We weren't like the locals who would still stay there and moan about black people. That was our contemporaries. It was as if we'd left them behind, and we travelled, even if not geographically that far, mentally."

During this period there were plenty of people who were well-known names around Camden Town and Holloway for being hard cases, such as the Phillips brothers. There was no shortage around Holloway either, with families such as the Flannigans, the Ball brothers and local boxer Dixie Dean.

It wasn't only being hard that earned you local celebrity status. One person known around Camden was Brian Monk. Monk had gained a reputation as a stylish dresser. He'd adopted designs in his suits that were heavily influenced by Italian and French styles. He was small in stature, but had neat dark hair, beautiful teeth and a head full of witty putdowns; it was enough to make him stand out from the crowd and be a pioneer in the new look.

In September 1962, *Town* magazine featured an article on three clothes-obsessed boys: Peter Sugar, Michael Simmonds and Mark Feld (later known as Bolan).

Jimmy West smiles as he recalls: "Monk was featured in an edition of *Vogue* magazine before that *Town* article came out about 'faces' in '62. It was Brian who used Bilgorri of Bishopsgate. He was way ahead of Sugar and his mob. As for relating to Mark Feld et al. … it is like comparing Peter Crouch to Ronaldo. Brian always claimed that he made Bilgorri vow to keep whatever he was making for him under lock and key, and only had private fittings. One time in Turnbull and Asser the assistant said, 'This one is very nice, sir.' Brian replied, 'All the more reason I don't want it.' When the interviewer at *Vogue* enquired, 'Are you a Modernist?' Monk replied 'No, I'm a plumber.'"

Dave Foley: "We knew Monk because he was local to us. I think it must have been later at the Scene in '63 we met Monk and got very friendly with him, and we used to go to parties and all sorts with him. We knew of Peter Sugar and Brian Monk before that though, because they were known in the area, they were local characters. I didn't really know Sugar. I'd seen him around but because of that thing with Monk, we wouldn't associate."

While Dave was learning the art of tailoring, he would often find himself at Alfred Kemp's in Mornington Crescent, near Camden. This was a great source of second-hand clobber that he could alter himself. When he got his first suit made it was at Charkham's in Oxford Street. It was a navy blue with a fleck in it, and he had the continental styling by having round shoulders. It cost £30 on the knock, and he had to pay

"We never had any problems with gay or black people. A bit later on, we'd go over to parties in Kilburn, and there would be Africans with all their tribal gear on. We'd take all our little firm with us, crates of beer, and never had any trouble. We weren't like the locals who would still stay there and moan about black people."
DAVE FOLEY

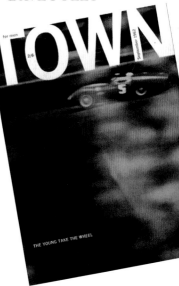

TUBBY HAYES QUINTET, OUTSIDE RONNIE SCOTT'S CLUB,
GERRARD STREET, LONDON, FEBRUARY 1964

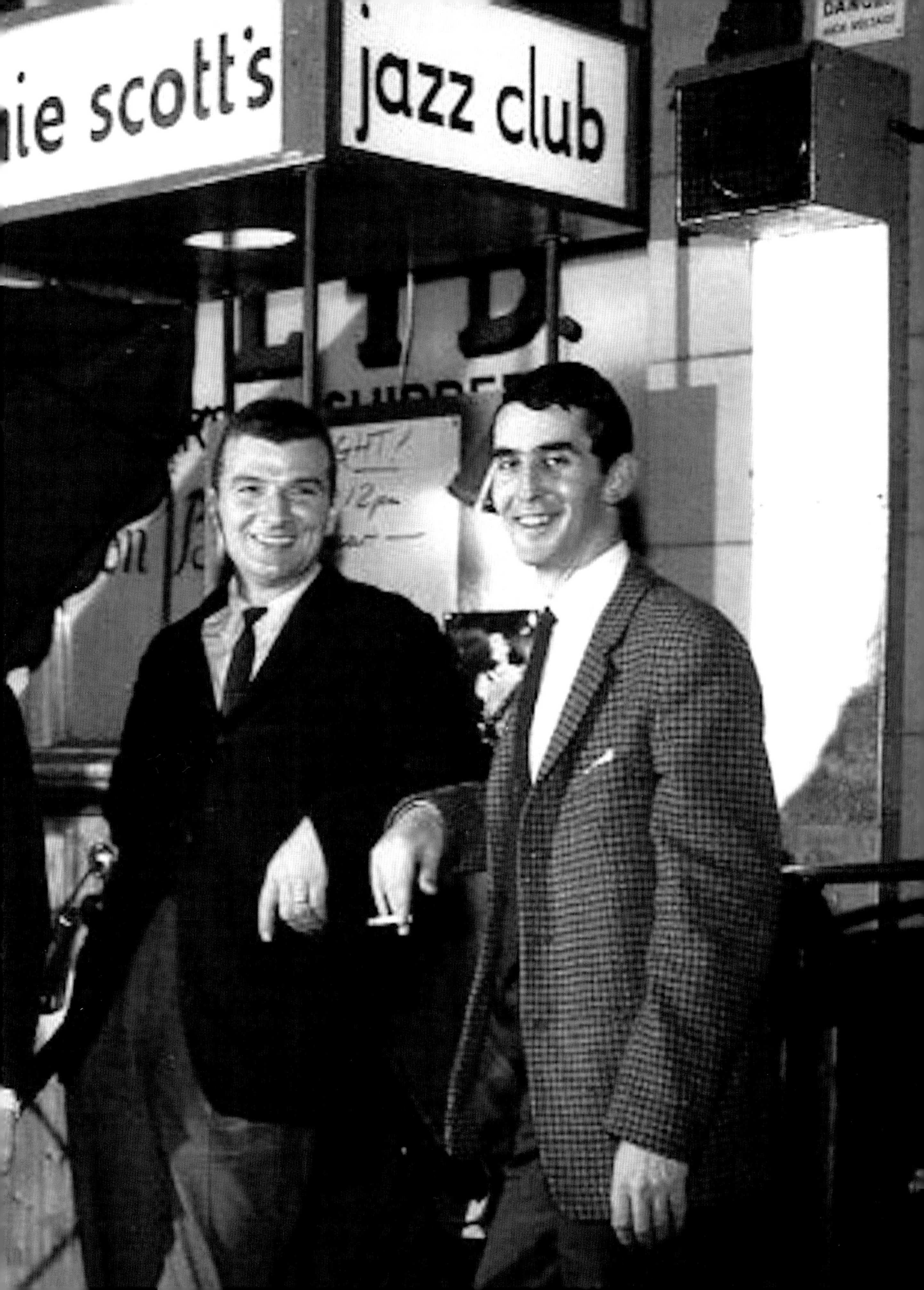
nie scott's
jazz club

"There was a jokey kind of saying at the time which referred to the Lyceum. People would say, 'When Curly hits the floor, everybody hits the floor.' Which meant nobody in that group would dance until Curly started dancing. He was no influence on us other than putting us on the firm at La Discotheque and later at Ronnie and Reggie's Esmeralda's Barn."
JIMMY WEST

for it weekly because out of his £3 10s, his mum wanted £1 10s for his keep. When Dave finally started work on his own suit, it was a two-button black mohair number with side vents. "I guess you could say that we were Modernists who danced the French Modern Jive," says Dave Foley. "It was slicker, it wasn't bouncy … more like ballroom dancing. The whole thing was to be slick and smooth. That's why we didn't like trad, which was bouncy dancing. That was a no-no."

The big dancehalls at the time such as the Lyceum were the place to show off the moves, full of teenagers high on testosterone. Willy Deasy from Islington remembers the friction: "One evening at the Lyceum, in the early days, there was a big fight between the north London and the south London [boys]. I saw this big guy hitting a young kid. I picked up a chair and whacked him on the back, but he just stood there, turned around and screamed, 'I'm going to kill you!' I thought to myself, fuck, he could do as well. I shot down the back of the Lyceum. Moke shouted for me to stand by the door; as the bloke came for me, Moke slammed this big heavy door in his face. We heard a scream, so Mokey and me ran outside and jumped on a bus at the Strand. When we finally looked up, we were in south London because we'd got

on the wrong bus. It was very territorial, especially north London and south London. I was an Islington boy, we got on with the east London [boys] and basically anywhere that ain't got a bridge in it. South London was Geronimo country!"

It wouldn't be long before these Modernists would look for alternative places to go. Dave Foley soon found the answer: "There was Tony Allen, a tailor at Marshall Street, top floor, right next to the swimming baths, and he told us about La Discotheque." La Discotheque was a small club above the Latin Quarter in Wardour Street that featured American rhythm & blues as its soundtrack.

'Curly' King was known around Soho. He'd earned a name as a bit of a thug and carried a fearsome reputation. He was a known associate of the Kray twins, and was often present at many of the clubs around this time. Jimmy and Dave became friends with King, and he and his friends would prove to be helpful allies.

"There was a jokey kind of saying at the time which referred to the Lyceum. People would say, 'When Curly hits the floor, everybody hits the floor.' Which meant nobody in that group would dance until Curly started dancing. He was no influence on us other than putting us on the firm at La Discotheque and later at Ronnie and Reggie's Esmeralda's Barn."

While others queued up for tickets and attempted to get past the notorious doorman at La Discotheque, Jimmy and Dave would saunter past with ease.

Dave Foley: "A 'Ticket' was a mug, a wally. It's what we called people who weren't hip. They were underlings. The whole thing was to get in without paying. Not that you didn't want to pay, and there were times when we never had the money anyway, but you wanted to be recognised by the people on the door, and then, bosh, you're inside. It was referred to as 'being on the firm', it was all part of the kudos.

"On entrance, Bert Assirati used to sit at the top of the stairs. If he didn't like you, you never got in, but if he liked you, he gave you an apple. That was the first place we heard Chubby Checker. A French bird came over to Lol and me and said, 'Le Twist?' Lol was sort of, 'Alright, darling,' and that was the first time we physically saw the Twist dance. I remember that Ray Nash was the worst conga player ever. They'd have a live band sometimes, and while the gig was going on, Nash would insist on playing with them but he couldn't play."

ESMERALDA'S BAR

50, Wilton Place,
Knightsbridge,
London, S.W.1.

Carmen Gimenez was a social butterfly in the West End and La Discotheque was one of the many places she would venture in to. "I met Ronan [O'Rahilly] when he was working at La Discotheque doing PR," says Carmen. "It was quite a large room, and on the right-hand side, the stage was at the end, that's where people danced. When you walked in, there was a kind of a hall with mattresses on the floor, and then a couple of steps up to the bar. It was kind of L-shaped. Up on the top floor was the casino. The cloakroom was on the first floor, and that's where we used to buy our purple hearts, by the hundreds! It was one of the croupier's wives that used to get them for us. I often ask Percy [Raines] how we survived all this. So many memories are blocked out … well because we were so blocked!"

Willy Deasy: "I was a bit of a loner until I had the mob to hang around with. I went to La Discotheque. They had two big mattresses on the floor so that if you were dancing you could cool down on them. It was very dark in there, so there was some heavy petting on them. One day somebody told the *News of the World*, and then the mattresses were gone."

It was during 1962 that Jimmy West, Dave Foley and Laurie Allan would be drinking around east London, especially in the Whitechapel Road, in the Blind Beggar at number 337, the Grave Maurice at number 269 and the London Hospital Tavern at number 176, which was run by twin brothers Brian and Kenny Bird. This was the Kray twins' territory, and they were a common sight in this trio of pubs. "We kind of skirted that criminal thing without realising what we were involved in. Curly King was a thug but when you got inside him, he was something different. He had a real presence, but when you knew him, he was sweet as a nut really. There was another guy called Roy McQueen who was an underling of his, who was kind of on his way up to being Curly King, again an East Ender," says Foley.

Carmen Gimenez: "As for Jimmy, Dave and Lol – I don't remember thinking of them as Mods. They were so well dressed, Italian-looking beautiful tailored clothes, because, of course, they made their own. Their shoes were highly polished. I mean they were immaculate. They used to go to East End pubs, they liked that little bit of naughtiness."

Curly King was both menacing and charismatic, and when he told them about a club that would draw the trio even closer to the underworld, they couldn't resist. Esmeralda's Barn was a nightclub at the Knightsbridge end of Wilton Place, next to Joan's Kitchen, that was owned by the Kray twins from 1960. They acquired Esmeralda's Barn as a result of landlord Peter Rachman trying to avoid paying the twins protection money; eventually, he offered it to them for a tiny amount of what it was actually worth. There was a discotheque in the basement with gambling tables upstairs that attracted regular visitors such as the artists Francis Bacon and Lucian Freud. The manager was Laurie O'Leary and sometimes Curly greeted members at the entrance. This became a regular haunt of the trio.

John Llewellyn, aka 'Laurie', was a friend of Lol's from school. He had his suits made at Lyon's the tailors in Kentish Town Road, and was a fan of the whole continental look.

"Jimmy, Lol and a guy called Lenny Gollop would go with me to Margate or Eastbourne and camp out. We'd find out all the

language school clubs where the foreign students would go," says Dave. "Me and Laurie also used to go to Hanover Square where there was a coffee bar where all the foreign students went. We'd go there and mingle because we wanted more than just London dames. We didn't like the 'Oo the fuck do you fink I am?' stuff. We didn't need that, we wanted a Bardot or a Swedish type of girl."

Dave and Laurie often went to see continental movies at one of the Classic Repertory Cinemas. Lol and Jimmy weren't as keen, especially as Jimmy loved American movies. Jimmy had little time for British cinema; he was completely Americanised. This, added to the underworld leanings, would lead to yet another phase.

Dave Foley: "I remember being on the back of Jimmy's Lambretta scooter a few times, but I always wanted four wheels. I passed my test as soon as I could. I bought myself a 1939 Ford V8, Pre-Ford Pilot, for £45 from a mechanic in Albany Street. Pointed front, running boards and a flat front windscreen. Lol had already bought a Mercedes from the same bloke. It was a 1937 staff car that the German officers had used during the war. We used to pull up outside this caff in Somers Town and get out of these motors. Lol bought a shoulder holster, and even tried to buy a gun. He couldn't get one, so he gave me the holster and I bought an air pistol. That idea came from us watching Belmondo in *Breathless*, where he played a free-flowing gangster. A couple of years later there was *The Decadent Influence,* which was another French movie where these two guys and a girl decide that they want to be gangsters. We also watched American gangster films.

"Around this period I had an off-white suit, because I'd made it myself. Men didn't go around with clobber like that much, back then. I used to get wolf-whistled at just for wearing a pair of white trousers down Kentish Town high street."

Carmen Gimenez says fondly: "We used to go to Ronnie Scott's a lot because by now I was going out with Georgie (Fame) and Georgie loved it, because he adored jazz. We'd go to the Roaring Twenties a lot to see Count Suckle. I loved it down there! Black bean stew, man. They had a cafeteria there with great food. The ladies of the night that worked in all the clubs like the Astor and stuff used to go down there. All the Jamaicans leaping about. My first date with Georgie was down there, and I nearly passed out because it was such a shock to me at the time, seeing all these black people leaping around. Going from La Discotheque to there was a huge leap. The black GIs at the Flamingo were bloody good looking, tall and beautifully dressed. They used to give Georgie albums and stuff that they got from the PX stores. He was like their little white soul baby. You'd walk into the Roaring Twenties, and it was full of Notting Hill Jamaicans, very different. It never felt dangerous – in fact it probably felt more dangerous at the Flamingo, if I think about it. The records down there, like Prince Buster and all the things I hadn't heard before, were just amazing. The music at the Flamingo was different, it was things like Jimmy Smith and Mose Allison. If you went into the Roaring Twenties, it was all bluebeat. It was very different, loose, and it was fun. I always remember Zoot Money's wife, Scotch Ronnie, down there dancing like crazy. She was amazing. Later, I used to go to

Hey, let's Twist!

THE BASIC STEP

The basic motion of 'The Twist' is a hip swivel. Imagine you are holding an outstretched bath towel; get the towel going back and forth and you will have 'The Twist' hip motion. *The Basic Step and Foot Position:* Place right foot back, toe pointing to the right, weight transferred on to this foot and remaining there for the following eight beats or movements. *Commence Twist as follows:* Keeping the knees towards each other, on count of one, swivel right foot to the left, left hip turning to the left. On the count of two, swivel right foot to the right, hip twisting to the right. Repeat this movement six more times, to complete basic figure. Keeping foot positions as above, transfer weight on to left foot and repeat 'Twist' for eight more counts, and all these counts are 'quicks' through the whole of that figure.

THE BOWLING STEP

Same as basic movement but lowering through knees as shown in illustration.

THE FIGHT STEP

Using four twist movements to transfer weight on to left foot. Lift right foot on five. Turning slightly left on six placing right foot forward on seven twist half turn to left on eight. (As in illustration). Ending with right foot back weight placed over it left foot pointing forward without weight. Repeat once more. When lifting foot on the 5th count use hands as in "boxing" up to 8th count.

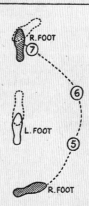

THE CHOO CHOO TRAIN

Footwork same as basic figure using arms as in train movement — left arm moving forward as right hip moves back, lowering through knees (as in sketch).

THE OVERSWAY AND REVERSE OVERSWAY

Footwork as in basic figure, weight on right foot, commence swaying back after four basic movements, using four more beats to achieve forward position. *The Reverse Oversway:* (See illustration) Footwork as in basic figure but with weight on left foot. Commence swaying forward after four basic movements, using four more beats to achieve forward position.

THE BACKSCRATCHER

With weight on right foot — left foot pointing to side dance four twist basic movements. Transfer weight on to left foot on five count lifting right foot for six and seven commencing to turn left — step forward on right foot turning left to back partner.

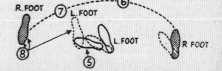

 **Beverly**  **Boysie Grant**  **Ezz Reco**  **Millie**

BLUE BEAT BREAKS THROUGH

NO one knows for certain where it came from. But millions know where it is today—high in the hit parade. Blue Beat seems to have arrived, and in more ways than one.

Jamaican songstress Millie flashed into the top ten with her bright, acy "My boy Lollipop". London group, the Migil Five are fast climbing chart with a BB version of "Mockingbird hill". Other record companies either signed or are interested in signing Blue Beat stars of tomorrow.

The giant Mecca ballroom chain has officially recognised Blue Beat and are uraging their bands to feature it all over the country.

by CHRIS ROBERTS

d the man who, two hs ago, predicted the rent boom—Blue Beat Siggy Jackson—says music is now spreading gly in the Midlands, chester, Liverpool, s and the North in ral, and various other of the country.

here must be more Blue clubs opening in the ry at the moment, for any other kind of c," he said.

s a promoter, I can tell that all the big do's— Leeds and Cheltenham ersity dances—who are ng for something dif- , are all going for Beat.

ITIONS

have at least some- like 25 Blue Beat acts r contract."

Where were all the e beaters going to ne from if the music came really big?

Vell, they don't all have e coloured. It is very ult to find all-coloured g bands around. I know e tried.

ut if you find a young that instead of devot- their attention to the and pop stuff, start ng Blue Beat, they can ne really great.

think you would find if a name group hed to playing Blue they wouldn't go down ell."

ggy added that he was giving auditions to groups all the time— an't afford to let any- slip by me," he said.

Among his catches is a

packing 'em in at Rich- mond Community Centre (birthplace of the Rolling Stones) every week.

"Most people in the bus- iness think they can easily play Blue Beat, but they can't. Their version is far from the way it should be.

"Mind you, it has many facets. Some people play it with a jazz idiom, others in a more commercial way."

Blue Beat — live — has already appeared on the West End club front—on Tuesday nights at the Marquee Club, and now on Thursday nights at the Flamingo Club, home of Georgie Fame and the Blue Flames.

They have used Blue Beat in their act for many months, and, in fact, have a special Blue Beat EP released by Columbia in the near future.

AUDIENCES

Owner of the Flamingo, Rik Gunnell, had felt an increas- ing need to provide a special music for the large coloured element in his regular audi- ences.

"Let's be fair—they have their own music. They dig it, as well as the R&B they come to hear. So why shouldn't we make a big thing out of Blue Beat for them."

He set up the first Blue Beat night at the club last week with Millie as the star —and was staggered by results.

"It was the biggest crowd we've ever had in there. Jam- packed. I tell you—Blue Beat is definitely here to stay on Thursdays, and possibly an- other night in the week, too."

The names you see and hear

the music — Syko and the Caribs, Ruddy and Sketto, the Exotics, Duke Vin and his Sound System, Brigette Bond, Mickey Finn, the Challengers, Earl Aitken, Boysie Grant, Beverly, and many others.

AUTHENTIC

Before any craze can sweep the country, it has to have some sort of national promotion. Which is where Mecca Ballrooms come in.

Their official recognition of the music and the dance, might be the turning point in Blue Beat's story.

"We have had Blue Beat going for us for a long time— a few months—played by Jeff Rowena," said Eric Morley, assistant director and promo- tions organiser.

"And I remember Ambrose at the Cafe Royal playing a form of it ten or twelve years ago, although no one knew what it was at the time.

"We have generally been right with trends in the past, and we now think that dan- cers are getting a little fed up of the beat stuff — the trend is going away from it.

"Mecca basically try to give the public what it wants.

And one of the happiest men behind the Blue Beat scene is Chris Blackwell, boss of Island Records, and one of the pioneers in the field, with many authentic artists on his books.

A few weeks ago he was worried about having no artists at all—major record companies were after them.

But we'll have to wait a few months before we see whether Blue Beat is break- ing out in spots—or all over.

London group the Migil Five are rapidly climbing the chart with a Blue Beat version of "Mockingbird Hill".

hmond and Dolphy — also scored a tremen- success at the 1961

tion lies in the blues and spirituals.

The musicians know each other's styles, and work in perfect harmony. "Medita-

for a stomach operation.

He has now recovered, and played with the group on their second French date at Marseilles on Monday.

> " What I fell in love with, with tailoring, was the thought that I can be wearing something that no one else has got. That was Monk's thing too. Everybody wanted to know what his next suit would be like. He'd always warn them off and tell them, 'It's at Bilgorri's under lock and key.' You'd never get to copy his suit."
>
> DAVE FOLEY

Klooks Kleek every week without fail. It had a fantastic atmosphere. I was going to the R&B sessions with acts like Graham Bond."

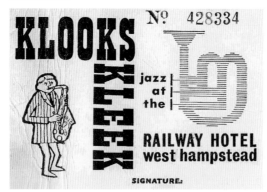

Dave Foley: "In Klooks Kleek, Jimmy and me often found ourselves in a bit of a bind because there would be a little firm here and a little firm over there. You know, little firms that didn't necessarily like each other very much, but because we made their suits, we'd have to entertain one lot for a while and then move on to another. Once we'd got to know Dick Jordan, which was made easier because we made suits for him and his business partner Geoff Williams, we didn't have to pay to get in because he made us honorary members. We'd go up the back stairs. Everybody else would be queuing up to get in, and we'd go in where the band went in. The bouncers used to hate it. Once they tried to throw me out. It was this bouncer called Bluebeard. I shouted, 'Get this monkey off my back!' and Dick came up and put him in his place."

Carmen Gimenez: "I remember coming out of the Flamingo on a Sunday at 5.30 in the morning, having spent Saturday night there, and sitting on the corner of Gerrard Street with a bag of chips, because we had to wait for the first tube home. The tubes ran later on a Sunday, so you couldn't get back anywhere. We used to take the speed to stay awake for days. We used to go to all the clubs, one after the other. There was the Scene, the Marquee, La Discotheque, the all-nighter at the Flamingo that started at midnight. Oh my God. I wasn't into the Lyceum and all of that though, and neither was Georgie. That wasn't my scene at all. We didn't like the ballrooms much as they were kind of poncy dress-up. I hated it. In the early sixties I was into Foale and Tuffin, Ossie Clark, then on to Chelsea Antique Market after that. Brian Jones [of The Rolling Stones] introduced me to that. We used to congregate on the roof of the café, it was great."

It was during 1963 that Jimmy, Dave and Lol got to know Ralph Berenson, who called himself Ralph Crawford. He was always the life and soul of the party, he'd do impressions and mimic accents. He could keep everyone entertained, so naturally he became a regular member of their clique.

"Ralph Berenson always carried import albums under his arm. That was his statement, as if to say, 'Look what I've fucking got, that you don't even know about,'" remembers Terry Smith.

In his autobiography Eric Clapton says: "A club I used to hang out in was the Scene in Great Windmill Street. I used to

watch, and finally made friends with, a small group of guys who hung out there and had a big influence on how I wanted to look at the time. They wore a hybrid of American Ivy League and the Italian look, as personified by Marcello Mastroianni; on one day they might be wearing sweatshirts with baggy trousers and loafers, on another maybe linen suits. They were an interesting bunch because they seemed to be miles ahead of anyone else in terms of style. I found them fascinating. They were all from the East End; there was Laurie Allan, a jazz drummer, Jimmy West and Dave Foley, who were tailors, and Ralph Berenson, a natural comedian and mimic."

Dave Foley: "One night, Lol, Ralph and myself were stood outside the Flamingo, around 4 a.m. in the morning. This girl called Alfie asked us for a cigarette, and we started chatting. Lol ended up going out with her for a while. She told us about this friend she knew who'd just left college, and was a bit timid, so she asked us to look after him. One evening she brought him down the Scene and introduced him as Eric Clapton. He's 17 and we're 19."

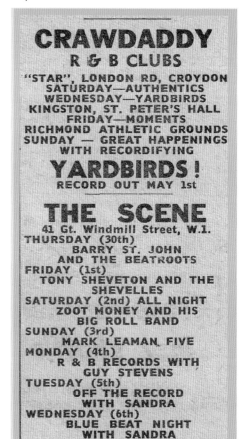

In 1963, the Scene Club in Ham Yard became the place to be– especially on a Monday night, when Guy Stevens, the man with the best record collection in the land, DJed.

Carmen Gimenez: "Originally, I was going out with Ronan O'Rahilly, and it was because of him I met and ended up going out with Georgie [Fame]. When the Scene had its opening night, I was there."

"We never paid to get in the Scene," says Foley, "because that was another thing about being 'on the firm'. We got in because we'd met Carmen, and she knew Ronan O' Rahilly. I was on the firm because I knew someone who knew someone. We wouldn't go with guests who had to pay. I took a few purple hearts, rabbit all night and drink gallons of water. That's why we used to stand by the toilets, there was a tap in there. Soft drinks at the bar, any money I had would go on drink. We were never pill-heads though, we'd only take a few."

Dave Foley: "The Jamaicans and the Africans generally liked the Roaring Twenties. The Flamingo would be Americans and Jamaicans, possibly Africans, because you had a lot of British jazz players such as Shake Keane that were African. We'd sometimes get to the Scene at eleven o'clock and there'd be no one there. We went there before Guy did it, and a girl called Sandra played the records, she was a mate of Carmen's. Ralph used to bring his own records, and she'd put them on. I used to dance to Nina Simone's 'Exactly Like You' with the big piano solo, and things like Charlie Mingus's 'Hog Callin' Blues'."

Carmen Gimenez: "There was Ralph Berenson, James West and Dave Foley. Those three were fantastically dressed. They'd have immaculate trench coats. They wore these wonderful gaberdine straight-legged trousers and lace-up shoes like the Americans wore. As for dancing, they were better than good. They'd do that slow block move, where they'd dance with their feet, but there was no waving of arms. They were great at dancing to jazz, sliding around the floor. They were very cool, and when I say cool, I mean very, very cool! They were always in one place at the Scene, as you came in, on the left by the wall. It's funny but years before, when it was Cy Laurie's, there was a group of guys there. One was called Andre, another was called Mick Delaney, and my God, they were smooth too. This was the days of jive, and could they jive! Cy Laurie's was amazing in those days, and everyone was real, cool jiving, slick twists and lots of foot movement, which was beautiful."

Brian Monk was a Scene Club regular too and would join the little firm congregated on the left-hand side.

Dave Foley: "Brian Monk had a friend called Tony Campbell. They had done National Service together in Cyprus, because they were at least two years older. He seemed to stop hanging around with Tony and joined our mob. He was a kind of local celebrity because of his clothing. I guess Jimmy and I were kind of Monk disciples. That's why we'd never talk to someone like Peter Sugar because there was a kind of loyalty, especially when he came on our firm. What I fell in love with, with tailoring, was the thought that I can be wearing something that no one else has got. That was Monk's thing too. Everybody wanted to know what his next suit would be like. He'd always warn them off and tell them, 'It's at Bilgorri's under lock and key.' You'd never get to copy his suit."

"People thought Monk was arrogant, but that's just the way he was," says Foley, defending his friend. "There was an incident at the Scene one night. A fella was being very loud and obnoxious. We used to stand over by the toilets where the alcoves were. On the far side, opposite the stage. The bloke carries on, and Monk, bearing in mind he's only just

over five foot, he calls this big guy over, grabs his tie and drags him in the loo. All you can hear is bosh, bang! The bouncers go in and throw Monk over their shoulder and run him out these big double doors. He's lifted his head up, and bosh, he hits the back of his head on them. So, we go out to see how he is, there's claret everywhere, and he says, 'Did I come a good second, lads?' He'd always have to say something, even in the face of adversity. That was Monk. Always had little lines to come out with. He was very distinctive and, for a little guy, he had a big ego."

Jimmy West, Dave Foley and the rest of the firm were never content with fitting in either. It was always about pushing boundaries, being one step ahead of the competition. New ideas were always being forged.

Dave Foley: "The Royal and the Lyceum were our early meeting places, dancehalls first, because of the suits thing. Once the Scene occurred, the style changed. I don't think I ever actually wore a suit to the Scene with a collar and tie. I may have worn a suit with a T-shirt and everybody would be thinking, 'Who wears a fuckin' two-piece suit with a T-shirt?' I remember going to see Graham Bond at the Marquee, and I remember wearing a navy double-breasted suit that I'd made, and I wore it with a white T-shirt. We were always trying to break the traditions down. On another occasion, I remember a period of buying Tootal ties in Oxford Street and wearing them with starched shirts with a stud collar, which was old hat but we kind of brought it back. Lol was never into the clobber that way. I mean he had suits made by a tailor in Kentish Town but not as passionate as us."

Cathy Roberts: "The first club I ever went to was La Discotheque and on that first evening somebody said to me, 'Don't bump into anybody or you'll get a knife in your back.' After we left there we went to Ronnie Scott's to see Stan Tracey because we'd met these two Mods, one of them was a guy called Johnnie Gillette. I went to Streatham Locarno and the Wimbledon Palais. That is where I first became aware of the Mod scene. I never liked The Beatles at the time. When The Who used to come on at the Scene as The High Numbers I used to go outside for a break. We definitely called ourselves Mods. My friend used to say, 'You'll never be a Mod,' because my hair would never go right, but we were Mods, yeah. I used to get my hair cut at Vidal Sassoon and it cost about £4.50. All our money seemed to go on clothes. When I bought a suit from Jaeger I was about 15 or 16. It was a Harris tweed and it was July! How did I afford that?"

Dave Foley: "We weren't involved in the scooter mob, the pill-heads or the teenyboppers. They'd kind of taken over the Scene Club, and it was time to move on. The Old Bill were forever raiding it anyway. We kind of pulled out of it because we weren't that. The Scene Club wasn't in any more in our eyes."

Willy Deasy: "I was working on the print and Johnny was in an insurance office. We all went for this job at Universal Drugs just off City Road. We had a mate working there as a stockman, and he was having all these black bombers out. They were made for the army, to keep them awake. He got these bombers, sleepers and other pills. We had a little goldmine for a while."

> "Gay clubs were OK, even though we weren't gay, it didn't really matter, we were all into clothes and they were all into clothes. One gay guy, who I think was called Martin, used to come down the Scene Club and one night he said to me, 'When I get my first crease I'm going to kill myself.' He was that scared of getting wrinkles."
> WILLY DEASY

DANCING ON TV'S *READY STEADY GO!*, FEBRUARY 1964

"If I could go back to those clubs for one night I'd go to the Speakeasy and the Bag O'Nails... That's where I first met Hendrix when they brought him over, the Speakeasy. I'd go for the big restaurant that you could sit in, glassed off from the dance floor... It wasn't a restaurant, it was a bloody glorified cafeteria, let's get real."

CARMEN GIMENEZ

"Mod was just a smart thing. We'd go to all the clubs because we were out every night of the week. We didn't drink or smoke then; I liked to pull girls, loved to dance and watch live bands. It was brilliant. All the foreign girls who were students used to go down La Poubelle and so we'd go down there trying to pull. Another place was Café Des Artistes in Earl's Court.

"I was getting ready to go out one Monday night. I was polishing my shoes, and when I got up and looked in the mirror I saw that some specks of polish had flicked up onto my shirt. I didn't go out. That's how dedicated I was. It was the only white shirt I had ready to go with the suit that I wanted to wear. I always remember a guy called Reggie Vincent who would always carry paper bags for when he had to sit down on the bus. That's if you could get him to sit, as he didn't want to crease his trousers.

"Gay clubs were OK, even though we weren't gay, it didn't really matter, we were all into clothes and they were all into clothes. One gay guy, who I think was called Martin, used to come down the Scene Club and one night he said to me, 'When I get my first crease I'm going to kill myself.' He was that scared of getting wrinkles. About a month later the guy that ran the Harlequin Club said to me, 'Hey, you know that guy Martin? He's topped himself!' He was so into being young and good-looking."

In March 1965, one person who never expected to have any input into the forthcoming tour of the Tamla Motown artists in Britain was Dave Foley, but he had a small part to play.

Dave Foley: "I left the Brown Brothers because I was on £12 a week at the time, and they told me they couldn't afford to give me a rise. I was about 19 at the time, so I set up my own business around the corner at my mum's place in Penn Road, and charged £15 a suit. I met Terry Smith down the Scene, and he asked me to make him a suit. I was already three quid up."

Dave Foley's mum had a flat consisting of his mum's bedroom, a kitchen, Dave's bedroom and a box room at the back that was supposed to be a bathroom, but it was never converted, so Dave started to use it for his workshop for tailoring.

Dave's friend Carmen Gimenez secured him the job of making the suits for Georgie Fame & The Blue Flames' tour with the Motown show.

Dave Foley: "I did their suits for that tour. Two lots of material, one jet black mohair and the other, brown mohair. Ivy League style, three buttons. There were seven members of the band, so I made the black mohair ones first. In my kitchen at Penn Road, they were all hung up after being pressed. My mother was so excited that Georgie and his band used to come around and have fittings in my bedroom. I had to deliver them to the Rainbow at Finsbury Park. Laurie came with me that night. As we got out of the cab with the suits hung over our arms, a small crowd rushed over, only to realise it was nobody famous. We went to the room where the band were changing. Speedy wouldn't wear his one as he wanted to wear his African robes. We left the suits and were given complimentary tickets to watch the show. As we were walking back down the staircase, we bumped into

these three birds, who were all giggling. We later sussed it was Diana Ross & The Supremes.

"I had to go to Rik Gunnell's second-floor office in Gerrard Street. Rik was at the end of this long desk, with his brother stood next to him. I asked for cash because I hadn't got a bank account. He refuses, then says he wants to make me a proposition. He then offered to set me up, get a work room and all the equipment I needed, plus he'd get me all the punters. I presumed he meant his stable of music groups. But then he said he'd take 52 per cent. I just said no, because again, whether it's arrogance or not, I thought I'm not selling out my own labour. I saw it as him poncing off my talent. What fanciful thoughts for somebody who'd done nothing. He couldn't believe that I said no to him. He looked at his brother, and then glared at me. I never ended up making the seven other suits in brown. I think I got a cheque for £110 for the first lot. I had to go to Newborough Street where there was a trimming shop called Bernstein and Banleys. They cashed the cheque because they knew me, and that was my first professional job."

Carmen Gimenez: "If I could go back to those clubs for one night I'd go to the Speakeasy and the Bag O'Nails. The Scotch of St James as well, which is where in fact, before the Speakeasy opened, we used to meet up with Eric Burdon and Chas Chandler of The Animals. That's where I first met Hendrix when they brought him over. The Speakeasy, I'd go for the big restaurant that you could sit in, glassed off from the dance floor. They let all the musicians and their ladies in free, so they were very clever there. It wasn't a restaurant, it was a bloody glorified cafeteria, let's get real. I mean, yeah, they were different from the Scene, but that was basically just a basement, a hole in the ground with a crappy bar at the end.

"Those days were so good. Running from the Marquee to the Scene to the Flamingo. Then later on, the UFO, that was one club that Georgie wouldn't come to with me. It wasn't his scene. It was all oil lamps and flashing lights. We did go to Middle Earth a couple of times and that was to see Zoot [Money] in Dantalian's Chariot. Oh God, that was dreadful. Then there was the Hippy phase with Eric Burdon, that was awful too. They were wearing these white long robes, and they looked like sheep. I couldn't believe it, I thought this can't be right. Georgie didn't get it at all. He always said that Zoot was a blues man, which is true. As for Eric being a Hippy, that was ridiculous. It didn't last long, and I'm not surprised. Eric was a great singer at the time and we had a lot of fun with him. For instance, one night in the Bag O'Nails he said, 'Do you fancy coming to Paris to see James Brown?' This is one o'clock in the morning. So, me and Georgie looked at each other and said, 'Why not?' We went home, grabbed some clothes and flew to Paris on a chartered flight. Totally mad!"

To dean
with love
Georgie
Fame

tography
E MORSE

Direction
RIK GUNNELL AGENCY
Tel; GER. 4973

GEORGIE   FAME

One person stands out as the leader of the pack when it comes to musical influences: Guy Stevens. He was totally focused on music throughout his short life, and became, for a few years, the main source of new music in London and throughout the UK.

Guy Stevens was born on April 13th, 1943 in East Dulwich, South London. Having passed his 11-plus, he went to Woolverstone Hall, a boarding school in Suffolk owned and run by London County Council.

John 'Pears' Perry: "We were in the same year at school. It wasn't a public school. You didn't have to pay to go there. It was an experiment by the London County Council. So, we boarded, but there were no fees paid. The idea was to provide a public school-type education to children based on their academic ability, and not the ability to pay for it."

One of his earliest ventures was to set up a rock 'n' roll club, charging fellow pupils a shilling and amassing a collection of records to play on the communal player, although rock 'n' roll wasn't well received by the teachers.

Graham 'Cartz' Cartwright recalls: "Suddenly Elvis took over my life. We started listening to early rockabilly. Of course, when we grew up, London was a hotbed of styles, trad jazz, modern jazz, R&B, folk. My school report said, 'He tends to drift through school' and I think Guy's was the same. I just wanted to get back and be in Soho all the time... Guy was expelled and I had to re-sit my exams because my brain was so full of rock 'n' roll, and girls."

John 'Pears' Perry: "Guy got expelled at the end of the fifth year. I'm not sure what for, because normally, if you were expelled, there would be a big thing during assembly about it, and you'd be hauled up in front of everyone as a kind of example. But his happened without anybody knowing why. It might have been smoking, because you could get expelled for that."

After getting expelled in July 1958, Guy moved to London and went to work for Lloyd's, the insurance brokers. It was during this period that he started seriously collecting records.

John 'Pears' Perry: "We were out and about in record shops together in 1961. We both used to love Chuck Berry, but it would be difficult to get hold of lots of stuff because there was no market for it, even in the States. The black artists didn't get the same exposure as the white ones. Occasionally you would hear a Pat Boone record, but it would be a cover of a record that had been made by a black artist that didn't chart.

"At school, we were avid readers of the Billboard and Variety charts. *NME* used to publish the Billboard charts and it was either *Melody Maker* or *Record Mirror* that had the Variety charts from the States. That's how we could see what was in the charts. We'd then get record shops to order

the records when they became available here, and go in and listen to them. That's how I first heard Jerry Lee Lewis 'Whole Lotta Shakin' Going On'. I didn't hear it on the radio, but I had that record on its release date."

Guy became quite obsessive about Chuck Berry and founded and ran the UK Chuck Berry Fan Club. At the time Chuck Berry was languishing in prison... He served twenty months from February 1962 to October 1963. Legend has it that it was Guy Stevens who flew to America and posted bail to get Berry released. He then took him out for a meal and gave him his bus fare home. Stevens then arranged for Chuck Berry to make his first tour of the UK. For all his help, Berry, allegedly, never thanked him.

In his personal life, Guy had met his dream girl, Diane Cox, and they married in 1962. A year later they had a son together, James. It seems that during 1963 he flitted between his mother's house in Forest Hill, which he shared with his wife, his son and his mother Lillian, and a flat just off Leicester Square with old school friend John 'Pears' Perry. John 'Woody' Wood, a close friend of Guy's, explains: "The flat was in Excel Court, Whitcomb Street. If you go in Excel Court it's the only house there. You'd walk through this archway into a courtyard. It was almost like a small double-fronted cottage. The whole front wall was painted with a really big harlequin. There were these two flats on the first floor; Guy lived in the front one. Pears was actually the person who officially lived

"We were out and about in record shops together in 1961. We both used to love Chuck Berry, but it would be difficult to get hold of lots of stuff because there was no market for it, even in the States. The black artists didn't get the same exposure as the white ones."
JOHN 'PEARS' PERRY

there but was not there all the time. He still stayed at his mum and dad's quite a bit. There wasn't a tap in the room but I think there was one in the sink in the toilet by the stairs. There was another couple of single-room flats upstairs. The flat's basement housed the Coffee An. Doug and Guido were mates of ours. There were quite a few other people used to crash now and again or be around listening to records. It was a very small flat (two small rooms) so it would be very crowded sometimes. There were only two beds, so there was a lot of sleeping on the floor."

John 'Pears' Perry: "It was in the first month or so of living at the flat, that we were robbed there. It was an open house. Whoever we'd seen in the evening would come back to the flat. The place couldn't be better located for everything. We were between Trafalgar Square and Leicester Square. Piccadilly Circus was three minutes away. People would always be missing the last tube, and coming back to our place.

"There was a window overlooking Excel Court, but there was also a window in the other half of the flat that you couldn't see, so unless you'd been inside you wouldn't know about it. It was the window in the kitchenette through which the thieves entered… The thieves took all our records, mine too. I had Chuck Berry, Bobby Freeman, Fats Domino, etc. too but I also had a lot of folk stuff, Woody Guthrie, Leadbelly, etc. They also nicked my camera, it was only a Kodak 127, but that's why I have no photos from then."

John Wood: "When you come out of Leicester Square and you go up to Chinatown there's a little alleyway, there was a little junk shop on the left. I was in there browsing around, and I found these records. I recognised them straight away and they had Guy's signature on some of them. So, I called Guy and he got the police involved. He managed to get nearly all his records back but the weird thing is that for some strange reason they sent a Black Maria around and took me, Guy and the records around to Savile Row police station. We were interviewed in this room with a big table… I really don't know why they were so bothered about it but we were there for bloody ages and it was just stolen records."

In March 1963 Ronan O'Rahilly had taken over premises in Ham Yard, off Great Windmill Street. It had previously been the Cy Laurie Club 11 jazz club in the fifties before becoming the Piccadilly Jazz Club run by Rolling Stones manager Giorgio Gomelsky. Ronan renamed the place the Scene Club and aimed to promote R&B. By May 1963 they had acquired Guy's services to provide an R&B record night on Mondays between 7 p.m. and 1 a.m.

Of course, even though the club was an early pioneer of American R&B music, it could not claim to be the first. Jeff Dexter, himself an early exponent of these sounds, remembers: "In the summer of 1961, Ian 'Sammy' Samwell hosted some lunchtime dance sessions at the Lyceum Ballroom in London, using his own collection of R&B and country rock 'n' roll records. Then in August, he was appointed the first resident DJ on Sunday and Tuesday sessions. He was playing in front of a fast-growing audience of a couple of thousand, mainly made up of the new exploding Mod scene."

You soon begin to realise that there was a whole world of rhythm & blues surrounding Guy at the time.

John Wood: "I first met Guy around '61, maybe '62. He wasn't even at the Scene when I first met him but he was doing stuff for the Pye R&B label. He'd got all these blues records and he started writing for *Sounds* magazine… Guy was obsessed with music all the time… Then I found out he had all these records. I was really excited about all that blues stuff, and I just thought, fucking hell, this is amazing! I can't remember how Guy got into DJ-ing because he was hardly an outgoing personality.

"I worked for Giorgio Gomelsky down at the Station Hotel in Richmond. I used to do the door there, sometimes when The Rolling Stones were playing there. That was really good, and the place I enjoyed seeing them the most, I think. It was electric in there, it really was. They were great at the Crawdaddy and Eel Pie but it was here I first saw them with a big crowd. It was really exciting. I took a few visiting music artists down the Scene Club from Fairfield Hall in Croydon… Giorgio Gomelsky promoted these gigs and it was somewhere for them to go after they had done their concert, because it was open late and played vaguely appropriate music."

Cathy Roberts was a young Mod girl from Wimbledon who remembers those days well: "I used to go up on a Friday night and stay with my friend June in Ealing. There was about four of us all sleeping in the lounge. We'd go to Henekeys on a Saturday afternoon to listen out for where the parties were. Then we'd gatecrash the parties Saturday night and on Sunday we'd go to the Crawdaddy Club to see The Yardbirds or the Stones. Monday night it was the Scene Club, because I always liked going out in the week because at the weekend it was too crowded. I rarely went to the Scene on a Saturday because hundreds of people used to go. On the quiet nights I used to chat to Guy Stevens."

There were meet-up places around the Scene, such as the lovely Victorian boozer, the Lyric, at 37 Great Windmill Street. Another would be the Red Lion at 20 Great Windmill Street, run by Doris and Fred. Doris looked like an ex-showgirl with plenty of makeup, always chatting to customers, while Fred just sat at the bar.

John 'Pears' Perry: "Guy had a lot of albums. At the time, albums were somewhat rare in that kind of stuff [R&B].

> "Guy kept bringing people back and those people brought others and I hated it... for a couple of weeks, but then I embraced it. I liked the people. I gave up going to work."
> JOHN 'PEARS' PERRY

You had to order them in. There were a couple of shops that we'd use. Dobell's in Charing Cross Road and Chappell's. They would order in records, because they had catalogues of the actual American record companies."

"Guy used to be happy ordering blind. There would be something like Muddy Waters, Howlin' Wolf or whatever, and he'd order it without hearing any of the stuff on it... I was never interested in something because it was rare, only because I liked it. Guy was a bit more of a collector, and he liked to have stuff that other people didn't have because it was rare or whatever. We had different attitudes. So, Guy had lots of albums of those kind of people, and Eric and Clive had a fair few albums. Eric had a thing about Albert Johnson. He'd only ever recorded about twelve tracks on an album. Eric had that album."

Lesley Gould: "The Coffee An was a habitual meeting place for me and friends. Doug and Guido, who were bit-part actors, ran it. Guy and Pears lived in a tiny flat above it. The Mods discovered it and crowded it out, much to our annoyance. I was neither Mod nor Rocker, though a bit of both in my clothes. I didn't know Guy very well. He was so obsessed by R&B music, he was of little interest to a girl. But he was the one who introduced me to Bo [Diddley] one night at the Scene. That was how I met Jerome and I became his girlfriend for a while and I got the job as Duchess's [Bo's rhythm guitarist] dresser and went on tour with them. It was organised by Don Arden. Other performers on the tour were Little Richard, The Everly Brothers, The Rattles [a German band], Julie Grant, Mickie Most, and a band called, I think, The Flintstones. They also had The Rolling Stones, who travelled in their own van.

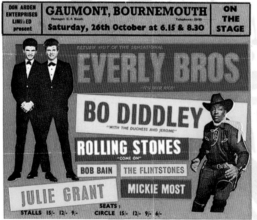

THE RATTLES

"The best night was a pre-tour performance, just Bo, Duchess, Jerome and me, at a US airbase. Many of the airmen were black and I imagine homesick and the appearance of Duchess in her gold lamé catsuit caused a sensation I will never forget. The noise and the atmosphere! You could have cut it with a knife. Even skinny 18-year-old me awash in some of the reflected glory of Duchess shaking a tail-feather, as she put it.

"The rest of the tour was a lot of coach travel in a coach that broke down several times and was fixed in the middle of Scottish moorland by Bo with one of my hairpins. He was very fatherly to me and taught me how to spit-shine his shoes. I broke up with Jerome quite soon and he used to go off with The Rolling Stones in their van. He

taught Mick how to play maracas and Mick gave him lessons in harmonica. Jerome was too bossy and possessive for me. I don't think he was used to adventurous white girls."

John Wood: "On a Saturday I'd get completely wasted, then on to the Coffee An for a chat, then back to Guy's flat and play more bloody records. Sunday morning, get up and go to the Tally Ho pub in Kentish Town which used to have big band jazz live from the likes of Joe Harriott, Tubby Hayes and Ben Webster. There would be lots of us from the Scene. It was quite a big thing that Sunday mornings you went to the Tally Ho. Then you'd go over to the Italian restaurant and have curry and chips. Then on to Ken Colyer's at 4 p.m. to see The Rolling Stones do a set. When they'd finish, they'd join us and come back with us to Guy's flat to chat, smoke and listen to records before we all went off to Eel Pie Island to watch the Stones' evening gig. So I'd see two Stones sets on those days but later on it would be the Stones doing Colyer's and The Yardbirds in the evening because they had taken over at the Athletic Ground. I also remember that The Beatles went down to watch The Rolling Stones at the Crawdaddy Club on a Sunday night."

Graham 'Cartz' Cartwright: "I've still got the Excello copy of the Slim Harpo LP that I played to Jagger before they recorded 'I'm A King Bee'. Some of us used to go to the Coach and Horses pub on the corner of Poland Street and Great Marlborough Street and drink Scotch with Muddy Waters. I always remember Guy giving Sonny Boy Williamson a lift to Victoria station where he had to catch the train for Southampton docks to get the boat home to America... I think when Guy dropped him off, that was the last time we saw him."

Mickey Tenner, a main face on the London Mod club circuit and regular dancer on the television show *Ready Steady Go!*, fondly remembers: "Guy would only do Monday nights. Peter Meaden, Guy and myself would talk a lot on these nights, discussing blues music. Even then, very few people would show up so I think Guy got fed up with it and he wouldn't have done it for more than six months."

On certain nights Guy could be found selling Scene Club tickets at Piccadilly Circus tube station. Membership of the Scene Club was one guinea (21 shillings, or £1.05), which

STUDIO '51
10/11 GT. NEWPORT STREET
LEICESTER SQUARE (Tube)
Friday. 7.30—11
JOHNNY MAYALL BLUES BREAKERS
EVERY MONDAY
8 till 11
and
SUNDAY AFTERNOON
4 till 6.30
Rhythm and Blues with
THE
ROLLING STONES

KEN
COLYER
CLUB

CHECKER LP 2974
high-fidelity

"Sandra complemented our music very well. You could see Guy had influenced her choice of records sometimes. Guy himself was like a mystery man in the background… but everybody knew how important he was."
MICK EVE

Have Guitar Will Travel
wire BO DIDDLEY

BO DIDDLEY

FAB
R. Mellin
45 R.P.M.
FAB. 37
©1968
JULIE ON MY MIND
(R. Mellin)
PRINCE BUSTER & ALL STARS
Fab Recording
Melodisc Records

DOCTOR BIRD
A Treasure Isle Production
DB 1061 A
©1967 Island Music
DON'T STAY AWAY
(Dillon)
PHILLIS DILLON

GIANT
45 RPM
GN 7A
A Production
WE ARE STILL ALIVE
DANDY

allowed you in for free on Monday nights, but there was still an entry fee on the other nights which varied according to the entertainment provided. Other nights would set you back a shilling (5p), except all-nighters on Saturdays, which were 5 shillings (25p).

"My first night down the Scene Club was on a Saturday in early December 1963. I was 17. Brian Jones was stood outside in the yard. After that I was there almost every Saturday night from December 1963 until September 1964," recalls Peter Gage.

"I remember my first impressions of the Scene quite well. In fact, I was impressed just walking down Great Windmill Street from Shaftesbury Avenue as it happens! You'd pass the snooker hall and the Windmill Theatre, then you'd turn left into Ham Yard, and suddenly you'd feel like you were in a *Johnny Staccato* TV episode, all seedy and subversive. Just what I was looking for! Ham Yard was a bit messy and you could imagine it being used by gangland heavies to do people over. But when you turned towards where the entrance to the Scene was, there was a crowd of Mods, 'geezers' and 'sorts' all gathering to get in line to join the queue that would take you down the narrow dark staircase. It was really dark down there; you could smell the sweat and the warmth, and the rancid smell of chewed chewing gum. It was a delicious smell that I would later measure all sweaty nightclubs by."

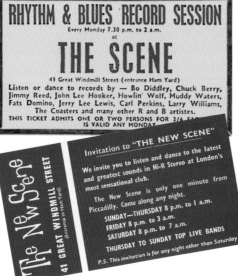

John 'Pears' Perry: "We had this episode where Woody and I were going into the Scene Club one night, and there were all these Mods packed out in Ham Yard. We were walking through them, and one of them said something about being shoved. Suddenly, me and Woody are having a row with them. Then, one of them threw a bottle which hit Woody on the forehead, and it came up in this huge lump. The one that had been giving me the mouth at the time, as the bottle came over from one of his mates, I just smacked him, and he went flat on his back… So that was the way it was, we didn't get on with the Mods. What Jimmy, Dave, Lou and Lol were interested in was American fashions such as Ivy League, and the kind of suits Gary 'US' Bonds used to wear. Where there was an overlap, was on items like Ben Sherman shirts, because they were seen as Ivy League, but the Mods took on the Ben Sherman shirts, and didn't pair them with Ivy League stuff, but with their little Crombies or whatever."

Adverts for the 1964 period reveal that between Thursday and Sunday the club would have put on live bands, presumably accompanied by DJs. Monday evening was R&B night with Guy Stevens. Tuesday was 'Off The Record' with Sandra and she also hosted a Blue Beat night on a Wednesday. During this period an act that did play the club was Georgie Fame & The Blue Flames. Their tenor sax player Mick Eve has fond memories of the club. "Sandra complemented our music very well. You could see Guy had influenced her choice of records sometimes. Guy himself was like a mystery man in the background… but everybody knew how important he was."

Peter Gage states: "You were given a stamp on the back of your hand and given a very cool-looking membership card. I became secretly quite proud to be the owner of that card. There was something about that whole place that you knew was going to have a big influence on your life. As the queue got closer and closer to the bottom of the cellar staircase, the music that was playing was incredible… for this punter, and a whole bunch of like-minded soul-searchers, this was musical nectar from the gods that we definitely didn't need to believe in at this stage. The queue was slow to move, but that didn't matter. I was amongst my kind of people, and I knew that a lifetime of influence upon me was about to start."

John 'Pears' Perry: "Guy could tell you how many it sold, where it was recorded, who played bass on it, how it charted and who later recorded it. All the facts and statistics… but it ain't music… We used to go and watch the Stones in the building that housed Ken Colyer's club, in the basement of Studio 51. We'd watch their rehearsals, and Guy would give them the benefit of his opinions on how they were playing a Chuck Berry number or whatever. Brian used to like hearing what Guy thought, but then, Guy was good at feeding people's egos."

John Wood: "The Coffee An was downstairs from the flat we were in at Excel Court. It used to be a girly bar but then it became the Coffee An. Doug and Guido were both down there. Everybody used to come back from the Scene and go down there. I was crashing around Guy's house, generally Thursday, Friday, Saturday but sometimes other days, sometimes not at all. I remember trying to get to sleep and he'd play a Jimmy Reed track. There always seemed to be a crash cymbal hit every now and again at random times on Jimmy Reed records just when you are least expecting it and you're just dropping off to sleep. Guy ran the Jimmy Reed, Jerry Lee Lewis and Chuck Berry fan clubs. He used to get all these people coming down from places such as Newcastle to listen to his records. I'd be trying to go to sleep as I was one of the only people working [as a draughtsman] while everybody else was just bumming around really. I had to get up and go to work the next day but these people would be just jabbering away discussing the merits of Jimmy Reed or whoever."

John 'Pears' Perry: "In the beginning at Excel Court, I was, like Woody, working as a draughtsman. I had been in an apprenticeship with an M&E contractor but I couldn't afford to leave home on 19s 6d a week so I jacked it in at ONC and got a job with Islington Council as an architectural assistant on £12 a week. First it was OK, travel was good – opposite direction to everybody else, but in no time at all every night was party night at Excel Court, Guy kept bringing people back and those people brought others and I hated it… for a couple of weeks, but then I embraced it. I liked the people. I gave up going to work."

Guy had written music articles for *Record Mirror* during 1963 and by February 1964 he'd started writing the R&B supplement for the weekly *Jazz Beat* magazine, which had started a month earlier. To gain such a wide

knowledge of the new fledgling R&B and soul sounds coming out of America was very impressive but Guy was still a rock 'n' roll addict at heart. In fact, early adverts for the Scene on Monday nights state: "Listen or dance to records by: Bo Diddley, Chuck Berry, Jimmy Reed, John Lee Hooker, Howlin' Wolf, Muddy Waters, Fats Domino, Jerry Lee Lewis, Carl Perkins, Larry Williams, The Coasters, and many other R&B artistes."

In an interview with Charles Shaar Murray for *NME* in 1979, Guy stated he'd got all his records mail order from the Stan Lewis Record Store in Shreveport, Louisiana. Although he may have used Stan 'The Record Man' Lewis for many of his purchases, he definitely got records from other sources too. Imhof's in New Oxford Street is a likely contender, especially for imported American LPs, which were often on display in the window. Transat Records, located in a bare basement at 27 Lisle Street, just behind the Empire Leicester Square, was the place for people in the know during this period. If you wanted elusive American 45s or rare albums this was the likeliest place to stock them. It only opened to the public for short periods on Friday and Saturday mornings.

Jeff Dexter recalls: "I had known Guy since he had come down every Tuesday to the Lyceum accompanied by Peter Meaden… The one good thing that he had at the Scene was he could experiment more with sounds because it was a lot smaller than the Lyceum. We had to get people dancing and it was a big venue. One place our paths usually crossed was on Friday mornings at Transat Records. Sammy, Guy and myself could be found picking through these imports because in those days sending an international money order to America wasn't easy."

Brian Crane, a Scene club regular, had different luck. "I was always on the lookout for new tunes and used Transat regularly. One evening I was at a club being held at the King Alfred pub in Lewisham when the DJ played a song called 'Confidential' by Sonny Knight. I asked where the DJ got it from and he wrote down the address of Ernie's Record Mart in Nashville. You simply sent him a list and some dollars and

RECORDED DYNAMITE

JAMES BROWN
AND THE FAMOUS FLAMES

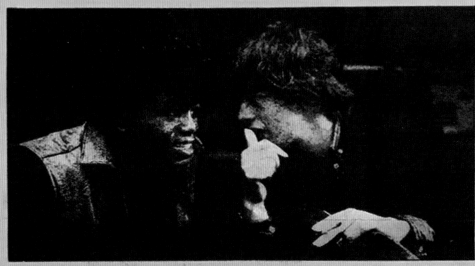

MICK JAGGER OF THE ROLLING STONES MEETS HIS IDOL JAMES
BROWN BACKSTAGE AT THE FAMOUS APOLLO THEATRE IN NEW YORK

NIGHT TRAIN

C/W WHY DOES EVERYTHING HAPPEN TO ME   SUE WI-36

SUE IS THE ONLY LABEL DEVOTED ENTIRELY
TO AUTHENTIC RHYTHM & BLUES IN THIS
COUNTRY !

SUE RECORDS 108 CAMBRIDGE ROAD LONDON NW6 · KIL 1921-2

Printed in England by MacNeill Press Ltd., London, S.E.1

THE HOTTEST LITTLE LP CATALOGUE IN THIS COUNTRY!

ILP907—I'VE GOT A WOMAN
JIMMY McGRIFF

ILP908—GOSPEL TIME
JIMMY McGRIFF

ILP911—MOCKINGBIRD
INEZ & CHARLIE FOXX

ILP913—THE SOUL SISTERS

ILP917—ROCKIN' PNEUMONIA
HUEY 'PIANO' SMITH

ILP918—THE BEST OF
ELMORE JAMES

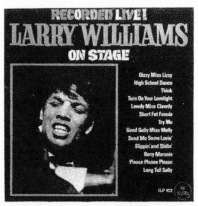

ILP919—PURE BLUES
VOLUME ONE

ILP920—50 MINUTES 24
SECONDS OF RECORDED
DYNAMITE!

ILP922—LARRY WILLIAMS
ON STAGE!

SUE RECORDS SUBSIDIARY OF ISLAND RECORDS LTD 108 CAMBRIDGE RD LONDON NW6 . KIL 1921/2

he'd ship over a box of records to you with their latest sales list. I also had a friend who worked at the Colony record store in New York. Guy Stevens was the man who influenced my taste and I remember buying off of him too. On some Thursday nights he would set up tables in the corridor of the Scene Club by the emergency exit. He'd have stuff on labels like Pye International and Sun Records by artists such as Carl Perkins and Sonny Burgess."

Peter Gage recounts: "When you entered the Scene itself you were in a dark space, enough to fit about 200 people in at a pinch. There was a supporting pillar right in middle of the floor.

Just to the right of you as you entered, there was the glass-windowed booth where Guy Stevens would sit. Facing you on the opposite wall to the entrance were the gents' and ladies' toilets, and on the side wall there were two of what I would call 'cubicles', sort of alcoves with a bench-type seat in them, where quite often blokes and girls would be able to be a bit more private, you might say. But round to the left as you entered the Scene was the stage, upon which sat a grubby white grand piano… I never heard the piano ever being played, and, if I remember, it took up a fair bit of the stage, but thankfully not so much of a space that you couldn't fit in a five-piece band like The Animals, or the four-piece phenomenon called The High Numbers, who later of course went on to become The Who… There was always a lot of dancing down the Scene… to the sounds of early Motown, Chess, Jimmy Reed, Major Lance, John Lee Hooker, James Brown, Impressions, Blue Beat sounds by Prince Buster and the incredible 'Carolina' by The Folkes Brothers. Most of these sounds had never been heard in the UK. Guy Stevens as the DJ had such an incredible ear for what the punters needed to hear. He was a major influence on the club, stamping his trademark on the whole future development of soul and blues music listening in the UK."

Stevens had been inspirational in getting the UK-based Pye International to release Chuck Berry, Muddy Waters, Sonny Boy Williamson, Howlin' Wolf and others from the Chess label.

John 'Pears' Perry: "Guy had, in some way, realised that Pye had inherited the British rights to the Chess/Checker catalogue, and some of the smaller record companies that used to come out under the London America label through Decca. Pye had no idea about this stuff, so Guy wrote to them, asking them why they hadn't released this, or that. Whoever was getting these letters, replied to him and asked him to come in for a chat. That was how he got involved with Pye… When the Stones started to be more successful, the first big tour they did was with Bo Diddley. Bo was brought over here through Pye, but it was because of Guy's influence that they'd brought him over."

Guy also made up tapes of his rare tunes for bands such as The Who, The Paramounts and the Stones to use in their early sets. He would charge a fiver for the privilege.

"Peter Meaden came around one night," Stevens told Shaar Murray in the *NME* interview. "He was the bloke who formed The Who, and he arranged to bring them round one day with

their manager, Kit Lambert. And they were really weird. They just stood there. My wife… made a cup of tea for each one of them and they still stood still. I played them 'Rumble' by Link Wray and put it on a tape for them – because by then I'd built up an enormous collection and Steve Marriott and everybody else used to come around and get material."

It was obvious Guy knew his stuff but he needed more than a DJ spot to channel his musical visions. That chance came when Chris Blackwell hired him in April 1964 to run a record label called Sue. Sue Records had actually started life in America when Henry 'Juggy' Murray set up the label in 1957. Based in Harlem, and named after his daughter, Sue Records soon started finding chart success with acts like Bobby Hendricks and the newly signed Ike & Tina Turner. Diverse in its musical direction, the label included jazz, blues, rock 'n' roll and soul acts and thus spawned subsidiary labels such as Symbol.

Back in the UK, Chris Blackwell had started a label after moving there from his native Jamaica in 1962. He'd founded Island Records after seeing how well the UK pressings of his unlicensed productions were selling – ska and calypso records were selling well here among the West Indian immigrants and in the emerging Mod scene.

In 1963, while on a return visit to Jamaica, Blackwell heard a tune on the radio that would change his life. He stood transfixed as 'Mockingbird' by Inez & Charlie Foxx filled the air. After discovering the identity of the tune and the vocalists, Blackwell found himself in New York acquiring the UK rights to the song. The meeting with Juggy Murray had been very successful; so successful that he had also become the licensee of all releases on the Symbol/Sue/Crackerjack and AFO labels.

Once back in England, Blackwell realised that the music didn't really fit into the Island label's ska output. So, along with his business associate David Betteridge, he set about creating a new label and finding somebody to run it. Guy Stevens was the perfect choice and for £15 a week he would steer the newly founded UK version of the Sue label on its course.

John Wood: "Once Guy got involved with the Sue label his tastes changed a bit. He liked things like Bobby Bland. I always remember, at the time, Eric Clapton used to say 'That bloody Bobby Bland! Two thousand steps from the blues. I hate him.' Subsequently Eric became quite a big fan of Bobby. Guy was also a big rock 'n' roll fan, so he had loads of Fats Domino, Little Richard, Jerry Lee Lewis, Chuck Berry and Bo Diddley."

Blackwell sent Guy to America to track down records, and while there he visited the Stax HQ in Memphis as well as Chess in Chicago, where he hooked up with Chuck Berry again as well as Little Walter.

In his interview with Charles Shaar Murray for *NME* in 1979, Guy stated: "I had every Motown single, every Stax... I went to Stax in Memphis in 1963 and they said, 'It's just a record shop.' I said no, no, you've got a studio, and they say, 'We're just a shop.' So, I went behind the shop and there was the studio where Booker T made 'Green Onions'. I said to them, 'Don't you understand the importance of what you're doing?' They were nuts. They thought the record shop was more important than the studio."

With its distinctive red and yellow design, it all looked so vivid and new. In December 1963 'Mockingbird' launched 'the 300 series' as its catalogue number was WI 301. This later became 'the 4,000 series' as Black Swan, one of Island's subsidiary labels, used a 400 prefix already. EPs had a 700 number while Sue LPs were just incorporated into Island's '900' catalogue.

Throughout early 1964 Guy released a varied selection of styles but still no hits came. In mid-July that year he placed an advert in Record Mirror stating:

Special Announcement: despite the fact that many record shops cannot be bothered or refuse to stock our records, we are still going to have a hit... following their sensational appearances over here, Inez & Charlie Foxx are selling big with their brand new American smash 'Hurt By Love' released here this week on Sue WI-323... hear it (or ask for it) at your local record shop NOW... and we bet you'll rave over it. – Guy Stevens. Island Records Ltd.

When the UK charts were published on 1st August the song peaked at number forty, although this was probably more to do with an appearance on the *Ready Steady Go!* television programme and strong pirate radio play from stations such as Radio Invicta and Radio London.

In December 1964 the Sue Records Appreciation Society was started to inform young hip kids of their new releases. The first newsletter rolled off the press in January 1965. Members would then regularly receive a monthly newsletter, release sheets, publicity material and a complete Sue Records catalogue. Every one of that month's releases would get a little review. Posters of current releases would sometimes be included, such as came with the May 1965 package, which promoted the Larry Williams LP. Williams had just toured the UK and on the last date of his tour in London he had been recorded live for this LP. Fan members were asked to actively promote the label by putting up enclosed posters, and phoning or writing to record shops or radio stations requesting they stock or play the records.

Guy set up a mail-order service from his flat at 23 Gloucester Avenue, NW1 to sell the back catalogue as well as new releases. Prices were as follows: singles: 6s 8d + 6d postage (about 36p); EPs: 11s 5d + 6d postage (about 60p); LPs: 29s 11d + 1s postage (about £1.55). This wasn't the first mail-order business that he'd run from these premises. He'd set up Atlantic Imports in 1964 to sell his other R&B stuff such as Sun and Pye label releases.

In the first two weeks of June, Sue were busy promoting their release of 'A Little Piece Of Leather', which had been a hit in the American R&B charts a couple of months earlier. There were appearances from Donnie Elbert on television shows such as *Discs A Go-Go, Scene At 6.30, Ready Steady Goes Live!* plus live appearances at the Crazy Elephant Club, Birmingham, the Cromwellian Club in London and the Mojo Club in Sheffield. Donnie's tune was a massive hit in the Mod clubs, but alas not commercially.

Sue benefited from Guy's amazing knowledge and diverse tastes so the label built up a back catalogue of artists and styles that included some great outlandish curios such as 'Stormy Monday Blues' by Little Joe Cook, who was in fact British singer Chris Farlowe under a pseudonym. Sadly, although the label found great success on the dance floors with songs such as 'Hitch Hike' from Russell Byrd and 'Daddy Rolling Stone' by Derek Martin, commercial success eluded them. The number forty chart position was never bettered and remained the label's biggest hit, although their *The Sue Story* LPs (three volumes) were big sellers over the period.

By 1967, Guy Stevens' world had changed too. The Scene Club had shut a year earlier but he'd fled the place long before. Music had changed as well, and Guy had embraced the emerging white rock scene which Island was getting more involved with. He left the Sue label, which eventually folded in 1968, and Guy was re-employed as an A&R man for Island, his wages increasing by a fiver, to twenty quid a week.

Terry Smith: "I remember going around Guy Steven's flat in the acid days, he had wall-to-wall records in his living room, and he was off his trolley kicking a football against them, smashing them up."

John Wood: "I guess I lost contact with Guy because I got married. I still used to see him now and again when he moved to Camden Town but he was getting more and more flaky and a bit harder to talk to."

Guy pursued his dream of that elusive hit but never quite got there. He would later produce records by artists including Spooky Tooth, Free and Stevie Winwood. He created a band and gave them the name Procol Harum (actually named after a friend's blue Burmese male cat whose pedigree name was Procul Harun, although somehow this mutated into Procol Harum). He had recorded a full demo tape of 'A Whiter Shade Of Pale'. Regrettably, Island, or more specifically, Chris Blackwell, showed little interest as at this point he was busy working alongside Steve Winwood and his new group Traffic. Sadly, the band left Stevens in the spring of 1967, signed to Decca's subsidiary label, Deram, and the song went to number one in June that year, selling tens of millions of copies worldwide.

——WI-301	Mockingbird/He's The One You Love INEZ & CHARLIE FOXX	
——WI-302	That's How Heartaches Are Made/Doodlin' BABY WASHINGTON	
——WI-303	All About My Girl/MG Blues JIMMY McGRIFF	
——WI-304	Jaybirds/Broken Hearted Fool INEZ & CHARLIE FOXX	
——WI-305	Hitchhike Parts I & II RUSSELL BYRD	
——WI-306	Gonna Work Out Fine/Won't You Forgive Me IKE & TINA TURNER	
——WI-307	Competition/Here We Go Round The Mulberry Bush INEZ & CHARLIE FOXX	
——WI-308	Daddy Rollin' Stone/Don't Put Me Down Like This DEREK MARTIN	
——WI-310	The Last Minute Parts I & II JIMMY McGRIFF	
——WI-312	I Can't Stand It/Blueberry Hill THE SOUL SISTERS	
——WI-313	So Far Away/Monkey Hips And Rice HANK JACOBS	
——WI-314	Ask Me/Hi Diddle Diddle INEZ & CHARLIE FOXX	
——WI-316	Send For Me/Bless You BARBARA GEORGE	
——WI-317	I've Got A Woman Parts I & II JIMMY McGRIFF	
——WI-318	Macks By The Tracks/Shine TIM WHITSETT	
——WI-319	Crossroads/My Baby's Sweet HOMESICK JAMES	
——WI-320	Got To Have Some/Why Did It Happen To Me WILLIE MABON	
——WI-321	I Can't Wait/Who's Gonna Take Care Of Me BABY WASHINGTON	
——WI-322	The Argument/Poor Fool IKE & TINA TURNER	
——WI-323	Hurt By Love/Confusion INEZ & CHARLIE FOXX	
——WI-324	Down The Aisle/C'est La Vie PATTI La Belle & the BLUEBELLES	
——WI-325	Shimmy Shimmy Walk Parts I & II THE MEGATONS	
——WI-326	New Dance In France/Carolyn BOBBY LEE TRAMMELL	

——WI-328	Dream Ba... ANITA W...
——WI-330	Set A Da... HOMESIC...
——WI-331	Just Got... WILLIE M...
——WI-334	Precious... THE WAL...
——WI-335	Dust My... ELMORE ...
——WI-337	I Done W... LOUISIAN...
——WI-339	I Sing Ur... J. B. LEN...
——WI-340	Watch Yo... BOBBY PA...
——WI-341	Yes I'm I... BIG AL D...
——WI-342	Rockin' C... BOBBY PI...
——WI-343	Oh! Mom... THE DAYL...
——WI-344	Like Long... PAUL REV...
——WI-347	I Don't W... JUNE BAT...
——WI-349	Driving Si... FREDDY ...
——WI-350	I Can't B... IKE & TIN...
——WI-351	Land of 1... CHRIS KE...
——WI-352	I've Got A... BETTY EV...
——WI-356	La De Da... INEZ & C...
——WI-359	Roll With... ETTA JAM...
——WI-360	Night Trai... JAMES BR...
——WI-363	Let's Stic... WILBERT ...
——WI-364	If It Ain't... Tu-ber-cu-l... HUEY ' PIA...
——WI-366	Sea Cruis... FRANKIE ...
——WI-367	Do-Re-Mi/... LEE DORS...

s Happened Before

fford To Do It

's No Big Thing

're Mine
HERS

y Home

Had A Feeling

I Feel/I Feel So Good

al Your Heart Away

/Please Come Home

s I & II

e Willie)/Hard Headed Girl

on
RAIDERS
e's Theme

deaway

t You Say/My Baby Now

es/That's My Girl

You/Your Love

u/Yankee Doodle Dandy
XX

/Good Rockin' Daddy

s Everything Happen To Me
E FAMOUS FLAMES

/Kansas City Twist

It's Another/
The Sinus Blues
H & THE CLOWNS

EP'S

———IEP706 The Soul of Ike & Tina Turner

LP'S

———ILP907 I've Got A Woman   Jimmy McGriff

———ILP908 Gospel Time   Jimmy McGriff

———ILP911 Mockingbird   Inez & Charlie Foxx

———ILP913 The Soul Sisters   The Soul Sisters

———ILP917 Rockin' Pneumonia and The Boogie Woogie Flu
          Huey ' Piano ' Smith & The Clowns

———ILP918 The Best of Elmore James   Elmore James

SUE
RECORD CATALOGUE

Sue
RECORDS

SOUL AND ROCK
THAT DOES NOT
STOP !

THE SUE STORY

THE ONLY LABEL DEVOTED ENTIRELY TO AUTHENTIC RHYTHM & BLUES IN THIS COUNTRY

Sue RECORDS

SUE
RECORD CATALOGUE

SUE RECORDS ARE OBTAINABLE AT ANY RECORD SHOP IN GREAT BRITAIN

available to record shops through :-

ISLAND RECORDS LIMITED 108 Cambridge Road, London, N.W.6.	KIL 1921/2/3
TAYLOR'S LIMITED 34 Pershore Street, Birmingham, 5	MID 5250
E.M.I. LIMITED 11/15 William Road, London, N.W.1.	EUS 2838
E.M.I. LIMITED 26 Progress Way, Purley Way, Croydon	MUN 3661
E.M.I. LIMITED 70, Fazeley Street, Birmingham, 5	MID 8301
E.M.I. LIMITED 30, Cannon Street, Manchester, 4.	DEA 6981
E.M.I. LIMITED 131, Renfield Street, Glasgow.	DOU 6061
SYMPHOLA LIMITED 14/18, Adelaide Street, Belfast, 2.	BEL 21939

Sue RECORDS

subsidiary of ISLAND RECORDS LTD.
108 Cambridge Road, London, N.W.6. KIL 1921/22/23

---

island RECORDS

IC

PHONE: KIL 1921/23
CABLES: "ACKEE"

FRIDAY, 19th FEBRUARY, 1965.

SUE   SET A DATE   Homesick
WI-330   Can't Afford To Do It

First great release on the exciting new 'pop' label

ALADDIN   HE'LL HAVE T
WI-601   GOTTA' LEARN TO   Jackie
           LOVE AGAIN

FRIDAY, 26th FEBRUARY, 1965.

SUE   JUST GOT SOME   W
WI-331   That's No Big Thing

ISLAND RECORDS LTD. 108 CAMBRIDGE ROAD, LO
TEL. KIL 1921/23

ISLAND RECORDS LTD.

Sue RECORDS   **BRIT**   **aladdin RECORDS**

RELEASE SHEET

FRIDAY, 5th MARCH, 1965.
SUE   IF IT AIN'T ONE THING IT'S ANOTHER
WI-364   Tu-ber-cu-lucas and the Sinus Blues
           Huey 'Piano' Smith & the Clowns

L.P. OF THE MONTH

SUE   ROCKIN' PNEUMONIA &
ILP-917   THE BOOGIE WOOGIE FLU
           Huey 'Piano' Smith & the Clowns

FRIDAY, 12th MARCH, 1965.
SUE   DO-RE-MI
WI-367   Ya Ya
           Lee Dorsey

ALADDIN   IT'S GONNA WORK OUT FINE
WI-603   DOLLY BABY   Owen Gray

FRIDAY, 19th MARCH, 1965.

IDAY, 11th JUNE, 1965.
ME   I HEAR VOICES
-379 Just Don't Care   Screamin' Jay Ha
61 Boogie Chillun   I'M IN THE MOOD
           John Lee Hoo

18th JUNE, 1965.
TURN ON YOUR LOVELIGHT
izzy Miss Lizzy
           Larry Williams

JUNE, 1965.
SIC CITY
ad A Little Money   The Pleasures

SING THE BLUES !
           Various Artistes

08 CAMBRIDGE ROAD, LONDON, N.W.6.
EL. KIL 1921/2/3

RELEAS

FRIDAY, 3rd S
SUE   I'M
WI-382 Som

SUE   TH
WI-386 Tell

FRIDAY, 10th S
SUE   Yo
WI-396 Run

FRIDAY, 17th S
SUE   DO
WI-387 PAR

SUE   YO
WI-390 Got

FRIDAY, 24th S
SUE   Bab
WI-397 Look

ISLAND RECORDS'

"Guy Stevens made these tapes up for me back in the day for ideas for me to use in my set as he thought they suited my vocal range."
CHRIS FARLOWE

Undeterred, Stevens then became part of the artist collective Hapshash & The Coloured Coat. He was fascinated by the vibrant concert posters that Michael English and Nigel Waymouth had designed. The band was accompanied by The Heavy Metal Kids (a mish-mash of musicians including Mickey Finn and Brian Jones of The Rolling Stones) and The Human Host. Their album was issued on red vinyl, with the sleeve cover designed by English and Waymouth, but the album's repetitive beats and chanting vocals did little to worry the pop world.

Earlier in the year a group from Carlisle, who had formerly been known as The VIP's, a tough R&B outfit, had arrived at the Island offices. They had moved on. They were now dressed in psychedelic threads and had changed their name to Art. Guy produced their sole album, *Supernatural Fairy Tales,* which was released in December 1967. As Art, though, they had only a short lifespan; vocalist and organist Gary Wright joined them, and by October they were going by the name Spooky Tooth. They were one of the few acts to incorporate both piano and organ at this time, although production duties for this band were handed to Jimmy Miller.

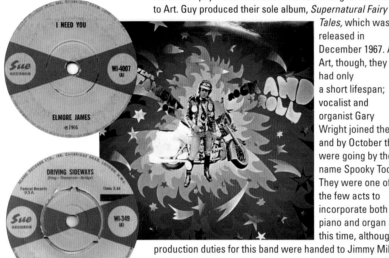

In 1968 Guy Stevens' *Testament of Rock 'n' Roll* was released on Island. The cover was an explosion of fiery colours with a black and white photo of Stevens clad in a Rocker's leather jacket, jeans and motorcycle boots, standing in front of a motorbike. That must have upset a few of the old Scene Club purists for sure.

Guy began dabbling heavily in drugs, particularly speed. He was given a year's sentence for possession and served eight months at Wormwood Scrubs prison.

In 1969 a Hereford band named The Silence came into Guy's radar. He christened them Mott The Hoople, as while serving his time in prison he had read a book about a circus freak with this name. He managed the band and produced their first two albums, then got dropped and reinstated before finally being sacked in 1972. The band were on the verge of splitting up when they covered 'All The Young Dudes', written and produced by David Bowie. The band went on to success, alas without Guy.

From 1975 Guy entered a downward spiral, pretty much the forgotten man. However, he was thrown a lifeline a couple of years later.

In 1977, Bernie Rhodes, who had known Guy since he'd been a regular at the Scene Club back in the day, proposed introducing Stevens to The Clash. Guy took them to a demo studio off Oxford Street. 'Janie Jones', 'London's Burning',

'White Riot', '1977' and 'Career Opportunities' were cut; but although Joe Strummer really liked Guy, he thought the demos sounded a bit lifeless and dull.

In 1979 Guy was asked to produce The Clash's album *London Calling.* CBS were opposed to the idea but nevertheless, from August 1979 onwards, the band went into Wessex Studio One. Guy would get them to warm up with Richard Berry's 'Louie Louie'. Tales abound of him running out of the control room into the studio, shouting, being aggressive, smashing chairs and pouring beer into the piano. The album made the UK top ten while the single 'London Calling' reached number eleven. Guy had his hit at last!

But it was too late and there is no happy ending to Guy's story. Sadly, Guy Stevens was found dead, aged 38, on August 28th, 1981, having overdosed on the prescription drugs he was taking to reduce his alcohol dependency.

Guy was immortalised by the song 'Guy Stevens Blues' by Free, 'Midnight To Stevens' by The Clash and the poem 'The Indiscreet Harlequin' by Paul Campbell-Lyons of Nirvana.

Fast forward to August 19th, 2008: my friend Damian Jones and myself found ourselves in a huge lock-up in Hackney from which singer Chris Farlowe ran his business. We were here to interview Farlowe for my forthcoming book on Mods, *The New Religion.* We were looking through his scrapbooks, when he produced three boxes of reel-to-reel tapes. I believe that the tapes date from 1965 as this appears to be the last release year on any of the tracks over the three tapes.

Chris Farlowe: "Guy Stevens made these up for me back in the day for ideas for me to use in my set as he thought they suited my vocal range." Damian bought the tapes from him that day and had them transferred over to CDs.

Back in December 1979, during the interview for *NME* with Charles Shaar Murray, Guy had revealed a love for a particular song: "Sue was formed by Juggy Murray in New York, and he started the label with Charlie & Inez Foxx's 'Mockingbird'; that was Sue 301. I went over to get a record called 'The Love Of My Man', which nobody has covered, and I hope Elkie Brooks isn't listening. 'The Love Of My Man' by Viola Kilgore [actually Theola Kilgore]. Unbelievable. Un-be-liev-able. Blitzkrieg, out the window, number one, easy. He owned the copyright. Chris went over and offered him $500. Juggy wanted half a million. It got to three in the American charts. If you check back you'll find it. One of the greatest records I ever heard in my life.

"I wanted it to be on Sue. The main thing was that I wanted everything good to be on Sue. I wanted Bob Dylan to be on Sue. That was why I started importing records for Island with David Betteridge and Chris. And it nearly bankrupted Island."

The strange thing is that 'The Love Of My Man' never came out on the UK Sue label, but another of Theola Kilgore's records, 'I'll Keep Trying' /'Coming Back To Me' (issued originally on the American label KT Records), was released as one of the last records issued on the British label, in April 1967. 'The Love Of My Man' was on the first of the tapes that Guy had given to Farlowe.

TAPE 1 (SM PHILIPS TAPE)

'Hi Diddly Dee Dum Dum' - The Dells (ARGO 5442)

'Some Day After A While (You'll Be Sorry)' - Freddie King (FEDERAL 12518)

'Yield Not To Temptation' - Bobby Bland (DUKE 352)

'The Love Of My Man' - Theola Kilgore (SEROCK 2004)

'You're Good For Me' - Solomon Burke (ATLANTIC 2205)

'Shimmy Shimmy (I Do The)' - Bobby Freeman (KING 5373)

'My Home Is A Prison' - Lonesome Sundown (EXCELLO 2102)

'I Smell Trouble' - Little Johnny Taylor (GALAXY 733)

'Little Boy Blue' - Bobby Bland (DUKE 196)

'I'm Hanging Up My Heart For You' - Solomon Burke (ATLANTIC 70.085)

'Slumber Party' - The Van-Dells (STAX 145)

'Do Anything You Wanna (Pt 1)' - Harold Betters (GATEWAY 747)

'There's Something On Your Mind' - Garnett Mimms (UNITED ARTISTS) (Garnet Mimms 1964 LP *As Long As I Have You*, United Artists UAL 3396)

'There's Something On Your Mind' - Jimmy Hughes (VEE JAY VJS 1102) (Jimmy Hughes 1965 LP *Steal Away*, VJS 1102)

'I Call It Pretty Music' - Stevie Wonder (LIVE RECORDING) (Stevie Wonder 1964 LP *The Original Motor Town Revue*, STMS 5092)

'Moon River' - Stevie Wonder (LIVE RECORDING) (Stevie Wonder 1964 LP *The Original Motor Town Revue*, STMS 5092)

'Pain In My Heart' - Otis Redding (VOLT 112)

'Hey Hey Baby' - Otis Redding (ATCO 103)

'It's Love Baby (24 Hours A Day)' - Hank Ballard & The Midnighters (KING 5798)

'I Done You Wrong' - Kip Anderson (TOMORROW 5103)

'Part Time Lover' - Little Johnny Taylor (GALAXY 722)

'Question' - Roscoe Shelton (SIMS 217)

'Baby Don't You Do It' - Marvin Gaye (TAMLA 54101)

TAPE 2 ('GREAT R&B')

'Daddy Rollin' Stone' - Derek Martin (CRACKERJACK 4013)

'Rock A Bye Your Baby With A Dixie Melody' - Aretha Franklin (COLUMBIA 4-42157)

'Don't Start Cryin' Now' - Slim Harpo (EXCELLO 2194)

'Somebody' - Jerry Lewis (DOT DLP 38001)

'Out Of Sight' - James Brown (SMASH 1919)

'That's The Way Love Is' - Bobby Bland (DUKE 360)

'Not Too Young To Get Married' - Bob B. Sox & The Blue Jeans (PHILLES 113)

'Laughin'' - Al Casey (STACY 950)

'Ain't That Just Like A Woman' - Fats Domino (IMPERIAL 5723)

'Lucy Lee' - Lloyd George (IMPERIAL 5837)

'Some Other Guy' - Richie Barrett (ATLANTIC 2142)

'Searchin'' - Alvin Robinson (TIGER TI 104)

'Thumbin' A Ride' - The Coasters (ATCO 6186)

TAPE 3 (SM EMI TAPE)

'Let's Kiss And Make Up' - The Falcons (ATLANTIC 2179)

'That's A Man's Way' - Wilson Pickett (ATLANTIC 2320)

'T-Bird' - Rocky Roberts (ROULETTE 4506)

'Old Time Lover' - Joe Tex (DIAL 3020)

'Welcome Home' - Walter Jackson (OKEH 4-7219)

'Hands Off' - Jay McShann Orchestra (VEE JAY VJ 155)

'That's Him Over There' - Nina Simone (COLPIX) (Nina Simone 1959 LP *The Amazing Nina Simone*, SCP 407)

'Don't Be Ashamed To Call My Name' - Little Willie John (KING 5147)

'Your One And Only Man' - Otis Redding (VOLT 121)

'Home In Your Heart' - Otis Redding (VOLT) (Otis Redding 1965 LP *The Great Otis Redding Sings Soul Ballads*, Volt 411)

'Lonnie On The Move' - Lonnie Mack (FRATERNITY F920)

'Tell It Like It Is' - Eddie Bo (RIC 969)

'Every Dog Got His Day' - Eddie Bo (RIC 969)

'Don't Jump' - Fontella Bass & Bobby McClure (CHECKER 1111)

'Looking For My Pig' - Joe Tex (DIAL 3019)

'My Babe' - Ramsey Lewis Trio (ARGO 5481)

'Organ Shout' - Dave 'Baby' Cortez (CHESS 1861)

'We're Gonna Make It' - Little Milton (CHECKER 1105)

'Satisfaction' - Otis Redding (VOLT) (although 'Satisfaction' was released by Otis Redding as a single in February 1966, I believe this version is from his 1965 *Otis Blue* LP, VOLT 412)

CHRIS FARLOWE

THANKS TO THE FOLLOWING FOR IDENTIFYING THE SOURCES OF THREE TRACKS: BILL SULLIVAN ('SOMEBODY' - JERRY LEWIS), PAUL NEWMAN ('IT'S LOVE BABY' - HANK BALLARD) AND CHRIS CASEY ('THERE'S SOMETHING ON YOUR MIND' - GARNET MIMMS).

Trippers are run out of town

POLICE escorted 20 trippers out of town yesterday after a fight in an amusement park.

Their coach-driver was ordered to drive the party—all men—back to London from Southend without stopping.

Fourteen other men who arrived in the coach missed the return journey because they were being questioned by police about the fight at the Kursaal amusement gardens. Six were later accused of conduct likely to cause a breach of the peace. They were allowed bail. One was also charged with assault.

The other eight will not appear in court.

Police with dogs were called to the amusement park when the fight broke out between Kursaal employees and members of the coach party from Battersea.

Four of the Kursaal workers were taken to hospital for treatment after being injured in the fight. All the 34 members of the coach party were taken to the police station.

Later 20 of them were allowed to return to the coach, which was escorted to the town boundary by a police car and motor-cycle outrider.

At the boundary, an Essex county police car took over the job of escorting the coach to London.

When the coach arrived at Battersea, other officers were on duty till the men in the group returned to their homes.

CHAPTER 5 : GANGS AND TERRITORIAL WARFARE

The summer of 1965 had many days of below-average temperature, and the beginning of September was still changeable, cool and windy. As the temperature got warmer around the middle of the month, the bright spell was welcomed by the public.

On Sunday, September 19th that year, crowds flocked to the coast to cling on to the last rays of the season's sunshine. In Southend-on-Sea, Essex, the Kursaal amusement park was doing a roaring trade. Crowds flocked to rides such as the Mont Blanc, Calypso, the Horton Scenic Railway and Aerial Flight. Soon, though, the pleasant atmosphere was shattered as a mass brawl broke out between the fairground staff and a group of young men out on a beano. As the tannoys called out across the fair for more attendants to leave their posts, from the Ghost Train to the Bumper Cars, families ran away in horror as the blood began to flow. To the Junction Boys, it was just another day out.

The Junction Boys were made up of a group of around twenty-five boys based around Clapham Junction in south London. They had become close friends around the period of 1960/'61. Their meeting points varied – the younger members would often meet up at the Windsor CastlePub on St John's Hill, Clapham; at Notarianni's ice cream parlour; or simply on the pavement outside Dunn's Gentlemen's Outfitters by the train station. Some of the older crowd congregated in the Essex pub, Grant Road, Battersea.

They'd then venture out en masse in a variety of vehicles, including at least twelve of them in an ex-police Black Maria, with at least two other cars following. The irony was not lost on them as often they finished the night in the back of a different Black Maria!

Roy Emberson: "In the early days, a few of us had scooters, but it really only lasted around a year to eighteen months until you was old enough to get a car.

"If you could be suited and booted in a car, you thought you had made it. We'd meet up in the Windsor Castle pub and Ray Cocklin had a Ford Consul Mark II, and we'd have a whip round to give him sixpence each because a gallon of petrol was only around 1s 10d."

They'd move out of the Junction and onto the Old Kent Road boozers such as the Apples and Pears, the Thomas A Beckett or the Kings Arms. Then on to clubs such as the Bali Hai in Streatham, where the entrance was adjacent to Silver Blades ice rink, the Stork Club and the Locarno, Streatham Hill, or maybe even Mr Smith's in Catford. If they went 'up

> "In the early days, a few of us had scooters, but it really only lasted around a year to eighteen months until you was old enough to get a car... if you could be suited and booted in a car, you thought you had made it."
> ROY EMBERSON

COACH PARTY TOLD 'GET OUT OF TOWN'

GEORGE 'COCO' FRANCIS. INSET: THE GANG

west' it could be the Lyceum, or later on, the Scene Club. The one very notable thing about the Junction Boys was the inclusion of a black man, George Warrington Francis, who was often referred to as 'Coco'. George had done a bit of boxing and could look after himself but sometimes he could attract unwanted attention.

"When George first came over from Jamaica he was 11, and he came to my school, the William Blake, in Battersea. At the time you seldom saw a black man," says fellow Junction Boy, Charlie Taylor. "Although we actually had a fight at school, from that day on we became friends and looked after each other. When we became the age where we could go out drinking, he wasn't allowed in to a lot of places. The Burnham Social Club in Battersea certainly wouldn't let him in because of his colour."

Kenny Moran was a regular face in George's company: "There was no racism at all from our crowd. When he was with us, he was a Junction Boy, so he got in to most places with us. A lot of people wouldn't call him Coco, so they'd call him George or 'Warry'. He was never offended by us calling him that because he knew us all. He could handle himself if it was needed though."

The group of friends never saw themselves as a firm, a mob or a gang. Their punch-ups could take place anywhere, from coastal resorts such as Torquay and Leysdown to the pubs and clubs of London. They certainly didn't ever see any of their exploits as Mods and Rockers-type violence.

Roy Emberson screws his face up at the thought. "We was on the piss and up for anything that came our way. We never had rows with Rockers. They never even came into the equation. Although we wouldn't have avoided them if trouble had started."

The Junction Boys are quick to deny that they considered themselves Mods but the similarity is stunning. Suits were from Henry London, shirts were from a black guy named Norman on the Fulham Palace Road, shoes were created courtesy of Stan's of Battersea.

"We were Mods in as far as we had mohair suits on, handmade shirts and handmade suits on. Dressing up became like a contest amongst us. Nobody ever said anything but everybody wanted to look the best, especially when Ravel's started making shoes down the Junction," states Roy.

"We were just fashionable. We knew where to get a whistle [suit] done," agrees Kenny. "All the stars used Norman for shirts. You'd have your initials on your breast pocket or your cuff."

Roy Emberson: "After Henry London, Brian Ritchie opened a shop. In fact, he'd originally worked for Henry, but opened his own place in the Junction, opposite Woolworths. We also used a place called Hymie's in The Cut at Waterloo."

Charlie Taylor laughs: "Brian Ritchie made me a suit and it was a black cloth with a mauve stripe in it. When I went for the fitting he said to me, 'This ain't arf gonna look nice.' I said I tell you what Brian, you fuckin' wear it. I look like

fuckin' Victor Silvester the band leader!"

Although they had gone through the scooter phase, transport often varied, from trips to Torquay or Leysdown on the back of a flatbed lorry to bundling in to Bernie McGhee's old 1950s ex-police van. There were also fights at places such as Battersea Town Hall and Wandsworth Town Hall, but the infamous coastal punch-ups of Mods and Rockers were avoided, as many members had already been nicked and previously served time or were currently serving time at borstal, a youth detention centre.

This didn't stop them getting tied in with Mods and Rockers reports in the newspapers though. The *Daily Sketch* on Monday 20th September, 1965 reported on the boys' eventful Sunday beano in Southend.

Thirty-four of them had set off on a coach trip that would see the lads eventually descend on the funfair. "There was little Stanley Price on a ride going round and his change came out of his pocket. When the ride finished, Price was furious and starts to have a tear-up with one of the blokes working at the fairground," explains Charlie Taylor. "It came over the tannoys: 'Fight! Security!' Then all the fairground boys converged from everywhere tooled up with chains and spanners that they kept on their stalls for these occasions."

"The boot was one of your main weapons, but we never went around tooled up. Nobody in our lot carried weapons," says Kenny Moran.

Fighting broke out all over the fairground, and Charlie ended up on the wrong end of a fairground boy's motorcycle chain. His blond hair turned red with blood, and he was taken to hospital to be stitched up. He ended up being handcuffed to a policeman, and knowing he was about to be arrested, asked to use the toilet. Once inside the cubicle he managed to escape from a small window and found himself outside wandering the street, covered in blood. He somehow managed to flag down a car, saying he'd been involved in an accident, and talked the owners of the car into giving him a lift back to the coach in Southend. Unfortunately for Charlie, the police were waiting again, and he was led back to the hospital once more in order to receive treatment, but this time handcuffed to two policemen.

The day out ended with four of the Kursaal workers going to hospital after being injured in the fight, and all thirty-four members of the coach party being taken to the police station.

A fairground worker said: "It was like something out of a cowboy film. Machines were overturned. Everyone seemed to be in a brawl. Then the police arrived and gave them some real Wild West treatment."

Later, twenty of the Junction crowd were allowed to return to the coach. It was escorted to the town boundary by five police motorcycle outriders. At the boundary an Essex county police car took over the job of escorting the coach back to the Windsor Castle pub at St John's Hill. The fourteen other men missed the return journey because they were being questioned by the police. Six were later accused of 'conduct likely to cause a breach of the peace', and one

"We was on the piss and up for anything that came our way. We never had rows with Rockers. They never even came into the equation. Although we wouldn't have avoided them if trouble had started."
ROY EMBERSON

ALL DRESSED UP AND SOMEWHERE TO GO

> "We did take a lot of liberties, but it's made us what we are today, and we're all right now and we're all straight. How nobody got killed I don't know, and how we didn't kill anybody I don't know because we did go over the top at times."
> ROY EMBERSON

was charged with assault. They were allowed bail. The other eight did not appear in court.

The following day the *Daily Sketch* printed an article entitled 'Coach Party Told "Get Out Of Town"' and a police spokesman gave this quote: "We called in every available police officer, locked them in their coach and escorted them out of the area. They were aged between 17 and 19 – Mods and Rocker types with long hair and ridiculous clothes."

Roy Emberson was somewhat displeased with the description. "What they wrote in the newspaper about Mods dressed in silly clothes and long hair was just absolute bollocks."

In the end the Junction Boys' exploits spanned well over a decade, until around 1973. Marriages and responsibilities as ever changed the lives of those involved. Despite this, they have remained friends and still meet up regularly to chat about those far-off days.

Roy smiles at the memories. "There was money over south London because of Chelsea and Kensington. There were some tasty areas such as Millwall, Bermondsey and the Elephant and Castle. All of them mobs over there had terrible names in the old days for people cutting you and what have you. We were all proud of our little mob. I was anyway, still am. That Battersea/Junction thing doesn't leave you. A lot of the things we done back then I'm a bit ashamed of. We did take a lot of liberties, but it's made us what we are today, and we're all right now and we're all straight. How nobody got killed I don't know, and how we didn't kill anybody I don't know because we did go over the top at times."

Early beginnings and Mod roots

Tony Ellis (London): "I was born in north London, but around 1956, my family moved to the Wimbledon/Putney area along the side of Wimbledon Common on a brand-new council estate, the Argyle Estate by Wimbledon Park Side. Lots of kids my age used to come back from church and play the latest pop records such as The Shadows, then when The Beatles came along, we all became Beatles fans. After listening to what The Beatles and the Stones were listening to, we soon got into the original American stuff. We had a club nearby, the Jenny Lind Club. In 1964, we used to go up there as young lads of 14 or 15 and see all the scooters outside. Mods used to come from all over the place, and the venue would be packed out. I bought my first reefer there, and that's where we danced to a local R&B group called The Hellraisers. They were the first proper band I ever saw, and they used to do the whole Stones-type thing with maracas, doing things like Bo Diddley covers. That got me really hooked on music, and it became a quest to track down the originals. Then as we became more Mod, we started going to the Wimbledon Palais, we saw The Who, Georgie Fame, The Move and all the chart sounds of the time. All the time, though, we were soul fans. We went to Radio Caroline and Radio London nights there too. They both played lots of soul sounds as well as Mod pop stuff such as 'Jump And Dance' by Carnaby, 'Liar Liar' by The Castaways. We just went on from there really."

Barry Quinnell (Eastergate): "Going right back to my primary school days there was a girl called Linda Beckenham, she was two years older than me. I remember that during the Beatnik days before Mods, she used to go up to people who weren't cool and make this square sign with her hands and say 'You're a square!' Remember, this is at primary school! So, move the clock forward, and we all went to Westergate Secondary Modern, and her and a bloke called Maurice Langridge both said around the same time that there was a club opening in Bognor called the Shoreline. They told us that it was part of this hotel for teenagers, and that if we went down there soon we could get free membership. So, we jumped on the bus and signed the membership form."

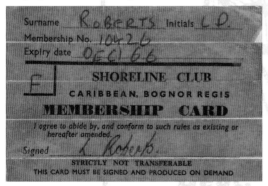

Tony Rounce (London): "I grew up in Stanford-le-Hope, Essex, despite the fact that I'm from east London. My mum and dad were on a list to move out, like a lot of areas of London at that time. They were pulling old houses down, particularly where I grew up, around the docks, because they'd been hit in that area so often by bombs during the war. People were scared in case everything fell down. So, they started building maisonettes and high-rises in the surrounding areas. We got moved from Silvertown to Plaistow, where we lived in a maisonette, and my grandparents lived next door. Then we got moved again to Stanford-le-Hope. It wasn't a new town like Harlow, Crawley or Stevenage for instance. It was a village that had lots of green land around it, and they were building houses to accommodate people moving out of London. It was the population explosion due to the baby boomers. It was a good thing for me because lots of young people ended up there."

Raymond Potter (London): "I was born in Bang'ole*, my old man was a totter, a horse-and-cart man. I'd got into the Mod thing when I was about 12 or 13. My brother had been into it with all the Mod scooters, so that's how I got into it. He was well into his suits, and that's what attracted me, because you could ride a scooter and still look smart. The whole area was all Mods. The scooter to have then was the Vespa GS – my brother had one and so did all of his little squad. There was loads of Mods and Rockers trouble around here, it was a big thing. It was bloody bad, and there were fights all of the time. At the top of Princess Road, they had a firm come down from the Salt Box, Hells Angels, so all the boys got on the roof with bottles filled with stones. When the gang turned up, they were pelted with them. That's how it used be. But the Mod days were the best days of my life without any shadow of a doubt."

Bill Fordham (London): "The family came from a flat in Shepherd's Bush but we moved into the brand-new Argyle Estate in SW19 when I was very young. So, I grew up there. It was a big estate with loads, and loads, and loads of kids. My brother, Steve, is three years older than me. He was a Mod who dressed to kill and frequented all the top clubs at that time, but I was a bit too young to hang around him. I remember everything about him hanging around with his mates – one of them was local face Pete Sinacola, and that's what I aspired to be. Steve's record collection was my first introduction to the sounds of R&B, Motown and Blue Beat. One thing that did happen to me was that I went to school two years early. They thought I was bright, so I started primary school as a young kid and then when I got to go to secondary school, they kept me back two years. All my mates were two years older than me, so when I was 12 and 13, they were 14 and 15. Plus I was small, and my mates were big, so I was always trying to prove myself to keep up with them."

Brian Wright (London): "I grew up in south Westminster, that had quite a large number of council estates. Although not many people know that. As a result of the baby boom, there was a big bubble of young kids of my age group. It was safer than now to be out on the streets in those days so we hung around on the streets a lot, and it was easy to get influenced by what you saw on other people. I was quite tall for my age, so I always hung around with older guys who were further down the road in terms of image and identity. I would have been 13 by the end of 1964. But bear in mind at that point I was six feet one, and shaving. From the age of 12 I had a part-time evening job delivering alcohol for a local wine office, so I had a disposable income. There were always jobs to be found, street markets were everywhere. It was easy to find out where guys got their clobber from so I started going to the same shops as them. One school year could be a massive difference. There was one geezer called Sonny who was that one year older, and by the age of around 14 he was

NEW! NE

WORLD'S FIRST

TEENOTE

Teenotel Week-end Special
COVERS

ALL FOR

ONLY

15/-

★ DANCES SATU
★ SNACK SU
★ MIDNITE FEA
★ BACON &
★ SNACK SU
★ FOUR FRE
★ TEENOTEL FACES
   CHANGING
★ Reduced Pric
   2/6 for

TOP GROUPS

No more d

ACTION AND THE VAGAB

N! NEW!

AND THE FANTASTIC

SHORELINE CLUB

AY and S

ER

RE FILM o

GG BREA

DAY LUN

COKES

CHES & SEA

S AVAILABLE

Annual Sho

eek-enders

Week-end

ND ★ 18th JULY

HURRY TEENAGERS
ALL NiTE rave
TO-NiTE
5 groups 5/- from 8 pm until 8 am
latecomers 10/- after 10 pm

the CARIBBEAN
the world's FIRST
TEENOTEL
RESERVATIONS at BOGNOR
NITE WEEKEND HOLIDAY
or "ALL-IN"

"There was a guy who lived in the flats just up the road from me, opposite the church I used to go to. He had a very distinctive name: a good-looking Italian-English bloke and he seemed a lot bigger than us at the time. He was a face we all looked up to, somebody you daren't even approach really. He was Pete Sinacola."
TONY ELLIS

wearing handmade three-piece mohair suits. By the time you're a teenager you go in search of your identity so it was only natural in a white working-class area to fall into the concept and image of Mod. There wasn't any choice. It was almost inevitable that you would become a Mod in south Westminster, given the fact that it was a grubby middle-class and white working-class kids area and there was nothing in competition with it. For instance, on Lupus Street, which we used to call The Front because it was on the northern perimeter of Churchill Gardens Estate, there were guys, older than me, on their motor scooters dressed in blue nylon macs and berets, bowler hats, even deerstalker hats. The influence of French neorealist films was part of that. There was a geezer who had a pram, and he sold fake fur, and these kids would buy a fake fur tail and tie it to the aerial on their scooter."

Tony Haddow (London): "I didn't have any older siblings, all mine were younger. But you had kids there that had developed from their Mod brothers. It was just us three mates on my estate, which was the Spur Road Estate in Edgware. I'd moved in there with my family when I was 2 years old. It was part of the massive rehousing project after the war. My mum and dad had managed to blag one of these three-bedroomed houses. Then all the flats went up and it created this melting pot like all the estates in London. Anyway, the three of us at school, were really into Otis Redding, Arthur Conley, Sam & Dave, all that type of sound, when we were 13 or 14. Then we started going to a few clubs, where there were a few black guys about. I went to college in St Albans, I did a year's full-time building course there when I was 15 years old. I met people from places like Watford and Welwyn Garden City. Fashion started to creep into the look. I finished the course and ended up at a plumbing and building college at Willesden around '66/'67. There, I started meeting people from Camden Town, Willesden, Kilburn, and that is when it all started happening. Because you're in that area, you start meeting black guys, and becoming mates with them. So, you end up talking music with them. There used to be a café on the corner by Willesden College, and they used to have a jukebox. You'd all go down there and you'd put on American soul like Otis Redding and Arthur Conley. Then you'd hear bits of ska such as Millie Small's 'My Boy Lollipop'. It all started to creep in. I started working all over London, so I'd go to different clubs and meeting people from other areas. Tunes like 'Longshot Kick De Bucket' and 'Return Of The Django' and 'Double Barrell' came out. 'Wet Dream' by Max Romeo got banned by the BBC and it's flying up the charts. We were going to record shops in Wembley, a couple in the Edgware Road, then Notting Hill, and over to Brixton. It wasn't hard to buy records if you knew where to go. We're buying 45s as they came in their droves from Jamaica. Lots of them just had bits of writing on them, and they had no middle. You didn't even know what you were getting. The earliest single I ever had was 'Rock And Shake' by Prince Buster, 1957, on a gold label. The ska thing was very big as well. When the reggae stuff came out, especially things like 'Wreck A Pum Pum' or 'Wet Dream', my mum would say 'Christ, what are you listening to now?'"

Ian Hingle (London): "Style is in my family. My dad didn't have any money, but he looked good. And my grandfather

fought in the First World War, regular soldier, and survived it. Out there from day one. His battalion got wiped out three times and he survived it without a scratch, mentally or physically.

"There are great photos of them when he and his brother got back. They just went for it. Dressed up in top hats, with capes open, so you could see the lining, and they had canes. They would parade up and down The Strand on the pull. Loads of clubs down there in the 1920s.

"He only had a humble job, my grandfather, no real money. He worked for United Dairies selling biscuits or something, but off he'd go, and out with face powder on, so he didn't look so pale. What he really got up to I didn't get a chance to ask, but there you go. Dressing up is in the genes."

Tony Ellis (London): "There was a guy who lived in the flats just up the road from me, opposite the church I used to go to. He had a very distinctive name: a good-looking Italian-English bloke and he seemed a lot bigger than us at the time. He was a face we all looked up to, somebody you daren't even approach really. He was Pete Sinacola."

Bill Fordham (London): "The first thing I got into was the Jenny Lind. That was a local club on our estate situated behind the Jenny Lind pub, which was a big Mod venue. My brother insists that it was here where The High Numbers played their first gig. I only got in there the once though because a bloke came up to me and said, 'I remember you. You were in here last week chatting my bird up.' I told him I hadn't been there before, but he just said he wanted me outside. Anyway, another bloke from our estate was laughing his head off and he told me if I didn't go outside with the bloke, that he'd give me a good kicking in the club. I am somewhat reluctant but thought that I could probably make a faster retreat from outside than from inside. We go outside, he comes for me and I catch him with a lucky punch. He managed to cut his neck on the railings. I run! The word goes out that I have 'knifed' him and if I return to Putney again, I'll get thrown over the bridge. So, at 14 years of age, I was a wanted man."

Tony Rounce (London): "I was observing Mod as it was going on, being in the fortunate position that a lot of youngsters weren't. I was encouraged by both my parents and my grandparents to listen to music and go beyond the boundaries of what was in the top twenty and explore artists that not many other kids did such as Bo Diddley, Sonny Boy Williamson, Leadbelly and whoever else. I was 11 or 12 when *Ready Steady Go!* started. My dad was only 29, so we watched it as a family. I'm getting the exposure to Mods, and I'm liking the image. I'm a bit too young for it really, but not too young for the records, and not too young to join the fan clubs of bands that I liked, such as The Yardbirds. As my taste is evolving, I'm going down a similar route to my parents and my grandparents of preferring black American music to anything else, but not to the exclusion of buying beat groups and such. I just needed a kick in that direction."

Barry Quinnell (Eastergate): "From when I was about 9 years old, and for the next four or five years after that, I was allowed to buy one record a week. My mum and dad were

BIRDCAGE BOYS.

"I don't really know what we were. There were a lot of youngsters like me, but we weren't Mods. Mods were always evolving. To me, we were Londoners. I always had my hair short and always dressed smart but wouldn't call myself a Skinhead. If you went out, you had to dress up. That was the way it was."
BILL FORDHAM

hard up, but as I was an only child I got more than others who had brothers and sisters. I'd buy things like The Swinging Blue Jeans, as well as things like The Barron Knights when they did pop stuff and The Searchers. One day I was in the Shoreline on a Sunday afternoon not long after it had first opened. The DJ played 'You're No Good', which I had a copy of by The Swinging Blue Jeans. I thought, this isn't the version I know. I went up to the DJ to ask who it was, and it turned out to be Betty Everett. I didn't even know she was a black girl. She could have recorded it at Abbey Road for all I knew. I spoke to a friend who knew it, but then he asked me if I had heard Doris Troy doing 'Just One Look', and then I found that The Beatles hadn't actually written 'Twist And Shout'. It totally politicised me. I got angry. I thought to myself, bloody hell, these black people in America are being downtrodden, and yet they're recording this wonderful music, only for whites to copy it and make fortunes out of it. That was a massive moment in my life. It was musically great, and politically fantastic for me."

Tony Ellis (London): "The clothes around '64 for us junior Mods were Hush Puppies dyed black or blue maybe. We couldn't afford the Yale T-shirts that some of the older Mods wore so we bought white T-shirts from British Home Stores and got iron-on fabric to make the Y for the Yale logo. We also wore Sinbad jeans which were highly coloured in lime green, orange or blue. They were sort of hipsters and quite short in the ankle. We weren't old enough for scooters at the time but all around the estate there were older Mods with all the lights on the front of theirs. We just used to sit there in admiration. There were a couple of Greasers on our estate, but it was mostly Mods. It all led on to not talking to people that weren't like us. The ones we'd grown up with, who just stayed normal, we didn't talk to any more."

Barry Cain (London): "I was born in 1953, so I was too young for the Mods and Rockers. I recall The Beatles in 1963 and

then I was into it all from there. I was brought up in the Angel and went to school in St John's Street there. Things were constantly changing in the sixties and Skinheads just didn't appear. From 1967 I started to notice them, not really more than that and there was that crossover time, which I call the Small Faces intermission. I mean you had The Beatles and that Mersey stuff and then The Small Faces and they were a different kind of thing. I had a friend at school, Tony Gibbs, who was the most sartorially elegant guy, 13 or 14 and showing off these grey herringbone trousers that he had and he was doing that, he was singing 'Stuck it up on a Friday night, sha la la la la lee…' and bowling along to that song. That was the first I noticed of the style of it all really. Tony lived in an absolute shithole in Northampton Buildings, near Exmouth Market, and he lived in two rooms in the basement. So, to have that kind of style coming out of there was something else."

Tony Ellis (London): "I think I became a fully fledged Mod around the time I took my first gear at a Who gig at around the time 'My Generation' came out. That was the turning point in a lot of our lives. The gear sort of put you into another bracket. They were French blues. We'd take twenty on a Friday night, and ten on a Saturday, that made for interesting times. Well, until my mum caught me. You'd got your mohair suit from Alexandro's in Putney. It was something like ten bob a month on HP. I got a brown mohair with a lime green button-down shirt with a tie. You'd end up with the girl's perfume on your shoulder from where you'd danced with them at the Palais. It would stay on there for weeks, because dry cleaning was too expensive."

Barry Quinnell (Eastergate): "I often wonder how my love of soul music and me being a Mod would have developed without the Shoreline Club. To me, it was massive for teenagers of that persuasion in the area. I lived in Eastergate and went to the nearby Westgate School. If you look at the

HOTEL

MODS OUTSIDE THE SHORELINE CLUB, BOGNOR, 1966
INSET: TONY ELLIS ON HIS SCOOTER, 1966
INSET BOTTOM: BARRY THANE, 1965

arthur alexander
JUST ARRIVED FROM U.S.A.
SHORELINE
EASTER MONDAY

MODS AND SCOOTERS, BOGNOR REGIS, 1966

map, Eastergate is about equal distance between Chichester, Littlehampton and Bognor Regis, all on the Sussex coast. Then going out a bit further, it's twenty-five miles east to Brighton and twenty-five miles west to Pompey. Before even leaving school, I had already got my membership to the Shoreline Club, and we all queued for the first all-nighter, most of us lying to our parents by saying we were all staying at each other's homes... 1965/'66/'67, those three years were pivotal, and I often wonder if the Shoreline hadn't existed whether I would have bothered to go further afield. Whether I would have gone to London and other places. Then, we had the Birdcage in Pompey, which put on some fabulous gigs with acts like Jimmy James & The Vagabonds with Count Prince Miller as the MC. They were fantastic nights."

Bill Fordham (London): "I don't really know what we were. There were a lot of youngsters like me, but we weren't Mods. Mods were always evolving. To me, we were Londoners. I always had my hair short and always dressed smart but wouldn't call myself a Skinhead. If you went out, you had to dress up. That was the way it was."

Bonny Staplehurst (London): "I was coming into it all as a mini Mod. Started that from 1964/'65. Stretch trousers, Hush Puppies. We had a cousin who was five years older and she influenced us. I think I got into the Skinheads in 1968 at school really. I went to school in Fulham and then I started going to football at 14, Chelsea being my team."

Jacky Abramovitch (London): "Thinking back, I'm not really sure what drew us into the look – me and my friend Gill were two grammar school girls, so God knows how that happened. I guess it was just exciting. I mean there wasn't anything else for us, because we were too young to do the Mod thing – well, we tried to do that in a kid way, but Skinhead was something we could afford to do and thought it looked great. Then there was the music; we really got excited by the music and in the end, well it was really to get the boys! Gill actually married one and they are still married today. We were really separated from the boys. We hung around but weren't really part of them then. I mean you were unlikely to go anywhere with a boy, unless you were going out with them."

Bob Wheeler (Slough): "A lot of people my sister's age used to go to the Ricky Tick in Windsor and also the Granada and the Carlton Ballroom in Slough. The Carlton was an amazing place, you used to get the Motown acts turn up at Slough high street! I guess I just caught the end of that Mod period. We were young kids really, but we wore parkas and had scooters. I had a Vespa 150 Sportique at that time, but not for long. A hostel was built on the Britwell, just opposite my house. I think it was for broken families, also kids that got into trouble, but they were all from London too. They were mainly Chelsea and West Ham boys, and all smartly dressed. They had all the top gear. They'd been running around London rioting for most of their lives, and suddenly they're put in the middle of nowhere. I tagged onto them, and we started going to football and places together. They were a big influence on me. The whole estate was basically Skinhead. Prior to that there was a lot of Greasers, I suppose you'd call them. They were a lot older than us lot, and they used to go in the Londoner pub. They were known as the 'Hole In The Wall Gang'."

John 'Bomber' Wild (London): "I lived in West London in the sixties and went to school just off Ladbroke Grove, at the time a very working-class area. Portobello Road Market was nearby and a great source of inspiration with its mix of people. We were a very mixed community. There were London working-class English, Irish and people from the West Indies, who had come in the late fifties. Judging by the surnames of many friends there were also a fair amount of Welsh families. The direct Great Western Railway link from the west obviously attracted Welsh families to London for work.

"Portobello was a bustling market – barrow boys selling fruit and vegetables, antique and second-hand goods dealers, then you had a strong Hippy radical type who frequented the bedsits and flats, as well as a number of squats in rundown Victorian and Georgian housing stock. To be fair the place was a bit of a slum. But brightened up with colourful characters, all nations gathered in a melting pot. I would be up the market at every opportunity visiting relatives and shopping with my mother. I'd been given the job of designated carrier of vegetables and food products purchased from the various market traders. Supermarkets were virtually unheard of at the time. The market was where I could source items of fashionable clothing and convince my mum I needed them. Fly jackets, Levis jeans and boots. You always had to have boots. Big T were my favourites, made by Tuf."

Maggie Brown (Southampton): "Firstly, I was born in 1956, I suppose it started when I was around 13. We all started going to the 'Teenage Centre' in Winchester; it was a totally different town back then. Everyone knew each other and there was a group of lads that used to come up from Eastleigh which is just a few miles away going towards Southampton. They were really friendly with the Winchester lot at that time, going to football etc.

"My cousin Richard was a big influence on me. He was a Mod and introduced me to soul, Tamla Motown, ska and reggae when I was about 13 years old. I remember his metallic copper and black Lambretta; I can see it now in my mind's eye. I suppose I looked up to him a lot because he was a Mod.

"This would have been around 1969 and the Teenage Centre was an old school at the back of the Guildhall in Winchester... A guy called Bob Dean was the DJ who played there most of the time. I can't recall the names of any of the other DJs. Some of the girls and boys were a couple or so years older than me, but it was all Mod and early Skinheads. I thought to myself, 'I love this look,' and the music just got into my head and, to be honest, I have never looked back. When the Teenage Centre closed we used to go to a pub called the Staple Inn – there was a hall in the backyard with a DJ playing in the corner. There used to be a café in Winchester called The Two Bare Feet but it was a bit before my time, but many of the 'old' Mods that I know today, talk about it very fondly!"

Paul Weller (Woking): "Personally, I think the Skin/Suede thing was all the younger brothers of the older brothers who had been Mods. Also, a reaction to dandy fashions and the Hippy movement of the mid-sixties, a very definite statement AGAINST dandyism.

"The styles changed so rapidly every week there would be one or two top boys you'd see out wearing something you'd never seen before and wanted immediately."

"It was definitely not continental like Mod, but still at its heart was the appropriated Ivy League American look and definitely West Indian influence, music and clothes."

"What was also so fantastic about it was that the styles were made up by the kids themselves. It wasn't brand led at all. Even with Brutus and Sherman, the kids picked up on them, and not the other way around. Levis Sta-Prest weren't aimed at Skinheads, the kids made them popular. There was no marketing involved or needed!"

David Rosen (London): "When I was 8 or 9, I had an older cousin, Eddie Rosen, and he was a first-generation Mod and that was his time, but by the time it had got to the late sixties/early seventies, it was our time. I somehow grew up subconsciously with all that American reference, maybe from the album covers, the MJQ, and they didn't look like your grandad or anyone, they looked sharp.

"I first remember seeing Skinheads in 1968/'69 in Kilburn, and then on the Edgware Road and them going down Church Street Market into Ernie Noads and Collins', the shirt shop.

"My first impression was that they looked like dockers. Monkey boots and donkey jackets, cherry reds. It hadn't moved into the American look, which kind of evolved into jungle greens, Levis with one-inch turn ups, Dr Martens which kind of looked like American army wear in my head rather than dockers."

Norman Jay MBE (London): "I was born in Acton, grew up in Ladbroke Grove and first noticed the Skinhead fashions in 1968, so I was 10 years old, just shy of my 11th birthday. I was too young to be fully involved, but I was an observer.

"I had a similar thing with the Mod thing. It left an impression. I was 7 in 1964. Two brothers lived half a mile from my mum's. The older one, Barry, was definitely Mod. The bloke who lived next door to him, Stuart, was the fucking coolest 15–16-year-old ever. He was the darling of all the black boys… He'd ride a scooter and he'd give all us little kids a ride on it with him up and down our play street. And that was what gave me my fixation with small wheels. Not necessarily the Mod thing, as I didn't get into that until the Mod revival in 1979/'80."

Tony Haddow (London): "I was born in 1952 and there was nothing. I was one of five, so money was tight. It was all hand-me-downs and everything. I suffered from the hand-me-downs because I didn't even have an older brother; they came from people on the estate. I certainly wasn't gonna wear my old man's clothes. One guy was called Bobby, and he had decent gear, so his mum always gave his old clothes to my mum. As soon as I could, I started earning money through paper rounds, milk rounds, gardening, and anything else I could do. I used to clean Max Bygraves' Rolls-Royce, because he lived around the corner from us, and I went to school with his son, Anthony. I was very industrious, and if I wanted something, I was willing to go and earn the money

for it. I was earning decent money as a 13-year-old, so I'd tell my mum that I wanted to go up to Watford, and buy something from the market. That's where they originally sold the American GI service trousers with one back pocket, which was an early Skinhead fashion. I remember buying a Mod-type cardigan with stripes down the front there. I mean, there was no education on it at all. If I saw it and liked it, I'd buy it, because it was my money. From there on, I started to get really interested with what clothes went together and made me look smart. By the time I was 15, I had DMs, 501 Levis, Wrangler cords and Ben Sherman shirts. That was very early for a Ben Sherman. I never owned a Brutus shirt. To me, they never seemed right, they had to be Ben Sherman or, later on, Career Club, the American shirt. Career Club shirts were real big buys for us. They were something we really liked. They were much better than Ben Shermans style-wise. John Simons was bringing them in from the States. I think he was more surprised than anything about the kind of people buying the gear. When I had my first number-one-grade haircut, a lady in Burnt Oak asked me if I had cancer, as the papers had not started reporting on this new fashion yet."

Clive Banks (London): "I was born in 1953 and grew up in Third Avenue from 4 years old. Mozart Estate, Queens Park. You would get your eight-track nicked out of your car and then go round to the Mozart and say, 'Look, it's mine, can I have it back?' It was all going on there. It was just a case of getting by. I used to have to go to the Ha'penny Steps, and the Wedlake Baths, because we had no bath indoors. Even then in the early sixties, it was all bombed-out churches and ruins.

"My stepfather was a milkman, and he was smart. He looked sharp. I worked with him from the age of 8. I'd do the round before I went off and did what I did. They used to go to these dinner-and-dance events, all independent dairy stuff, and mum would look incredible, sort of Dusty Springfield with the hair. They were occasional events; therefore, they were momentous for them.

"I was too young really for the Mod thing, but my wife Moira, who is three years older than me, was a complete Mod. She grew up in Hounslow, got a job at 15 at Philips Records, and she saved up for THAT green leather coat she had to have. She went to Twickenham and Eel Pie Island, and Richmond and Rod Stewart did knock about with them and incidentally she still works with Rod today, which is fantastic."

Ray Butters (Whitley Bay): "I'd led a pretty sheltered life, but I was aware of the Mods and Rockers stuff because of what had happened at the seaside riots. That was as much as I knew about gang culture. There were a couple of Skinheads at school, but I wasn't allowed to be one because I was in care at the time.

"We used to go to a club on Friday nights called 'Waggers' in Ware in Hertfordshire. That's where I got into it. That's where all the gangs from the area used to go. I first heard ska and reggae there, because all the Trojan stuff was popular at the time.

"I moved from County Durham to Waterford in Hertfordshire. I was an apprentice compositor in the printing industry. That was where I got into being a Skinhead. Then I moved to Whitley Bay on my own."

"By the time I was 15, I had DMs, 501 Levis, Wrangler cords and Ben Sherman shirts. That was very early for a Ben Sherman. I never owned a Brutus shirt. To me, they never seemed right, they had to be Ben Sherman or, later on, Career Club, the American shirt. Career Club shirts were real big buys for us. They were something we really liked. They were much better than Ben Shermans style-wise."
TONY HADDOW

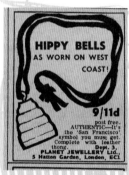

1967

By 1967, Mod was most definitely in its death throes. Marriage, and the expectation that they would settle down at a relatively young age, would see a cull of many of those involved. Also, other cultures had replaced it and had become more newsworthy. Psychedelia, drugs, student militancy and Hippies were some of the buzzwords of the moment. These were seen as the new enemies to morality, and became the social problems that the newspapers decided to focus on. Besides which, Mod culture was seen by some as too expensive to keep going. The originators saw the new generation coming up through the ranks, diluting their passions. Some would blame commercialisation, as they watched their original ideals being exploited.

The Hippy dream had always seemed too good to be true. Over in America, in June 1967, there were people searching for a new way of life. Thousands of young people descended on the Haight-Ashbury neighbourhood of San Francisco. They wanted to form an ideal community – a money-free, self-sustained anarchist society. They were anti-greed and opposed to self-interest. But by August 1967, the place was full of runaway kids with no money. They were overdosing on drugs, and sexual disease was rampant. Even 'free love' comes at a price. It didn't take long for the whole idea to be exploited by unscrupulous outsiders, and destroyed by the media attention to the subculture. Just three months after it began, in October 1967, the death of Hippy was declared.

Not that it held much sway here in Britain. Because, although there were certainly people wandering around in kaftans greeting each other with the word 'Groovy!', in the run-down estates around London, the sun didn't shine quite as much as it did in San Francisco. The reality was grey skies and grey concrete. For some, their world wasn't that beautiful.

Tony Ellis (London): "From around '67 my friends who earnt more money than me bought clothes from the Ivy shop. When my mate John was on holiday on the Isle of Wight at a holiday camp, some blokes came up to them and asked if they were from Richmond. Because that's where the shop was, and it was a very localised look, not many had heard of it in those days. The legend hadn't spread at that point. But it was stuff like the Pringle jumpers, crew-necks and Career Club shirts and things like that. Then you had the shoes, the Smoothies or Royals as they call them now. That was a big part of the look as well. It was just what working-class people did. It just evolved into what you did. If you were the sort of bloke who bought soul music or went to the Palais or wherever, you were that kind of person. You might have been a Mod or not but you dressed like you were because that was the way it was done. I think the Mod thing certainly informed us how to dress, it certainly informed how I dressed apart from my Hippy period. It was just who we were, on our estate there weren't many Greasers and the others who didn't dress like us, we didn't speak to. It was like a brotherhood of drugs."

Barry Quinnell (Easterham): "In later years, there was this thing to calling yourself a Suedehead. If you'd asked me at the time, I would have said I was a Suedehead. I would never admit to being a Skinhead. But if you look at photos of me from that period, taken around Bognor, I realise that I was a Skinhead even if I didn't want to be called one. The thing is when you are inside something, it evolves so slowly that you don't particularly compute it. You don't suddenly say, 'Ooh, I'm this type of thing now.' I mean, I was into Modernist stuff before a lot of my school friends. I can remember when chisel-toed, Cuban-heeled shoes were Mod. Or when the first lot of anoraks, the blue ones with the zip up the front, which you could buy in Millets, were Mod. At one point you had to have a reefer jacket and a pair of chisel-toed shoes, which came after winkle-pickers. That was the nuanced change from Rockers to Mods. My cousin Danny would wear the Rocker-type suit with the drainpipe trousers and Cuban-heeled boots at roughly the same time as I was buying the Mod stuff. A little bit after that you got the checked hipster trousers with the big white belt, tab-collared shirts. If I went to the Roaring Twenties I could never go there without putting a proper suit on with a shirt and tie. But I have to say I've never had a number-one-grade haircut. I just couldn't do it because that is so obviously Skinhead. I remember the first time I followed the Skinhead fashion was probably before it was called Skinhead. On Sunday afternoons in 1967, the year that we got wind that the Shoreline would be closing, a lot of people would hang around Bognor after the all-nighter, lounging around the town, behaving badly on come-downs. One Sunday in particular, there were some lads from Redhill with a bloke called Big Les. They all had braces and steel toe-capped boots. They were scrappers, you had to be careful with them, and you needed to be their friend otherwise you were likely to get a pasting. They were absolutely Skinheads but I don't think the word existed then. They were pre-Skinhead… but trust me, they were Skinheads more than anything else."

Ian Hingle (London): "Simply, different areas had different styles. I was always a bit too young for the Mod thing, though I used to wear some of the things they wore. I mean I couldn't afford a Fred Perry 'cos I was still at school. So, I would buy the same style top, but it had a penguin on it from Smith and Western, which was like a pound less, or something. I couldn't afford proper Hush Puppies, so I bought Plush Happies from Dolcis, which were ten bob less, or something.

"The one thing you couldn't scrimp on was Levis. You HAD to have Levis. I know up north it was Wranglers, but we had to have Levis. I got mine from a shop called Alfs on Wandsworth Bridge Road. They sold workwear, you know, Tuf boots and donkey jackets and Levis. And they were a lot of money. They were all imported and I've got a figure of 42/6 in my head. You just couldn't walk into any shop and get them. They were rare.

"When I was about 15 or 16, so 1966/'67, there was a whole group of young people and no one could give us a name… The press couldn't call us anything. You know, Punks, Teds, Skins, whatever. We were none of them. We didn't have a name, so it was just 'youths'. 'Youths involved in brawl' type of thing. It was completely freestyle. A mixture of Mod stuff, Hippy…It was military jackets, some guys grew their hair… It was just a sort of mish-mash.

"Then I started to hang out with a group of black kids, who I met in the record shop I worked in. I was always into soul and reggae, though it wasn't called reggae then, more ska, and 'cos I used to hang out with them, I started to dress like them. I was a sort of sponge. So, I ended up getting my hair cut really short. The only guys I knew then who had their hair really short, was these black guys or a nutcase. I mean real hard cases that were around real dodgy areas like Clapham.

"I had my hair cut then with scissors, not clippers, so it was a proper haircut, but short. There are photos of me then, this is in 1968 and I'm wearing flared trousers and a crew-neck sweater and the trouser length was short, so they floated above your feet when you were dancing, which I think was the idea.

"So, it was nothing like any other style really. It wasn't a Hippy look 'cos we had cropped hair. I used to say to my black mates, 'Why do you wear flared trousers?' and they'd say they'd get photos from back home in Jamaica and the styles back there would be influenced from America, 'cos they had family there.

"Birds then would come up and rub your hair when it was cropped and back then I had really tight curly hair and it was really tight, thick and coarse and you couldn't see through it, not like geezers with straight hair, which you could see through and which looked a bit silly."

Phillip Ellisdon (Watford): "Watford was sort of a Mod town because of the Trade Union Hall, famous for Mod groups like The Who, Yardbirds, Them, Zoot Money and others, then the Watford Top Rank became the Mod place. Even as kids, we all had Mod hairstyles and were wearing paisley silk shirts. I was only 15. This is early '67, and one Thursday night we were in the Top Rank when someone said that a friend of ours, Gary Armstrong, was down a pub called the Red Lion, which was next door to a twenty-four-hour café called the Busy Bee, which was a famous Greaser hangout, but good for buying pills. So, we go down there and find Gary Armstrong with these guys from the East End of London. Anyway, these guys had Skinhead haircuts, the braces, Ben Shermans, all the gear, and they just looked… wow. I thought it was so cool. We got talking to them and that was it. The next day we went to work, and during our lunch hour, me and a guy called Steve Hickman went down to this barber in Watford called the A1 and asked for a number one, and they whipped all your hair off. We were now Skinheads."

John 'Bomber' Wild (London): "We would see large groups of West Indian men and youths at the funfair at Wormwood Scrubs where ska music and reggae was being played. Guys wearing their trousers high up their ankles and wearing bluebeat trilby hats, long overcoats and leather coats too. As well as a fair amount of teenage-type Mods, also all mixing. My dad always told me to keep away from the fair when it came to the Scrubs, as usually trouble flared up. But obviously with such a vibrant gathering of the styles and music, it became a focal point of coolness and inspiration to us younger kids. We could not resist. Hanging out at the switchback ride and the dodgem cars. Pounding ska and soul music, and the odd pop tune.

"Portobello was also the inspiration for clothing, I would copy a lot of the older Mod kids on my estate, who would be wearing Levis with a thin one-inch turn-up, always with a steel comb carefully placed in their back pocket of the jeans, and usually, a pair of suede Chukka-type boots called Foresters. These lads were who I looked up to as they paraded around the estate in leather coats and suede bomber jackets, often riding or tinkering roadside with their scooters, usually Vespas.

"There seemed to be a definite and spontaneous look emerging amongst us younger kids. Everyone wanted to own a pair of Levis jeans, which incidentally, you could only purchase in our area, at a man's shop on Portobello Road called Temples. Elasticated two-coloured snake belts, white Fred Perry tennis shirts and Tuf 'BIG T' boots were popular. Nylon fly jackets, later known as bomber jackets, topped the look off. The regulation college-boy haircut our parents insisted on was now being exchanged for a French-style crop. This would have been around 1967/'68. I later purchased my first pair of monkey boots, a dull-looking pair from Czechoslovakia. But all the kids around my estate were impressed. This was the look, heading into the street styling of a Skinhead look. But we did not have a name or a label, everything was spontaneous."

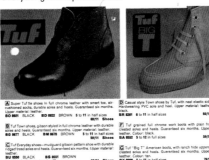

[A] Super Tuf tie shoes in full chrome leather with smart toe, air-cushioned socks, durable soles and heels. Guaranteed six months. *Upper material:* leather.
BO 8821 BLACK BO 8822 BROWN 5 to 11 in half sizes 59/11 Shoes

[B] Tuf Town shoes, gibson styled in full chrome leather with durable soles and heels. Guaranteed six months. *Upper material:* leather.
BG 8677 BLACK BM 8678 BROWN 5 to 11 in half sizes 59/11 Shoes

[C] Tuf Everyday shoes—mudguard gibson pattern shoe with durable ridged tread soles and heels. Guaranteed six months. *Upper material:* leather.
BU 8550 BLACK BS 8551 BROWN 5 to 11 in half sizes plus size 12 59/11 Shoes

[D] Casual style Town shoes by Tuf, with neat elastic side gussets. Hardwearing PVC sole and heel. *Upper material:* leather. *Colour:* black.
BR 8281 6 to 11 in half sizes 59/11 Shoes

[F] Tuf grained full chrome work boots with plain fronts, stout cleated soles and heels. Guaranteed six months. *Upper material:* leather. *Colour:* black.
BA 8552 5 to 12 in full sizes 59/11 Shoes

[G] Tuf "BIG T" American boots, with ranch hide uppers and thick cleated soles and heels. Guaranteed six months. *Upper material:* tan.
BX 8909 5 to 11 in half sizes 79/11 Boots

Bill Fordham (London): "In '67, while I was still at school, the other place I'd have to go to was the Streatham Locarno. I'd do paper rounds, and have to earn enough money to get into the Locarno, which was a big place. When you went in the big band was playing all the modern stuff, the stage would revolve and the DJ would come on, and that's where you heard music being played properly. It was mainly Tamla and Atlantic stuff. The stage would revolve and you'd hear the opening bars of Joe Tex's 'Show Me', then you'd hear Rufus Thomas, Ben E. King and lots of Tamla, but no ska or anything like that. It was very white; it was only later on that trouble started when some black kids started coming in. I think they were the new generation, who were a bit more assertive, and that's when trouble broke out.

"The other place to go to was the Croydon Suite, which was one up from the Locarno because the Locarno was something like 12/6 to get in, which was a lot of money for me then, but it was fifteen shillings for the Croydon Suite, but it was more upmarket. When I first started earning, I was on six quid a week, so I was still going to these places in '68. Then we started going to St Mary's in Putney, but now it was called the Ska Bar. The DJ there was Neville The Musical Enchanter. This music came out, and it was the most stunning music I'd ever heard. I was trying to work out what the music was, so I went to this record shop, and found out that it was '54-46' by Toots & The Maytals. But, that first time I heard those opening bars at the Ska Bar, it was brilliant. Everybody was dancing, but there was this strange friction. There were these black guys who'd come down from Hackney, north-east London, on one side, and all these black guys from Brixton, south-west London on the other. So, you had these two sets of rival blacks, and a small band of daring white kids in the middle of them, trying to look cool."

Brian Wright (London): "There was a kind of division of labour in our grammar schools so around '67 lots of middle-

class kids were drawn to The Doors, Grateful Dead and Frank Zappa. Working-class kids tended to be into the sharp stuff like Motown, reggae, ska. You could kind of define people's backgrounds by how they wore their school uniform. The kids with the long hair, scruffy shoes and a Doors LP under their arm or us lot who pressed our trousers with turn-ups and wore them with braces, shiny shoes, white tunic shirts with the detachable collars, and you did your tie in a Windsor knot so that it stuck out ninety degrees and then dropped down so it was very defined. The thing about Mod was that we copied each other. If somebody had an umbrella with a cane handle and a gold ring, the next week everybody had one. The same went for fads of trilbies, black and white spotted ties and so on."

Barry Quinnell (Eastergate): "In those days you didn't want to lose touch with people, but that wasn't easy, you'd bump into people more by luck or at one of the usual haunts, such as the coffee bars or hanging out near the church in the high street in Bognor. That's where all the Mods would park their scooters. You would just chat to people who came into your life that day, providing they looked the part. One day I remember bumping into Tony Cropley, a local lad who said to me 'I'm going to this fucking Isle of Wight Festival to see what it's all about.' Anyway, a couple of months later I bumped into him again and he was a changed man. He was going, 'Fuckin' hell man, the vibe was really cool man, like really cool.' He'd gone to that festival as a Mod and he came back a complete Hippy. I thought, bloody hell. What's happened to him? But he wasn't alone. That festival had an effect on a lot of people."

Tomorrow brought out 'My White Bicycle', and suddenly I took an interest in pop music again for the first time in six years because I'd been buying ska and R&B since I'd got into music. What really did it for me was hearing The Doors do 'Love Me Two Times'. That changed my life completely. I suddenly bought beads to wear around my neck, grew my hair long and turned into a Hippy; 1967 was a definite turning point in my life. I moved to Ladbroke Grove in 1970. Hippies were mostly from the middle classes, and I started moving amongst middle-class people, and they've got a different take on music to what we have. They like the esoteric stuff whereas we like a good solid beat to dance to. Four years I was into that music. I'd been to see The Doors, Love and The Grateful Dead. Then when Lynyrd Skynyrd came out, and the Crosby, Stills & Nash albums, I didn't like them. It got a bit silly and I just thought, fuck this! It was great going to Middle Earth and the Roundhouse. Whereas, in the early sixties, I'd gone down Drury Lane to Anello & Davide's for my boots, three years later I was going down there to go to the Arts Lab, which was really a crash pad for Hippies. I went back to collecting R&B, ska, reggae and rock 'n' roll. In 1971, if you came around my house, you'd hear The Spaniels or Charlie and Inez Foxx playing. Maybe Elvis Presley or ska. The Grateful Dead album had been pushed aside. By then I was buying most of my records from Musicland in Soho which had opened up in Berwick Street. Two Hippies ran it, dressed in stuff like mauve and purple velvet. There's always been a style to it. I mean the Hippies had a style. In '71 though, I was a weird thing. I was the only guy with long hair amongst Skinheads. I made friends with Skinheads eventually around '72. We'd go to clubs together."

John 'Bomber' Wild (London): "I had an aunt who worked at the joint UK/USA Air Strike Headquarters in Northwood, Middlesex, who would give me second-hand American clothing pre-owned by American airforce kids. To my delight this is where my very first button-down collared shirt came from. I would get farmed out of the city during some of the school holidays to a place called Carpenders Park, a London overspill estate near Watford, where most of my family had been moved to after the war, from Paddington. My delight was always seeing the sizable group of Mods on scooters who hung about by the tube station. And of course, the anticipation of going to my aunt's house, to see if the American kids had any cast-offs of clobber for me. I had already accumulated two button-down McGregor shirts, a pair of Converse basketball boots, although we called them 'bumper boots', and a basketball.

"We attended our local youth club called the Seven Feathers in London W10, and played football, table tennis and listened to records. At the time pop hits with a reggae flavour were popular, Johnny Nash's 'Cupid', 'Stir It Up' and 'You Got Soul', together with all the big Motown hits. Thursdays would also see the TV room in this vast community centre youth club packed with youngsters for *Top Of The Pops*, followed by *The Man From U.N.C.L.E.* The buzz tune of the time was by Steam, 'Na Na Hey Hey, Kiss Him Goodbye', a catchy pop tune that always reminds me of the pre-Skinhead times.

"There seemed to be a style evolving from the remnants of Mod for us younger kids, names like Peanuts were touted about, but I really cannot recall a specific name."
Soul music was still the main dance music in many of the youth clubs and discotheques. One song that certainly

MOD DAYS AT THE CAXTON CLUB, LONDON

Bill Fordham (London): "There was a girl called Pauline, from Fulham, that I'd met at the Caxton, and we went out for a while. She queued up to get the Beatles *Sgt. Pepper* album. So, we went back to her place. We went into her bedroom, and her old man used to get the right hump about it. The music never appealed to me, it was always black music at the time. Although I did have an argument with somebody because I reckoned that 'Sunny' by Georgie Fame was better than Bobby Hebb's version."

Penny Reel (London): "One day I heard Pink Floyd on the radio. They brought out 'Arnold Layne' and 'See Emily Play'.

bucked the trend was 'Al Capone' by Prince Buster. It had originally been released in 1964, but it would take until 1967 to make an impact. In February that year, the song became a hit for Prince Buster, making number eighteen in the UK charts and staying for thirteen weeks.

1968

In April 1968, because of fears of race riots in America, Ike & Tina Turner were in England for the first time in two years on a Don Arden-arranged tour. Ike told Alan Walsh of *Melody Maker*, "I fear that this summer when the colleges get out, there will be a war in America. It happened when Dr King was killed. The clubs closed and we lost work. What I'm trying to do is line up a European tour for the summer during this trip."

LESTER OWERS WITH HIS COUSIN AND FRIENDS, 1968

The irony was that, although there were race riots in America, racism in Britain would be put in the spotlight after the austere Shadow Defence Secretary, Enoch Powell, delivered his so-called 'Rivers of Blood' speech to a Conservative Association meeting in Birmingham on April 20th, 1968.

In the speech, one line stood out: "In this country in fifteen or twenty years' time the black man will have the whip hand over the white man."

He had just returned from the United States when he made that speech. Only two weeks before, Martin Luther King had been assassinated, and America was in the grip of race riots. Powell's concern was that Britain would go the same way, and that immigration would erode the national character.

The speech would divide the nation.

Melody Maker then spoke to various artists in the music business to see their views on racialism in Britain. At the time, racial harmony was enforced by the Musicians Union and it took a firm stand against discrimination. It forbade its members to play in South Africa during the apartheid era, for instance.

The answers from the artists were quite interesting. Among those they spoke to were Geno Washington, who had come to Britain in 1961 as a member of the United States Air Force, but had gone on to a career as the singer in an otherwise all-white seven-piece band.

Geno stated: "Discrimination, man? What's that? It's never affected me in Britain. In spite of my permanent sun tan. I've never had any trouble. Discrimination is just something I read about in the press." Jimmy James, Kenny Lynch and Selena Jones all told similar stories.

However, Florida-born Herbie Goins, who stayed on after doing his US National Service, said, "There is some prejudice inside the business. It happens, but it's not big with me. Outside the business it's hell. Like looking for a flat or in restaurants, when you can tell the other customers don't really appreciate you being there. You can tell by the way they act."

Joy Marshall and Madeline Bell were in agreement. Jamaican Eddie Thornton, however, said that even though he felt he'd been received well, "It made me very depressed to read Mr Enoch Powell's speech, because people will climb on the bandwagon. I've found the British people are the most tolerant in the world."

Later, Laurel Aitken would record his answer to Powell's speech in the song 'Run, Powell, Run', in which he emphasised that black Britons were calling for equality rather than the hostility that Powell so greatly feared.

Later that year, a resistance movement against the Vietnam War, which began simmering on American college campuses in 1965, boiled over into a global movement. On March 17th, 1968, an estimated 10,000 people in London demonstrated against American action in Vietnam and Britain's support for the United States. The protests began in Trafalgar Square and culminated in clashes outside the United States Embassy in Grosvenor Square. More than 200 people were arrested, and St John Ambulance volunteers reportedly treated eighty-six people for injuries; fifty were taken to hospital, including up to twenty-five police officers.

While the students and other middle-class youths chanted "Ho, Ho, Ho Chi Minh!" they were surprised to be confronted by some 200 Millwall 'end' Skinheads chanting "Enoch, Enoch!" and "Students, students, ha, ha, ha!"

It is said that some of these were the sons of dockers from the Millwall area. The dockers believed their jobs were under threat because of the influx of immigrants, and they organised their own march to the House of Commons in support of Enoch Powell's immigration policy.

Penny Reel (London): "When I went to the demonstration against the Vietnam War in '68, I saw my first Skinheads. They were working-class kids, hardnuts, they were Millwall supporters and they were football hooligans. They were definitely the first Skinheads I ever saw. My theory is that they were the younger brothers of Mods, who then adapted the style to Skinhead. They had very short hair, whereas Mods had it in a college-boy style. These guys had number-one crops. They wore braces, red

GRAHAM STUBBS AT THE MARINA, SOUTHSEA, 1968
INSET: SANDRA SMITH (NÉE SANDERS) AND FRIENDS, MARINA, 1968

SANDRA SMITH DANCING WITH GLENN MILLER
(CAROL STOKES LEANING ON CHAIR), MARINA, 1968

socks and Ben Sherman shirts. By this time, I was going to Middle Earth, so me and these Skinheads I saw were enemies. In '65 there'd been Mods that didn't pick on you, but these Skinheads would approach you and pick on you, and give you aggro. The march was mostly Hippies or left-wing people opposed to the Vietnam War. On the fringes of it there were these Skinheads taking the piss. They were jeering at us with chants of 'Fuckin' Hippies. Dressing like a woman. Long hair like a woman. Beads around your neck like a woman. Flowers in your hair like a woman!' It's strange because I came from Hackney, and we're all working class around here. Strange the same class of people picking on each other."

It seems ironic that part of the uniform the Skinheads adopted was the surplus jungle greens that the soldiers were issued with in Vietnam, known as OG 107 fatigues, which were widely available and relatively cheap in army surplus stores. These were often paired with cherry red Commando boots.

Clive Banks (London): "I do remember buying a pair of jungle greens. They had to be the right ones though. I got mine from Laurence Corner and you had to go through all this crap to get to them. Parachute trousers, gas masks, life rafts... You didn't get the khaki or camouflage ones, you wanted solid darkish green. I think that idea came from films like *The Great Escape*, and war films in general. McQueen again, he just looked so cool. Anything he's wearing, we'd want it. We want to be part of his world. I also bought monkey boots from Laurence Corner, rough old things but an important thing at the time."

To many, Skinheads were seen as a dissident group who wanted the security of working-class identity. They became a metaphor for racism and violence. In their labouring clothes of vests, braces and heavy boots, they believed in a lifestyle of hard work, patriotism and the defence of their local area. They formed gangs named after their local leader (the hardest) or their territory. They despised the middle classes, deviants of any kind and Hippy liberalism.

Not everybody was the same. Some felt frustrated that in their quest to be expressive, their own youth and immaturity denied them what they wanted from society, magnifying their lack of power. Getting to school-leaving age gave them power and freedom. They could move on from the routine authority dished out by the teachers at school. Obviously, you can suffer this at a workplace too, but at least you have the option of walking out that you really don't get at school. Being old enough to work also gave them the benefit of earning a weekly wage. Consumer spending power was key to the lifestyle that revolved around new clothes, records, clubs, and for some, drugs. This combined with getting to an age where you are self-conscious about your appearance and often in pursuit of the opposite sex.

Away from the school gates and playing on your own street corner, your boundaries start getting wider. You start to meet new characters who may influence your decisions, and you can become a stranger when venturing into other areas.

Geoff Deane (London): "I lived most of my early life in council flats in Hackney and by the end of 1967, early '68, it was already happening. My little mob were wearing Levis, thin braces on show, cherry red boots, steel toe-capped Dr Martens with the steel exposed, army greens, chunky knit cardigans and Sta-Prest, though there was no name. The only name that was given to it was 'Peanuts' and 'Pinheads', 'cos the hair was short, but people hadn't gone that extreme, which happened later when it went to a number-one crop with a razored-in parting.

"We then moved to Chingford and I thought, even though I was only 13, that coming from Hackney, I was a right geezer and about to move into an area of right fucking yokels, but I was completely wrong. There was a kind of organisation about things in Hackney, but it was fucking mayhem when you got outside that part of the East End.

"The crew I was in was called 'The Jelly Tots' and everyone then had an area... For a long time, I used to get the train back to Hackney every night, just to hang around in the flats, did that for about a year, but eventually you make new friends and they were all into it. Everyone was into the same thing."

Norman Jay MBE (London): "1968 was a pivotal year for me. It was the year I bought my first records and it was the year I first went up to Shepherd's Bush Market on my own. I had got my first transistor radio that year from Woolworths with a single earpiece. I loved pop music and was always hearing the music in our house.

"I loved the classic ska stuff. I was old enough to be buying it at the time and I know the effect it was having on my white mates when I played the records to them for the first time. I bought reggae consistently from Christmas 1967 up until 1971/'72. Off the top of my head, my favourite tunes would be either 'Israelites or 'It Mek' by Desmond Dekker, 'Sufferer' by The Kingstonians and 'Everybody Needs Love' by Slim Smith. I can remember going to buy them and being scared that the big boys were going to snatch the money from my hand. Another one was 'Long Shot Kick The Bucket' by The Pioneers. Some of them were commercial ones and you heard them everywhere. This was what everyone remembers – the populist end – and rightly so.

"That year, over my local park on a Sunday all the kids would come and play football, forty a side. Mostly black guys, but a couple of cool white dudes and an Asian family, Bobby and his brother.

"I remember all the older kids in the park, and we thought they were big men, sideburns and that. But we were too scared to play against them, because they had Dr Martens on. They were just scary, it looked aggressive, but it looked great. Braces of all colours, white and red socks. And collarless 'union' shirts. You also saw monkey jackets, which looked like copies of the England football team tracksuit top.

"Looking back, it was an aspirational time. If you didn't have the money, you begged, borrowed or stole the clothes. Cheap copies would suffice though. No one really got mugged off if they wore a cheap market Crombie. No one got laughed at because they wore a Leon Patten shirt. They had the most colours, most checks and paisleys. They were shit quality, but you wore them for school. No one could see the label, so you could get away with them thinking it was a Brutus.

"I also discovered what Levi jeans were. A kid a year older than me, Mickey, was just more clued up. I mean a year then was a big difference. Anyway, he came over and asked a couple of kids who were playing in the game with us and who were wearing jeans, 'Are they Levis?' and I thought, 'What the fuck is Levis?' I noticed his were still wet. He'd been in the bath with them half an hour earlier, and then came straight over to us.

"It was a year before I really cottoned on to it all. I remember the white kids, but also some of the black kids, started to wear button-down shirts and I loved that."

Pete Schaffert (Kent): "I first heard Jamaican music when I lived in north London in the sixties. I had a couple of older cousins who had some records, one of which was the LP *Prince Buster's Greatest Hits*. It was the track 'Al Capone' which really started me on a lifetime of collecting JA music. This cousin got so fed up with me playing the LP over and over that she ended up giving me the LP. I still have it today, and it plays through. The other cousin gave me a handful of 45s, mostly Pyramid label rocksteady tunes by Desmond Dekker, Austin Faithful and Derrick Morgan. He was also a Skinhead of the time and is where I first encountered the clothing of the day, this would have been '68 or '69. It was after I left London and moved to Kent that I started to get into the current fashion of that time, although I refused to cut my hair very short. In fact, very few of my mates went for the shorter hair. We had all the 'Skinhead' clothing, but had shoulder-length hair."

Bob Brooks (Reading): "Around 1968/'69 drugs were still quite a big thing in Reading. It was mainly blues, purple hearts, bustaids and acid. There was no cocaine, it was mainly amphetamines. Everybody I knew was doing them. A lot of blokes used to drink as well, but I never went through that apprenticeship of drinking. I'm sure it's because of amphetamines, that even to this day I'm not a beer drinker. When I went out I preferred getting blocked. Just before going out of a night, I used to go into the bathroom, wash and shave, take five amphetamines, get changed, and by the time I left the house I was buzzing. On a Thursday me and a couple of friends used to go in this guy Tony's Thames 500-weight van, and pick up this kid who lived right by Reading West bridge. He'd take us over to Piccadilly Circus and on to Wardour Street. We'd end up at the Coffee An café, go downstairs, where it was pretty dark. There'd be an Italian kid sat in the corner. We gave him all our money, and I think it was something like 1s 6d a tablet. All our wages had gone on a big bag of them. Then on the Saturday night we'd be outside Vincent's Car Showroom by Reading station selling the gear. You had to keep your eye out for the local drugs copper, Gowers. We used to double our wages. Another time, we were going down to Minehead or somewhere, and there were five or six of us in the back of the van. In the back of the van there was a little six-inch by six-inch trap, and if you lifted it up it was full of amphetamines for the trip. Anyway, we got pulled by the cops. We had to get out, and were stood between the cop car and the van shitting ourselves that they would search the van."

Phillip Eddison (Watford): "We'd be popping blues on a Saturday night, ready to take on the world, dancing all night up the Rank and then a gang of you walking up and down Watford high street till the Wimpy Bar opened in the morning, then down Cassiobury Park, laying on the grass during the 'comedown' feeling crap till about 5 p.m., then go home and eat your dinner your mum had left in the oven for you. Work on Monday and meet up to talk about Saturday night and plan where and when to get our blues for the next weekend."

The music

The R&B charts were compiled weekly from specialist dealer returns around the country. Each year they compiled a survey on the half-year in accordance with the inauguration of the chart in July 1965. However, the 1967/68 chart marked a change of style as ska and reggae were now integrated into the charts, because even though many would argue against its right to be classed as R&B, it was the dealers who insisted on including it in their returns.

Soul was obviously the biggest genre dictating the charts, and Otis Redding was the runaway success of the 1968 survey, sadly due to his untimely death, which ignited a buying spree. Otis and four of his backing band, The Bar-Kays, were killed after his plane crashed into Lake Monona as it was coming in to land at Madison Municipal Airport, Wisconsin on December 10th, 1967. This would lead to Redding taking the top two positions of the top R&B albums, with *King And Queen* with Carla Thomas sitting at number one followed by *History Of Otis Redding* in second place. The albums *Otis Blue*, *Live In Europe*, *The Dock Of The Bay* and *Pain In My Heart* all made it into the top thirty.

The biggest-selling soul compilations that year were *This Is Soul* and *British Motown Chartbusters*. Best-selling soul singles that year included: 'Gimme Little Sign' – Brenton Wood (Liberty), 'Soul Man' – Sam & Dave (Stax), 'Respect' – Aretha Franklin (Atlantic), 'Tell Mama' – Etta James (Chess), 'Higher And Higher' – Jackie Wilson (Coral) and 'I Was Made To Love Her' – Stevie Wonder (Tamla Motown).

From a ska/rocksteady/reggae perspective, Dandy was a major surprise in the album charts. The consistency of sales for his *Rock Steady* album was an inexplicable deviation from the expected run of ska album sales, which were usually small compared to singles. The other bestselling ska-related albums were the compilations *Club Ska 67*, *Club Ska 67 Vol. 2* and *Blue Beat Special*.

The overall success of ska and reggae artists in the 1968 R&B survey shows that, in all, eight artists made the top sixty: The Ethiopians, Desmond Dekker, The Maytals, The Mohawks, Jackie Mittoo, Norma Frazier, Derrick Morgan and Stranger Cole.

Some of the best-selling ska singles were 'Train To Skaville' – The Ethiopians (Rio), '007' – Desmond Dekker (Pyramid) and 'The Champ' – The Mohawks (Pama).

The bestselling R&B labels were:

1. Stax
2. Tamla Motown
3. Atlantic
4. Volt Import
5. Stateside
6. Track
7. Giant
8. Chess
9. Pye International
10. Coxsone

SKINHEADS IN COVENTRY PRECINCT, OCTOBER 1969

SKINHEAD COUPLE, OCTOBER 1969

CHAPTER 6: CLOBBER

Clothes

When you're a teenager, there is no better way to express yourself than the clothes you wear. Individualism is key, and the only real way to stay individual is to have clothes made. Here we speak to a man who just wanted to be known as 'Alec' about his influence in helping create these dreams.

Alec (cloth merchant): "I was first and foremost a Mod. I went to the clubs and on the scooter runs from around '62/'63, yeah, I did all that.

"At that time, I was a trainee hotel manager with Forte and that was the career I was looking to get involved in. Then one day a mate of mine turned up at the hotel with a large bolt of cloth and asked me if I knew anyone who would want it. I think there were five or six suit-lengths in it and he was looking for £3 or £4, I think? Anyway, I was only earning £10 a week in this job, but I took a punt on it. As it happened, I quickly sold a couple of lengths at the hotel to two guests and the rest I punted out at the Scene, I think? Well, outside, if you know what I mean. Anyway, this roll of cloth brought in £20 and it was relatively easy. You have to remember, then, nearly everyone wore a suit, with the Mods being fussier on the quality of the cloth than the normal man in the street. I went back, spoke to my mate and mentioned I'd like to do another roll of it, only this time more quantity, but only if it was mohair, because that is what I had been asked for in the clubs.

Mohair – that was all the guys wanted.

"I knew that market, and knew if I got the right stuff it would fly out. A while later my mate came back and said he couldn't get any, but a mate was looking into mills up north, to see what he could do. Well, once I heard that, on my next day off I drove up to Bradford and knocked on a few mill doors. Soon I was being offered suit lengths of black and midnight blue mohair at £2 10s a time. I bought up as much as I could afford.

"Then it was mentioned at my day job that I was in line to be promoted to become an under-manager. So, I did that for a while, but my wages stayed the same. I stayed a while longer and still no wage increase.

"Out I go again and flog the cloth. Well, it flew out. It was sold out in an hour and I got at least £5 a suit length. Again, I more than doubled my outlay. So, I jacked in the hotel job and went back up to Bradford and did a deal for cloth, buying more of it, and therefore got a better price for it.

"I went to a different club each week, to sell that. I'd leave it in the motor and then if I saw a well-dressed Mod and later Skinhead in the club, I'd ask if they were looking for cloth, as I had a few pieces that would be cheaper than any tailor could provide. Streatham Locarno, Tottenham Royal, the Flamingo, the Scene, they were all on my list. Before long,

I was well known for good cloth, so the chaps would seek me out if they saw me in any of them.

"Within a year, eighteen months or so of doing that full time, this was 1966/'67, I was making £100 a week. A bus driver then, which was considered a really good job then, was getting £20 a week. I was rolling in it. I had a nice car, nice house and wined and dined out all the time. I knew of only a couple of other merchants doing what I was, but they didn't know the score with the clubs so the field was clear for me really. They mainly sold directly to tailors and there were plenty of them about in the 1960s. Five in Berwick Street alone. One cloth merchant name comes to mind, Flash Ronnie. A legend he was. I also sold to the tailors and they used us, because it got round having to deal with the mills directly. We did the legwork for them. Made their life easier. There were stories of tailors in Soho in the mid-sixties making and therefore selling 100 suits a week! They couldn't get that cloth quick enough. I reckon at one stage I was responsible, cloth-wise, for 80 per cent of suits in London.

"Don't forget there was no purchase tax on cloth then, so very little overheads, apart from getting up to buy the cloth. Purchase tax was the forerunner to VAT, which came in 1973 and that changed things dramatically. Prices went up 20 per cent to cover that.

"As mentioned earlier I later sold to Skinheads, who also loved a bit of the Tonik [a mohair blend], probably more so than the Mods. That was all they wanted, Tonik. I know other colours came in, but black and midnight blue remained my biggest sellers."

Slowly, though, more 'readymade' suits came in, and Burton's and similar shops made a range of tailored suits that some punters went for. Times were changing, and it got looser and more casual in general as styles evolved.

"So the game slowed down, but I kept at it and am still in the game now. Most high street tailors have gone, but enough keep going for me to keep ticking over.

"I'm an old man now, but still well known. It has given me a good living and that'll do for me."

Brian Wright (London): "The prime shop was Austin's in Shaftesbury Avenue, which imported American gear. It was pricey but lasted for ever. You could buy American-style suits off the peg with a good cut on them, and original button-down shirts made by Oxford, Dehavilland and Hathaway, who were the original makers. Interestingly, when you heard later on Mods in other parts of London talking about Ben Shermans, we never wore them, because growing up in Westminster, you are only up the road from the West End, Covent Garden or Soho, so your reference groups are those people in that area. Nobody even bothered to open a shop then selling Brutus shirts or whatever. We did buy Sta-Prest trousers because they did look the part."

> "...I later sold to Skinheads, who also loved a bit of the Tonik, probably more so than the Mods. That was all they wanted, Tonik. I know other colours came in, but black and midnight blue remained my biggest sellers."
> ALEC

David Rosen (London): "It was quite functional clobber really when you think back. I even recall bib and brace overalls and butchers' coats being part of it. Even white waiters' jackets from Denny's in Soho, teamed with Levis, which had been bleached, with a Ben Sherman or a Fred Perry. It appealed to me once I realised you pop into Millets in Kilburn and pick up a SkyJump Harrington, a pair of Levis and monkey boots. I had just had my bar mitzvah, so I was around 13 coming up to 14. I was first-generation Skinhead, and it was the first multicultural thing, black, white, working-class background, all in it together really."

Clive Banks (London): "I missed all that Mod stuff, but there was some impact from it. I went to Somers Town school at 11, back of Kentish Town. I had to get a blazer and I got mine from Alkit and Sons on Cambridge Circus. I had my one made which had the 12-inch vent in it. I want THAT, that is what I WANT. I wanted it to be sharp and I also wanted a pair of grey flannels that would stay pressed. You went all over to find what eventually became 'Sta-Prest' and were readily available and in all kinds of colours. I went back to Alkit when I was 13 or 14 and they made a three-piece suit for me, bottle green, 12-inch vent, and my dad helped me with that. I found out recently that it was John Moss's father's shop, Culture Club and all that.

"A real misconception of those times is that we had a lot of gear. I didn't know anyone who had a lot of gear. We had a coat, or we had a great suit. You wore the same thing, which you really looked after."

Geoff Deane (London): "Our shops of choice back then were places like Mann's of Aldgate, which had shelves and shelves of Ben Shermans, and in Tottenham High Road there was Silvers, where you could get an off-the-peg Tonik suit, which was nice. I had a windowpane check mohair suit from there.

"How we got the money at 14 is something, really. I mean, I was always doing jobs on the markets. My youngest is 16 and the thought of him earning some money and buying himself a suit? He's years away from that. But we were more advanced. I've always been clothes bonkers and that is really where it started for me. I just became fixated. I mean you're young and you don't know anything, but you know that 'that' is right and you want some of it. I guess you are looking for some degree of identity, I don't know. You are brought up by your parents and mine were good people, but life isn't that exciting and then suddenly you see this thing and it's like it's come from a different world and it's like wow!

"You then realise what a dramatic impression your turnout can have. It really makes a difference. People say you shouldn't judge it that way – of course you fucking should! It's the most important thing in the world to judge someone by appearance, 'cos if you are looking for a shorthand for what bird I might get on with or what bloke I might get on with, or who I might have something in common with, it's obvious you are going to go by first impressions. I mean, back then looking at people who you admired by the way they dressed, how bad was that? It was better than looking at a fucking drug dealer and saying I want to be like him, ain't it? It made me get an array of stupid part-time jobs and spend a stupid amount of money on clothes, which continues to this day."

"We'd had the older boys who were Mods and they influenced us to an extent, but at this point, it seemed to collect its own momentum. Somehow it seemed to start between us. I mean that word 'common' was a real thing with us. Nobody wanted anything that was seen as 'common'. So as soon as everyone was getting the same thing, you was skidding on to something else. If you went down the Tottenham Royal and thirty blokes have got the same deckchair-striped Ben Sherman shirt on, you're like 'I ain't wearing that piece of shit again…'

"When the Harringtons caught on and everyone had the black one, and I had a black one at the beginning, we all did, suddenly we were like the fucking rainbow parade. Sky blue, maroon, all kind of really lairy colours, just to sort of be different."

Tony Haddow (London): "I always wanted to be a bit different because the newspapers would try to cover fashions, and every time they'd list what they were wearing. You'd roll your jeans so that there was a quarter of an inch turn-up, you'd wear white socks, you'd wear boots with just the right amount of sock showing, then there'd be braces, then everyone starts doing it, so all that lot goes to one side, and you take it further. That's when the suits started coming in, and mohair became the big thing, and you'd get down to Soho and start getting your suits made. I had a tailor in Berwick Street that I used to go to all of the time. It was the whole procedure of choosing a cloth, getting measured up, telling him what you want, being phoned up and asked to go for a fitting, going to the fitting, approve it and going back the following week with a pocket full of money and telling him he had done a brilliant job. Then, you've got a night out in your new whistle and you feel good. I had a red Tonik, gold Tonik and blue Tonik among others. I had a whole mixture of suits and trousers made and a camel Crombie made. Then the Prince of Wales check and dogtooth-check suits. I remember watching a film on TV with somebody like Ryan O'Neal in it, and as they walked away, I notice their jacket had an off-centre vent, so immediately I wanted that. I went and told the tailor I wanted the vent off-centre by an inch, he looked confused but did it."

Clive Banks (London): "I think my influence was coming from seeing things on telly. *Peyton Place*, Ryan O'Neal as Rodney Harrington in that coat, which became known as the Harrington. I had one in a bottle green colour, but I really wanted one with the open vent at the back of the jacket, not sewn down and I didn't like the idea of the elasticated cuffs, I wanted the button cuff. You would go deep and hard to find that, so it was nearer a golfer jacket and you'd not necessarily find it, but I wouldn't take a substitute. You wanted the one you wanted. You might find it off a mate, or a lot of that stuff ended up in old men's shops. You know, flat caps and all that. But every now and then you'd find something in there. Most of the stock was 'forget it', but occasionally…

"Other influences were Steve McQueen and Paul Newman in the film *Cool Hand Luke* where he cut off the heads of the parking meters. I was him. So cool."

Austin Myers (Shipley): "It all started in our area around '67/'68 when this boy, Tommy Hawthorn, moved up from London. He was an ardent Chelsea fan, and he knew the real hard-core Chelsea fraternity. He made friends with the Shipley community because he knew we had a reputation as handy lads, and most of us were Leeds United supporters. I saw him as a 13-year-old and when I saw how he was dressed, I thought my God, that's what I want. His boots were Dr Martens but were steel toe-capped. They weren't shiny, they were dull with a yellow band around the top. White Sta-Prest, a great navy-blue single-breasted raincoat with the collar turned up and a pork pie hat. He looked the dog's bollocks. I thought that's how I wanted to look, and everybody thought the same. He was a cool, good-looking guy and he suited the Skinhead look. I'm not kidding, it spread like wildfire amongst the Shipley youth."

Jean Brooks (Reading): "When we were going to the Crescent Club we were wearing jeans and Ben Sherman shirts a lot, but we were soon wearing Sta-Prest, and also Trevira skirt suits. We never ever wore trousers. We would go to Oxford Street in London, looking for them. Plus, there were shift dresses with holes in the back. They were always dark colours, navy, blacks, greys, green with the Tonik sheen on it. A bit after those came the midi-dresses, always worn with lacy tights with the holes up the side. The girls were very smart. Shoes came from Ravels and Sasha in Oxford Street. You'd never wear anything manmade, all our shoes and handbags were made of real leather. The hair as we went on got longer, and they'd have it put up in a bun with little ringlets at the side that you used to stick to the side of your face with eyelash glue. At this point there were also a lot of false eyelashes and Biba make-up. The in places then were the Kings Road, Chelsea, Petticoat Lane and Kensington Market. There were a few shops catering for us in Reading, but everybody was wearing it and we didn't want to look the same as everybody else. We'd maybe buy our sheepskin coats from Brahms in Reading, and they were expensive at something like seven guineas. You'd have to use provident cheques, which was basically on tick, because there were no credit cards. If you wanted a leather or sheepskin, then you needed a provident cheque, but we weren't old enough, so mum had to use them and when we paid our keep you'd pay for that too."

Geraldine Choules (Reading): "Because I worked in Heelas [a department store in Reading] we used to get a bonus every March. We'd get the train to London and blow the lot on clothes. All our money went on clothes and going out. We never had savings, but then we never really spent that much going out. You may spend money going into a club, but then we had gone out to dance. You may have only had a couple of halves of lager during an evening. I used to drink Watney's at the time. Men would offer to buy you drinks, in fact I used to play 'Spot The Grot', which was basically where you'd get someone to buy you a drink, then later you'd have to move quick if you noticed him coming over. You'd go over to the bar when the slow dances came on! The thing is that you have to remember we weren't paid anywhere near as much as the boys. There were no equal rights back then. The gap between what females were being paid compared to men was massive."

Jacky Abramovitch (London): "We wore what the boys wore. Sta-Prest, men's shirts, Harrington jackets, but we didn't have the boots; we absolutely didn't have the boots. We wore brogues instead. And then we went into mohair suits and things and that to me is what people think Suedehead is…

TOP: JEAN HADDOW (TONY'S SISTER), 1968
BOTTOM: TONY HADDOW AND SANDRA, SPRING 1969

"We'd had the older boys who were Mods and they influenced us to an extent, but at this point, it seemed to collect its own momentum. Somehow it seemed to start between us. I mean that word 'common' was a real thing with us. Nobody wanted anything that was seen as 'common.' So as soon as everyone was getting the same thing, you was skidding on to something else. If you went down the Tottenham Royal and thirty blokes have got the same deckchair-striped Ben Sherman shirt on, you're like 'I ain't wearing that piece of shit again.'"
GEOFF DEANE

TONY HADDOW AND SANDRA, BUTLINS, BOGNOR REGIS, EARLY 1968
INSET TOP: HEATHER DURY, WATFORD, 1968
OTHER INSETS: JEAN HADDOW, 1968

"I bought my first pair of Levis in 1968 from the money I earned as a paperboy. I got 15 shillings [75 pence] a week and the Levis cost 59/11 [£2.99] at Millets. So, I virtually blew a month's wages on my first pair of Levis. Then I saw some lads wearing sleeveless pullovers with their jeans… and wanted one. My mum knitted me one in chocolate brown! It was quite a hit and my mates regularly tried to buy it off me."
CLIVE KNIGHT

They would have been from East Ham high street. Bought some bits in a shop called Granditer's. You could buy second-hand Ben Shermans down Petticoat Lane… Also, in Petticoat Lane we were buying mohair material and having clothes made. We also bought off the peg in a place called 'Terela' and I ended up working there on a Saturday. I got the job, by just walking in and asking. I guess I looked right? The shop was in Green Street in Forest Gate. They sold suits, but I can't remember any trousers, so it was skirts and jackets and dresses with a keyhole back, sleeveless. You chose the colour and the size and they were made of men's suiting obviously. It was a hugely successful business, when I was working there. With my mohair suits, I'd wear shoes from Anello & Davide, which had a bar across them, sort of tap shoes, which we called 'dolly shoes'. I'd dye those all different colours. I had bottles and bottles of shoe dye. Then you'd look down at the end of the night and it would be peeling off. All the girls would have worn them. I never got a sheepskin, just couldn't afford one, but Gill did and she has just given it to her daughter. Shirts-wise, it was Ben Sherman. I really can't discuss any of the others. It was about buying the best really. You only had limited money, so you got the best, I do remember Brutus though as they had bright, different patterns."

Tony Haddow (London): "Around 1968, I found this shop that did military badges and ties, and lots of army-related stuff, in Holborn, Kingsway. I went in there one day, and told them I had a blazer but I wanted something on the breast pocket. I wondered if they could do my initials inside a kind of badge. The bloke asked if I wanted it done in 22-carat gold thread. So, they made it. I was always looking for new things to move on, basically."

Geoff Deane (London): "I saw a bloke called Weedon one day in around 1969/'70 in a barathea blazer with his initials on the pocket, in a kind of yellow cotton. And I thought I fucking like that, so I went to Visatelli, who was my tailor, and I said I'd like a monogrammed blazer and I mentioned I'd seen it in a cotton thread and he said he could do me one in metal wiring, 'cos that was what people used to have it done in. So, I had a barathea blazer, with GD in silver metal wire, which I had for about three months. Can't remember exactly how much, but around that time a made-to-measure pair of mohair strides were about £13 and a suit off the peg for about a score [£20] so I guess the blazer was about £30.

"Anyway, after three months, it's lost its shine a little bit, so I thought I'd wear it for school, but for school, you've got to have the school badge on haven't you? So, I had four press-studs fitted on it, and whenever I saw a teacher or my mum and dad, I put the badge on, but the minute they were gone, I whipped it off and I was walking around with my initials on. I was probably only about 15."

Bernard Jennings (Ruislip): "The Oldfield in Greenford was quite big. I remember everyone there had blazers, and they all had step vents in their blazers where they'd had them made. Most of them had their initials on a breast pocket badge but because I was a member of the Chartered Insurance Institute, I had a real badge with gold braiding and a Latin motto and a matching tie as well. These were worn with white shirts and always tailored checked trousers,

usually in Prince of Wales, nothing too loud. We used to iron the trousers with brown paper over them and that's how you got the sharpest crease in mohair. Trousers always inevitably split on the crease because that's where they got the most wear because of being pressed. These would be accompanied by flat tops or wingtips buffered within an inch of their lives. We spent hours shining shoes. Everything had to be sharp, and of course you daren't sit down on the tube for fear of losing the crease in your trousers. White macs were big too because you wanted to look like the FBI."

Andrew Vaughan (Orrell): "The barathea blazer was usually worn with the Prince of Wales trousers and would always have an 'Ancient and Loyal' Wigan Town crest sewn on the breast pocket. I remember Peter Halliwell's mum sent his Upholland secondary school blazer to the dry cleaners and it came back minus the school badge but complete with an 'Ancient and Loyal' badge on it. His mum went mad. He was elated! It did seem at the time that every youth in Wigan had one of these blazers and some lads would put piping around the edges of the blazer to tart it up a bit… these were basically our going-out clothes. When we went to the football or elsewhere, we'd have our daytime clothes on… Ben Shermans and tank tops but matched with Wrangler jeans, always Wrangler in Wigan, never Levis, Dr Martens boots and if it wasn't too cold a Wrangler jean jacket. On the jean jacket you'd stitch the badge off the back of the jeans onto it. The more badges you had the better you looked. Some lads had scores sewn on there. It was obvious that they didn't own so many pairs of jeans so you had to assume that they were hard bastards and had simply taxed some young urchin like me for them."

Clive Knight (London): "I started to wear the clothes in 1968 I think, when I started looking at what people were wearing. I bought my first pair of Levis in 1968 from the money I earned as a paperboy. I got 15 shillings [75 pence] a week and the Levis cost 59/11 [£2.99] at Millets. So, I virtually blew a month's wages on my first pair of Levis. Then I saw some lads wearing sleeveless pullovers with their jeans… and wanted one. My mum knitted me one in chocolate brown! It was quite a hit and my mates regularly tried to buy it off me.

"1968 was also the year of my cousin's wedding and I had my first three-piece mohair suit in lovat green, made to measure at Burton's. I used Burton's all over, like the Edgware, Burnt Oak and Kilburn branches. Even after my Skinhead phase, I continued to use Burton's to make high-waisted 'bags' as worn in 1973/'74/'75."

Lester Owers (London): "Clothing from around late '68 for me was Austin's and the Squire shop exclusively, and then moving to the Village Gate, with forays to Kensington Market. I got married in a Village Gate suit. I must have bought four suits and about five jackets from the Village Gate. I never shopped anywhere else really. You would never find me in a Levis, Mr Byrite or anywhere near Carnaby Street. I once bought two Ben Shermans from Take Six in East Ham, but I never would get caught in a Brutus or Jaytex. The Skinhead thing was too uniform, and not individual. The Ivy was more timeless and I have more or less gone back for years and dressed in that style. I'm a Brooks Brothers addict."

Phillip Ellisdon (Watford): "Everybody wore white socks at the time. I went into the Co-op in Watford, which was in a building called Gade House, to buy some white socks as mine were dirty, but they didn't have any. As they'd sold out, I decided I would buy a pair of bright red socks. My mate, Barry Preston and his girlfriend Linda, who were with me at the time, said I'd look a dick, but I bought them anyway and put them on in the stairway of the shop. Because I was a dancer, I just wanted to be different, and show them off while dancing. Soon, a few of my crowd started wearing them, then a few from the Top Rank did too, and soon it became a bit of a fad. It was a Watford thing at the start, but it did pick up at other places. As far as I'm concerned, I was the first person to wear red socks at that time."

Tony Rounce (London): "It was always a case of me liking that Ben Sherman or trousers or whatever, but if I buy them and make them last, then that's another five or six LPs I can buy. I used to go to a shop right by Grays station to buy clobber. That little shop stocked everything that the budding Skinhead or Suedehead could want. People had started telling me about the Ivy shop around this time, and I went on a pilgrimage over there. Me and a mate caught the buses over to Richmond, which was like the other side of the universe to me. Having seen the prices, I thought maybe I should walk around to Soul City and buy some records instead. I guess I didn't have to dress to impress any girls at that time. I didn't want to. I was more concerned with reading the discography of Solomon Burke so I guess I was a bit shy to be honest."

Clive Knight (London): "I came across this high-shine mohair fabric with a sort of Prince of Wales check woven into it. It was what can only be described as pea green and it was not cheap. I could only afford a pair of trousers to be made; the full suit was beyond my means. I collected the trousers from Burton's in Kilburn on the Saturday and wore them for the first time at Hammersmith Palais on the Sunday. On the tube train down my mates were really impressed with my new trousers until, on the walk from Hammersmith station to the Palais, a bloke walked past in the full suit of the same fabric. Mugged off does not come near to how I felt. I was the butt of jokes for the rest of the evening."

Norman Jay MBE (London): "Looking back now, I can still see my mate back then called Ernie. He was a black guy and he wore the DMs, the bleached Levis with red braces and the union collar shirt. His hair was a low-cut skiffle style with big sideburns. He looked great."

Phillip Ellisdon (Watford): "You had to have the turn-ups on your Levis jeans of only half an inch. If it was any bigger, you looked a gimp. You had to have a Levis jean jacket and Levis jeans, worn with Dr Martens polished so that you could see your face in them and white Fred Perry. You looked and felt the nuts!"

Clive Banks (London): "I'd wanted a pair of Prince of Wales trousers with the half-inch turn up, which was a very important detail. The shop would do that for you and it was a mystery how they did really, because it wasn't your mum doing it like normally. They were doing it for me, and despite the fact that I'm paying them to do it, it felt special. The other

ALL PHOTOS: IAN HINGLE, 1968

"Looking back now, I can still see my mate back then called Ernie. He was a black guy and he wore the DMs, the bleached Levis with red braces and the union collar shirt. His hair was a low-cut skiffle style with big sideburns. He looked great."
NORMAN JAY MBE

MAIN IMAGE: SHEEPSKIN STYLE AT THE LADY GOMM CLUB, 1970
INSET: COLIN STAPLEHURST (LEFT) AND FRIEND, 1969

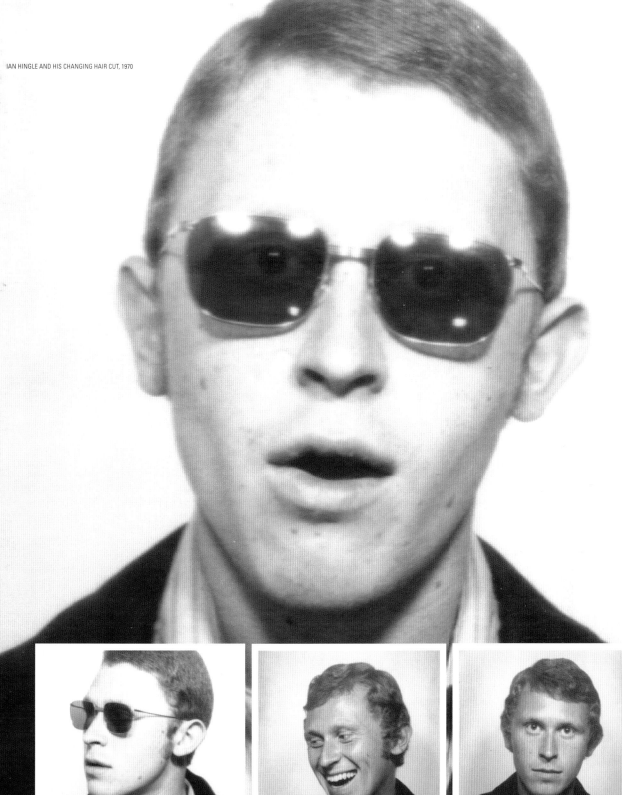

IAN HINGLE AND HIS CHANGING HAIR CUT, 1970

> "We used to go upstairs at Ronnie Scott's, the Roaring Twenties in Carnaby Street and clearly see gangs of Skinheads from other parts of London who dressed quite differently and some were very hard and aggressive-looking; whereas we prided ourselves on looking quite American, they didn't."
>
> BERNARD JENNINGS

thing I really wanted, and this again comes from Rodney Harrington or possibly Steve McQueen, would be a herringbone jacket, which just looked great."

Lorraine Le Bass (Southampton): "The shops were great. It was just lovely, that even though there were only two boutiques in Southampton, you could actually get the clothes of the day... I was lucky because my mum would make clothes for half of what they'd cost in a shop. Plus, they were exclusive, so my friends would ask where I'd got them from. I also had a cousin who lived in London who would send me down clothes you couldn't get. Once, she sent me down a brilliant two-tone dress which was green with a red thread going through it. Everybody thought that was fantastic. I was lucky, because London was far ahead of Southampton."

Bernard Jennings (Middlesex): "We went to a tailor in Brewer Street. I always remember going in with a mate, Geoff, and he tried on some Sta-Prest , then he put his jeans over them. He went to walk out and the guy in the shop asked, 'Will you be taking the Sta-Prest then, sir?' and Geoff was embarrassed and said 'Oh yes, of course, I'll take them.' They were well aware that a lot of stuff got nicked from those shops."

Geoff Deane (London): "I loved a bit of Prince of Wales. One month the blue stripe was in, the next, 'Nah, fuck that, I'm wearing red... 'Just a classic. There was a bloke at my school called Dave Cohen, who was, shall we say, lively, even though he was young and still at school. He was little, but immaculate. He had gold-rimmed glasses, always wore a nice button-down shirt and once, a three-piece Prince of Wales suit on with a matching overcoat and I was like... that's proper money, but they were on it. Proper tea leaves."

Phillip Ellisdon (Watford): "I used to have a green Tonik suit with a red Tonik to match the socks, Florsheim brogues, white Fred Perry and a red hanky in the suit top pocket and I thought I was the bollocks up the Top Rank on a Saturday night; it's where I met my wife Lori forty-six years ago."

Barry Cain (London): "I had a suit made in '67/early '68 and that was at Alfie Myers, which is where my dad got his suits made on Old Street, and he took me there for my first blue mohair suit. That would have been about thirty quid then. It was brilliant, all the fittings. That was really important. In the end I had about three suits made there. Wish I still had them, though I still have one of his hangers. My dad was always well turned out. He'd sit there indoors, with a shirt and tie on. He had a certain style about him, my old man. Anyway, it was during that crossover period, that hipsters started happening. Extra wool, big check or stripe hipsters with the big belts. But I had this allergy to wool, so I had to wear long johns under them and live in fear of anything happening to me and I'd be sitting there in these long johns. You were surrounded by these fashions. At school and round where I lived."

Bonny Staplehurst (London): "For the clothes, we would go down to East Lane, Walworth, and there were shops down there where you could get mohair suits, nice shirts there. Ben Sherman if I had the choice, but I liked Brutus 'cos of the short sleeves. Would also go to Petticoat Lane and The Cut, near Waterloo. Actually, I had a couple of sheepskins,

'cos my mum had a sheepskin coat, which was like a family heirloom, a real one. All the family wore that at one time or other. My mum paid £7 for that. It was one that John Motson wears... I got my first one in Petticoat Lane. I gave £35 for that, a lot of money then. I must have been given the money. We didn't have hundreds of outfits. I only had two suits, and you wore your jeans, and Sta-Prest, and of course your Crombie. I got mine down the Old Kent Road. I also had a lovely Prince of Wales check coat, which I got from The Cut. I didn't have anything bespoke made, I got all mine off the peg. It was a boyish look I suppose, but we'd make it more feminine. I'd wear big gold-hooped earrings. I even had a trilby, which I got in Chelsea. Our dad used to wear a trilby all the time, so it was kind of in the family."

Bernard Jennings (Middlesex): "We never thought of ourselves as Skinheads. We always wanted to distance ourselves from Skinheads because I was a grammar-school boy and you just thought of Skinheads as secondary modern louts in a way, so therefore what we did was pick up on the fashion elements side of it. So, when I left school, the first thing I did was get a Crombie coat made. I wasn't going to go to a local shop and buy a cheap Crombie so we used to get our clothes made by a tailor called Paul Simon in Berwick Street. He was a fat Jewish guy and he'd always tell you where you could buy cloth and how much you needed. When we were getting our shiny suits made, I made sure I bought the proper Dormeuil Tonik rather than all the cheap shiny Toniks that people were wearing. It was very much for the fashion and the music, and I never got involved in the football stuff, braces or Dr Martens type of thing. We were a bit snobbish about it really. I suppose it was a kind of Hard Mod look although we'd seen pictures on *Ready Steady Go!* of these Mods, and we thought they looked a bit poncey with their odd hairstyles. You didn't want anything to do with that so it was college-boy haircuts."

Barry Cain (London): "When I was out then, it was definitely the Skinhead look. The clip-on braces and that. They were cooler than the leather-end ones. Mind you, the guys who wore them were usually harder. Not sure why, but you were always a bit wary of them. I used to buy a lot of clothes on Chapel Market, 'cos I was around there then and I used to work in the market when I was about 12, on a stall selling pets. I used to stand in the middle of the market and I'm only 12, all day Saturday and up to Sunday lunchtime, holding two mongrel dogs saying, 'Two pound the dog, thirty bob the bitch...' They also had a big aquarium full of fish, hundreds of fish and kids used to say, 'I want that one' and I'd be standing there chasing the fish round the tank. They'd say, 'No not that one, that one!' We used to get the black guys then, buy the pet rabbits and take them home and cook 'em because that was what they were used to. Shrewd move really, 'cos it was fresh meat. Anyway, I did the sitting in a bath wearing the jeans, but it never used to work for me. I'd buy them from a stall, cheaper. There was a big old boutique up there, next to Woolworths. Always bought Ben Sherman, never Brutus. When we used to go out, I'd wear a tapered white shirt with a college tie, and sometimes with the old fob, with the waistcoat. Yeah, yeah, oh yeah. It was all Crombies and Dunn's macs. Never had a sheepskin though. Never had the money. It was hard being a Skinhead really. I used to earn a few bob, but I was the only one on my estate who stayed on to do A levels, so I wasn't earning any money, like my mates were."

Bernard Jennings (Middlesex): "We used to go upstairs at Ronnie Scott's, the Roaring Twenties in Carnaby Street and clearly see gangs of Skinheads from other parts of London who dressed quite differently, and some were very hard and aggressive-looking; whereas we prided ourselves on looking quite American, they didn't. They had tramline partings and long sideburns, and to us it looked distinctly unsmart. In a way you wanted also to look a bit like Georgie Fame I suppose. You'd see pictures of Georgie in a nice Shetland wool crew-neck jumper, and it was all very conservative. We'd wear these crew-necks, because they looked great with a button-down shirt. Whatever colour you bought, you'd get the matching socks. I wouldn't do it now but I remember yellow crew-neck and matching socks. There was a lot of white sock-wearing in those days too of course. White socks always went with loafers. Levis jeans and trousers were cut quite short but you'd never have them five inches above the ankle or anything silly. The girls, particularly, wore their jeans much shorter, and wore white socks with loafers. But mainly, I seem to remember girls wearing knee socks and flat shoes. We never bothered with turn-ups on jeans, unlike some."

Bill Fordham (London): "In '66 I was only 14, I did a few jobs here and there. All I had to do was earn enough money so I could get out on a Saturday night. I could get down the Caxton easily because it was just pennies to get in, and we always used to bunk the fares anywhere we went. We never paid on the trains. For clothes there was a shop in Kingston called Osbourne's; he was a second-hand clothes dealer. I'm pretty sure that when the ocean cruise liners would dock, people would leave clothes behind, and he would buy all this stock up. It was brilliant gear in there, my brother used to buy some stunning stuff. It was just trying to get something to fit but I remember getting a mohair suit out of there. I left school in March '67 as I was 15 and three months and that was the legal requirement to leave. I got a job in the print room in an office in Victoria. I was only on about £6 a week but I had money coming in for records and clothes. I got my first suit made up, a Tonik mohair at George Doland's in the high street in Victoria."

Bernard Jennings (Middlesex): "At the tailors I had a tonik suit and a navy-blue work suit, a couple of blazers made. With the blazers I had a step vent, patch pockets and a kind of boxy style. Three buttons because you always wanted that 'three over two' look. The top button was always undone, and you used just the middle button because it was the American influence. We never went in for four buttons, double-breasted or those deep vents. We used to see the guys with all that but they tended to be tail-end Mods – well that's how we thought of them. It was all single-breasted and quite a narrow profile. Things like Harry Fenton was OK, it was quite Italian-looking, but with the other American influence, we were always juggling between the two. We didn't wear Brutus shirts in our area; there were Career Club shirts and Gant shirts. The ones that were available on the high street were Ben Sherman and they were reasonably well made actually even though they were made in this country. I always remember that when you bought shirts at John Simons, there was a five-shilling difference between a

long-sleeved and a short-sleeved shirt. So, we used to buy the long-sleeved and wear that for a while, and then convert them to short. My mum used to sew, so she used to shorten my trousers or change shirt appearance… we'd get them cut so they were quite long, cut at the elbow and flapped a bit. They also had sewn-in box pleats at the back – we thought it made the shirts too tight, so we'd pick them out. They had to be nice and loose, because you wore tight trousers, so the profile was a bit baggy on the top and tightish profile with the trousers. A few years later we were wearing hugely tight shirts and baggy trousers. It just turned around. Things came and went quite quickly.

"There was a big craze for bowling shirts, so you had to buy authentic ones. You'd go to markets where you'd pick your way through piles of imported bowling shirts. I always remember I had one with 'crop duster' written on the back. I was particularly proud of that one because it didn't have too many bowling insignias on it. They had pyjama collars on them and you'd turn it up. That was when we were wearing ultra-bags for trousers. They were never like the northern soul bags, these were decent ones. We used to buy the soul magazines, and you could see the adverts for clothes that you could get made to measure for northern clubs, and we'd look at them aghast. The whole northern soul phenomenon was not something we came across because of where we lived… It was funk and everything that was released last week. That's what we were interested in. The type of clubs we were going to were full of West Indians and they don't want to hear stuff they've heard before. They're always searching for something new. They want to be amazed all the time. There was no singing along to what you were familiar with, there was a huge changeover of music, and I suppose the fashions were changing just as quickly. We were wearing Frank Sinatra hats for a few weeks but they were always getting nicked. We'd call them 'snap brims', they had to be the right shape of hat. It was very difficult to find. You wouldn't think 19-year-old blokes would be influenced by Sinatra, but he was a smart guy. West Indians wore pork pie hats, but to me, they never looked right on white guys."

Bob Wheeler (Slough): "We used to go to the Ivy shop in Richmond. We used to get our loafers, Gibsons and Royals there. There was a cobbler called Gunns in Slough where you could get your brogue shoes. Our Crombies and suits we used to get at Jacksons and pay them off weekly. It then became mainstream fashion and you could buy your Toniks from high-street shops."

Paul Weller (Woking): "I started going to Woking Football Club dances on a Thursday night. That's what opened my eyes to what clothes were really about. I think by 1970 most people had longer hair and less crops were about. We still wore Dr Martens with jeans or Sta-Prest but not if you were going out. Woking was probably a bit behind the changing styles; it took time to filter down. There were always a few 'tasty' older geezers around who really knew how to dress. Incredible Tonik suits, some in petrol blue and gold, blue and green, wine and blue mixes, two-tone. I remember seeing older lads at school wearing black Sta-Prest (with a sheen to 'em) and Royals wingtip brogues and also Smooths [a plain cap version] especially on brown. Just incredible. I bought

> "The Skinheads were born of the Ivy Leaguers who came into our shop and it became distorted through Brutus, etc… all these brands were born of the Career Club and all the other makes of American shirts we sold."
> JOHN SIMONS

MEET THE CROMBIE BOYS

Photograph by Red Sanders

The kids call these overcoats Crombies, but they are rarely the genuine article made from the celebrated Crombie cloth. Still, there is a touch of real class tucked in the top pocket – a pure silk handkerchief. This gentlemanly fad started in London, swaggering out from the East End on to the football terraces where it was caught like measles and spread to places as far apart as Highgate and Barnes. Now you can see Crombie boys getting off the football specials from the Midlands and North. It's a look for boys (and a few girls) between 12 and 20 who want to give themselves a group identity that swings away from the aggressive look of skinheads and rockers; some South London Crombie boys have even been seen with rolled umbrellas. Shoes must be black and clumpy, shirts thinly striped and open necked, trousers knife-creased. When the 'Crombies' are shed as the weather gets warmer, the word is that the ceremonial order will be two-tone mohair suits – one of the gents in the chair has already been for a fitting. Shirts will have unbuttoned down collars. Black and white patents will probably be *the* shoe.

"I can remember almost every item of clothing that I wore. From the moment you bought that Ben Sherman, resplendent in its own box, neatly folded and smelling just perfect, you were hooked. We basically thought we looked the dog's bollocks and you know what? We probably did."
ANDREW VAUGHAN

a black pair of Smooths off a kid at school but they fucking crippled my feet. I gave up on them after a couple of months."

John 'Bomber' Wild (London): "I had become obsessed with clobber throughout the whole period, right from the beginning of Skinhead and through to the Smoothie era and beyond, when styles changed constantly. It was certainly very competitive to keep one step ahead, and my circle of friends were equally into the style. A few of us had part-time jobs to accumulate the funds to buy clothes. The obsession ran into all items of clothing: trousers, shirts, shoes, jackets, nothing was left untouched. I had a good contact who sold me Levis Sta-Prest at knock-down prices, although it was probably knocked-off prices. Grey, black, ice blue, airforce blue, white and pea green… Shirts, my favourite was always Jaytex, although I had Ben Sherman, Arnold Palmer, Southern Comfort and Brutus at various stages.

"Shoes also were in a constant rota of what was in and what was out. At my youngest, my first pair of loafers were the Frank Wright black tasselled version. Although I was never entirely convinced by them… soon I saved for my first pair of Royals wing-tipped brogues. Once purchased, the Royals were taken to the cobbler and an extra leather sole would be added, which gave the sole a thicker wedged look. It was just a little detail that some of us did.

"Bespoke suits and jackets were really out of my reach, so an off-the-peg Tonik suit was purchased often worn with a plain button-down and a selection of ties usually sourced from my old man's wardrobe."

Bernard Jennings (Middlesex): "The other place we looked at lovingly was Austin's in Shaftesbury Avenue. I did buy a suit in there but sadly my younger brother wore it on New Year's Eve and went in the fountain at Trafalgar Square in that suit so that was the end of that."

Raymond Potter (London): "My wife had her first Crombie overcoat made at Burton's, ticket pocket, red lining, everything. She was 13 or 14 and still at school. She wouldn't take it off in case someone nicked it."

Becky Potter (London): "I had it made to measure in Burton's. I wore it to school, and I told them you don't think I'm taking this coat off in class? No way. I had to go and see the head master and everything. I loved that coat. I had all the tonik Trevira suits going, and that was my school uniform."

Raymond Potter (London): "We used to wear Blue Beat hats with our Crombie coats. If you went to Brixton market you

could get any colour you wanted. I always liked something that matched, so if I've got a brown Crombie on, I want a brown hat. We also wore gold-rimmed glasses but they'd be plain glass. They weren't spectacles or sunglasses, they were just clear lenses, but they were all the fashion, so everybody got into it."

Lorraine Le Bass (Southampton): "I used to definitely prefer Brutus over Ben Sherman shirts. The colours were better, and they were a bit cheaper than Ben Shermans. Also, luckily for me, my brother didn't want to keep trying to nick them because he preferred Ben Shermans. We used to buy them from a shop in East Street called Shirt King. We used to get all our shirts there. It was very reasonable, you could afford to get a shirt when you wanted."

Geoff Deane (London): "Clothing styles we liked became more available, but not really the stuff that you wanted. Like, there was Brutus and Jaytex, which was everywhere, but you would have your throat cut in our mob if you wore either of them, 'cos they were like idiot shirts, they were a sign of a true mug. It was basically Ben Shermans, and Arnold Palmers, but the shirt was the tartan Harry Fenton, which came in three tartans and it was a superb shirt in a limited run. Not like Ben Shermans, which were all over the place. Those tartans… You got them from their shops in the West End. They were incredibly hard to get hold of. As soon as they came out, they were gone. I got one in the end, a green tartan, which wasn't the one I wanted, but I used to wear it with ice blue Sta-Prest, and maroon Royals. You could see that coming."

Phillip Ellisdon (Watford): "The problem with Ben Shermans was that everybody pretty much had the same shirts. With Brutus they had a bigger range and they were cheaper, so you could have something that was slightly different to everybody else. A lot of people bought the Brutus because they wanted to be a little bit different, you know."

Paul Weller (Woking): "There were two boutiques in Woking. One was called Squires, which sold more Hippy/hairy fashions: flares, cheesecloth, scoop-neck T-shirts with bell sleeves, etc. The other was called Flaks and was run by an older cat with a great moustache and a trendy dresser. He also sold the more West End Hippy clothes but at the same time he also had Brutus, Ben Sherman shirts and eventually Levis Sta-Prest trousers. Flaks is where I bought my first Brutus short-sleeved checked shirt. It was dark blue based and had petrol blue and red in the check/tartan. It was the greatest thing I had seen at that point and I guess so did at least three of my mates too, 'cos we all had the same shirt!"

Clive Knight (London): "As for shirts, well, Ben Shermans cost more, but had some great fabrics. Brutus had that great short-sleeve look with the notch in it. Brutus were also cut a bit tighter than Ben Sherman. But to really impress it was a Career Club or Arnold Palmer. I couldn't afford those shirts but a mate who was an apprentice could, and we used to swap clothes around so I got to wear them even if I did not own them."

Clive Banks (London): "We'd dream of a Brooks Brothers shirt. We'd have picked the name up from the TV or the movies. People like Jack Lemmon, that was what he was wearing, very Ivy League. The Ben Sherman always seemed

100

to be a different type of shirt, heavier material. We'd have one, of course, because Brooks was hard to find, but occasionally someone would bring back one from a trip to the States. Brutus means nothing to me; I didn't fancy the check shirts, not for me. A lot of that look, to me, looked aggressive, violent really."

David Rosen (London): "As for the brands, the absolute brand we all loved, for all of us, was first and foremost Levis. Then Dr Martens. The Harrington jackets weren't the Baracuta; no one knew about them in those days – it was SkyJump, that was the brand. It had a tartan lining, and was basically a cheap English version. It was only years later that we found that it was actually Baracuta we aspired to, and we only then discovered Baracuta when John Simons opened a Covent Garden shop in the late seventies. It was funny to then learn that what we were all into was actually an old British brand and not American as we thought. The American brand was called London Fog."

Norman Jay MBE (London): "I had a mate in my primary school called Desmond, and his mum, who was lovely, used to dress him up like a dandy. He was the most colourful black kid in our year. He was the first kid to wear bell bottoms and then he got a button-down shirt on and we are all thinking, this is great. It wasn't a Ben Sherman, it was a Brutus, because I don't think they made kids' sizes in the Bens back then. Only the older kids had Ben Shermans. Anyway, for me they were quite dull, because I only ever saw plain or pastel colours. Brutus came in with checks and we aspired to Brutus, and if you couldn't afford that, you wore a Leon Patten. You got them at Shepherd's Bush market. Sort of moody rip-off. Most of the kids at my school wore them. I would have got my first Fred Perry around then too, a red one, which I persuaded my mum to buy me."

Andrew Vaughan (Orrell): "I can remember almost every item of clothing that I wore. From the moment you bought that Ben Sherman, resplendent in its own box, neatly folded and smelling just perfect, you were hooked. We basically thought we looked the dog's bollocks and you know what? We probably did. Even though we didn't know it back then, the Ben Sherman shirt was a direct copy of an American shirt. However, the Bens came in superb gingham checks. To have a red and white checked shirt was brilliant. With it we'd wear two-tone parallel trousers. The lucky ones had their own suit but alas that was not me. These trousers were made in a Tonik material that would gently change colour as you moved. They were mainly in a green/blue or red/blue combination. Ours were sixteen inches wide at the bottom with an inch turn-up and sat proudly on top of your Royals or Como shoes. Royals were a heavy black brogue, made of cordovan [horse leather] and were shone to perfection. I bought mine from a little shoe shop at Orrell Post that has long since gone. My dad took me and, before we left the shop, we had to have the obligatory 'Blakeys' metal tips banged into the heels. I bought my Frank Wright Comos from the same shop. These were generally in an oxblood colour and were sometimes known as 'Smooths', and that basically described them."

Bob Wheeler (Slough): "There was always the influence from my missus, who liked longer hair. She was always getting me to grow it and buying me things like Budgie jackets and all that. Everybody used to take the piss, and I'd throw them away and go out and buy the proper clobber. There was always a mixture."

Coleen Wheeler (Slough): "I was a Hippy before I met Bob. I remember being away at the coast with my mum and dad and my mate Sandra. It was when there was first talk of Hippies. We said to my mum and dad, 'We'll see you in about an hour.' So, we went off and we bought a budgie bell to hang around our necks, took our shoes off, put a band around our hair. An hour later we met up and my mum said, 'What the bloody hell has happened?' We just told them that we were Hippies now. I was about 15 at the time. After I met Bob, he kind of converted me a bit so one day I wore my Tonik suit and the next day I'd wear my Hippy dress. I made him try on some velvet flares in a shop called Just Pants. He put them on and I told him he looked lovely. He eventually bought some striped trousers, some checked ones like Rupert trousers. He only wore them once. He said 'You made me buy them!' My brother David had been a Mod and was in a band because he was six years older than me. I used to go and watch him, so when I met Bob, although I was 17, I'd been going out to pubs watching bands so I was a lot more grown-up in music than Bob was. I told him I was into Jimi Hendrix and that kind of stuff and he was going, 'Whaaaat?' Bob never liked my music."

Geoff Deane (London): "On a holiday I'd met a bird from Liverpool, Margot from Toxteth, and got engaged. She's got four brothers on the docks, four brothers unemployed, so a very classy act. I've always been a bit of a romantic and a bit soft with the women. Anyway, I'm about 15. I've never had the money for a sheepskin, 'cos they were big dough, something like £75 for a good one which was always out of my reach. I've come back home and I'm in love and we're corresponding, writing each other letters. My mum and dad definitely ain't well pleased though. Margot's invited me up there, and I'm having it, I'm giving it, I'm going up to see my bird.

"So, my mum says to me a few days before, 'You still going up to Liverpool then?' and I'm like yeah, yeah, don't try and stop me and she basically said, 'I'll get you a three-quarter-length sheepskin if you don't go.' And that was that. What might have been, eh? It wasn't one of my nicest choices, but it was a three-quarter-length sheepskin, and a black one as well, 'cos the white fur ones had become common, so…"

Clive Knight (London): "I never bought a sheepskin, because wearing one made you a target. One acquaintance had his sheepskin razored by a local thug in Finchley. Another mate went up to Liverpool for an Everton v Spurs FA Cup game in his 'sheepy', got rolled by a bunch of scousers when they heard his London accent. His sheepskin was nicked and he rocked up to school on the Monday with one of those black eyes that look like you've got a golf ball under your eyelid. I learnt by other people's mistakes."

Where can you buy the best American clothes in England? The answer, is from the legendary retailer John Simons. His Ivy shop in Richmond, where he sold the real deal in American Ivy League clothing, as well as the likes of the Baracuta Harrington. John was responsible for giving the garment its name, in honour of the TV character Rodney Harrington, who wore the jacket in the US TV series *Peyton Place*. In the late 1960s, the Ivy was the destination of choice for Skinheads and later Suedeheads who had heard of the exclusive and expensive wares he had to offer…

Truval shirts

LESTER OWERS, PONTINS, OSMINGTON BAY, 1969
BOTTOM: TONY HADDOW AND STEVE SMITH, 1968

KEN THOMSON **TRYING IT ON**

At the Harrogate Men's Wear Conference where Peter Golding wins an Oscar

The Men's Wear Association of Britain – the most important group of retailers in the country – elected its youngest-ever president at their Harrogate conference this year. Barry Reed, managing director of Austin Reed, had a few harsh words to say to manufacturers in this country: that they had better watch it if they did not want overseas manufacturers to capture the growing market for fashion clothes in Britain. He decried the way some retailers and manufacturers seem to fear fashion for men, and made the point that fashion did not always mean Carnaby Street, or 'mod'. His observation that at exhibitions in this country the foreign exhibitors often seemed far superior to British was unpopular, but true. There is never the overall style at British clothing exhibitions that one finds in Paris.

But some encouragement could be found in the awarding of an 'Oscar' (for best design at the exhibition) this year to rainwear m[...] who have engaged a y[...] to overhaul their rang[...] ing's 'About Town' r[...] available at Dhobi W[...] tailers in the spring, [...] flared coat in plasti[...] cloth which won the a[...] Twenty-six-year-old Peter Golding has already worked for European manufacturers with success and some of his clothes have already reached the British market. He was the first designer of men's clothes to be made a member of the British Society of Industrial Artists and Designers, and earlier this year did an important collection for the International Fashion Council in Amsterdam.

By the mid-sixties, John would be making regular buying trips to New York to pick up shirts such as Lion of Troy and Career Club by the dozens, plus three-button jackets and straight trousers and the like that no one else was selling in the UK at the time. One thing was for certain: he knew his stuff and he was prepared to educate his customers, if they wanted to know the score.

John Simons (London): "We opened the Ivy shop in Richmond in 1964, and by 1965 we had created the look we had set out to achieve in the shop and that look remained throughout the sixties. We wanted that young Harvard graduate look, the Ivy League look, which was around from the fifties, which some of us had grown up with, and in the shop we wanted to create that look. We weren't looking back. We were looking forward. We were running around the East End like blue-arsed flies, going in and out of doors, saying, 'Can you make this? Can you make that?' We'd be looking to order a dozen and they'd want 1,500! No, we could only order a dozen, all we could afford.

"Then I'd started going to America in about 1966 and a whole new world opened up. I was running up and down the stairs of the Empire State Building where the wholesalers were, shouting, 'Got any clear-outs, got any clear-outs?' By buying their old stock, I got to know them all."

John Simons was born in Hackney, east London, just after the start of the Second World War. From an early age, he was surrounded by well-dressed uncles who steered their young nephew the right way when putting an outfit together. Upon leaving school, he took an apprenticeship at Cecil Gee, the men's clothes shop, learning the art of window display there, while also studying the craft at Central Saint Martins School of Art.

So good was he at window dressing that he soon picked up freelance work doing the same thing at Austin's in Shaftesbury Avenue, which gave him the exposure to classic American clothing. He would later also work for Burberry, soaking up the history of that brand.

His work location, bang in the heart of the West End of London, exposed him to the buzzing lifestyle of Soho in the late 1950s. He hung around at Sam Widges, the iconic coffee bar with its fantastically stocked jukebox, quickly absorbing the jazz he heard there. He also played tenor sax in a couple of modern jazz line-ups. He partied at clubs like the Florida, the Mapleton and the Flamingo. He studied the look and haircuts of Italian waiters and the art in the various galleries around town.

This was simply a great education. It also marked him out as a Modernist, but never a Mod.

From 1955, John was designing and selling suits in person or from a market stall on Petticoat Lane in east London, working under the name of 'Far Out Tailors'. Then in the early sixties he moved to his first shop, which he called Clothesville, and which was directly underneath the Hackney Empire. He'd design a coat in the morning, perhaps in colourful corduroy with a button-down collar, a local manufacturer would deliver it within a few hours and it would be sold by closing time.

From here he ventured out west to Richmond, where his customers came from all over to pay homage. Marketing men, Skinheads and all the stops in between arrived by the hour. It was a big move for a kid from Hackney, but John embraced it. He followed his nose, he just knew. Instinct won the day.

John Simons (London): "Some of the stock I was buying included Career Club shirts, Royals shoes. We had Bass Weejuns in 1969, and we got those in from Switzerland where they had a warehouse. Our blazers came from firms in America making blazers in hundreds of colours for dance bands and the like. They were all Ivy-style blazers. They were chopped out, and very nice, but they were cheap and they were what we used to buy. There were adverts of people like Bob Hope in old *Esquires* showing a myriad of colours. Not only that, but I was going home thinking, I've seen this film actor wearing this, where can I get it? My source material at that time was the whole world of jazz, I was heavily into jazz, still am… the whole world of film, when you had real film stars who dressed out of this world, you know. People like Tony Curtis, Fred Astaire, Cary Grant…

"As it transpired, there wasn't an absolute market for that look, but it was there in the film industry, the advertising industry. Then it began to tap into the unspoken needs of the young tough guy in town and he began to have his hair cut short, neat! You know, like Anthony Perkins kind of look, crew-neck sweaters, narrow jeans, short in the leg with loafers, so we did create a 'Modernist' look. We created a clientele. The Mods that came in to us, wore little narrow suits and little hats and things, but they weren't harsh, it wasn't a harsh aggressive look. But it spawned other looks. How that developed into a Skinhead look, I don't quite understand, but I'm here to tell you it did! The Skinheads were born of the Ivy Leaguers who came into our shop and it became distorted through Brutus etc… all these brands were born of the Career Club and all the other makes of American shirts we sold. I don't really remember seeing them in the shop until the very early seventies, possibly very late '69."

WHERE CAN YOU BUY THE BEST AMERICAN CLOTHES IN ENGLAND?

...ond, Surrey.   26 Brewer Street, London, W.1.

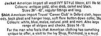

Jacket American import all wool IVY STYLE Blazer, £11 10s 6d. Colours: antique gold, olive drab, camel and black. Sizes 36"–42", regular fittings and long.
Shirt American import Travel 'Career Club' in Oxford cloth, tapered body, back pleat and hanger loop, soft flare button-down collar, 38s 6d Colours: white, blue, maize, natural, pink and mint. Also large range of stripes and checks. Sizes 14–16
For the man who feels that American clothing has something unique to offer, a visit to the Ivy Shop, Richmond, is a must. Browse through the most comprehensive range of Stateside ...

The late 1960s saw him open the Squire shop on Brewer Street, Soho. Here, he continued to sell the Ivy League look: loafers, wingtip brogues, sharply pressed trousers, coupled with a continental sensibility. Graphic designers, advertising execs and visiting Italian and Spanish overseas workers were regular customers here. As were the Suedeheads.

John Simons (London): "They got the look absolutely bang on. Nice navy blazer, buttoned-down shirt and a nicely knotted tie. But let me tell you, these were London 'Jack the lads' and not Harvard graduates, take my word for it…"

Lester Owers (London): "Around late 1968/'69, I used to go to the Squire shop, which I'd heard about through one of my mates. A few of us went up there before a West Ham match. Because I was buying records, I would do Cheapo Cheapo's in Rupert Street market, then go over to the Squire shop in Brewer Street or Musicland in Berwick Street. You did it as part of the circuit. Most of the time we'd bunk on the trains.

"At the Squire shop, we found American gear, which was far different to what was around at the time, like Ben Sherman or Jaytex. On the bottom of their Career Club shirts there was 'Made in the USA' stamped on the outside. I remember wearing one in Southend and a girl asked me if I'd got it at the Squire shop, because their stock was so unique. A pair of Royals in Squires was seven guineas. A Baracuta jacket was about fourteen quid and shirts were about three quid. You'd have a set of rubber soles put on the shoes so you didn't wear out the leather.

"Then we started shopping at Austin's in Shaftesbury Avenue, which was basically like an old boys' shop. Alpaca jumpers were twenty quid, which was more than a week's wages. The trousers came in a dead length, so they could cut them down and alter them to your requirements."

Tony Haddow (London): "We'd go to John Simons on a Saturday, and it would cost me eight quid to buy some shoes off him, which is all I was earning in a week, as an apprentice plumber. I had plain tops, brogues, Gibsons, loafers, tassel loafers, the whole lot. My old man used to take the wicked piss out of me polishing my shoes up. He told me to spit on them and buff it, this that and the other until my plain caps were gleaming. The shoe shops like Ravel were crap, I wanted more than that, so that's when you find out about Squires or the Ivy shop in Richmond, but it would cost you three times more. Plain caps were my absolute favourite. I used to break them in so that I had two or three creases on the toe cap. I had a certain way I wanted to break my shoes in, so I got very meticulous about it, and my old man used to scratch his head. He thought there was better things that I could spend my money on, but I was happy. I'd then go upstairs and put my Dansette on, and corrupt my brothers and my sister by telling them to listen, while he'd be downstairs, shouting, 'Can you turn that fuckin' thing down?' while watching *World at War* on BBC2."

Geoff Deane (London): "I didn't really have the money then for the Ivy shop or the one in Tottenham called the Bronx shop, where they were doing Bass Weejuns and Royals, so we went to Blackmans in Brick Lane and they did a grained wing-tipped brogue for the same price as a pair of Levis,

which was just under £3 then. They were fantastic, leather-soled, but the only thing was they only did them in brown. So, we bought them and dyed 'em black. I didn't want brown shoes, 'cos in them days, black was definitely the thing."

Tony Haddow (London): "John Simons… knows what he's done, he's proud of it, and so he should be. He made me very happy when I walked out of there on a Saturday, and I'd done all my dough and I'd got the next thing that I wanted, and I was early getting it."

David Rosen (London): "It shifted very quickly and I soon worked out that it was coming from the world of Ivy League. I then made that pilgrimage to Richmond by bus. I used to hear about this place, it was like the Holy Grail. Everyone in the clubs was talking about the Ivy shop, or the Squire shop and I didn't even realise the Squire shop is in Piccadilly and all you've got to do is jump on the Bakerloo Line and go half a dozen stops and you're there. Instead you're schlepping over to Richmond.

"I bought a pair of fantastic fringe and tassel moccasin loafers, which I've still got. They were very soft and it said inside them, that they were specially made for the Ivy shop or Squire shop. At the end of the day, it all comes back to Johnny Simons. At one time him and his business partner Jeff Kwintner had Thackeray's, the Ivy shop, Village Gate, the Squire shop and they were really where it was at."

Shoes

Steve Ellison (London): "The original Skinheads were in my mind, very smart. Of course, they wore the Dr Martens and I remember them being mottled-coloured. They would take two or three different-coloured polishes and rub them in and mix them on the boots. They also cut the bit where the steel toecap was and that peeped through then. Very cool that. I never wore monkey boots though. They were very cheap back then; fucking soles would fall off and all these nails were poking out."

Bernard Jennings (Middlesex): "We started out shopping at the Ivy shop in Richmond. Then it became aspirational. You wanted to get all your stuff at the Squire shop if you could afford it but in those days a pair of wingtip brogues would be five guineas, but then all their shoes were the same price. A nice pair of flat tops or a pair of Gibsons, those were the three main styles around '67/'68. I was still at school and I was the first guy there to wear a pair of wingtips to school. Soon another chap, who was a lot younger and smaller, started wearing them, but they were his older brother's. He was about five foot nothing, wearing these size 11 wingtips padded out with newspaper on the inside, clumping around in them. His brother was a big face in North Harrow, 'cos you knew who all the faces were, big gangs of brothers, that sort of thing, but quite well dressed."

Austin Myers (Shipley): "The plain cap Royal was quality because it had an edge around the shoe that distinguished it. We'd put segs [small metal plates on the sole] in so people could hear you coming. It was important to have a presence. I used to love walking onto a dance floor with the sound of segs in the shoes, much to the annoyance of the dancehall owners."

Phillip Ellisdon (Watford): "If you went to the Top Rank with metal tips on your shoes, the bouncers would check the bottoms of your shoes. If you had them on, they had a screwdriver and they'd pull them out because they used to scratch the dance floor."

Bernard Jennings (Middlesex): "We bought our loafers at John Simon but I can't remember what make they were if I'm honest. In the same way I remember wingtips being called Royals and they were made by a company in Northampton that made them all for export, and John Simon started off by importing them until he realised they were made in England, so thereafter he went directly to them. We asked how come he was still charging the same amount of money, but he just did. All the shoes were a standard five guineas. Five pounds and five shillings was an awful lot of money in those days. It was more than my dad ever paid for a suit so he was horrified when he found out how much we paid just for shoes."

Steve Ellison (London): "There was an Ivy League shop on the Walworth Road, which was more local to me. That was called 'Rufus' and they had a nice wooden table in the middle of the shop, with all the shoes arranged on it. You just couldn't believe the shoes in there. Fringe and buckle, fringes on their own. The bollocks, really was. So many different styles, it was brilliant. I remember a blue fringe and buckle, never seen them before or since.

"I mean I loved a shoe. The brogues, wow… like a Walkover, with the brogue line going straight to the back of the shoe. Me, my brother and my dad all got a pair from Timpson's on Rye Lane. Worked out at £7.50 a pair. I got a size 8. Finally grew out of them and my dad carried on wearing them. Lasted years. That was the first place that had those brogues. Timpson's of Peckham.

"With the Lotus tassel loafers, when you were dancing, the tassel would fly off, but if you went to the Lotus shop, which was on the bend of Regent Street, opposite the Café Royal, they would have a drawer full of replacement tassels. Funny thing is I can't remember that shop ever selling the shoes.

"I'd also go to Blackmans in the East End and Harry's in Brixton market. You'd go in and he'd lock you in the shop, in case you did a runner with new shoes on, ha ha. Most of my mates got the Solatio range. Not the greatest quality, but we liked the style."

Clive Knight (London): "Later on when I got a Saturday job, I started going up Petticoat Lane on a Sunday morning. Many a shirt was bought at Reiss's. Also, at any opportunity, often school holidays, John and me would go to the Squire shop in Brewer Street where I was almost in seventh heaven. I bought my tan Gibsons there. I wanted oxblood but my mate John got in first. One of our rules was never to wear the same as someone else."

David Rosen (London): "If you went to the Ivy shop or the Squire shop, all you would see would be Royals; there is no other brand in 1970/'71."

Clive Banks (London): "Shoes-wise, we'd get them at Dolcis. Smooths with welts and they had to be oxblood. We wanted the particular roundness of that shoe and if we couldn't get

that, we'd get a loafer and stick a coin in it, I'd have seen that on TV I guess. Shoes were a major purchase, a lifetime event. They were special and only worn on special occasions. I'm not even sure we wore them in as we wore the good ones so sparingly. We'd also get a plimsoll type of thing from Anello & Davide, maybe in 1969/'70."

Raymond Potter (London): "It was either Dr Martens or jodhpur boots which we got from Millets in Surrey Street or Hollidges. Hollidges was in Broad Green, down in Croydon. We'd go down there and get twenty pairs made with steel toe caps, specially put in because they didn't make them normally. Even as Skinheads we wore desert boots. I used to dye them all different colours. Suede coats, leather collars, Crombie overcoats, bomber jackets, reef jackets, Tonik suits, Hush Puppies, red socks, army greens with Dr Martens. I used to buy a pair of shoes first, then me strides, then a shirt, then the jacket. I always started feet first, hundred mile an hour. My old man, his boots were always highly polished, so I was the same, especially the boots, you could see your face in 'em."

Geraldine Choules (Reading): "Our dad liked the Skinhead boys because they were smart and well turned out – they weren't wearing the Dr Martens then, they were wearing the army boots. Our dad worked at Arborfield Garrison, so he could get the black boots and supply them to the local Skinheads. Our mum didn't seem to mind the Skinheads, but then I don't really think she knew what was going on."

Lorraine Le Bass (Southampton): "Mum also could not believe it… now I was even wearing sensible shoes. I was buying black leather loafers from Ravels. Actually, they were quite expensive for the time, but then Ravels was quite an expensive shop. I really had to save to get a pair of them. My mum used to say that it was great to see me go out properly dressed. A proper coat on, a sensible pair of shoes, the only thing she wasn't too happy about was me wearing red tights."

Bill Fordham (London): "You had your two different sets of clothes: one for going out and the other for football. I was a Shed boy at Chelsea and so you had your jungle greens and your Docs. This was around 1967. I had a mate over in Bermondsey so we'd go over there to army surplus stores. I remember even before, around '64/'65, when I was at school in Clapham, there were these older kids from Bermondsey there who were young Mods, and they were the first people I saw wearing boots. They were called Tuf boots, just working men's boots, but they'd wear them to school. So, I started wearing them at school too. The other thing is while people go on about monkey boots, everybody round our way called them Noski boots, because Surrey docks were all timber docks and the boats that came in, came from Russia. All the crews would sell all their gear to get money. The term came because that's what everybody called Russians, 'Noskis', at the time."

Phillip Ellisdon (Watford): "The ultimate shoes for a Skinhead were the Florsheim Imperials brogues (I still wear them today). Everybody wore them because they had a double-thick sole, so that if you kicked somebody with them, they felt it, you know. That was the shoe of the day, and you had to save up your pennies to get them as they were from the

BRUTUS WILD STREAKS

. . . in the trim, slim shape of today.
Young men with a flair for fashion show a
definite preference for the shaped silhouette
and body-hugging fit of the BRUTUS shirt. An
easy ride for you.

BRUTUS

COLIN AND BONNY STAPLEHURST AMONGST FRIENDS,
CIRCA 1968/9

BRUTUS

TRIM FIT

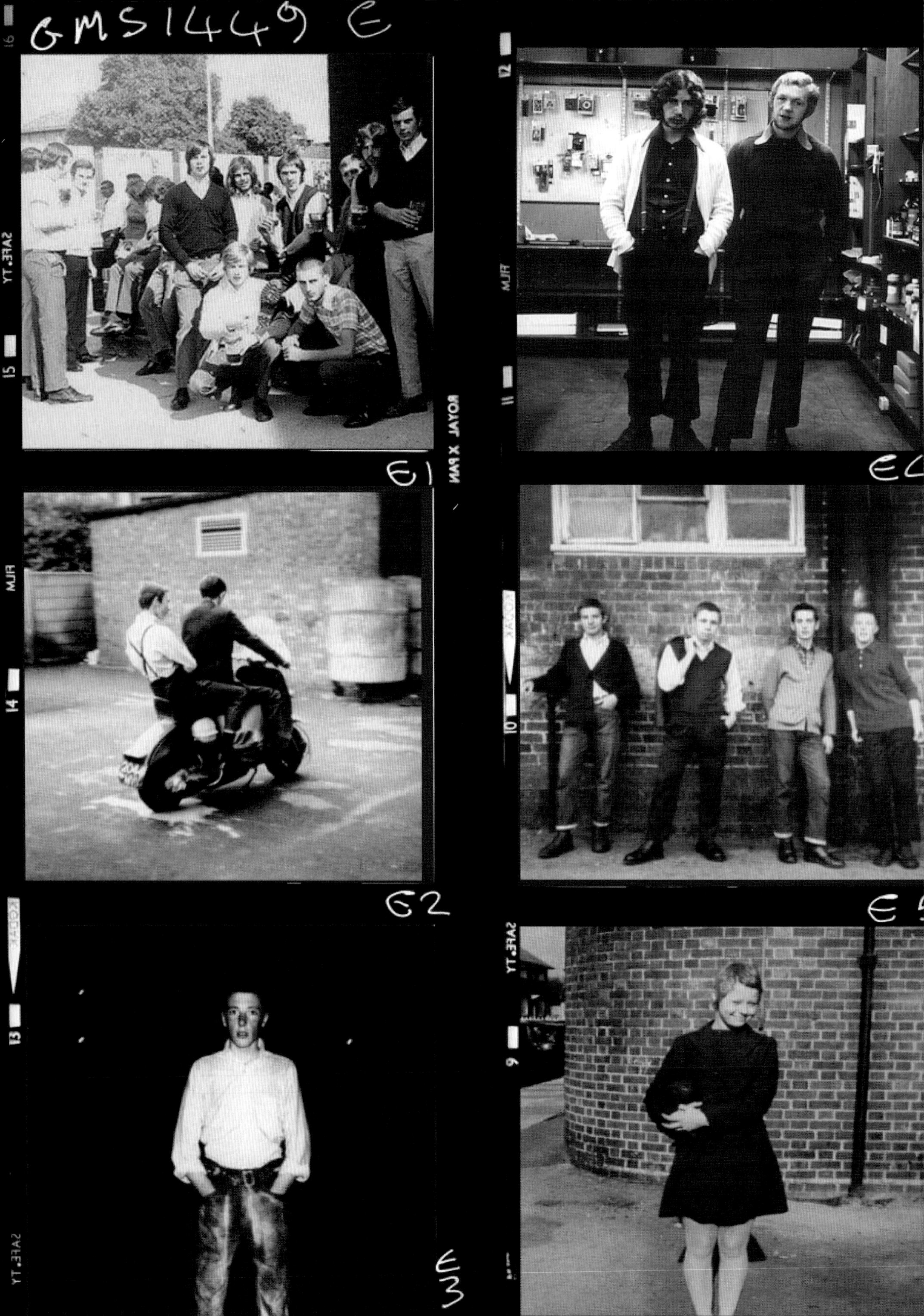
GMS1449 E
E1
E2
E3
ROYAL X PAN
SAFETY
FILM
KODAK

E7

E10

E8

E11

E9

E12

JEAN HADDOW, 1968

POLISH THOSE DANCING SHOES! BRIXTON, 1968

USA and only available in the Squire shops in those days. They looked cool with white Sta-Prest, Ben Sherman or Brutus and a Harrington jacket or Levi jacket, not a hair out of place."

Paul Weller (Woking): "The last pair of what I consider to be Skin/Suede shoes were Solatios, though we called them 'sugar tops' in Woking. They were quite bulky shoes but looked OK with the wider-legged trousers being worn. I think platforms came after this, which I fucking hated."

Hair

Tony Ellis (London): "We used to get our hair cut in Putney Bridge Road by our friend Andy Phenopoulas. A Greek guy, from our class. That is where all the local lads went. He used to cut our hair in the garden of the estate where he lived, not far from Putney Heath. It was cheaper because he may have done twenty of us at a time. He started cutting the partings in as well. The hair got less Moddy and more of a French crop. Then it got shorter than that. They certainly weren't using the name Skinhead at the time. That was still quite a rare look at the time. Nobody on our estate was involved with the '67 'Summer of Love' look from what I remember."

Austin Myers (Shipley): "I was the first guy to walk into my school, Salts Grammar, with Dr Martens boots and a shaven head, and it shocked the teachers to the core. Our school was steeped in a tradition of school uniform and very strict rules and regulations around that. The Skinhead haircut became a problem for me at a grammar school. There were a lot of restrictions placed on me as an individual and others who wanted to be Skinhead. It was discouraged, and so I had to walk around school and attend lessons with a school cap on for two weeks until the hair had grown a little. Even though nobody at the school knew what a Skinhead was all about then, they felt it was actually some sort of cult and they were worried that half the boys from my school would be walking around with shaven heads. This was around '68/'69."

Bernard Jennings (Middlesex): "*Peyton Place* was on TV, and as well as giving the name to the Harrington jacket, they also featured lots of other clothes that you looked at, as well as hairstyles. It was quite short college boy and that's what we used to have. Obviously there were all the Americans in the Ruislip area from the two huge airbases, one in West Ruislip and one in South Ruislip. So you were often noting off-duty airmen who had regulation haircuts. All the local barbers were quite happy doing them, so that's what we used to have. So in a way we were just trying to look like off-duty American airforce people, they weren't GIs. That was the influence. We saw these guys and obviously they had way more money than us English fellas. When I was waiting for the bus to take me to school I used to count the cars and 50 per cent were American and the other half English."

Barry Cain (London): "The Skinhead haircut was unique, extreme actually. Up until that point, there hadn't been anything near as extreme as that. They actually looked violent fuckers. Up for anything. The reality was that loads of us weren't [laughs]. There was always one or two who would have it, but for the rest of us, it was just a fashion thing. The music pulled us in."

Bernard Jennings (Middlesex): "People would have flat-top crops. Retired military men in the US continue to have those military haircuts. A lot of the young lads in our area had that look but I never did. Our look was more an Ivy League preppy look. We wanted to be Ivy. And of course with the Ivy shop, we quickly realised what Ivy meant. You may not be able to name the ten universities but you realised that Ivy was a very middle-to upper-class American style and that's the look you wanted."

Jean Brooks (Reading): "We used to have to tell the boys who owned motorbikes or scooters to meet us around the corner of the club because our dad wouldn't let us on them. I got in trouble once though, because I went to school with long hair, and because my mate's aunty was a hairdresser, I came home with a Skinhead haircut. Mum was like, 'What the fucking hell have you done to your hair?' I just said, 'I've had it cut, I'm a Skinhead!'"

Jacky Abramovitch (London): "As for my hair, well to think about doing that today, I just can't imagine, but back then I did it in a heartbeat. I was 15/16 and I had virtually no hair, long sideboards hanging down. I gradually grew the back a bit. Not as short as the boys, but for a girl it was really, really short."

Bonny Staplehurst (London): "I really liked the short haircut, just liked the style. I had mine pretty short, but I always had the long bits. Again, at school a lot of the girls had it. Some of the Skinheads looked really horrible, but I thought we looked really quite nice! I was really going for a Julie Driscoll look, which was my thing. We went to a barber to have it cut, not a hairdresser. We went to one in Church Street, Pimlico. They would just look at you, obviously a bit odd, but they would cut for you. The boys didn't really have it that short at first, only later did it get really short. It was more like a college boy. My brother had one of those. You could still get a comb in it. I've got a photo of me trying to blow dry it… Most of them were more like the crew cut, sort of astronaut cut."

Maggie Brown (Winchester): "In those days you were either a Skinhead or a Greaser – I loved the neatness of the early Skinheads. A lot of girls had their hair cut like Julie Driscoll… I think we all wanted to be her as she had the ultimate Mod look! Personally, I think that was when the 'feather cut' was born."

Clive Knight (London): "My first crop was in 1968 and that was a number one. I had started knocking around with a different bunch of lads who were neither schoolmates nor Chelsea

Above left, a typical London skinhead in 1969. His head is comp[letely] carefully tended sideburns. "The barber took them off once," he is re[...] my nut." At the same time, fashionable young men were wearing [...] (above right), thus showing in the streets of London a contrast in [...] Roundheads and Cavaliers of 300 years before.

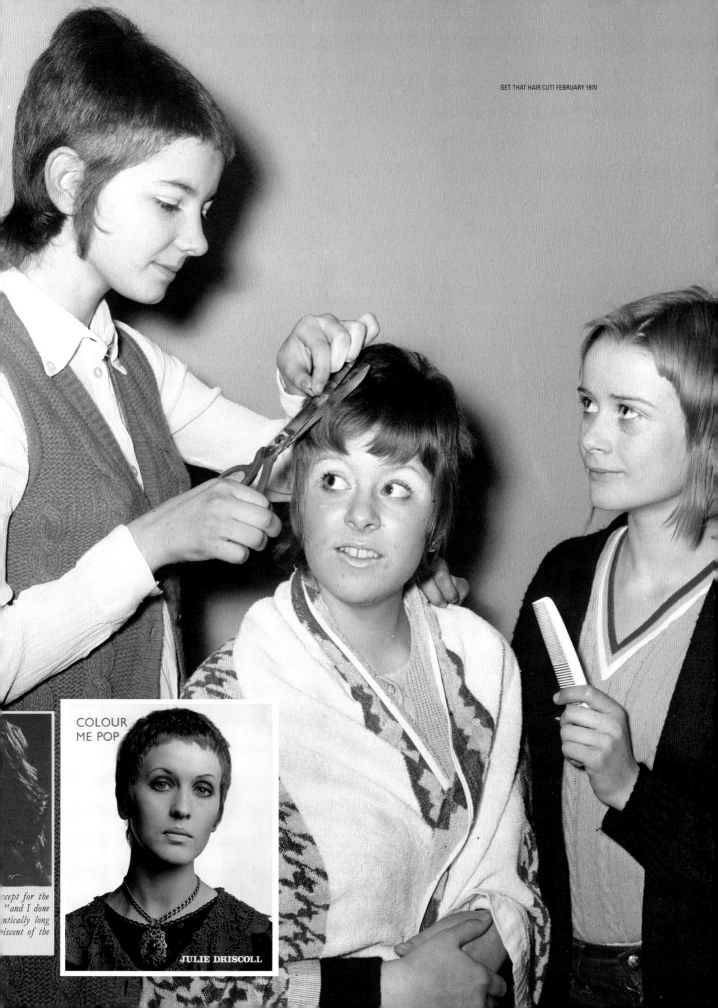

COLOUR
ME POP

cept for the
"and I done
ntically long
iscent of the

JULIE DRISCOLL

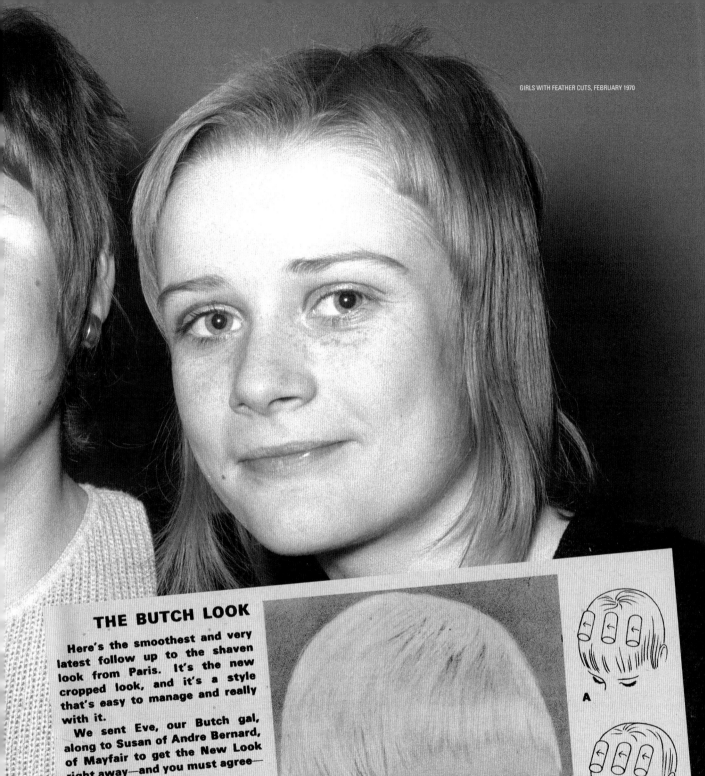

THE BUTCH LOOK

Here's the smoothest and very latest follow up to the shaven look from Paris. It's the new cropped look, and it's a style that's easy to manage and really with it.

We sent Eve, our Butch gal, along to Susan of Andre Bernard, of Mayfair to get the New Look right away—and you must agree— it's real cool.

The Butch hairstyle relies solely on expert cutting, and it's simple to set. Here are the instructions (and they are also illustrated in diagrams A and B).

Use six small rollers, made of cotton wool. Taking the crown of head as focal point, place three rollers at back of head from right to left, thus forming a circle. Comb left to right. Place three rollers at front, this time from right to left. Comb fringe, nape and side into place and secure with pins.

To comb out: Brush in circular movement, as rollers were placed. Back comb if needed, and spray lightly to keep in place.

GET OFF AND MILK IT!

supporters. My dad always said that they'd get me into trouble, ha ha. He was almost right. I moved between groups of like-minded lads but the one thing was that as I moved, I also moved further away from the troublemakers to the group of friends that I still see on a regular basis now after nearly fifty years.

"Prior to that first number-one crop, I had always asked the barber for 'a one inch and same length all over, please'. Then one day someone rocked up with a number-one crop and within days we all went up to the Stanmore barber and had the same. My mum went ballistic and said I looked like a convict, but my dad had been in the army and just said it looked smart and neat. Remember, in 1968 a lot of lads had that Hippy long hair look going on. I remember nagging the barber to put a razor parting in it and him telling me my hair was too thin for it.

"I didn't have that crop for long and it was all Paul Newman and Steve McQueen's fault. One of my mates, John, has seriously wiry hair so didn't get a number one, but stuck with a longish crop. John also had the bluest of eyes and the local girls used to say he looked like Paul Newman. At some point in 1968 we went to see the 1967 film *Hombre* and agreed that John did look like Paul Newman. So, some of us decided we also wanted to look like Paul Newman. Then *Bullitt* came out and, well, that was signed, sealed and delivered. No more number-one crop for us."

RAY AND BECKY POTTER, WADDON ESTATE, CROYDON 1969

Becky Potter (London): "My mate Sally Bond was a Skinhead and had dark hair. Her haircut had long side bits and a parting. It looked smart. I asked her where she got her hair cut and she told me it was the barbers. So one day we skipped out through the fence in the school at lunchtime. There was a hole in it, I don't know who made it, could have been me. So we got to the barbers up the road, and Sally got hers cut first. I said I want the same as her but the barber said it wouldn't suit me as I had blonde hair. When I got back to school, I was only there half an hour before I was summoned to see the headmistress. 'What on earth have you done to your hair? Your mum is going to go mad. How am I going to explain this?' Blah, blah, blah. When I got home my mum wouldn't answer the door to me. When she finally did, she slammed it shut again. 'You're not coming in here. You

look like your brother!' she shouted. Anyway a couple of days later I went up the Top Rank Suite with a Ben Sherman shirt on, and all the girls loved it and kept rubbing my hair."

Raymond Potter (London): "I got involved in the Skinhead thing around '68/'69. Everybody had long hair at one stage of the game. I always had mine cropped off, and everybody I knew changed to how I was. They'd gone from Mod to Hippyish; I just went from Mod to Skinhead. My older brother was three years older than me, and he was my big influence. To me, around this area, the Skinheads were still Mods, but just with a shorter length of hair. If you'd been a Mod and went to a Skinhead, it was never any different. Later the Suedeheads may have driven motors such as Minis and MG sports cars, but the Mods and Skinheads around here were always on scooters. Other people reacted differently though. They'd see your Skinhead and think you're trouble."

Scooters

Another continuation from the Mod days was the use of the scooter. Scooters were loved for their sleek styling and it was usually Vespas and Lambrettas that found favour.

Phillip Ellisdon (Watford): "We all used to ride scooters, following on from the Mod era. I had a Vespa GS 150 and was the only Vespa owner, the rest of the boys had Lambrettas. Over South Oxhey they had a load of lads on scooters called the Bailey Boys – they all used to hang outside a shop called Baileys, hence the name. If you were not from the estate, they would chase you off it. Lucky for our boys we were mechanics and had tuned our scooters and we used to ride past them just so they could not catch us, we were too fast for them.

"Everyone used to hang around Arthur Francis Scooters in Watford on a Saturday morning – people came from all over the place to get the scooters fixed or tuned at Arthur Francis. We used to get to know other Skinheads from different areas. Everyone was called 'John' – it was always a nod and 'Alright John' whenever you met someone. There were no fights, it was all about the scooters, yet see them come in to the Top Rank and there was a good chance they would end up in a scrap!"

Mauro Antoniazzi (Birmingham): "We all used to meet in the village. All our scooters would be lined up. We'd be in and out of cafés, and used to go to a lot of youth clubs. I had these two-tone trousers, I had loads of pairs of them. My favourite pair were these blue and purple ones. Wherever the light caught them, they changed colour…

"One day I'd spent all day polishing the scooter and cleaning the chrome on this Saturday morning. I'd put all my best clothes on. It was a beautiful sunny day so I decided to go round the block on it. The traffic was quite heavy on the Mosley Road, and this dog ran out between the traffic and went under my wheel. It knocked my steering to the right, and I smashed head-on into a car coming the other way. All I can remember is the shock of it all, and then suddenly it was like being in a washing machine, everything was spinning around. All of a sudden, I was on the floor, and when I opened my eyes, I couldn't move or breathe. All I can remember seeing was a car, right up against my shoulder. I thought I was dying, these were my last moments. Somebody came over and lifted my head and talked to me, and I was just trying to get a breath. I eventually got my breath back and started breathing, but I still couldn't move. The ambulance came, all the traffic was still, and people were lined up all along the road, looking.

"I was taken to the hospital. They had to cut my lovely trousers off me because I'd broken my left leg above the knee, and it was at a strange angle. I'd dislocated my shoulder, and had cuts and bruises, but luckily, I'd had my helmet on at the time. I was in a plaster right up to my thigh, with my arm in a sling, and off work for about six or seven months. It was the most terrible time. I could only wear one shoe because I had the plaster on.

"I was gutted about my clothes, but even after that I still had my scooter fixed. I was back on the road in no time. My mum was worried whenever I went out after that.

"Only about two or three months after I'd had the plaster off my leg, one of my friends had bought a brand new GP200, and decided we were going to have a race. My friends called for me one night, and it was quite dark already. I sneaked my

scooter out so my mum didn't hear. I didn't have my crash helmet on, just my trilby. We got to this long road and we started racing each other, going real low at full speed, overtaking each other. All of a sudden, my mate in front braked really quickly. So, I braked and lost control, and the front wheel locked. The scooter just went on its side and dragged me along for about a hundred yards. I must have blacked out for a time, but my friend lifted the scooter off me, and thought I'd died.

"I was OK but because I didn't have my helmet on, it had scraped all the skin off my face and arm on the tarmac. I didn't end up with any scars on my face. When I got home my mum was absolutely horrified. The scooter, because it had the crash bars, it slid along with them, sparks everywhere. But it was fine. After that I became a bit more conscious safety-wise.

"I had my Lambretta for three or four years and they were the best years of my life. We used to go to different clubs in town, Top Rank, Locarno, Rebecca's, Barbarella's, parties, and the occasional blues parties. It all changed when we learnt to drive cars and passed our driving tests. Gradually we sold our scooters and bought cars. Sadly, I sold mine to a friend to buy an Austin Mini Mark II. Wished I had just covered it up at the back of my garage, worth a fortune now."

> "Everyone used to hang around Arthur Francis Scooters in Watford on a Saturday morning – people came from all over the place to get the scooters fixed or tuned at Arthur Francis. We used to get to know other Skinheads from different areas. Everyone was called 'John' – it was always a nod and 'Alright John' whenever you met someone. There were no fights, it was all about the scooters."
> PHILLIP ELLISDON

Supplied By
arthur francis ltd
Vespa · Lambretta · Honda
St. Albans Rd, Watford, Herts.
Tel: Watford 20304

MAURO ANTONIAZZI

Skinheads & Cherry Reds

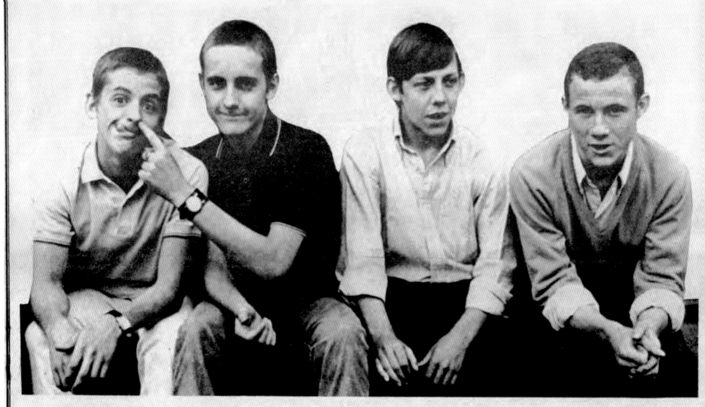

They are the people you may see on the fringe of things, at free concerts shouting out for their favourite football team when everyone else wants to listen to the music, hanging around outside the Roundhouse trying to annoy people with long hair, or you may see them just hanging around on the street. They are the kids who have short cropped hair, wear boots and levis with braces. They don't really have a name as such, outsiders call them crop-heads, prickle heads, bullet-heads, spike-heads, thin-heads, bother boys, or agro boys.

The lack of a name is strange, for most groups of people with an image of their own eventually get a name, Mods, Rockers, Hippies, Heads. 'We are not mods really. Some people call us Mohair Men because we wear suits at the weekend, mohair men waiting for the agro. We're just sort of stylists really because we keep in with the styles.'

The thing they are known by is the gang and the area they come from. Like Mile-end, the Highbury, the Angel. The gang will have a hardcore of members with the rest of the bullet heads in that area supporting this gang against gangs from other areas. 'There's about 30 of us here from the Town (Summerstown), you know, King's Cross and all of them areas. If we ever got into trouble, the geezer's down there'd back us up; like there was 120 over the Hampstead Fair, geezer's we knew, and everyone would back us up if we was in trouble.'

Trouble is the key activity of the gangs. Known as a 'bit of agro' — a bit of aggravation. Trouble can start at some event such as a football match, a free concert 'like up at Parly Hill' or at just about any other time. At the

CHAPTER 7: LABELS

One of the earliest pieces on Skinheads, if not the earliest, was published in *Rolling Stone* magazine, dated July 16th, 1969. Up until this point, in most articles about them, they are still referred to as Mods. Here the writer puts forward many suggested names for the group, and although this does not include 'Skinheads', the title of the article is 'Skinheads and Cherry Reds'. Strangely, the picture accompanying the piece features four boys who, although they have cropped hair, do not appear to have a graded cut.

They are the kids who have short cropped hair, wear boots and Levis with braces. They don't really have a name as such, outsiders call them crop-heads, pickle-heads, bullet-heads, spike-heads, thin-heads, bother boys, or aggro boys.

The lack of a name is strange, for most groups of people with an image of their own eventually get a name, Mods, Rockers, Hippies, Heads. "We are not Mods really. Some people call us Mohair Men because we wear suits at the weekend, mohair men waiting for aggro. We're just sort of stylists really, because we keep in with the styles."
ROLLING STONE, JULY 16TH, 1969

The article is quite lengthy, and features a crew of kids from Somers Town, who talk about the territorial fighting against gangs from St John's Wood, the Edgware Road, Tufnell Park, Archway, Burnt Oak, Mile End, Kilburn, Holloway and Highbury. There's talk of football, fashion and aggro between them and various targets that include students, Pakistanis and Greeks. Yet they talk about their admiration for West Indians.

While 150,000 young fans were peaceably communing with Mr Bob Dylan on the Isle of Wight, eighty miles away in north London, a gang of youths were doing their best to kick in the face of a 13-year-old boy. The youths were peanuts, or skin-heads. In contrast to the hippies' vague and shaggy line of gentle co-existence, they preach an alarming new doctrine of destruction.
DAILY MIRROR, SEPTEMBER 3RD, 1969

The *Daily Mirror* printed a one-page article on youth cults in September 1969. 'The Age Of Identity' was a guide to the youth cults that Britain had had to endure so far, featuring Teddy Boys, Mods and Rockers, Beatniks and Hells Angels. The latest perceived threat to this island's respectability was given its own separate feature. Written by Jeremy Hornsby, 'No Love From Johnny' featured a 16-year-old Upton Park Skinhead. The piece ends with a psychiatrist stating, "Predictably, these youngsters with their violent creed are reacting against the cult of peace and love preached so long by the hippies and the flower children." And so began the *Daily Mirror's* obsession with exposing the new Skinhead cult.

In the old Mod days, the press had mocked the girls of the period for choosing to have their hair short, and wear clumpy 'granny' shoes, stating that the girls had begun to look like the boys. When boys grew their hair so that it reached their shoulders, like Mick Jagger of the Stones, the press criticised the boys for looking like girls. On October 10th, 1969, the *Daily Mirror* ran a feature on the fact that Skinhead girls were cropping their hair, wearing jeans and boots, along with the boys. The article was written by Felicity Green and entitled 'Unisex Isn't Dead – It's Just Had A Short Back And Sides'. It described a young couple from Finchley: Glenda Peake, 16, and Tony Hughes, 18. As well as featuring photos of the couple, there are two short interviews with them, plus a guide to Skinhead lingo (Aggro = Aggravation, and so on).

This way of dressing is very comfortable really, and the braces make a nice change. In the evening though, I think the blokes look tasty when they're got all up in their mohair. The girls wear mohair too. Longish jackets, like the blokes, and a skirt – mind you, not too mini.
Glenda Peake, 16

First, there's your Ben Shermans and your narrow braces and Sta-Prests worn at half-mast to show off the steels. This winter we'll all be wearing sheepskin jackets. We wear this casual gear during the day if we're meeting our mates or something. But in the evening, when we go to Mecca or Top Rank dancehalls, we like to dress formal. Got to anyway. They wouldn't let you in without a tie.
Tony Hughes, 18
DAILY MIRROR, OCTOBER 10TH, 1969

Ian Hingle (London): "I always thought of myself as more of an observer really. I thought I was too old to be a Skinhead, 'cos a lot of them seemed around 15 and I was 18/19. So, I started to grow my hair and I was going for a more American student look. I even had a moustache. A lot of people were trying to grow one then. So, really skinny trousers, not denim jeans, cotton jeans, loafers, though I couldn't buy Bass, well you probably could, but I didn't know where to go.

"Then I went to university, up north, Bradford, studying economics and politics. The others up there were all scruffy, so I thought I'd go back to my roots! When I was back in London, I got my hair cut shorter and bought a Harrington. I mean I had just got rid of all that stuff, but by way of a reaction to the scruffy students I think, I bought one again. I was on my own like that for about six months and that lasted about six months until the *Daily Mirror* came out, you know the famous one, with the headline.

"I was up in Bradford the day that came out and all the kids up there were Teddy Boys really, slicked-back hair, like Rockers. Greasy hair, Brylcreem and all that clobber. And that article came out and the next day they all shaved their heads. They bought things like Tuf boots, 'cos they had no idea. I mean this was a street style, led by the streets, so they didn't know, did they? I thought, bollocks to that, I don't want to be associated with these idiots, so I started to grow my hair again… I wasn't really happy up there, I was like a fish out of water. I had to look Bradford up on a map: 'Oh, there it is,' that sort of thing."

STAFF AT *SUNDAY TIMES*, FARRINGDON ROAD, 1969

he public were only just discovering the ways of the Skinheads in the papers, but they'd been reading for the last couple of years about 'filthy Hippies'.

n London, the area of Piccadilly Circus had been a meeting place for Hippies sleeping rough. Known as the 'Dilly Dossers', they would soon be catapulted into the nation's consciousness, when a group led by a character known as Dr John (actually Phil Cohen) took over an empty five-storey mansion at Hyde Park Corner. Number 144 Piccadilly would be known as the London Street Commune – a place for all homeless Hippies to seek refuge. It outraged the public.

A news story appeared about a group of Tottenham Skinheads, armed with airguns and rocks, attacking the premises, as if on some moral crusade. The Skinheads were finally beaten back when water-filled carpet boules and ink-filled balloons rained down on them.

THE SQUAT, 144 PICCADILLY

Musically, 1969 proved to be the peak year for reggae music in he UK. Songs such as 'Return Of Django' by The Upsetters, 'Liquidator' by Harry J. All Stars and 'Long Shot Kick De Bucket' by The Pioneers would all become Skinhead classics. But the song that probably turned a lot of people on to the sound was 'The Israelites' by Desmond Dekker & The Aces, which reached the number one spot in March that year.

On December 10th, 1969, the BBC disclosed the world of Skinheads to an even wider audience when they screened heir *Man Alive* investigation programme called 'What's The Truth About Hells Angels And Skinheads?' Reporter Harold Williamson missed out on a trip to California by reporting on Hells Angels much closer to home, at a pub called the Oddfellows Arms in Oldbury, near Birmingham to be precise. The actual report is quite grim viewing as we see 18-year-old Sylvia wed a self-named 'Hitler' in the backyard of the pub

with a BSA motorbike manual as a bible and an oil seal as a ring. When interviewed, 'Hitler' states: "If it was legal, we'd go around hanging Skinheads."

It's not until the last twenty minutes of the fifty-minute programme that you actually get to see the Skinhead section: Danny Harkin and the Chelsea Skins at an away football match in Newcastle. Then you see kids playing pool at a youth club before the camera switches to four young Skinheads who mainly talk about 'hating Pakis' and being very dismissive about the local Greasers having the nerve to liken themselves to America's Hells Angels. When questioned how long they will remain Skinheads, one replies "I don't know. Up to about 18 I suppose, I don't know. I mean you don't get many Skinheads over 19 or 20."

Steve Thompson, 16, is the next to be interviewed, at his parents' house. Steve's father is very understanding of his son's choice. Having been a Teddy Boy himself, he states, "You get the feeling when you are a teenager, like when I was a Teddy Boy, that they appear to be having a go at you. I now realise there's no such thing, but when you are a teenager, there is a little something there. You get a crowd of you, a little bit of chit-chat, and for a bit of devilment you probably do aggravate older people. I went through this phase; the only thing is, these boys seem to be going through it a couple of years before we did. He's just 15, but that makes sense… It seems these days, they are growing up quicker all round. So, he's doing at 15 what I was doing, possibly at 17."

Chris Difford (London): "In '68/'69 and a bit of '70, I was living on Combe Avenue, a council estate on Blackheath, a modern collection of *Clockwork Orange*-style houses and flats. Everyone on the estate was in and out of the gang, there was little choice at the time. I daubed on a wall in white paint, 'Combe Avenue Killers'; we were far from that."

Bill Fordham (London): "The funny thing is that as time progressed into the later sixties, I think people took it into a bit of a parody of what we originally were, in that we had short hair and boots in '67 and they then started cropping it all off to go one bit further, but we didn't think that was terribly smart actually."

THE 'PRINCE' WHO IS 'KING'

AND suddenly Prince Buster has bust on the scene. The King of Blue Beat has found success here via his "Al Capone" single and has also landed in the national R & B charts and if that doesn't make too much sense, well . . . he is selling his records to the main core of blues enthusiasts.

The Prince-who-is-King to thousands of blue-beat fans is quite an enigma. A ravingly happy character from Jamaica who says he can't understand why "Al Capone" has been singled out for special attention. Why can't he understand? Simply because there is a shatteringly long list of his titles available in Britain right now and they really are all much of a muchness. Take a look at a new quarterly-published list of available singles in Britain and the mind boggles at the flood of material by the Prince.

MANY RELEASES

I counted nearly 50 by his Highness under his own solo name—and only "Ten Commandments", "My Girl" and "Big Fight" appeared twice . . . with different flip sides. There are 17 by the Buster All-Stars, including "Al Capone". Buster and Cool turn up on one. Buster and the Torchlighters have one, as well. Then there is another ten split between Buster Jnr., Buster's Band, Buster's Group. All this lot out via Blue Beat, which is a label belonging to Melodisc and the indefatigable blue-beat booster Ziggy Jackson.

Even if Buster hasn't been in the charts before to any extent, these singles sell astonishingly well among the coloured population. Back home in Jamaica, Buster has long been one of the biggest sell-out stars . . . and his influence has spread through the States. Odd thing here for the prolific one: his "Al Capone" is available there on no less than five different labels!

PROTEST

What of the Prince instrumentally? Usually he accompanies himself on drums —the African variety, and they fall somewhere between the Conga and Bongo categories. He was born on May 24th, 1938—his dad was a railroad worker. Says Buster: "Living was hard. That's why my blues are really a form of protest against all the things that bug me. I have to remember my background: how my ancestors were slaves and are still fighting for full freedom. So if you can dance to something of mine like 'Soul Of Africa' . . . well, great. But I want you to listen to the message as well".

He was once a professional boxer, but avoided getting badly marked. He started singing in a club for the equivalent of a couple of bob a night. He's toured Spain and France and has visited Lon-

Prince Buster with a Nigerian princess of whose tribe Prince is an honorary chieftain.

don several times for exclusive West Indian concerts. I once went to a Press reception for Buster, watched him sell his curious form of blues. As ever he yelled his opening announcement . . . "This is my personal dedication to all of you—LET'S DANCE TO-NIGHT!" And, blow me down, after a couple of numbers even hardened journalists were jigging their own form of blue-beat steps.

On sheer weight of issued material, Buster simply HA[ ] to break through. But as wit[ ] Millie's blue-beat break[ ] through of three years ag[ ] it could be a mere spasm o[ ] enthusiasm. There's no re[ ] evidence of blue-beat takin[ ] over on a really wide scal[ ] It just has its own non-fickl[ ] and enthusiastic followin[ ] that's all.

CHAPTER 8: SOUNDS

Ska music had already worked its way into the West End of London by 1967. In fact, it was totally established as a major sound. It had filled dance floors at places such as the Flamingo in Wardour Street, the Limbo Club in D'Arblay Mews, the Roaring Twenties in Carnaby Street and the Marquee on a Monday night.

The thing that the Flamingo and the Roaring Twenties had in common was a major crowd-pulling DJ by the name of Count Suckle. He had come to England after stowing away on a banana boat in the late fifties, and soon set up an established sound system in Ladbroke Grove, west London. He had some great contacts back in Jamaica, and artists including Prince Buster would send over exclusive tunes for his set. By the time the sixties arrived, Suckle had a big enough reputation and following in places such as Brixton and Ladbroke Grove to get him a gig in the West End.

The Flamingo had already established itself on black styles of music, although many of the bands performing it were white. Throughout the fifties the club had gained a reputation for providing the best in modern jazz, with the likes of Tubby Hayes, Tony Crombie, Ronnie Ross and Ronnie Scott playing live on stage. In early '62 Georgie Fame & The Blue Flames, Zoot Money and Chris Farlowe had slowly changed the soundtrack to rhythm & blues. The records played over the sound system, between live acts, were a mixture of R&B, soul, blues and ska.

In 1961, the Flamingo finally got the man they wanted on the decks to provide the latest offerings from Jamaica. They gave him Sunday nights. His selections drew people in to the West End, but to Suckle it wasn't enough, he needed more nights. However, the club was doing very nicely with its other genres of music, particularly R&B, which both the black American GIs and the white pilled-up Mods loved. Luckily a chance meeting with Jamaican singer Owen Gray led to Suckle fulfilling his ambitions. Gray informed him that the Roaring Twenties club at 50 Carnaby Street was after a full-time sound system. Count Suckle took the reins behind the decks, and introduced a whole Jamaican-style night, bang in the centre of town. Black people flocked to hear the music, while white Mods and tourists made up the rest of the crowd.

By 1964, Suckle felt that he'd outgrown the confines of the Roaring Twenties. He'd also got fed up with the numerous police raids that the club attracted. He went in search of his own club, and found some premises below an old cinema in Praed Street, Paddington. He prided himself on offering great live acts too, which included soul acts, artists such as Garnet Mimms, Maxine Brown and Edwin Starr, as well as jazz organist Jimmy McGriff and the reggae stars he knew. The membership card for the club was pink and on the back were the warnings: "There is no whiskey allowed in this club. No drugs of any kind. No dangerous weapons. Please keep this card with you always, otherwise you will pay again."

A licensed bar obviously attracted passers-by, plus you could get great food there too – curried goat, rice and peas, roti, callaloo, all served out of a hatch on paper plates.

Penny Reel (London): "I was collecting ska and reggae from 1961 to '66, so I had 'Push Wood In The Fire' by Jackie Opel, several Maytals records such as 'Hurry Up', 'Alleluyah', 'Six And Seven Books Of Moses' and 'A Man Who Knows'. I bought most of my records in the market. But I also used Words And Music at the top of Arcola Street, Rita and Benny's (R&B Records) in Stamford Hill, a shop in Church Street called the Music Box and one in Kingsland Waste called Teachers. So, all around here [Hackney] I was buying ska records. But it was mostly from Nat, who was the guy who ran a stall at the top of Ridley Road market. He had all the Blue Beat, Island, Rio and R&B catalogues. In other words, pretty much all the releases of that genre. It was a big stall. When I first went there in 1960, he had a box with five records in it. Stuff like Beresford Ricketts, Higgs & Wilson, Jackie Edwards, Owen Gray. That was all he had. Me and my friend Martin left them, but gradually I got into the sound and finally bought some in '61. Every week I'd go down to his stall, and I bought tunes by Lloyd Clarke or Derrick Morgan. I knew very little about them, so I was buying them blind. I thought they came from New Orleans but when I asked Nat, he told me they came from Jamaica. I didn't believe him, but then I found out he was telling the truth.

"Dalston and Hackney had been filling up with black people since around 1958 and '59, people who had come to our shores from Martinique, Trinidad and Tobago. As a couple moved out to Essex, their place would be taken by a black family. Suddenly the whole of Cecilia Road was black, then Colveston Crescent, Montague Road and Sandringham Road soon followed. People were aghast. They'd stop my mother in the street, and have conversations about how these people put shit through your letterbox or ate dog food, you know, made-up stories like that. It was the general feeling amongst the older generation. I liked black people. I started moving with them, just around that music stall to begin with. I loved the way that they were just ordinary guys, and they loved their music. I loved their music too, so we had that bridge, that connection, to meet these people."

Geoff Deane (London): "The music then is still my go-to music now. It was all singles really, until 'Tighten Up', and I was buying most of it from Music Land on Ridley Road, which I now know, though I didn't know then, was part-owned by Chris Blackwell who owns Island Music. You'd go down there and the van would arrive with all the new stuff and after a while they started making stuff here as well, so it wasn't only coming from Jamaica. You'd have all the Skinheads and the Rude Boys there too. They would get first pick, 'cos we were a little bit fearful of them."

Tony Ellis (London): "I started collecting records in '61 when I bought The Shadows. I got the bug straight away because my dad had it. It just kept growing. First The Shadows, then

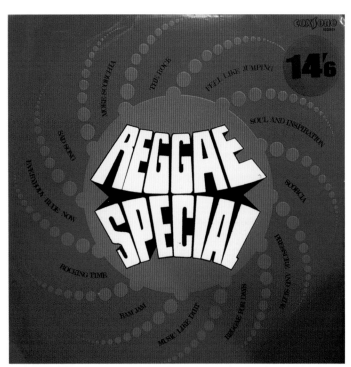

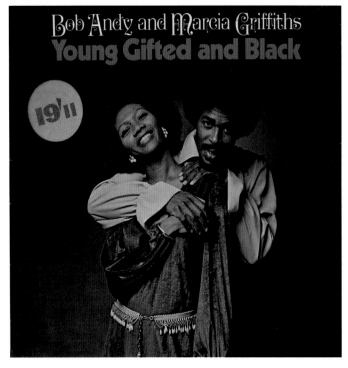

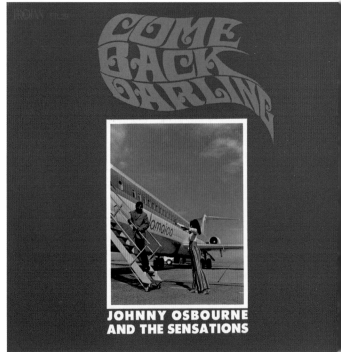

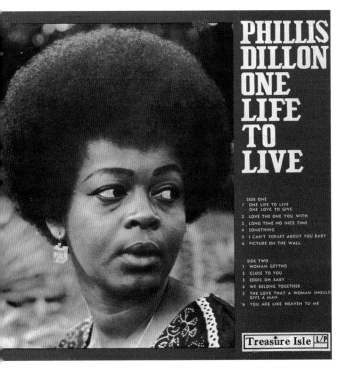

PHILLIS DILLON ONE LIFE TO LIVE

SIDE ONE
1 ONE LIFE TO LIVE
  ONE LOVE TO GIVE
2 LOVE THE ONE YOU WITH
3 LONG TIME NO NICE TIME
4 SOMETHING
5 I CAN'T FORGET ABOUT YOU BABY
6 PICTURE ON THE WALL

SIDE TWO
1 WOMAN GETTHO
2 CLOSE TO YOU
3 EDDIE OH BABY
4 WE BELONG TOGETHER
5 THE LOVE THAT A WOMAN SHOULD GIVE A MAN
6 YOU ARE LIKE HEAVEN TO ME

Treasure Isle L/P

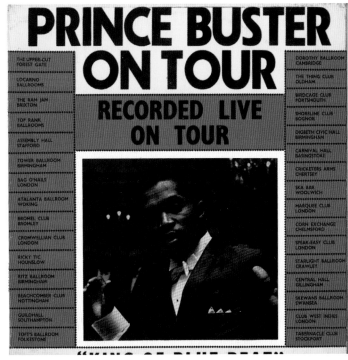

PRINCE BUSTER ON TOUR

RECORDED LIVE ON TOUR

THE UPPER-CUT FOREST GATE
LOCARNO BALLROOMS
THE RAM JAM BRIXTON
TOP RANK BALLROOMS
ASSEMBLY HALL STAFFORD
TOWER BALLROOM BIRMINGHAM
BAG O'NAILS LONDON
ATALANTA BALLROOM WOKING
BROMEL CLUB BROMLEY
CROMWELLIAN CLUB LONDON
RICKY TIC HOUNSLOW
RITZ BALLROOM BIRMINGHAM
BEACHCOMBER CLUB NOTTINGHAM
GUILDHALL SOUTHAMPTON
TOFT'S BALLROOM FOLKESTONE

DOROTHY BALLROOM CAMBRIDGE
THE THING CLUB OLDHAM
BIRDCAGE CLUB PORTSMOUTH
SHORELINE CLUB BOGNOR
DIGBETH CIVIC HALL BIRMINGHAM
CARNIVAL HALL BASINGSTOKE
CRICKETERS ARMS CHERTSEY
SKA BAR WOOLWICH
MARQUEE CLUB LONDON
CORN EXCHANGE CHELMSFORD
SPEAK-EASY CLUB LONDON
STARLIGHT BALLROOM CRAWLEY
CENTRAL HALL GILLINGHAM
SKEWANS BALLROOM SWANSEA
CLUB WEST INDIES LONDON
TABERNACLE CLUB STOCKPORT

"KING OF BLUE BEAT"

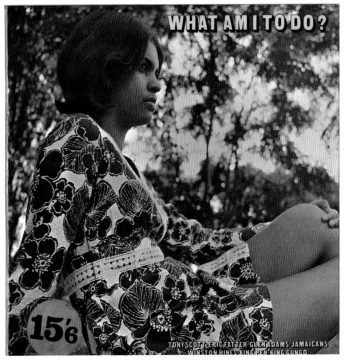

WHAT AM I TO DO?

15'6

TONY SCOTT·ERIC FATTER·GLEN ADAMS·JAMAICANS
WINSTON HINES·KING PEN·KING GUNGO

> "The funny thing is that as time progressed in to the later sixties, I think people took it into a bit of a parody of what we originally were, in that we had short hair and boots in '67 and they then started cropping it all off to go one bit further, but we didn't think that was terribly smart actually."
>
> BILL FORDHAM

came the blues, then British R&B, American R&B and then soul. My first soul record was 'In The Midnight Hour' on black Atlantic, that was a big club sound before it made the charts. Ska obviously too, when tunes like 'Phoenix City' by Roland Alphonso, 'Broadway Jungle' by The Flames, and 'Don't Throw Stones' by Prince Buster were all big in the youth clubs. We had a couple of hip blokes in them. One guy, Keith Appleton, who talked in a Jamaican accent from time to time, even in the early sixties. He had one deck, and he was a bedroom selector [a reggae word for a DJ]. He used to play in the Croydon Estate youth club, which was just a few miles away from where I lived. This is around '65/'66, and he was only about 16 or 17. He told us he only needed one deck as he was a selector. I have no idea where he'd seen that."

Tony Rounce (London): "I was lucky in that the guy who ran the local record shop, the Melody Inn, was Martin Hubbard. It was opened in 1965 by Martin and his wife Sandy. They were only in their late twenties. Her parents were fairly well off and bought them the shop as a wedding present. It was a tiny little shop but Martin really knew his stuff. The time period really captured me perfectly as a teenager with money. The first record I went in there to buy was 'I'll Keep On Holding On' by The Action. Martin looked at me very derisively and said, 'There's a better version of that you know. Have you heard of The Marvelettes?' Luckily, I had and mentioned 'Please Mr Postman'. Then he put the record he was talking about on the turntable and said, 'Now, you're going to buy this one, aren't you?' He wasn't scary but I didn't want to upset him, so I bought it. Luckily enough there were other record shops in the area such as the local Rumbelows, where the girl who worked there wouldn't laugh if you walked in and asked for Major Lance or whatever. So, I wandered over there and bought The Action's version too. Now that Martin had started pushing soul at me, he wouldn't sell me pop records any more. He was one of the first guys I knew who imported LPs and singles."

Tony Ellis (London): "While I was a kid at school, there were some kids on the estate who had pork pie hats, polka dot shirts, jackets with flaps over the breast pocket, you know, they seemed to have a lot of money. Anyway, they played 'Madness' to me by Prince Buster. I'd never heard anything so outrageous in my life, but I went and bought it anyway. I took it to the music club at school, where they all laughed at me because of it. So, I was an early victim of prejudice against ska and Jamaican music. I was one of the first kids around our way to have my own record player in my bedroom. My dad built me a record player with a separate cabinet, so we all used to come back from the Jenny Lind Club if it wasn't a good night, and pile into my bedroom to play records. It was probably blues stuff like Sonny Boy Williamson or a Pye International LP. That was unusual because in most families it was forbidden to have mixed sexes alone in the bedrooms of your parents' house."

Brian Wright (London): "I was buying records at just run-of-the-mill shops. There was one in Victoria near the Shakespeare pub but we used to go to Coxsone's Downbeat Records in Atlantic Road, Brixton. We used to get our ska stuff down there. Sir Coxsone used to sell white-label records that had come straight from Jamaica. So, he used to invent the title of the tune and the name of the band. People used to think they

were so hip because they were in on the scene, but he was making it all up. I had heard ska stuff probably on pirate stations and through Georgie Fame & The Blue Flames, but on the whole, I'd give most credit to discovering most of it in the Caxton [Club] to be fair. We used to go to Soul City in Monmouth Street, and that's where you got your imports from. We were getting tunes on Gordy, Tamla or Motown but not UK Tamla Motown."

Tony Ellis (London): "My mate, Peter Hill, who lived on another part of the estate, his sister was about two years older than us and she had the Derrick Morgan *Forward March!* LP. The picture of Derrick on the front in his pork pie hat strolling forwards just kind of fascinated us. I'd never seen anything like it. Never heard anything like it. It was just another world to us. I wouldn't say I was fascinated with it at the time because it just then sounded like novelty music. But it came into context a bit later on when we went to the church youth club, and these brothers who I mentioned had played 'Madness' to me, started taking these records over there and we started dancing to them."

Bernard Jennings (Ruislip): "I was from Ruislip, and there were dozens of kids into this new style. The big meeting place would be up at Burton's in Uxbridge. There was also a West Indian club on the high street in Uxbridge. I always remember my first night there, and I was blown away with just how good the music was. They had a very good sound system, and I spent years and years trying to remember and buy every record I heard on that first night there. Things like 'Save A Bread' on Island, 'Inez' by Lester Sterling with Tommy McCook & The Supersonics, 'The Higher The Monkey Climbs' by Justin Hinds, but this was the re-recorded rocksteady version, and you have to remember all this stuff we were hearing had just come out. That was the wonderful thing, going up to Rayners Lane record shop to buy all the new James Brown singles and paying a shedload of money to buy them on import. They came out on UK release weeks later, but you just had to have them. We'd also go up to Shepherd's Bush market on a Saturday morning. There was one very good record stall in the market and there was also the Pama shop, which was a very big shop and also had a downstairs listening room. We'd just listen to everything that was released that week, you know, the assistant putting it on for ten seconds, bang, taking it off quick and they'd ask, 'Do you want it or not?' If you didn't like the initial sound you were scared of wasting their time. If you declined it went onto this big stack behind them. You'd stand there with a big long line of people behind you waiting. Reggae records always had good intros but it was make or break in those first ten seconds."

Tony Ellis (London): "I was buying records from HMV in Putney. It was soul mostly. Singer sewing machine shops sold records. They had stores in Putney and Knightsbridge. Near Harrods, they had a store there stacked with soul music. They had Homer Banks' 'A Lot Of Love' there, which was a big tune on the Mod scene. Around Wimbledon station there were a few second-hand shops. I bought 'Jerk And Twine' by Jackie Ross there on a demo for 2/6. There were quite a few demos to be found because DJs who got sent them didn't want this black stuff, so they'd chuck them in the second-hand shops… I only knew 'Jerk And Twine' because I'd heard it on *Ready Steady Go!* I dread to think what I left behind. We also used to sneak off to Soho to look at the striptease clubs as young boys might want to do. There'd be more shops around there with demos in; in later years I got P. P. Arnold's 'Everything's Gonna Be Alright'."

Barry Cain (London): "The big song for us was 'Return Of Django' by The Upsetters. That was the number one, the Skinhead stomp record."

Tony Ellis (London): There was a lot of us who hung around together in Putney. Not a gang as such, but just teenagers who hung around Putney high street, sit around in the old Joe Lyons tea houses or going to W. H. Smiths to listen to records in the booths. Then the HMV opened up just down the road, and they had a hip manager there. He started playing imported stuff. I saw my first import there, 'Mellow Moonlight' by Leon Haywood. So he was somebody who had an influence on us, and that took us into another realm of soul: imported soul. We used to read these charts in the *Record Mirror*, you know, the top ten soul records, so we'd go along to Transat Records in Soho. The top ten records would be something like Little Mac & The Boss Sounds, 'In The Midnight Hour'. I'd never heard it before but it just sounded so cool with a group name like that. Then you'd see the Sue label with names like Edgewood Smith & The Fabulous Tailfeathers. I mean, what the fuck! So I used to collect all the release sheets and Sue publicity material. That all went alongside interesting blues as well. So I had my first Lightnin' Hopkins LP, *Dirty House Blues* on the Realm label, which came from the influence of the *Mike Raven Blues Show*. Around 1968 when the British blues boom started, we were still listening to soul music and being slightly Moddish, hair maybe a bit longer, but then we branched out in going to the Blue Horizon club in Battersea run by Mike Vernon. We'd go and watch Fleetwood Mac when they first started, plus bands like Savoy Brown, Freddie King backed by Chicken Shack and The Black Cat Bones

featuring Paul Kossoff of Free. It was a fantastic club held in just a little upstairs room above a pub. Just seeing Freddie King doing 'You've Got To Love Her With A Feeling' was wonderful."

Tony Rounce (London): "Dave Godin had a shop in Deptford first of all but I never went there. Even though it was just down the road from Millwall, funnily enough, my trips over there to see the football would be, see the match, jump on the train at New Cross or New Cross Gate then go back home. I'd never venture into Deptford high street, that was like uncharted territory. But when Godin opened up the shop in Monmouth Street, just at the back of Covent Garden, I started going. It was probably around March 1968, so not long before I left school. One Sunday evening I was listening to Mike Raven, who was now on Radio 1, play Bobby Bland's 'A Piece Of Gold'. He'd said that it was not being released over here but if you popped over to see Dave Godin and his friends over at Soul City Records they'd probably be able to find you a copy. I bunked the next day off school, went up there and bought it with another couple of things. I got chatting to Dave, and he asked me what other artists I liked. I'd been a member of the Tamla Motown Appreciation Society, so I'd been reading his enthusings for a few years by that time. It had been around this time that me and my school pal Dave had started our Motown fanzine *The Motor Town Revue* so I asked his advice on it. Godin gave me some hints such as: 'Keep it interesting, keep it short, keep it fluent, don't be opinionated, stick to the facts and no gushing superlatives.' He then said if we could get the magazine off the ground, he would take fifty copies for Soul City every month. That was about a third of our print run. It only ran to three issues. We'd have kept going but my friend started going off and doing things such as interviewing Edwin Starr without even considering asking if I was interested, and secondly, we fell foul of the two girls who ran the official Motown Fan Club. They got EMI to send us a legal letter telling us to cease using the words 'Tamla' and 'Motown' in our magazine and telling us to put in an apology in our third, and what turned out to be our last, issue. We were 15 or 16 years of age at the time. Ironically I ended up becoming very good friends with somebody who was working for the fan club at that time. After we stopped our magazine I could go around her house and listen to all the new promo records and test pressings from EMI."

Bernard Jennings (Ruislip): "We used to do a little bit of DJ-ing around 1969 at the local youth club. We got my younger brother involved because he talked well, and he was called Boss J. So we brought the records and he played them. We mixed the tunes with soul but it would have been around 75 per cent reggae because that's what youngsters wanted. They were usually a week ahead of you, we used to bump into these young lads anyway at Shepherd's Bush market and they'd end up buying more than you did. It was quite competitive but in those days there were only ten or a dozen released each week, so if you bought most of them you were usually OK. I remember one of the biggest stirs happened when certain records were put on for ten seconds before you bought them – one was when 'Monkey Man' came out. It had a big impact, but the biggest impact of all was when The Melodians' 'Sweet Sensation' came on in the shop. I think everybody there bought a copy, it was just so good. Flipsides

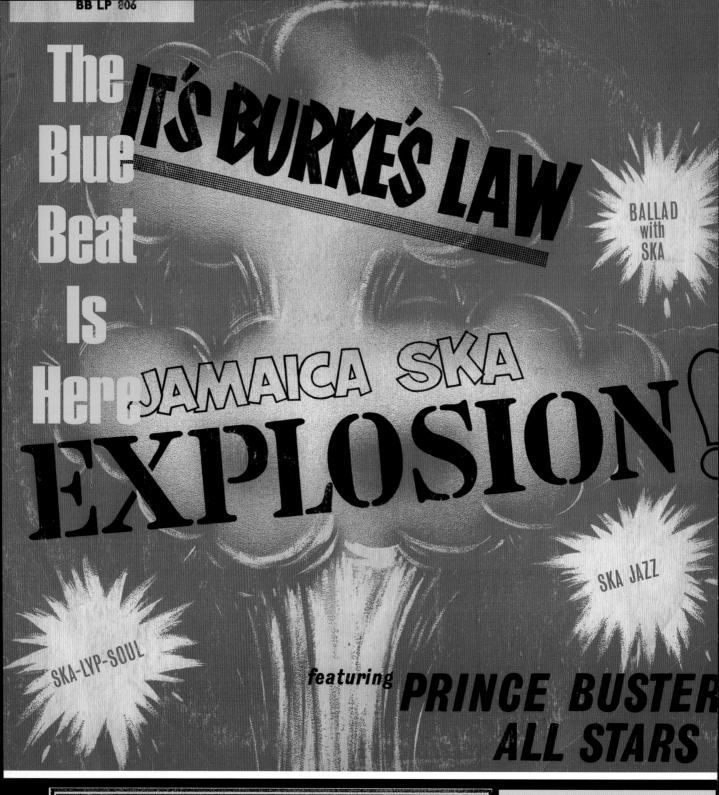

BB LP 806

The Blue Beat Is Here

IT'S BURKE'S LAW

BALLAD with SKA

JAMAICA SKA EXPLOSION!

SKA JAZZ

SKA-LYP-SOUL

featuring PRINCE BUSTER ALL STARS

"While I was a kid at school, there were some kids on the estate who had pork pie hats, polka dot shirts, jackets with flaps over the breast pocket, you know, they seemed to have a lot of money. Anyway, they played 'Madness' to me by Prince Buster. I'd never heard anything so outrageous in my life, but I went and bought it anyway. I took it to the music club at school, where they all laughed at me because of it. So, I was an early victim of prejudice against ska and Jamaican music."
TONY ELLIS

were always just as interesting, it was probably older and maybe an instrumental. It might be Sound Dimension or The Skatalites. You'd always eagerly flip it over to see what you'd got on the back. I think the best B side was 'Marcus Junior' by the Soul Brothers, and then there was 'Worries A Yard' by The Versatiles on the Crab label. We liked big drum rolls on tunes. We used to go to a shop in Rayners Lane that was run by a guy who was an obsessive and he'd scour London record shops to buy anything to do with soul, so he taught me a lot. There was also a record shop in Ruislip Manor. They'd realised quite quickly about this reggae thing but they didn't really know anything as it was an old-fashioned shop. Still, they had a big box full of all the Crab label stuff and early Island bits. There'd be blokes nicking it, putting it inside their sheepskin coats as soon as it was put out."

Jacky Abramovitch (London): "I loved the music at the clubs, the early reggae and Tamla Motown. We didn't listen to anything else… No pop music. We were really sniffy about any of that. We were purists. There was that tune 'Young Girl' by Gary Puckett, which I secretly liked but I would never admit it. We would go to the Ilford Palais and the Top Rank. There would be a bit of trouble, but it didn't really bother us and the thing is, we didn't really drink. Alcohol wasn't really our thing. I don't remember any pills then either, maybe later, but not then, we were too young really. I just wasn't aware of the people I was with doing it either.

"These are my top ten tunes – they aren't necessarily the best, but the ones that take me there in an instant, when I hear them. I really remember how we used to dance to them. If you put any of these on now, I could do the dance. For example, when 'The Israelites' came on, we'd hear one beat and everyone knew it. I would immediately bend down and start the moves. I always thought he sang 'baked beans for breakfast'. Nobody knew any different. For years and years, I thought that was what he said. It still makes me laugh now. Nobody questioned it… nobody said that is so strange. I don't know if I was just thick or what. It seemed perfectly OK to me.

"Anyway. Here are my top tunes. 'Long Shot Kick The Bucket', 'The Israelites', 'Spirit In The Sky', that was the Tottenham Royal and everybody in the place would all be in a line and do this kind of move to it. Huge tune. Then 'Double Barrel', 'Young, Gifted And Black'. 'Train To Skaville' is probably the one that takes me back instantly. 'Monkey Man', 'Love Of The Common People', Nicky Thomas version, 'You Can Get It If You Want', Desmond Dekker and 'Guns Of Navarone'. 'Ride A White Swan' – we was like, do we like it? I can't really explain the joy we had searching out these records. We'd get them mainly in shops, not markets. We would love the B-side too… My husband, who I met in '72/'73, was a DJ. He died in 2010 but he had boxes and boxes of records and I've still got them. The time we would spend trying to find unusual things. if I had to name one song to represent me from that time it would be 'Black Pearl' by Horace Faith."

Andrew Vaughan (Orrell): "Back in my home town music was everywhere, or more poignantly, black music was everywhere… Black music and the dance floor. The

adrenaline rush that goes together. The working-class love of black music. But back then was it the girls or the reggae that got me onto the dance floor all those years ago? Probably a healthy mix of them but those dance floors were my bombers, my dexys, my high. School discos and the under-18 discos at the Orrell British Legion and Billinge Higher End Labour Club. Billinge was on a Monday night and the Legion on a Friday. All getting dressed up, chewing gum and smoking fags. Bit like our fathers and grandfathers before us. Working-class boys growing into working-class men. Looking smart on a Friday night. It was either soul music that very soon afterwards we'd know as northern soul, or reggae music, which I loved then and still do now. But back then in 1969 (or 1970 or 1971 or so) in some sweaty club… they'd play all the sounds of the day: 'Skinhead Moonstomp', 'Long Shot Kick The Bucket', 'Wet Dream', 'Double Barrel', 'Israelites' and all the rest. Fantastic! We'd stand there nestling our bottles of shandy (always shandy, Bass Shandy, always pretending it was beer) watching the older lads and girls dancing while shuffling our feet on the edge of the dance floor."

Tony Rounce (London): "Soul City was a fantastic shop. It was a bit like a boutique, in that it didn't cater for people off the street. Everybody who went there, went there because they knew what it was and what it sold. It wasn't like when I eventually started working Saturdays at Record Corner in Balham, the records we sold there were different. I mean, they sold James Brown and we sold James Brown, but we sold to local black kids and local white kids, plus Africans, Jamaicans and all sorts. Soul City was predominantly white. The only time I really remember any black people coming in was when they had the occasional signing session. Garnett Mimms did a signing there, for instance. You'd find a few older black people, who maybe danced to these records down at the Cue Club. I think that may be where the shop became unstuck, in that you didn't get the regular bread-and-butter people buying their copies of 'Mr Big Stuff' or whatever. And of course, they didn't stock any reggae so there was no incentive for black kids who bought a bit of soul and reggae. They'd rather jump on the train and go to Record Corner, or there were a couple of shops in Paddington or R&B Records in Stamford Hill, where you could buy a bit of both. Back then the soul scene was relatively small."

Norman Jay MBE (London): "With music, when the Jamaican DJ came on over rhythms and versions, I got bored of it and maybe I was trying to deny that I loved The Temptations, and that I had rediscovered Marvin Gaye, because my dad had all the original Marvin Gaye singles from the early 1960s. I had also discovered the Philly sound and all that kind of coincided with a period of my life when I was really quite happy and I'm discovering myself. I never really listened

BAF 1

"SWAN LAKE"

THE CATS

Sole Agency:

South Eastern Entertainment Agency   Tel. 690 2481

"The big song for us was 'The Return Of Django' by The Upsetters. That was the number one, the Skinhead stomp record."

BARRY CAIN

to songs that intently, I just liked the rhythm and the choruses, but then I remember discovering the Detroit Spinners' 'Ghetto Child' in 1973 and that was me! Fucking hell... I identified with that. 'Smile in your face, but all the time they want to take your place, backstabbers...'I know that...

"I was into that early seventies stuff, and I'm still into my sixties. I was a soul boy. I'm a dancer. I could do all the moves. Because I never drank or did drugs, my recall is excellent and total. It was a happy time. I had tons of records. I did my first gigs around then. People would say, 'Get Norman, he's got the records.' I was a total music geek. I played at my cousin Anne's birthday. She was 11 and I was 9. I played two dozen records, A-side, then B-side."

Bonny Staplehurst (London): "I remember buying the record 'The Liquidator' at a shop in Brixton, under the arches, and me and my mate Angela would be the only two white girls in there, and they would play the music and I thought, 'Ooh I like that,' and I remember buying it and every time I'd go into places, I would ask for it and I did that at Chelsea. They used to have a DJ there, a fella called Dave something, can't remember, and you could request a record at the ground, and I asked for 'Liquidator' and it went down well. Still played down there to this day. I bought loads of records, loved my music. I've still got most of them. The funny thing was I didn't know what half the things they were singing about meant. Like 'Wet Dream'. I was playing it indoors and no one mentioned it. I played it on a school journey and the teachers didn't twig. If I had to pick out one tune, I'd go with 'Swan Lake' by The Cats, which is one of those tracks that whenever you hear it, you go, 'Aahhhhhh' – great record.'"

Clive Banks (London): "Songs like 'The Liquidator' were popular around the pubs, Prince Buster and, if I'm honest, loads of songs by people I didn't know – really it was a mixture. Not really specific genres. You'd hear a bad northern tune you'd never heard of, bad British versions of American records, but also a lot of Four Tops and Temptations. Even if they had come out in '65/'66 you would still hear them then, along with Psychedelic Shack later. For a three-year window, there was a real melting pot. All sorts going on."

Norman Jay MBE (London): "The big records that always remind me of that Suede, late Skinhead period are 'Tears Of A Clown' by Smokey Robinson, 'Hey Girl Don't Bother Me' by The Tams, 'Band Of Gold' by Freda Payne, always loved that, 'Give Me Just A Little More Time' by Chairmen Of The Board, 'Na Na Na Hey Hey' by Steam, which the terraces then appropriated, and 'The Liquidator' by Harry J. & The All Stars. I remember going over Chelsea and hearing that and I was shocked!"

Maggie Brown (Winchester): "The first reggae single I ever bought was 'Israelites' by Desmond Dekker. A lot of Trojan, Pama and other LPs and singles followed later. The first Motown single I bought was 'I Heard It Through The Grapevine' by Marvin Gaye; again, a lot of Motown records followed which I still have in my collection today.

"When I was a teenager my love was only for Tamla Motown, soul, northern soul and ska and reggae... you know, the general stuff you would hear at clubs at that time. When it comes to Motown, I am not generally a great lover of the more known tunes, for example 'Baby Love', 'Jimmy Mack' and the stuff everybody knows – can't stand them if I am perfectly honest. I prefer the Motown records that didn't get so much airplay in the UK. The likes of Marv Johnson, 'Baby I Miss You', 'Come On And Stop' and 'So Glad You Chose Me'. Artists like Earl Van Dyke's 'Soul Stomp', Junior Walker's 'Cleo's Mood', 'Shotgun'... it really would take me too long to tell you all the tracks that I love but I think you get the picture.

"Reggae and ska... well I still absolutely love this music today. I think it lifts the mood and makes you happy. There are many tracks that I love and again, it would take so long to list them all. Some of my favourites were 'Dry Acid' by The Upsetters, 'History Of Africa' by The Classics, 'Everything Crash' by The Ethiopians, 'Pharaoh House Crash' by Prince Buster, 'Landlords & Tenants' by Laurel Aitken, 'Without You' by Donnie Elbert, 'Dollar In The Teeth' by The Upsetters, 'Woman Capture Man' by The Ethiopians, 'Poor Rameses' by The Pioneers, 'Moon Hop' by Derrick Morgan, 'Hong Kong Flu' by The Ethiopians, 'How Long Will It Take' by Pat Kelly... well, anything by the wonderful Mr Pat Kelly. Early bluebeat, rocksteady, I love it all! I would have to say ska, reggae, bluebeat and rocksteady are probably my favourite musical genres.

"So many northern soul and soul tracks, Billy Butler 'The Right Track', 'Mockingbird' by Charlie & Inez Foxx, 'Compared To What' by Mr Flood's Party, 'Keep On Keeping On' by N. F. Porter, 'Baby' by Carla Thomas, 'Little Queenie' by Bill Black's Combo, 'Sliced Tomatoes' by The Just Brothers, 'The Champion' by Willie Mitchell, 'Everybody's Going To A Love-In' by Bob Brady & The Con Chords, anything by Otis Redding and Aretha Franklin and ultimately Etta James. Oh my goodness, the list is endless!"

Bernard Jennings (Ruislip): "Geno Washington & The Ram Jam Band was my very first big night out. He was good, very shouty, but the one we liked most was Jimmy James & The Vagabonds. We'd go and see The Coloured Raisins and they were very good. Herbie Goins & The Night-Timers was a bit

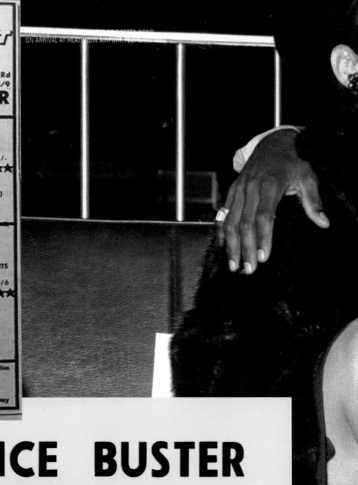

PRINCE   BUSTER

FABulous

GREATEST HITS

MSI

UPSETTER

THE UPSETTERS

RETURN OF DJANGO

146

MIKE RAVEN WITH WIFE MANDY, JUNE 1969

twice
voted top
"pirate"
radio
show

THE MIKE RAVEN BLUES SHOW

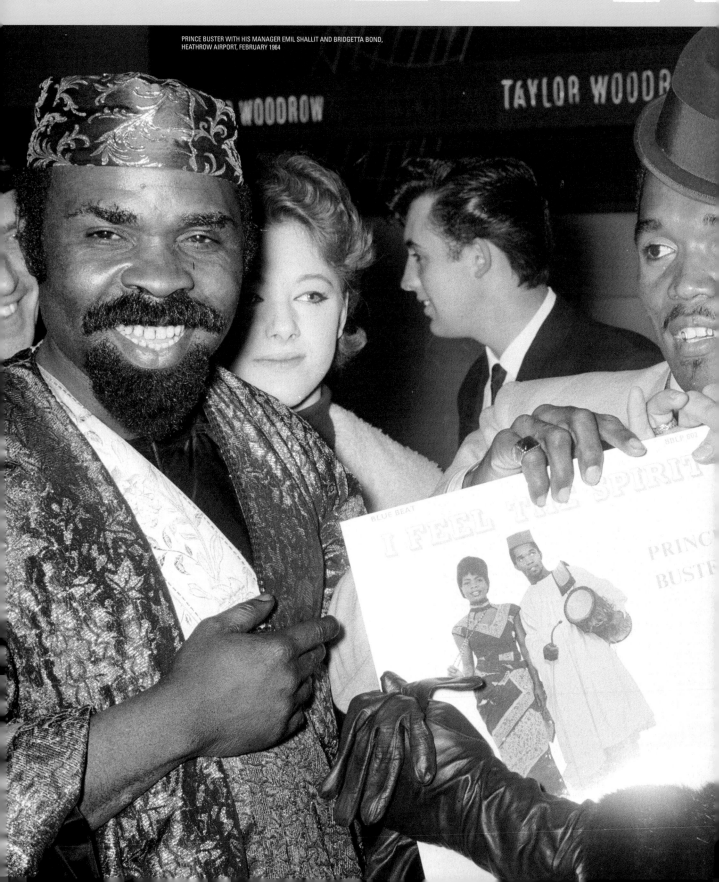

PRINCE BUSTER WITH HIS MANAGER EMIL SHALLIT AND BRIDGETTA BOND,
HEATHROW AIRPORT, FEBRUARY 1964

of a throwback to the R&B days for us. Then of course there were the purely reggae groups such as The Pyramids, and The Cats, who recorded 'Swan Lake'."

In the readers' letters section of *Record Mirror*, dated October 25th, 1969, one contribution headlined 'BBC & REGGAE (are they trying to hush the music?)' stated:

So far this year, eight reggae records have made the Top Fifty. This proves that the public have caught up with the music despite Radio One trying to hush it up.

Once the deejays realise that reggae is a valid musical form, and they stop pretending that it does not exist, then we will get records by people such as Prince Buster, Dandy, and Derrick Morgan into the charts.

Mark White, chief assistant of Radio 1 at the time, seemed a bit miffed and replied:

The BBC does not have anything against reggae/bluebeat music at all. This is rubbish. Earlier this year, Mike Raven was devoting a segment of his show to this type of music, and reggae discs are still being featured in our programmes.

The BBC would use many arguments to justify the lack of reggae on their playlists, including that the production level on the records wasn't up to their standard, and that the genre didn't really fit in with their usual playlists. In 1971, Nicky Thomas wrote a tune called 'B.B.C.' in which the lyrics address the lack of reggae airplay on the radio.

Black music generally was pretty much in the minority on BBC playlists, but in the end they had to recognise its popularity and they secured the services of two ex-pirate DJs. The first was the golden-voiced Mike Raven, who had begun his career on Radio Atlanta, Radio King and Radio Luxembourg presenting shows based around American rhythm & blues and soul. BBC Radio 1 snapped him up in their first year, 1967. He would present his *Mike Raven Blues Show*, starting with the opening tune of 'Soul Serenade' by The Mike Cotton Sound, and play the best new American releases, as well as a handful of ska tunes.

Bernard Jennings (Ruislip): "We didn't really mind stuff like 'Skinhead Moonstomp' because even though it was at the commercial end of things, you didn't really hear any of this on the radio. The only music we heard on the radio that we liked was seven o'clock on a Sunday, the Mike Raven show. He played soul up to about half seven, one or two R&B things after that, and then it was blues. Blues wasn't of much interest to us. So, we'd listen until 7.30 and then leave home to go to the youth club. But later he started to add a bit of ska and reggae to his playlist. Even though it was at the commercial end, we thought it was great. You couldn't wait to see which ones he was going to play. A lot of radio though was hairy white music, which we avoided of course. Interestingly though, when I was at school, we had a few outings with the lads in the sixth form. There was a huge range of styles and I was probably the only one who dressed as I did. But we used to compromise so we might end up at places like the Regent Street Poly, always rammed there. I remember seeing Cream there. I also went to Klooks Kleek in West Hampstead and saw Julie Driscoll and Brian Auger. Just like

everyone else who's ever seen Julie Driscoll, I fell in love with her immediately. We went to see The Crazy World Of Arthur Brown at the Clay Pigeon pub. He had something but he was a bit hairy for me. At school most of the other sixth formers I was with were more in that direction. The big album doing the rounds at school was *Electric Ladyland* by Hendrix, and that was getting played in our common room, so me with my Four Tops and my James Brown LPs just didn't get a look-in. We called white boys with guitars 'twang music'. I remember years later ruminating whether or not to buy The Average White Band because we realised they were white, and we'd never bought any white music up to that point, but we eventually did."

Mauro Antoniazzi (Birmingham): "Most of my friends were Jamaican. I grew up with them and used to go to parties they had, you know, blues parties everywhere. I loved the music, we were all into reggae. We used to go down the road to a shop that bought them in from Jamaica before they were released. So, we could listen to them there and buy them. They were incredible. Magical times really."

The boss at the time in reggae circles, though, was Emperor Rosko. Rosko (real name Michael Pasternak) was born in California. He came to Britain in 1965, having also lived in France. He worked for Radio Caroline, and then Radio Luxembourg, where he was known as Le Président Rosko. In 1967 he joined Radio 1. Because he produced his own shows, Rosko wasn't bound by draconian playlists, and he would play the latest soul and reggae releases in his show. The Skinheads loved him. Apart from his DJ-ing he even got to record a version of Prince Buster's 'Al Capone' on Trojan Records.

Interview with Emperor Rosko

"My greatest memories were showing up in clubs where they didn't know what I looked like, and the Rosko Roadshow would be booked to play at an all-black reggae club in Birmingham or Manchester or somewhere. We'd roll up at about three in the afternoon, and they wouldn't let us in. They'd be saying, 'But you not him, man!' I'd have to start doing my shtick in order to convince them that I really was The Emperor. Those were the things that really made me laugh.

"The Apollo Club in London was another one that was absolutely hysterical, because they would book me for ten o'clock even though I wouldn't go on until two, so what are you going to do? That's when the crowd would start to wake up at that club. Luckily, in my youth, I could stand it but if they did that to me now, I'd be sound asleep. The first time I went to the Apollo, the guy said to me, 'Here's your bottle of Bacardi, we'll let you know when to come on.' I said, well, when are you going to start? And he said, 'Well, we've got to get everybody in.' I'm looking outside and the queue is out of sight, two or three blocks down the line. So I'm saying, well, it's already full, and he says, 'We're gonna get 'em all in. Don't worry.' Little by little, they got them all in. No doubt the fire department would have had a shit fit if they'd seen how the place was overloaded. I went on at two, half smashed out of my brain, and everybody loved it.

"When Otis came over, the record company asked me to do the tour. Back in those days, I was a little more famous than

I am today, and they would go to my agent and asked how much to get Emperor Rosko on board because they knew they'd get a lot of plugs on the radio, I guess. I actually went on the bus with them, which was most unusual. Sometimes I followed the bus in my car, so sometimes I'd be in the car, other times in the bus. All over the country, every night, two or three thousand people at a theatre somewhere. The Stax tour was probably one of the most exciting soul tours, mainly because of Sam & Dave and Otis Redding. The rest on their own would have been great, but they took it to new heights and blew everybody away. It was unbelievable. Of course, starting in the second half of the show would be Sam & Dave, and they'd be so good that Otis had to be better than good to follow them. He was the star. We used to laugh together, what a great time we had. I was back on the air in French Radio Luxembourg a couple of weeks later, that was my main gig, and somebody came in and told me Otis Redding had just died in a plane crash. I was speechless and I couldn't do the show. I was emotional to say the least. I only have to think about it now and I get teary-eyed. I got his albums and just said, 'Ladies and gentlemen, I can't talk, let him sing.' I played two Otis albums non-stop, and that's how I dealt with it.

"Radio Caroline changed the whole horizon of music in the UK, because back in the day, the BBC played an hour a day of pop music and that was it. Obviously, they had their favourites, so when it came down to reggae and soul and stuff, very little got played. So suddenly here comes Radio Caroline, and Luxembourg to an extent, but that was in France. Caroline started playing all kinds of music twenty-four seven, and that woke up the country big time. I mean, it was colossal. The French Radio show *Minimax* did for the French what Radio Caroline did for the British, because they were stodgy, so they called up Ronan O'Rahilly at Caroline, and the new major stockholder in French Radio Luxembourg was Jean Pruvost. He... wanted to change the old stodgy station and make it sound like Radio Caroline. Of course, it's impossible to do. It's like changing government. So, we said we'll give you a show in the afternoon like Radio Caroline. They sent me over because I could speak a semblance of French. It was amazing because I met John Pruvost and he told me, 'Anything you need. The budget is wide open.' I thought I would test him here because I was going from £75 a week to suddenly about £500 a week plus expenses, just to get me back to France because I really didn't want to do it. I was really young back then and I didn't see the opportunities, but they were there. The man said to me it was an open budget, so to test the old geezer, I said first of all they'd have to build a new studio, self-operating, because in those days the union played the music and the DJ did the talking. There was no disputing on this so they would not give in to that. When they found out I was building a studio self-op for a DJ, they went berserk and threatened to call a national strike of all four radio stations at the time. So we said, you can have an engineer in the studio, but Rosko's gonna play the records and your engineer can be his assistant. You're still hiring somebody, it's just a different technique. So that's how we got by that. Then they spent a couple of hundred thousand pounds building this fantasy studio that I kind of semi-designed, right with a first-floor balcony overlooking the street. That was where thousands of kids later would come to cheer at the window. We put in cart machines, which were the new thing back then. We had a

battery of six or four across the front. It was a super studio. I was taking ten people a night out for dinner on their bill because they'd said anything you want, it's all yours, just make it happen. They had a timeline, I think they had ninety days to do all this. At the time slot I was going to start back then, we were up against a show on the radio station France Numéro 1, which had been number one since time immemorial. They played two or three hours of French pop music but not like The Emperor. So that was the target to beat.

"So, then I said we need jingles, and the old man, Jean Pruvost, didn't know what a jingle was. So, I played him some PAM stuff in English but I said we need this in French, which means I need to take a load of French singers to Dallas, Texas, then you need to buy all the jingles, and they have to agree to let us sing the English jingles in French. Me and my buddy translated 90 per cent of them into French. Once again, unbeknown to me, had I taken the time to tell the French people at the publishing company that I was the writer and producer of all this stuff, I would be a very wealthy man now because they pay into your pension for that, and I would have five times the pension I have now. Once again that's hindsight. I was young and had money in my pocket.

"We had two French singing groups, The Gams were one and I can't remember who the guys were. We flew them over, and got them into the studio, where we had a whole week. We did a hundred jingles in French, and everybody lost their voice. It was just insanity, but we had a great time. We came back with these jingles, and all the French were standing around going, 'My God! What is this?' So, then the studio got finished, the press got going with 'The new revolution is here!' because the old man owned the papers. We kicked off and I was playing one French record and one American or English record to keep it fifty/fifty. It took off and everybody went crazy. The music was fresh because I didn't allow too much slow stuff, and we took over the number one spot within about two months. All went well until the French Revolution because I refused to slow down for that. They said, 'Fine, you're fired.' So, I left and went to England. Radio 1 became my home from '67 when they started to '76 when I went back to the US. I was on Caroline at the same time and they were just sorting out what pirate DJs they wanted for the launch of Radio 1. Everybody said, you must use The Emperor. Derek Chinnery, who became the boss of the station but at the time was just a producer, flew over to see me operating in Paris. He was watching me in the studio, which was as good, if not better, than what the BBC had at the time. He said to me, 'Obviously, you don't want to leave here.'

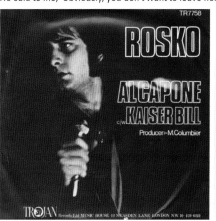

"I remember the press saying, 'Great show! The Emperor's fantastic... but what's he talking about?' The news guy came on after my show, and in a posh voice said, 'And now the news in English.' EMPEROR ROSKO

EMPEROR ROSKO, RADIO 1, PARIS, 1967

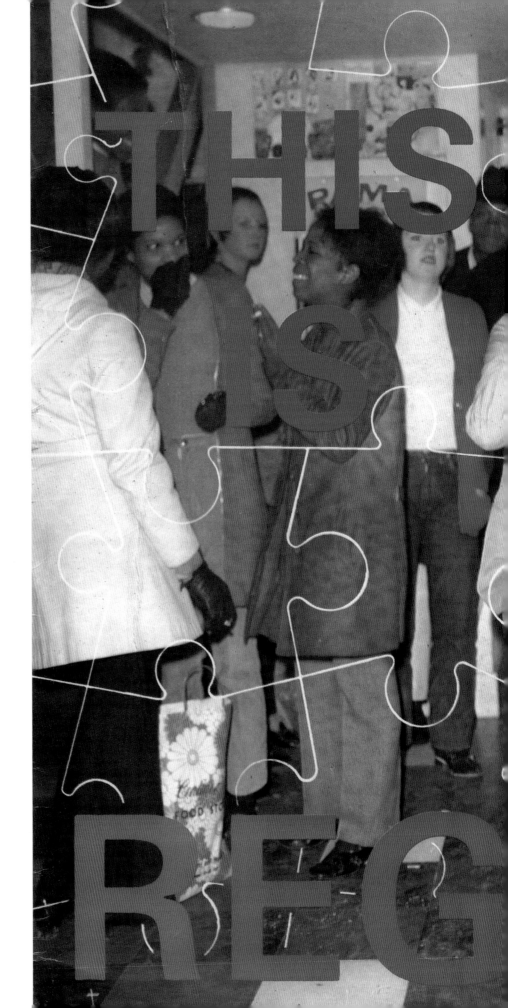

I said not for what you're going to pay… I said what I will do is send them a tape every week, so he agreed to that. Radio 1 launched, and I was there on the day they launched. I was midday spin, and I remember the press saying, 'Great show! The Emperor's fantastic… but what's he talking about?' The news guy came on after my show, and in a posh voice said, 'And now the news in English.' That made all the press. As I said, I was there until '76, during which I wrote a show called *Rosko's Round Table*. They based the Radio 1 Club on my roadshow which was running around the country. It was the time of my life.

"Johnnie Walker liked his soul music, but I never noticed anyone championing it to be quite honest because I was too damn busy, but I certainly did. I did more reggae than anybody back in the day. The BBC, of course, didn't understand at all. They were just not into that. Stand-out records for me were anything by Otis, and everything on Trojan. I liked ska, a lot of it from the fifties and the sixties. I liked the sound of that era. Reggae, when it changed and they wanted to make it their own, they kinda lost me on that. I remember when 'Wet Dream' by Max Romeo came out, I played that for weeks on the BBC before they discovered what it was about, and then they had a shit fit!

"Mods and Skinheads was something I never paid a lot of attention to, except to admire from a distance. If it was a good song, that's what I played. If it appealed more to Mods or Skinheads, then it did.

"I never met Prince Buster, but I did admire him. The first version of 'Al Capone' was recorded for AZ Records in France, and was a big hit. I don't remember recording another at Chalk Farm but it's too far back. I remember I got a couple of grand advance from the record company [for the 'Al Capone' single] and I haven't to this day seen a royalty sheet, and I know that they probably sold about a hundred thousand copies."

One thing that could always be found at parties during this period was the budget-priced reggae compilations. There were various ones, including *Club Reggae* (Trojan), *Reggae Special* (Coxsone) and *This Is Reggae* (Pama). Probably the best known were the *Tighten Up* series on the Trojan label, which showcased previously released singles – 14s 6d was the asking price, so therefore affordable. The other attraction of the albums were the covers, which usually involved an attractive West Indian girl in some form of undress. Volume 3, released in 1970, came complete with a poster of a naked girl, carefully posed so as not to reveal too much.

Paul Weller (Woking): "My favourite records of that time are 'Band Of Gold' by Freda Payne and all on the Invictus label, Chairmen Of The Board, who had an amazing run of great singles, 'Sex Machine' by James Brown, a lot of early reggae, 'Liquidator', 'Return Of Django', '54-46 Was My Number', 'Bang Bang Lulu', 'Swan Lake', 'Double Barrel', all big tunes. The *Reggae Chartbusters* were the albums I had because they were less than a quid and with 'all the hits'. Same with *Motown Chartbusters;* it was an economic thing. Every fucker had those albums and every party you went to they were playing them."

Pete Schaffert (Kent): "I played some records at a few school discos and took great delight in dropping Max Romeo's

'Wet Dream' on the turntable, much to everyone's delight, except the teachers. And I also blew a school speaker at a Christmas disco when I played The Cimarons' version of 'Silent Night'. When the bass kicks in at the start, it's a real boom. I guess that was the limit of our rebelliousness.

"Being still at school at the time, money was tight with only a paper round or two to fund record buying. Consequently, the Trojan various artists LPs were essential buying. The *Club Reggae* and *Tighten Up* series were bought as soon as they hit the shops and they never failed to hit the spot – a good cross-section of hits and club favourites for a budget price. There were no books about the music back then, so any sleeve notes were invaluable.

"At school, and in society in general, we were seen as very strange to be fans of this music. Lots of people wore the clothing, but very few were into the music as deeply as myself and a few mates. I had decades of 'It all sounds the same' comments thrown at me as I strolled around the playground with my cassette recorder blasting out tunes I'd recorded."

Andrew Vaughan (Orrell): "Do you remember the first time? Too fucking right! Because you just do. You just remember such moments. Back then Slater's was my shop. Was 'our shop'. A town-centre shop like many other shops in many other towns but this had the gear we wanted. The gear the big boys wore. The gear we talked about in the playground and our den in the woods, us sharp-looking pre-teens. The clothes that came into our lives around the same time the music did. Oh, and the music. The bloody music and in our dens and hideaways, our front rooms and youth clubs we listened, we looked and we loved. In our little town and throughout the country we all had the same thoughts, the same clothes, the same music and the same loves. It all goes together. Girls, clothes, music, football. I'd buy all the *Reggae Chartbusters* LPs that were released and the *Tighten Up* volumes that had the best sleeves known to man!

"My Dad said, 'What is this? You better not let your mum see it.' That was ten minutes after he'd 'studied the tracks' and glanced at the cover of a beautiful naked black girl. You didn't find many of those in Wigan.

"I was enthralled. It helped that I'm a cricket man and the West Indies team and Clive Lloyd at Lancashire was one of my heroes. I embraced everything that was Jamaican (or Guyanese in Clive's case). Many around were looking to Detroit for their black music of choice but for me there could only be Kingston, Jamaica."

Just as the early ska songs had delved into the rich vein of rhythm & blues coming out of America, reggae music often covered versions of the latest soul offerings such as 'Rescue Me' by The Ebony Sisters or 'Walking Up A One-Way Street' by The Clarendonians.

Favourite topics that reggae songs would cover would include anything to do with space, because of the moon landing by Neil Armstrong on July 20th, 1969. These would include songs like 'Moon Hop' by Derrick Morgan, 'Splash Down' by The Crystalites and 'Apollo 12' by Sir Washington.

tighten up

with all
the best sounds
from the
West Indies

> "It was supposed to be a six-week tour, but it ended up being for three months. Buster was the star, and we were nobodies. We had half an hour to do our own thing on stage, before he joined us and then we'd back him. When we did our bit, we ripped the place apart. When he came on, even though he was the star, he couldn't match us. After the gig, he told us, 'When you go on stage, don't get the crowd involved. Play your little t'ing and come off.'"
> FRANK PITTER

After all the Rude Boy fascination with guns, James Bond films and Westerns would feature heavily, giving rise to songs such as '007' by Desmond Dekker, 'El Casino Royale' by Lynn Taitt & The Jets, 'For A Few Dollars More' by The Upsetters and 'Death Rides A Horse' by Roy Richards.

The subject of sex remained ever popular: 'Play With Your Pussy' by Max Romeo, 'Don't Touch Me Tomato' by Phyllis Dillon and 'Sex Grand National' by Fay, for instance.

One person who would forever be associated with the more risqué side of the music would be Judge Dread. Born Alex Hughes, English and white, he was hardly your expected reggae star, but he went on to be one of the most commercially successful artists in Britain with his sexual innuendo and double entendre-laden songs such as 'Big Six' and 'Big Seven', notching up eleven national chart hits. The BBC banned more of his songs than those of any other recording artist.

He'd first heard Jamaican music when he lodged as a teenager in a West Indian household in Brixton. Hughes was heavily built, and got to meet Jamaican artists Derrick Morgan and Prince Buster through his job as a bouncer at London nightclubs such as the Ram Jam in Brixton. Among other jobs, he was even a debt collector for Trojan Records.

With an emerging new market coming from the Skinheads themselves, obviously they were catered for as well. Trinidad-born Joe Mansano would use The Rudies, and occasionally The Cimarons, as a backing band and record tunes such as 'Skinhead Revolt', while Lambert Briscoe, a Brixton-based sound-system operator, joined forces with The Cimarons and Eddie Grant to create the band The Hot Rod All Stars on the Torpedo label to record heavy Hammond organ-based tunes such as 'Skinhead Moonstomp' and 'Skinheads Don't Fear'.

To find these kind of records you had to seek out specialist music shops such as Derek's Records in Wood Green, Hip City in Brixton and Joe's Shack (belonging to Joe Mansano). Musik City had a chain of shops including in the Portobello Road, the high street in Deptford and Ridley Road in Dalston.

David Rosen (London): "I also picked up straight away on the music and that had just gone beyond ska into first-generation reggae, which we bought from Musik City – with a K – in Kensal Rise, and this wasn't even Trojan, this was Pama. 'Red Red Wine', Tony Tribe, early Ethiopians, really lovely stuff."

The story of 'Skinhead Moonstomp'

In 1965, Frank Pitter was studying to be an engineer. He dreamed of following what his father had done, making parts for aircraft. He knew it was a good profession, but there were distractions. Every so often, a music programme would fill the TV screen at home, and Frank found himself mesmerised. *Top Of The Pops* every Thursday and *Ready Steady Go!* every Friday. Frank had always loved music; when he'd been a young boy, his father had played the guitar, and Frank would jump and dance around to it. But now in later life, he could see his destiny on the small screen.

"I started to watch these pop groups on TV, and my interests shifted a bit," remembers Frank. "I'd see these pop stars, not

'THE PYRAMIDS'

so much the Jamaican artists but bands like The Who, The Beatles, The Troggs and The Dave Clark Five. I'd watch *Ready Steady Go!*, and see all the American artists coming over, but what led me to playing the drums was Keith Moon. He was so exciting to watch. Then there was The Beatles, with Ringo. It was all the fame and the glory that attracted me. I wanted a part of that, so I decided to start a band."

Frank found himself peering into the window of a music shop in Tooting, his eyes drawn to a Pearl drum kit. He pleaded with his father to let him buy the kit; at first, he was reluctant, but somehow, he was persuaded, and soon Frank could be found learning his craft… until one day the living-room ceiling came down.

This didn't put him off, however. He hooked up with an old school friend, Neville, and they were soon joined by Michael 'Mik' Thomas on bass. They didn't have a vocalist but rehearsed as an instrumental band playing current pop music.

"I had a vision," says Frank. "I thought reggae and ska music was nice to listen to but I didn't think it would last. I wanted to be like the pop boys, making money and being famous. I wanted a mixed-race group, black and white together. I thought, with this as a base, we could go somewhere. We had a white guy called Les, a guitar player who was great at lead and could do good Chuck Berry covers. When it came to practice, he couldn't turn up, so we decided to stay as a trio but we realised we needed a singer. We got a guy called Johnny Orlando, but he was a bit big-headed, you know. We were doing Rolling Stones stuff as well as R&B covers by John Lee Hooker and mixed it with pop. The band needed a name, so I'd called them The Bees. I loved The Beatles, so just shortened it to the Bees."

The band rented a community hall in Balham. They would practise there twice a week, and were charged a pound – it seemed Frank was always paying for it. One evening, a guy called Roy Ellis wandered in with a trombone, and asked to join in. The band declined. He came back for a second visit, and introduced the band to Monty Neysmith, a keyboard player. They offered him a place in the band, but at first he declined as he had come over from Jamaica to study law. Finally, Monty agreed, and after several attempts to join the band as a trombone player, Roy Ellis was taken on too, singing vocals.

Both Roy and Monty were heavily into ska and reggae, and this had an immediate effect on the band, whose repertoire

TL 1021) ON RELEASE

now included these alongside some pop and American soul numbers. They soon realised that by playing ska music they were getting more of a connection with the owners of black clubs. At the time Geno Washington & The Ram Jam Band were doing straight soul sets, while Jimmy James & The Vagabonds would mix soul and ska, and The Bees were now more akin to them.

"We had a good residency in Dalston at the Four Aces, playing twice a week. Other clubs that we played a lot were the Cue Club in Paddington, with Count Suckle, the Roaring Twenties, the El Partido in Lewisham, the Pama Club in Harlesden, the Ram Jam Club in Brixton and a club we called the Billy Club in Cricklewood. The Bees were very active. It was while playing at the Four Aces that we met up with Laurel Aitken. He was impressed with us, and booked a studio for us in the Old Kent Road. It was there that we recorded Junior Walker's 'Shotgun' and another song called 'Every Day You Gotta Cry Girl' with Laurel Aitken. We also did 'Jesse James Rides Again'. That and 'Shotgun' were both minor hits.

"I think at the time, Siggy Jackson, head of Blue Beat records, was kind of Laurel Aitken's management in the UK. So, coming up to the end of 1966, we were in with Siggy and Emil Shallit, the owner of Melodisc, of which Blue Beat was a subsidiary. Siggy told us that there was a UK tour coming up with Prince Buster. He'd been over many times before. He'd been on TV doing 'Wash Wash' and 'Al Capone'. He had decided to do his first UK tour, but he needed a band. So that's where we came in, and the whole connection was now there. We added two brass players to the band to do that tour.

"The tour was such a success. Everywhere we played it was a packed house. It was supposed to be a six-week tour, but it ended up being for three months. He was the star, and we were nobodies. We had half an hour to do our own thing on stage, before he joined us and then we'd back him. When we did our bit, we ripped the place apart. When he came on, even though he was the star, he couldn't match us. After the gig, he told us, 'When you go on stage, don't get the crowd involved. Play your little t'ing and come off.' We only had that little half hour to show the world what we could do, and try to make a name for ourselves. It wasn't just playing. You could be raving and doing these physical things. Buster, from Jamaica, he don't do these things, he don't know about it. Jimmy Cliff could do it, but Buster only had one little move so we were showing him up everywhere. Roy Ellis and Monty would dance, and it would be electric.

"Buster had a minder who protected him. He was so big that he looked like a bloody rhino! He told us, 'Buster said you don't rave the people up!' The next place we play, the people are there to be raved, so we done it again. His minder warned us and told us that if we did it again, he would beat us up. We were thinking, him alone? There were seven of us in the band including the new brass section, plus our road manager, making eight of us.

"The next time we play, I think it was Coventry, and we did it again. Buster's bodyguard came in the dressing room and beat up all eight of us. I was knocked out. I didn't even know what happened. After that we had to carry on the tour, but we had to hold back a little bit."

After the Prince Buster tour, President Records approached The Bees to record them, and this is where Eddie Grant came into view. Eddie was on the President label with his band The Equals. He'd written a few songs, and used The Bees as a backing band to record them. He also supplied them with a new name: The Pyramids. 'Train Tour To Rainbow City' was one of the tracks recorded and chosen to be released as a single. Eddie Grant just talked over the song, he didn't sing, but it still meant Roy Ellis was sidelined. The band didn't tell anybody, and Roy had to learn the song for their live appearances.

Frank Pitter: "We were playing in France, and we got told to come back to England because the single had got into the British charts. We had our own identity now, and were a chart band as The Pyramids so we dropped the name The Bees altogether.

"We made other singles, such as 'Bakerloo Line,' under the name The Pyramids. We became popular for doing sessions with other artists such as Toots Hibbert, Millie Small, The Pioneers, Jimmy Cliff, Desmond Dekker, Jackie Edwards and others. We were working around the clock, touring all over the country, then coming back to the studio to back sessions with these people. There were no motorways, apart from the M1, so it was up and down the country in a Transit. We were in demand and a lot of other labels contacted us, but we were locked into a contract with President so we couldn't move.

"The next time we play, I think it was Coventry, and we did it again. Buster's bodyguard came in the dressing room and beat up all eight of us. I was knocked out. I didn't even know what happened. After that we had to carry on the tour, but we had to hold back a little bit."
FRANK PITTER

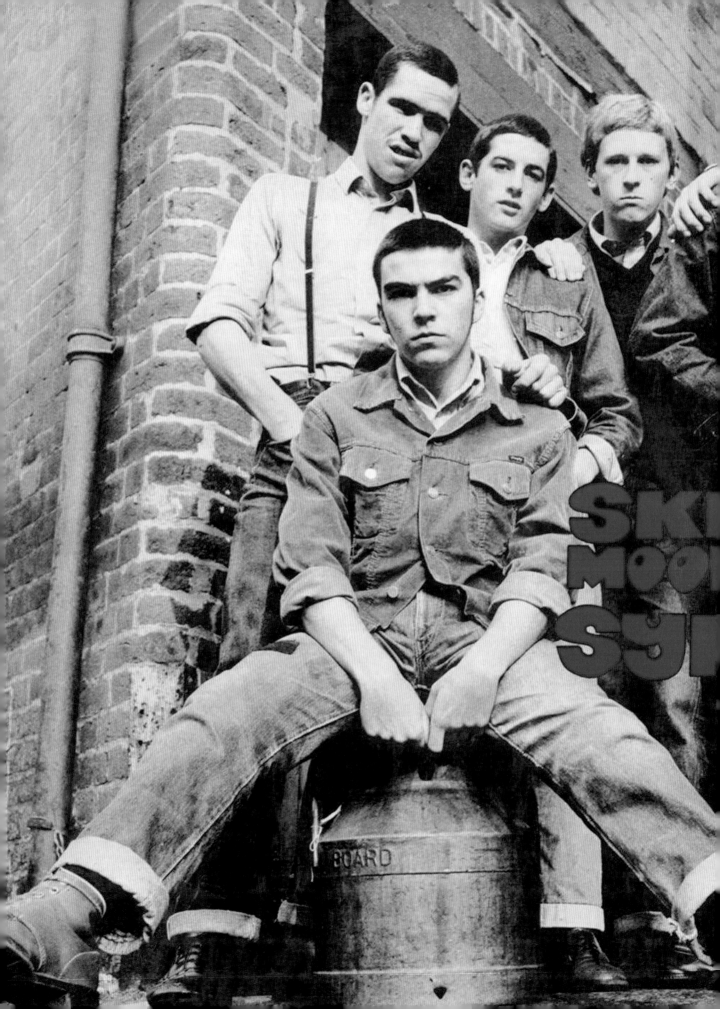

REGGAE by Roger St. Pierre

Stamp Skinheads, Stomp!

THERE'S nothing new in a ska record being banned but there is a novel reason behind the refusal of Britain's ballrooms to play Symarip's "Skinhead Moon Stomp."

Said the record's much-perplexed producer Graeme Goodall: "The ballroom proprietors have put a ban on the record because it is too popular. All the kids stomp their feet to it and the ballroom people are worried this might damage their dance floors!"

"We have been pleading with them to help us promote th record because it is still virtually impossible to break a reggae record on Radio One play alone."

Despite the ban, "Skinhead Moon Stomp" which leads off with the inspired introduction "I want all you skinheads to get on your feet, untangle your braces and put your boots on your feet" – has already sold more than 20,000 copies which isn't bad going at all.

"It's the first record on B & C's new Treasure Island label and was produced by my new Philligree Productions company," said Graeme.

Just exactly who, or what, is or are Symarip?: "Spell it backwards and you might get a clue," said Graeme, "actually, it's the Pyramids who have had more than a few ska hits under their own name of course, The are in process of changing their name completely so we coined the Symarip tag just for this one disc."

Just to make sure that the ban wasn't simply a manufactured publicity stunt I checked it out with the manager of one of London's leading ballrooms: "Yes, I have banned the record. I had to, the kids were stomping with the beat and all my decorations were falling down!"

One ska man who has never had trouble with being banned is Owen Gray who, along with Jackie Edwards, was an original pioneer of the scene over here.

"It's fantastic to see the way things are mushrooming now after all those years of struggle. I had to put out a lot of soul material both on record and on stage in order to survive but ska is really my scene and now I can devote myself to it," the lean, soft-spoken 26-year-old told me.

Owen's career could hardly have started in more glamorous fashion. It was a work-mate who persuaded him to enter Vare John's Talent Show which was a big attraction in Jamaica, both with live audiences and on TV.

The newcomer won at his first bid and went on to win three more times.

"But everything over there was so small-scale and restricted. When Jackie left for Britain in the spring of 1962 I could have stayed at home and taken over his crown but I decided to follow his lead instead and I arrived in London a few weeks after him.

Owen soon became a major attraction on the club scene and his records sold in large numbers but only to the immigrant population.

But the built-in resistance among soul fans for material of non-American origins kept him out of the charts despite some fine recordings.

Now Owen has been teamed with another singer in exactly the same boat, Britain's ultra-talented Elkie Brooks.

Together they have recorded the old pop hit 'Groovy Kind of Love" reggae style and it is already picking up a lot of club plays.

"Then we met Graeme Goodall, who had been doing his own little thing with Chris Blackwell at Island Records. They had a little two-track studio in the Fulham Road. Goodall had the Doctor Bird label, so we thought we could work with him. We did some session work there, but I think President Records heard about the connection.

"We used to get a statement from President every three months of our record sales. At the time we all thought we were millionaires. We'd had a number two in Germany with 'Mexico Moonlight', a slow ballad. We were called to the offices in Denmark Street. They had an accountant called Dane, and he gave us this long statement. There were more expenses on it than the amount we'd earned. That was when it went downhill with President. We were unhappy and wanted to leave but we were still under contract. We approached Ed Kassner, he was the owner, and asked to leave but he said no.

"Graeme Goodall played us 'Moon Hop' by Derrick Morgan, and we loved it. We went in the studio, and we recorded our version within half an hour. It was like a Sam & Dave riff which Roy used at the start. We'd seen the build-up of the Skinhead crowd as far back as the Prince Buster tour in '67. We saw it getting stronger, because they were claiming ska music as their own. The Skinheads were basically a turnaround from the Mods. They were the same people, but just dressing different. Roy changed the lyrics to be about them and just captured the phrasing based on Sam & Dave. 'Skinhead Moonstomp' was born.

"President Records heard about the song, and started threatening us. Of course, we denied it, but they said if we wanted to leave them, we'd have to make an album for them for nothing. So, for their subsidiary label, Jay Boy, we went under the name E. K. Bunch and recorded 'Banana' and others. We recorded it with no real great care, and eventually they released us.

"Monty, the keyboard player, came up with spelling The Pyramids backwards, and after jumbling it up we got the name Symarip, and that went onto the 'Skinhead Moonstomp' single. Boom, it was in the charts within weeks. Then we made the LP. Graeme Goodall had a guitar player called Phil Chen, from Jimmy James & The Vagabonds. He played guitar on the single and most tracks on the album.

"The Skinheads had been following us, so we kind of reflected that. The whole album and the single were built up around Skinheads. So, we dressed up like them, and we weren't afraid to say it. They started worshipping us like gods. We didn't get to play many black clubs after because they'd say Skinheads were racist, but I know that was the opposite, because they embraced us. How could they say it was racist? They even called it Skinhead reggae, because it wasn't coming out of Jamaica. Laurel Aitken saw it and got involved, as did others. We were the first though; they came after us to jump on the spark.

"We never had a problem with violence at our gigs, but still we got banned from places like the Hammersmith Palais, the Locarno and other clubs. In fact, they never banned us, they banned the audience because of the part of the song about stomping, and they were following the words with the motion.

"There was a troublemaking side to it, but they weren't Skinheads. It was big gangs, and the real Skinheads were getting the blame for a handful of idiots, but the stigma made it bad for the real ones. It may have only been ten out of a hundred, but in the press, they got a bigger slice of it, you know. The only thing I could say they were racist for is claiming the music as their own! But they embraced it with love.

"When 'Moonstomp' was released the BBC didn't want to know. It was such a fast-moving song, and the stigma stuck straight awa[y] but the sound mashed up the crowd. I think Graeme Goodall put Emperor Rosko onto it. You could pay money to have your song played on the radio, but I think Rosko saw the position too, that this was something different. I think he ran it more, and he used to big up. We've got a lot to thank him for. It was also an extra boost to g[et] banned by the BBC, so in a way they did us a favour. It hit the cha[rt] so quick, it didn't linger. I bless Rosko for that."

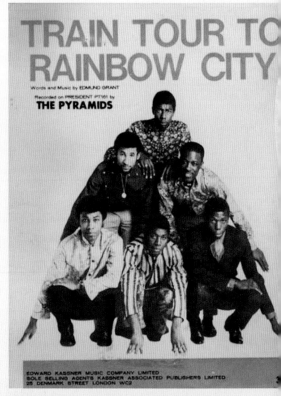

THE PYRAMIDS
ON STAGE ARE GREAT

A CHART HIT THE
PUBLIC SHO... ...RATE

SYMARIP

SKINHEAD MOONSTOMP

TROJAN RECORDS

® 1970

1. 3, 4, 5, 6. B & C Music
2. Island Music

1. Skinhead Moonstomp (Naismith/Ellis); 2. Phoenix Reggae
(Alphonso); 3. Skinhead Girl (Naismith/Ellis);
4. Try Me Best (Ellis/Roberts); 5. Skinhead
Jamboree (Naismith/Ellis/Chen);
6. Chicken Merry (Naismith)

TBL-102A

...AVOY ("FORMERLY" "WITCHDOCTOR") CATFORD
...DAY, SEPTEMBER 7th
THE PYRAMIDS
SUNDAY THE
...EVE MAXTED SHOW

treasure isle

SKINHEAD MOON STOMP
(Ellis & Naismith)
SYMARIP
Producer: Graeme Goodal
A Philligree Production

TI-7050 A
Copyright
Control
Time 2.55 sec.

...ner of the recorded work reserved · Unauthorised public performance broadcasting and copying of this re...

165

RACIST GRAFFITI FROM BACK IN 1952. KBW MEANT 'KEEP BRITAIN WHITE'

CHAPTER 9 : RACISM

Mr Jagmahan Joshi, convenor of the Black People's Alliance, which represented fifty-two immigrant associations, was quoted as saying, "If the state is not able to extend protection, we will. We will not be going out to bash Skinheads. We will take whatever measures are necessary to protect Pakistanis from violence."

The Pakistani Workers Union wrote to the Home Office requesting an emergency meeting with the Home Secretary, James Callaghan, to discuss police protection for Pakistanis in the East End of London.

Tony Haddow (London): "I don't know of anyone that I know that went out and beat up Pakistanis. Really there weren't that many Pakistanis back then, they were mostly Indians. Pakistanis came in a different wave. The Indians were new, and they were blue-collar workers and things like that. You know, I really get angry with what the press did with the whole thing, because they created the monster that it became, and they're still doing it today. They alarm everyone by sensationalising everything and presenting it out of proportion. I worked in Southall on one of the first supermarkets, and we were putting in all the wastepipes for the freezer cabinets. I remember all that stuff being in the papers, and me having to work there in the evenings, with all these Asians walking about, and I was conscious of them looking at me because of what the papers had said. I've never been racist at all. My old man was at one point, but I think most of them were. It was all 'Bleedin' immigrants coming here, nicking our jobs.' Which was all bollocks anyway because we'd asked them to come. I was totally the other way. I completely embraced that culture. My old man learnt not to be racist by meeting a lot of my mates. I never had time for all that racist bollocks."

Bob Wheeler (Slough): "The Skinheads got a bad name because of the people like the National Front, especially outside Chelsea. I remember going away, and we got to the services [on the motorway]. It was quite a handy lot, Lewisham, Streatham, Stockwell and the rest. Hickey [Steve Hickmott] and all his lot were with us too. We got off the coach and walked into the services, and there were the National Front handing out leaflets. There was a fella with us, Black Pete, good as gold. They said, 'Not you, sooty.' Everyone just stopped, turned around and beat them up. I had loads of black mates. The music was the thing that bound us together. Once you are young, and you have mates like that, it goes on for ever. The papers twisted a lot of it as well. They made out as if every Skinhead was basically a National Front supporter but it wasn't true. Fairly rapidly though you wanted to distance yourself because you didn't want to be identified as a troublemaker in the clubs or whatever."

Pete Schaffert (Kent): "I never encountered any racism among my friends. I had grown up in Willesden in the sixties and had black mates. The only violence I really saw was at football matches. When in Kent, I used to go to Gillingham's home matches, and when Southend or Millwall visited, you kept your head down. They used to wear white butchers' coats on top of their clothes and you knew to give them a wide berth."

Bernard Jennings (Middlesex): "What we felt we were doing was embracing West Indian culture. There wasn't a lot of aggro between white guys and black guys in those days. Well, not that I remember. But you were aware to never tangle with West Indians because they didn't use fists, feet or boots as they were nearly always tooled up by carrying knives. You'd never bother because you knew you'd always come out second best."

David Rosen (London): "I was at the Jewish Free School up in Camden, a nice comprehensive, and I regularly took my life in my hands in getting home going through Camden and Kilburn to get to Maida Vale."

Tony Haddow (London): "When the West Indians arrived here and got off the *Windrush*, how fuckin' cool did they all look? They're there with their hats and their jackets. They look like demob suits really, but worn with attitude. They're happy to be here. If I came from Jamaica and got off a boat here, I'd turn around and get back on again!"

Look who's talking

"Is this some of the 'Alien-occupied territory' Powell's talking about?"

"When the West Indians arrived here and got off the *Windrush*, how fuckin' cool did they all look? They're there with their hats and their jackets. They look like demob suits really, but worn with attitude. They're happy to be here. If I came from Jamaica and got off a boat here, I'd turn around and get back on again!"
TONY HADDOW

ENOCH GOES FOR VOTES, JANUARY 1970

DAILY Mirror

6d.   Monday, April 13, 1970 ✻ ✻ ✻   No. 20,618

A defence plan to beat the 'Paki-basher' mobs..

DON'T GO OUT ALONE

PAKISTANIS were warned last night not to go about on their own, but to move in groups to protect themselves from "Paki-bashing" by young skinheads.

"We never attack first," said Mr. Abun Ishaque, chairman of the Pakistani Workers' Union.

He went on: "But when our people are attacked, it is their duty to help themselves.

"We are asking our people to move about together, and look after themselves."

At secret meetings yesterday of several coloured people's organisations, it was decided to stage a huge public meeting in Stepney, East London, next Sunday.

Victims of the skinheads will be there to tell the stories of how they were beaten up.

Police will be asked to the meeting.

Mr. Ishaque said: "If the meeting attracts skinheads looking for trouble, we will be ready for them."

Protection

Suggestions that Pakistanis should form vigilante groups were turned down at yesterday's meetings. It is known that police chiefs do not approve.

But Mr. Jagmahan Joshi, convenor of the Black People's Alliance, which

By MARK DOWDNEY and ROGER TODD

represents fifty-two immigrant associations said: "If the State is not able to extend protection, we will.

"We will not be going out to bash skinheads. We will take whatever measures are necessary to protect Pakistanis from violence."

Emergency

The Pakistani Workers' Union wrote at the weekend to the Home Office requesting an emergency meeting with Mr. James Callaghan, the Home Secretary, to discuss police protection for Pakistanis in the East End of London.

Extra police have been moved into the Bethnal Green area in the past few days.

Their orders are to combat what the police call "recent reports of rowdyism."

YOUR DAILY MIRROR

FROM today the price of your Daily Mirror is increased by a penny, from 5d. to 6d.

The increase, which was approved by the Prices and Incomes Board on February 5, has been delayed for as long as possible.

The prices of other popular newspapers—the Daily Express, Daily Mail and The Sun—have also gone up to 6d.

Daily Mirror

'The Who' drummer in midnight drama

MAN DIES AS SKINHEADS MOB A POP GROUP CAR

5d. Monday, January 5, 1970 No. 20,535

TRILBY STYLE, MAY 1970

LONDON — Who drummer Kei Moon has been cleared of all charg surrounding the death of his chauffe last January.

The chauffeur, Cornelius Boland, 2 was crushed under Moon's Bentley whi Moon was driving it from a parking to escape a mob of skinheads.

Moon pleaded guilty to three charge drunk driving, driving without a licen and driving without insurance. But th court wiped out all three charges.

As recounted in the courtrom in Ha field, the story began when a group jeering skinheads stormed the car Moon, his wife, and several friends we leaving a club. They threw stones a coins, kicked the automobile, and tri to overturn it. Amid the panic, accordi to the prosecutor, Boland either got o or was dragged out.

Moon, who said he had hired Bolan in anticipation of getting soused, too the wheel of the slowly-moving car. the scuffle outside, the chauffeur w knocked into the path of the car.

Under the circumstances, the jud told Moon, "You had no choice b to act the way you did and no mos culpability is attached to you."

The new decade had hardly started before the *Daily Mirror* had the word 'Skinheads' in their headlines: 'MAN DIES AS SKINHEADS MOB A POP GROUP CAR'. The story referred to an incident in which Keith Moon, drummer of The Who, had been to the Red Lion pub in Hatfield, Hertfordshire, which was owned by his neighbour's son. The pub had been full of Skinheads who had taken exception to Keith Moon's display of wealth. Outside in the car park they surrounded the car and began throwing coins at it. Neil Boland, who was Moon's minder and chauffeur, got out of the car to confront the tormentors, and in the ensuing mayhem, Moon accidentally ran over Boland, who sadly died in hospital. Moon was later charged with drink-driving without a licence or insurance on top of killing Boland. But he was cleared of all charges, as it was ruled that the death was an accident.

The paper seemed fixated on the 'new menace', as later in that month they even ran a pointless article about John Lennon, who had cut his long hair. The journalist asked some Skinheads if Lennon had done enough to join their ranks. The most interesting part is that after it mentions the singer's hair is about half an inch long, it continues: "This would qualify him for membership of a new fringe set emerging on the scene, who have slightly longer hair than the Skinheads. They are called the Suedeheads. And they might suit the peace-loving Lennon better because they don't go in for all that bovver."

On February 3rd, 1970, Skinheads were featured in the *Daily Mirror* in an article entitled 'Aggro: The Cult Of The Bovver Boys' written by journalist Ray Weaver. It was accompanied by three separate incidents of aggro: the trouble at a club called Snoopy's in Ruislip, Middlesex from a fifty-strong Skinhead gang called the 'Willesden Whites', an interracial fight at West Ham Technical College involving Skinheads and Asian students armed with hockey sticks, and trouble at Richmond railway station with an attack on a train crew.

There is also a drawn illustration of a male Skinhead (based on the picture they had featured of Tony Hughes in 1969) along with a description: "Skinheads began in London and the Midlands about a year ago as off-shoots of the Mods. The essential distinguishing marks then were cropped hair – as short as one eighth of an inch – and large boots, ranging from steel-capped industrial type to imported American Dr Martens at 95s. a pair."

It went on to name some of the London gangs: the Willesden Whites, the Burnt Oak Mob, the Kilburn Aggro Boys and the Hendon Mafia. It continues with: "Many of the original Skinheads have tried to turn respectable. They are letting their hair grow longer, have switched their boots for heavy American black brogue shoes and wear button-down shirts,

ties and suits. These Suedeheads, as they are called, prefer to stay in their home area, prepared to defend their own club or pub if attacked."

Mauro Antoniazzi (Birmingham): "I was living in Moseley, Birmingham and in 1970 had just left school at 16

> "I was living in Moseley… and in 1970 had just left school at 16. I used to see some lads on Lambrettas riding around and thought how cool they looked. I thought, 'God, I want to be like that.'"
> MAURO ANTONIAZZI

WATFORD SKINHEADS, 1969

AGGRO: THE CULT OF THE BOVVER BOYS

YOUTH workers, parents and police have been unable to curb the skinhead cult and its vicious characteristics of "aggro"—sudden violence, big boots, football rowdyism, vandalism and gang warfare.

Daily, more victims are added to the list of people who have met trouble crossing the paths, innocently or otherwise, of the cropped-haired "bovver boys."

The present inter-gang exchanges could develop into a lethal war. Claims are being made by some mobs that "shooters are needed for self defence."

Already there have been cases of shots being fired in a London Tube station gang clash, and from the open rear doors of a mini-van being chased by a police car.

In Hertfordshire, where the police are 400 men short of their establishment of about 1,200, Chief Constable Raymond Buxton has produced a report for his county's police committee spotlighting the increase in street fights involving rival gangs, the rise in vicious assaults on the police and the lethal types of weapon carried by mob members.

Heavy overtime has become a necessity for the police. The danger with the work is correspondingly greater. A tactical patrol group has been established for use in trouble spots.

Support for the police chief's efforts comes from those with the power to act.

Owen Stable, Q.C., Deputy Chairman of Hertfordshire Quarter Sessions, has asked for a tougher line in the courts.

His comment: "Every case of violence towards the police, however minor, is an assault punishable by two years' imprisonment. That includes roughing up and causing no injury at all. No quarter will be given to anyone convicted of laying a finger in violence upon the police. Anyone unwise enough to think the police are hired and paid by the ratepayers for use as a punchbag by any layabout is making a very grave mistake."

Mrs. Brenda Swinson, St. Albans City Bench magistrate, says: "We are seriously concerned at the frequency of offences arising from rival gang fights and intend to deal severely with all future offenders. There was a time when I did not mind walking alone on a street at night. But I would not do that now."

Many of the skinheads deny they look for trouble, and claim that trouble looks for them. But as they run through their anecdotes of aggro, this explanation sometim... the ring of conviction

A 19-year-old toolm... his piece: "We had and-dumb guy in the bumped into someo... boozer and knocked The guy said he shoul... another. Our m... understand, and befo... us could explain, ... We got the geezer w... and fixed him good. you understand.

"Then the other... were motoring me... from Northampton... us stopped at a caff... the others. There... greasers there. Ther... of mixing it. Mos... arrived—they were... and started on us. J... our crew arrived an... able to handle them.

"When you have... coming to you for n... have got to be ready... Iron bars and lavate... are OK—but now sh... needed too."

A night at Snoopy's

REQUEST TIME: disc jockey Chinnery and skinhead fans at another club.

SCENE: Snoopy's Club, Ruislip, Middlesex.
TIME: 10.15 p.m.

ABOUT 600 youngsters aged between 14 and 18 were dancing to music from the Pat Kelly group and the discotheque offerings of "The Judge," 26-year-old Geoff Chinnery.

Snoopy's Club, at Bourne Secondary Modern School, was in its eighteenth month of providing first-rate Saturday night entertainment for 1,000 members drawn from a large area of central Middlesex.

Suddenly the "Willesden Whites" arrived—a gang of about fifty skinheads armed with iron bars, bottles, glasses, knives and hand straps hacked from tube trains.

The invaders stormed the main entrance to the school, lashing out at the stewards. It was only a matter of time before the defenders were overwhelmed. The mob moved on into the main hall, where the club members retreated in terror.

There is no point in being brave when facing a well-armed band of hooligans. The clash was brief but brutal. Then the raiders fled—before the police arrived. Several stewards had to be severely injured and some of the youngsters had to have hospital treatment for cuts and bruises.

Damage to the club was severe. On the recommendation of headmaster Harry Hull the local education authority allowed one further club night, then cancelled all other bookings.

LONG-HAIRED Geoff Chinnery said: "Snoopy's Club was an answer I found to the complaint that there was nothing to do in the area.

"For the eighteen months it ran, it was free from trouble. We had some great groups on stage and the kids of the area looked forward to Saturday nights.

"The Willesden Whites raid seemed to be some sort of reprisal for a roughing-up one of their gang had in this area. But anything that happened to one of them had no connection with Snoopy's Club. I think it was an act motivated by jealousy. We had a top club—they didn't.

"I cannot blame the authorities for cancelling our hall bookings. Their reason is understandable.

"And as long as this skinhead type of warfare continues I will not run another club. I feel that it exposes youngsters, who want no part of violence, to unnecessary danger."

Headmaster Hull explained why he recommended the closure of Snoopy's: "Apart from the danger of further raids and damage to school property there was the very real possibility that the school name itself would become associated with skinhead gangs. There was also the chance that pupils would carry out reprisals and worsen an already worrying situation.

"Three months ago I did not have a skinhead in the school. Now some pupils have adopted the hairstyle and wear boots. They form only a handful out of more than 300 boys. I feel they are trying to make an impression, wear this uniform, group together and attempt to present a united face to the world.

"To order them to let their hair grow or stop wearing boots would be to make them martyrs. I prefer to leave them alone—unless their actions interfere with the running of the school.

"Gang fights in the school hall could interfere with the school. I felt I had to take the action I did. I know there is damn all for the kids to do, apart from attending one or two youth clubs. But these children are not interested in table tennis nights.

"I don't really know what is the answer to this problem."

Incident on Platform Si

SCENE: Richmond Railway Station, Surrey.
TIME: 11.28 p.m.

THE last train from Richmond to the West End was about to leave Platform Six. Driver Jack Weeds walked from the cab at one end of the train to the other closing windows and looking for any damage. Three girls sat talking in one compartment.

Driver Weeds completed his check, got into the cab and prepared to start the train. In his right hand he held the master control key — steel, twelve inches long and weighing about two pounds.

In the back of his mind was a report he would have to complete on an incident earlier in his shift when a sniper shot at his Euston-Watford train and a child was showered with broken glass.

His alert had stopped trains on that line while a search was made for the gunman. Such a disruption in service requires solid report work later.

A babble of raised voices interrupted him. He looked along the platform and saw a group of people around an open compartment door.

Said Mr. Weeds: "I walked through what seemed to be just a bunch of gawpers. In the compartment three skinheads were involved in an argument with the girls. One of the girls was cowering in the corner, holding her head.

"I told the blokes in the compartment to get out and leave the girls alone. I realised that I still had the master key in my hand when one of the skinheads shouted. 'Look out, the bastard has got a spanner.'

"One of the blokes looked at me hard like—then belted me. It was a beautiful punch and caught me right on the point of my chin."

MR. WEEDS, ex-welterweight boxer and solidly built—"I was a coalshovelling fireman for thirteen years"—was knocked out for the first time in his life.

"I went down like a stone. Blacked right out. When I came to I realised that I was being kicked. I got boots in the back, in the guts, on the head, everywhere. If I moved one way a boot came the other. I tried covering my head with my hands and they kicked my hands. The backs of my hands were a mass of bruises.

"I still had the key in my hand, but one little creature —he looked about 15—kept working on that han... and jumping on it... the key go. When h... there on the deck th... the mob. They... youngsters—except... who punched me a h... He was about twen... kids were actually... around with excite... would dart forward... boot and skip aw... with delight.

"Suddenly it end... one yelled, 'Cop... the whole lot skitt... like rabbits."

The West Ind... guard and a pass... tried to help Driv... Their rescue att... short-lived and... became on-the-grou... of the boot brigade.

All three men re... pital treatment. ...head's leader was ... the police. He... twenty with a crim... He is now in priso... months. The youn... in the gang, howeve... Said Mr. Weeds:... it happened so quie... violently is the ... aspect. I was ... aggressive and k... myself, 'Why did ... why are they so vi...

BOOT-IN DOWN WA

SCENE: Water-lane, West Ham, London.
TIME: 9 p.m.

A PAKISTANI student was walking to his lodgings from West Ham Technical College. Close to the college was a cafe used as a skinheads' hang-out.

A group of almost forty youths appeared on the dimly-lit street. They closed in and formed a frightening circle round the student. Suddenly the Pakistani was on the pavement and the boots began to seek out their human target.

Another student raised the alarm at the college. Three Asians ran out. They were members of a hockey team and had just returned from a match. They picked up their sticks on the way to the door.

As they went into the battle area police arrived. The skinheads fled into the night—and the hockey-stick-carrying trio were arrested. Two skinheads were later held.

In court the Pakistanis were found guilty of being in possession of offensive weapons and bound over for twelve months. They were also ordered to pay £5 each towards legal costs. It...

wa... the... the...

an... ski... tol... stu... pra...

fie... Pr... col... the... pea...

Dossier compiled and written by C

Levis, clip-on braces and boots

SKINHEADS began in London and the Midlands about a year ago as off-shoots of the Mods. The essential distinguishing marks then were cropped hair—as short as one-eighth of an inch—and large boots, ranging from the steel-capped industrial type to imported American Dr. Martens at 95s. a pair.

Jeans, Levis or light-coloured trousers, short on leg length, allowing the boots to be emphasised, were suspended on narrow clip-on braces. Flannel or "skinny grandad" short-sleeve vests completed a summer outfit. A sheepskin jacket tops the gear for winter.

The youngsters attracted into the cult describe themselves as "working class". Their ages ranged from fourteen into the twenties—an unusually wide span for a craze.

Football teams became the first focal points for skinhead groups. Soccer provided something to shout about and something to support, and produced a ready-made set of "enemies" in the opposition supporters

THE record of havoc across the nation is well-enough known. The police have suffered. A chief superintendent in West Bromwich said: "There used to be a time when it was a pleasure for a policeman to be on duty at a football ground. Now we have had to multiply our Saturday strength. It is considered a dangerous chore today."

The Saturday "bovver" for the skinheads did not provide enough excitement. The other six nights of the week had to be filled.

Gangs developed in defined areas—the Willesden Whites, the Burnt Oak Mob, the Kilburn Aggro Boys, the Hendon Mafia.

Across-the-border r a i d s developed. Any opposition became aggro. A fight led to a defeat, a defeat to a reprisal, a reprisal to a declaration of war.

Clubs and dance halls were regular targets. Many publicans shut down discotheques because of skinhead gang fights and threats to "do the place."

Individuals also became victims, the declared targets being Asians, hippies, rockers, students, "queers" and anyone who might "screw" (stare) at a mob or get involved in an argument.

MANY of the original skinheads have tried to turn respectable. They are letting their hair grow longer, have switched their boots for heavy American black brogue shoes and wear button-down shirts, ties and suits.

These suedeheads, as they are called, prefer to stay in their home area, prepared to defend their own club or pub if attacked.

Said an 18-year-old: "We are like a family, see. At some stage you got to decide which family you are going to join—the hairies or the skins. You can't be nothing. Nothing means you're a nobody. Who wants to be that? So you become a skin.

"If trouble comes to someone in the family you got to help sort it out—even when it means knuckling a brother skin. You get fights in every family, right? So we're just a normal family."

INSIDE the discotheque clubs used by the skinheads, the youngsters go through their simple dance step routines to the music of reggae, or bluebeat, originating from the West Indies.

At the Cherry Tree, Welwyn Garden City, Geoff Ward took on the job of running the discotheque after trouble had forced others off the scene. He gathered a team of £5-a-night bouncers.

Ward says: "We soon knew why the others packed up. A mob of skinheads arrived and tried to force their way in for free. We invited them into the car park to sort the matter out. They haven't been back since."

-LANE

they had not used weapons and that echnicality.

he seventh case of e i n g attacked by college. The day ior police officers anged meeting of involved in any reve the s k i n head e.

ver, are not satisay, 20, is Viceaffairs) of the on. He explained be taken to make treatment given to try to get action

from authorities, trade unions and employers aimed at curbing what was termed "fascism," and set up a system of self-protection for students going home from college buildings after dark —such as leaving o n l y in groups or with escorts.

Said Mr. Spray: "At this college about 40 per cent. of the students are from overseas, a large proportion of them Asians. They work extremely hard and in the evenings can be found studying in the library.

"These unwarranted attacks have upset them and if they continue or grow in number, a serious situation will develop, maybe forcing the students to leave."

GREGOR. Pictures: RAY WEAVER. Graphics: JOHN HILL

> "I help to run a boxing club and amongst the fifty youngsters in it there are twelve skinheads. One of them is a Great Britain champion. They are all good kids who would walk away from trouble. If you want to give publicity to skinheads then these are the ones who should be getting it."
> E. TURNER

I used to see some lads on Lambrettas riding around and thought how cool they looked. I thought, 'God, I want to be like that.' On my way home from work one day, on passing a garage I spotted a Lambretta TV200 for sale, £99. Which was a fortune. I went in and put a deposit on it, and arranged to pay for it on HP. The arrangement was that I paid a certain amount until I had paid it off and then I could take it home! It took me nine months and when I made the final payment, my dad came with me and I pushed it home because I didn't know how to ride it. Once I had mastered riding it, practised in the alleyway behind our house, I was on the road.

"It was not long before I encountered two Lambretta riders, Paul Morris and Tony Simmonds, who I used to see all the time, and we became good friends. Paul's SX 200 was incredible and was fully loaded with mirrors, spotlights, and chrome crash bars, and we all wanted our scooters to look like his.

"Gradually more and more joined our group and we would go on rides together. We were all Skinheads who eventually turned Suedehead. There was nothing better than seeing all our Lambrettas riding in convoy. We went to Weston-Super-Mare, Coventry, Stratford-upon-Avon."

The *Daily Mirror* continued its fascination with the perceived threat from Skinheads throughout 1970. In a feature dated February 9th that year, they printed a selection of letters giving the latest 'Public Opinion On The Bovver Boys'. The results were amazingly quite balanced. While some referred to the subjects as 'mere thugs' and 'violent people', there seemed to be more letters giving favourable accounts, including these three:

"I help to run a boxing club and amongst the fifty youngsters in it there are twelve skinheads. One of them is a Great Britain champion. They are all good kids who would walk away from trouble. If you want to give publicity to skinheads then these are the ones who should be getting it."
E. TURNER, BELMONT, SURREY

"There are just as many good decent skinheads as there are bad ones. We are not all complete idiots. I am sixteen, work hard five days a week in a City office, don't get into fights and don't take drugs. I wear all the skinhead clothes and love Reggae music, but when I am twenty I won't be a skinhead – unlike the chap in your article."
R. WARREN, LONDON N16

"Skinheads have been around much longer than one year as you seem to think. I am a skinhead girl and I had my hair cropped about three years ago and I am nowhere near being the original peanut. What did happen a year ago was that newspapers discovered 'boys with close-cropped hair' and called them Skinheads. They just didn't get the publicity before."
(MISS) M. NAMETT, LONDON N10

Tony Haddow (London): "By the end of '69, early 1970, it got too tiring. There were too many people involved and too much involved in the papers. We had a bad reputation and I think the fashion had gone as far as it could do really. We didn't know where else to take it, and felt we'd done it all basically. You might have gone from a Crombie to a camel-hair Crombie, but where do you go to after that? I finished my

apprenticeship in 1970, I literally went self-employed straight away, and started earning almost triple what my dad was earning, and he was a really good plumber. By '71 I was looking for work and I phoned up a company in London advertising for plumbers. They told me all the jobs on the London sites had gone. They then offered me a job working in Gibraltar, and I was out of it. From there I went pretty casual. I went travelling around Morocco at the end of my contract, and ended up in Jersey in the Channel Islands with a load of money in my pocket. Jersey in the early seventies was brilliant, lots of really good clubs playing soul music."

Brian Wright (London): "The time naturally arrived when you didn't feel part of it any more, by virtue of age, culture, dress and music. Its dynamics were forever changing. If I look back to, say, 1964, there would have been more Motown than '68, when it was Stax, Atlantic, Chess and so forth. It was changing every week and evolving. When you get to 16, you go to work, you've got money in your pocket so you don't feel the same as the younger ones because you don't identify with them any more. Your manor, your natural hinterland has got bigger than just Westminster or wherever. Some kids were getting engaged at 17 or 18. It was the done thing. You took a bird to the Wimpy bar and bought her a knickerbocker glory, and the next thing was an engagement ring! They then spent the next four or five years sat at mum and dad's flat saving for a house, because Westminster Council weren't building any. So, people just naturally drifted away. The mates I had of my age group started spreading out. One of them bought a car, then you could go anywhere in London, or even outside London."

David Rosen (London): "Once you moved away from the Skinhead look, if you wanted to wear a Harrington, you'd then wear it with a nice pair of Levis, white or denim with the one-inch turn-up and instead of wearing kind of 'bovver boots', you just progressed into a loafer and you were kind of doing the Ivy League/Mod/Suedehead 'jazzers' look, without anyone really realising it."

Paul Weller (Woking): "I was 12 in 1970 and that's when I got seriously into clothes. I wanted all of it. I was part of the 'over-counter-culture'. There wasn't much money around but I had a Saturday morning job and then a paper round and the rest I would bug my poor mum for! My mum bought me my first pair of Levis, maybe 501s but they had a zip fly, at the Co-op for thirty bob (£1.50!) and with them and my Brutus I felt I was in. That's kind of all you needed to be part of it, certainly at 12 anyway. Now I can see how we'd be looked at in disdain by the older originals."

Everybody had heard of the Skinheads and Hippies thing. Peter Wyngarde, the actor, even included a novelty record entitled 'Hippie And The Skinhead' on his LP that year.

Rolling Stone magazine published another article in 1970 concerning Skinheads. In truth, they needn't have bothered. It wasn't that much different from the article a year earlier.

Have you heard about our Skinheads now?

They're the rage. The Hippies are all but… boring… if not forgotten. It's Hippies vs. the Generation Gap on television plays. The Hippie season must be past.
ROLLING STONE MAGAZINE, 1970

They chat to 'Reg', who pontificates about violence towards both fighting rivals and Hippies.

"I don't like hippies, you know, but sometimes when I feel really rotten, I can understand why they get away from it all, I can really understand it, you know, it really gets you down, doing nothing at all," Reg admits. "But I don't know why they have to dress like that, I can't stand it, having their hair long like that… There was one in the paper and he and his mates admitted they hadn't washed their hair in three months, they're filthy and dirty and they make me fucking sick. I can understand hippies sometimes, but why they have to go round like that I can't understand, but some of their outlooks are alright, like world peace; as much as you say that Skinheads like violence, this world peace lark is all right, isn't it? It's a bit different from fighting in the streets." 'REG', ROLLING STONE MAGAZINE, 1970.

In a strange turnaround, some members of the Dilly Dossers, who had fought against the Skinheads, spent their time selling the alternative Hippie underground newspaper *International Times* (*IT*). During 1970, there was an idea that there would be a separate newspaper dedicated to Skinheads, but it never developed further than a regular column, edited by Paul Thompson, entitled 'Yell'.

The Hippies weren't alone in being shown the exit door. They were swiftly being followed by the Skinheads. The media had made it impossible to continue with the convict-short hair and brutal image.

Barry Cain (London): "It all started petering out for me really 'cos of school. I'm knuckling down, and taking loads of pills didn't work with that. I was 17 and it had had its days. I mean Suedehead brought it back a bit, but really it was all over. I had dropped acid not long after and there was no going back. If the original Skinhead had dropped acid that could have been interesting… I didn't really do much else. The dope was useless really, like Old Holborn, and it gave me a headache. And then I went to the Isle of Wight festival in 1970 with my mate and we must have been the straightest two fuckers there. We didn't even look like Hippies, but a month after I got back I dropped acid and everything changed. I only did it a couple of times and it was really profound. By then, the Skinhead thing had gone. Long gone."

Jacky Abramovitch (London): "By 1970, I was moving away from it. We had gone on to the next lot of fashions. For me, this was Biba, Mr Freedom, really bright colours, bright yellow satin trousers. My hair had grown. There I am, head shaved, and then it was down to here… I must have slowly grown it out even when I was still wearing the Skinhead clothes. I started to go to Kensington Market around then I think? The music, though, absolutely stayed. Even now for me, it is still there. Sadly, we didn't have many photos, because no one had a camera. I think we have some from the photo booths. Looking back, it was a great time. We discovered so many things. We didn't have the internet, so we'd spend hours listening to the radio just to hear that one tune. I discovered so much great music and the clothes just had to be right."

Tony Haddow (London): "We started growing our barnets again and the fashion changed because we were getting such bad publicity, and plus after a couple of years you've had enough. I've been through so many different phases of so-called fashion. You know, I was in the whole Soul Boy scene, it's a kind of 'been there done that' kind of thing all the way through. Some people, they become a Skinhead and that's how they look for the rest of their lives, and that's all they think about. I've never done that, to me it was just a stage of my life."

"By the end of '69, early 1970, it got too tiring. There were too many people involved and too much involved in the papers. We had a bad reputation and I think the fashion had gone as far as it could do really…"
TONY HADDOW

MARINA, SOUTHSEA, 1968

SEVENTEEN-YEAR-OLD JANET ASKHAM AND FRIENDS, HUDDERSFIELD, JUNE 1970

A BREAK FROM DANCING, MARINA, 1968

THE CHURCH OF ASCENSION CLUB, WEMBLEY PARK, CIRCA 1970/1

THE CHURCH OF ASCENSION CLUB, WEMBLEY PARK, CIRCA 1970/1

THE CHURCH OF ASCENSION CLUB, WEMBLEY PARK, CIRCA 1970/1

THE CHURCH OF ASCENSION CLUB, WEMBLEY PARK, CIRCA 1970/1

> "I always remember going to the first Reggae Festival that was put on at the Empire Pool, Wembley, circa 1969. The Pompey lot loved their reggae music – well the lot I knew, anyway. They had an old clapped-out white van, I think it was a Transit or a Bedford, everybody called it the 'Ska Car.'"
> BARRY QUINNELL

Bernard Jennings (Middlesex): "From around 1970/'71 onwards I worked for John Simon at the Village Gate but that was just a Saturday job. Because I worked in the City I had an annual train pass which meant I could do a Saturday job in London and it didn't cost me anything to travel. But the style was more flared trousers and the collars getting wider and wider. I was still working there when I got married in 1976. I didn't give it up until about a year after that. I got a discount and it was a buzz working in the King's Road. I used to double my money because it was all on commission and people were coming in and buying shedloads. Decent money plus a bit of discount so I'd go home with a mixture of money and trousers. I remember I was once working at the Marble Arch branch and Miss World, Eva Rueber-Staier, came in and the manager pushed us Saturday boys out of the way to serve her. She wanted half a dozen men's suits because they are usually better quality than women's. So, they had to be radically altered and I always remember this West Indian tailor on his knees, looking up at Miss World, eye level with her crotch, and as he tried to chalk the measurements his hands were shaking."

Brian Wright (London): "The shops no longer sold Mod gear. Austin's shut down, and the Squire shop became Village Gate. Village Gate and Cassidy's, which were at one time competitors, started selling velvet suits with soppy collars and flares, so you drifted away. I would say that most of my mates did go that sort of flower power and Hippy direction. Afghan coats and things, but then got into the Mr Freedom, Village Gate, Cassidy's look of velvet suits, roll-necks, cheesecloth shirts and all that. Being tall, and very self-conscious, I never fancied myself in fashion. I still don't wear fashion; I try to wear a classic look. Some of my mates had the confidence and the good looks to get into the checked trousers, hacking jackets and riding boots or whatever followed."

In October 1970, plucked guitar chords and handclaps introduced a new sound across the clubs, youth clubs and radio airwaves in Britain. T. Rex announced a whole different style from their former acoustic offerings under the banner Tyrannosaurus Rex. The elfin lead singer, Marc Bolan, had once been in love with the early Mod style, but now he was the antithesis of the look. His long, dark, curly hair fell around his shoulders, and his clothes were brightly coloured, with huge flared collars. In just over two minutes, 'Ride A White Swan' heralded a whole new sound that would change music in Britain, and make the Skinhead style redundant overnight.

The Skinheads had been untouched by the illusion of 'Swinging London'. They didn't buy into the use of clever words and lyrics found in psychedelic songs. To them, music was for dancing to. It meant good times, and hopefully 'pulling birds' at parties and clubs. They hadn't been disciples of the Timothy Leary mantra of 'turn on, tune in and drop out'. They were just out for fun.

With bands such as Slade and The Sweet, there was a merging of glamour and Skinhead working-class hardness. These bands may have looked effeminate in their clothing and make-up, but most members of the bands had the type of build that suggested they could have just stepped off a building site.

Andrew Vaughan (Orrell): "Prior to 'Hot Love', T. Rex had a huge hit in late 1970/early 1971 with 'Ride A White Swan'. I loved 'Ride A White Swan' with its mystical lyrics and catchy tune… to this day I still haven't a clue what Bolan is actually singing, never mind what it means. At 11 years of age I loved it in the same way I loved 'I Hear You Knocking' by Dave Edmonds and 'Black Skin Blue-Eyed Boy' by The Equals. They were chart hits, they were on the radio, they were great tunes and more importantly they were on *Top Of The Pops*, along with *Match Of The Day* the must-see television event of the week."

In November 1970 Edgar Broughton was in the *Melody Maker* complaining about his gig at the Top Rank in Brighton. He launched a general attack against concerts being held at Top Rank suites. "Apart from about fifty people, who were sitting down and quite prepared to listen to the music, the rest of the people there were Skinheads and 'suits', who were walking around with pints of beer doing their best to spill it down people." The band decided not to play and walked out.

Edgar Broughton continued: "We really thought it would be a nice thing to do Top Rank suites, but we now know our audience won't go, because of certain violent elements that seem to exist there. I mean it's very difficult for the suites to switch from soul and Tamla to putting on underground stuff. The way they are treating the switch leaves a lot to be desired."

Now the *Observer* proclaimed the end of Skinheads.

TOO MANY CLOSE SHAVES SPELL END OF THE SKINHEAD

The skinhead 'uniform' of cropped hair, short trousers and braces made them stand out – especially to the police.

London's Skinheads have disbanded. When we weren't looking, the bovver boys slipped out of their braces, grew their hair long and quietly demobbed.

Football club secretaries, policemen, community relations officers and hairdressers have known all about it for some time. Gordon Borland, secretary of Millwall Football Club, was happy to admit last week that he had not seen a Skinhead around the place for months. "I think they're a dying breed."

Bob Wall, Arsenal's secretary, told me: "Vandalism in the ground has diminished and Skinheads have just disappeared." Crystal Palace manager Bert Head recently had 700 fans accompany his team to Manchester and was moved to comment on the excellence of their behaviour.

Sergeant Sullivan, who works at Bow police station in the East End, where it all began, agreed: "The old guard has gone," he said. "The braces and the cropped hair have gone; the trousers are getting longer and the boots are disappearing." The 'new guard' were now wearing not-so-short trousers, shoes, and Ben Sherman shirts.
OBSERVER, DECEMBER 13TH, 1970

Brian Wright (London): "I guess at the start of the 1970s I did make certain accommodations for the look, because it got harder and harder to buy the things that you'd always had. I still saw myself as some kind of a Mod, but not an out-and-out Mod because it was so hard to maintain it. You just couldn't get certain shoes, because they'd been and gone, as had the shirts. Whereas I might have always had button-down shirts or tab-collar shirts, I would then maybe get ordinary collars, cut away as much as possible to show off the tie. I guess I unwillingly reinvented my look, trying to keep as faithful as I wanted to be. Put it this way, I've always had a Harrington jacket, since around '66. I've got five right now. I've always had a fly-fronted mac, so I've always had certain signifiers that I wouldn't be without. I've always had Tootal paisley ties, original ones from the sixties. We're all peacocks who like to make a display. We all belong to a club. You define your club by what you wear, and so wherever I could, I would let people know that that was the club I still belonged to."

There was one highlight in 1970. Horace Ové was a British-born filmmaker who filmed the 1969 Caribbean Music Festival at Wembley Arena. This was turned into a documentary called *Reggae*, which was successful in cinemas and was shown on BBC television. It featured the crowd wandering over to the concert, including some fantastically well-dressed black kids, and some white Suedeheads discussing their love of reggae. The footage also captures Roy Ellis, lead singer of The Pyramids, bare-chested with braces, half-mast jeans and boots, dancing energetically. On stage were some of the greatest reggae acts ever.

Barry Quinnell (Eastergate): "I always remember going to the first Reggae Festival that was put on at the Empire Pool, Wembley, circa 1969. The Pompey lot loved their reggae music – well the lot I knew, anyway. They had an old clapped-out white van, I think it was a Transit or a Bedford, everybody called it the 'Ska Car'. They were great guys, and about twenty of them went up in this van."

In April 1971, reggae was back at the top of the charts as Dave & Ansell Collins' 'Double Barrel' toppled T. Rex off the number one spot, where it had been sitting for six weeks. When the group were introduced, Tony Blackburn declared: "It really is nice to have a brand-new number one record, particularly when it's as good as this…"

Which was strange, as Tony Blackburn was known for calling reggae music "boring and monotonous" and regularly deriding it on air.

FILMMAKER HORACE OVÉ
DIRECTOR OF *REGGAE* DOCUMENTARY

"I guess I unwillingly reinvented my look, trying to keep as faithful as I wanted to be… We all belong to a club. You define your club by what you wear, and so wherever I could, I would let people know that that was the club I still belonged to."
BRIAN WRIGHT

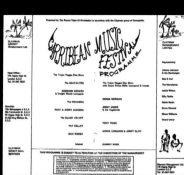

1st CARRIBEAN MUSIC FESTIVAL 1969

MONDAY SEPTEMBER 21st.
EMPIRE POOL, WEMBLEY
Souvenir Programme 2/6

CARRIBEAN MUSIC FESTIVAL

A GROUP OF SKINHEADS JUST EVICTED FROM THE SPANISH CITY,
WHITLEY BAY, MAY 1970

TREBLE
GREEN
SHIELD

DAILY Mirror

THE CUP FINAL

SPECIAL FOUR-PAGE PULL-OUT INSIDE

5d.   Saturday, April 11, 1970   •   No. 20,617

SKINHEADS SOCCER RIOT: 60 ARRESTS

CARDIFF FANS DAVID 'DICKY' ROGERS, DES O'CONNOR AND GARY BONTER DISPLAY TROPHIES TAXED OFF THE OPPOSITION, 1970–1 SEASON

By PAUL CONNEW

THREE-HUNDRED rioting Soccer fans — many of the skinheads — were turned off a football special train b railway police last night.

Then sixty-one of the troublemakers were arrested as they went on t rampage in a town.

Trouble began when the fans began smashing up the train taking them on the thirty-mile journey home to Coventry from Wolverhampton.

Windows were broken by flying bottles, seats slashed, and the communication cord pulled repeatedly.

The fans were celebrating Coventry's 1—0 away victory over Wolverhampton.

This put Coventry into the European Fairs Cup competition next season.

Terrified

As the riot worsened, rail police were called in. They managed to turn the 300 rioters off the halted train at quiet Bescot junction, near Walsall.

But the stranded rowdies then began a two-mile hike, shouting and singing, towards the centre of Walsall.

Terrified residents dialled 999 as the mob passed—shouting insults and throwing bottles.

Finally, Walsall police broke up the mob.

A police spokesman said: "The cells are packed tight. We haven't had a chance yet to count the total number arrested—but it is certainly over fifty."

Big police guard for Cup Final

By MIRROR REPORTERS

MORE than 700 uniformed policemen will be on duty in and around Wembley Stadium for today's F A Cup Final between Chelsea and Leeds United.

This is the largest uniformed force ever gathered for the Final.

Scores of plain-clothes officers will also be on duty—on the watch for pickpockets and on guard to nip any crowd trouble in the bud.

The Final has produced a record bonanza for ticket touts. Some £4 stand tickets were fetching more than £60 yesterday.

One tout said: "You can't lose. Leeds are the team of the moment and every football fan in London is willing to pay to see Chelsea win the Cup for the first time."

But some touts may find themselves out of luck.

For many of their would-be

Leeds victims have bee guaranteed tickets—thanks the generosity of fans w could not make the trip London.

The Leeds United Su porters' Club reported yeste day that dozens of fans h telephoned them — offeri tickets at face value.

Deluge

A club official who handl yesterday's deluge of calls s last night: "The phone h never stopped ringing.

"People from all over country, who had clb bought too many tickets couldn't make the trip, offer us all types of tickets."

He added: "As it was t late to post them, we arrang various meeting places London where the ticke could be handed over to o fans today."

WHAT IS FOOTBALL COMING TO

CHAPTER II: FOOTBALL

SKINHEADS SOCCER RIOT – 60 ARRESTS

Three hundred rioting Soccer fans – many of them Skinheads – were turned off a football special train by railway police last night.
DAILY MIRROR, APRIL 11TH, 1970

After Bobby Moore had lifted the World Cup for England in July 1966, football changed considerably in this country. The media spotlight fell upon the new and glamorous young players such as George Best, Rodney Marsh, Bobby Moore and Charlie George. They were good-looking, fashion-conscious, and had more in common with the pop stars of the day. Some even went on to have their own clothing labels and boutiques.

With the teenage market so strong at the time, the game began to attract more girls, as well as teen boys. But don't be fooled into thinking that girls were only there to flutter their eyelashes at their latest footballer pin-up. Some girls had their own hard reputation, and were just as keen on joining in the fighting as the men. Others would help their boyfriends by hiding weapons.

In June 1975 in American soft-porn magazine *Oui*, an article entitled 'Blood In The Stands' appeared, covering the history of British football violence. It interviewed two Manchester United fans discussing girls:

"Who's going to carry stuff to an away game? Thing is, they never think to search the birds." And his eyes wandered after a likely pair, two girls in United's colours, wan-faced, expressionless, arm in arm. "They're the ones who carry the stuff in their handbags for the boys. Razors, knives, steel combs."

"Or down their tits," Rhino chipped in. "I seen one once, at a Leeds game, pulled this fuckin' big iron bar outa her jumper, passed it on to the bloke that she was with. Bomp! Got rid of it the same way."

"Girls can be worse than the boys," Moey said, "egging them on, like, slipping them things. There's one comes to United's games regular, hefty piece. I seen her with two hundred blokes running along, following behind her."

'Youth Ends', the special areas in a stadium reserved for youngsters, were vibrant, loud and full of testosterone.

Clive Knight (London): "In 1967 I was tall for my age and knocked around with a bunch of lads who were two or three years older than me, who went to the same school as me, and who were all hard-core Chelsea supporters. In 1967 we went to the FA Cup semi-final against Leeds at Villa Park, coach courtesy of a local soft drinks company, Schweppes. These older lads were wearing those mottled black Tuf boots with highly polished toecaps and they had turn-ups on their jeans, though no Levis at that point."

One of the most attractive things about going to football was that it gave people the chance to be somebody. You could slave away all week in some dead-end job where your bosses treated you like dirt, or you might be on the dole. Come Saturday, you could be on the terraces with your mates, dressed up in your clobber, shouting and punching your way to be noticed in a sea of fellow supporters. You could be king for a day. You could be a face. Of course, there would be a hierarchy in the group, and the hard nuts were ultimately the leaders. The generals.

In the football grounds of the late sixties and early seventies, the meeting place for all the wannabes was the End. These attracted all the local gangs, firms and crews. These were the places where territorial violence spread like a plague. They were the catwalks for street fashion, and the castle to be defended at all costs.

The goalposts marked the End because there were no seats behind the goals at football grounds, just open terraces fitted with crash barriers. Each End had its own sets of armies separated by estates and areas. The Arsenal had the Kington and the Angel mob, and they formed the North Bank End. Chelsea had the Shed, with lots of little firms. Manchester United had the Stretford End, made up of various gangs. Leeds United had a mixture of districts such as the Seacroft Boys or the Harehills Boys. West Ham's North Bank was full of little gangs from Barking and Ilford as well as hard nuts like the Mile End Mob.

Each End had various characters who could go beyond the 'king for a day' tag and be deemed leaders. At six foot two, Johnny Hoy was a legend on the Highbury terraces and a reputed friend of Arsenal hero Charlie George. Hoy would meet the others in the Long Bar of the Gunner pub opposite the ground to organise the day's events. He gained further reputation when he was highlighted in an article on football gangs in an issue of *Time Out* in April 1972. By 1974, the Clock End at Arsenal had become the hooligan area.

Arsenal had a big reputation in those days for fans disembarking from trains to away matches, singing, "Arsenal boys, we are here, shag your women and drink your beer, la la la la la la la la. Arsenal! Arsenal! Arsenal!"

Another would be: "I was born on the North Bank, balls are made for kicking, when you go down to the North Bank, knives are made for sticking."

The 1972 *Time Out* article by Chris Lightbown also describes the leaders of the other main London hooligans. For West Ham, it notes that there is no overall leader, but that the North Bank has individuals such as Ilford's Johnny Williams and Rollo, as well as a family from Barking, the Coopers.

Frankie Parish is named the leader of Tottenham's Park Lane End, described as a "5'6" dynamo who has led their Park Lane revival… every Smoothie worth his Crombie has either seen or heard of Frankie Parish".

"Girls can be worse than the boys, egging them on, like, slipping them things. There's one comes to United's games regular, hefty piece. I seen her with two hundred blokes running along, following behind her."
MOEY, MANCHESTER

PITCH INVASION! AUGUST 1971

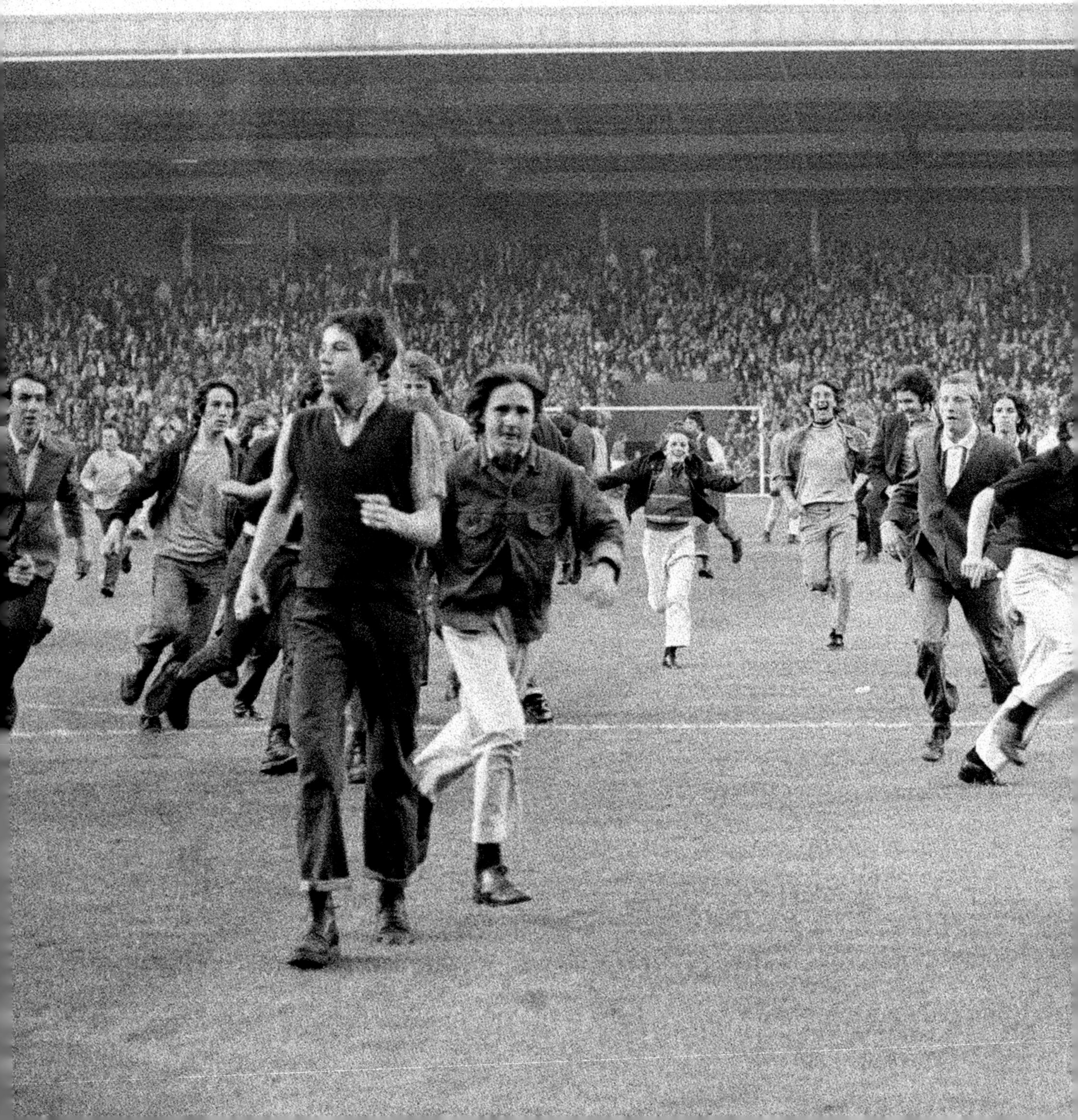

Chelsea's undoubted leaders are named in the article as H. J. Greenaway and 'Eccles'. Micky Greenaway was the man who got the Shed (Chelsea's Fulham Road End) singing and chanting, reputedly after seeing how the famous Kop End in Liverpool encouraged their team. His booming voice could be heard leading one of the songs he invented, the 'Zigger Zagger' song (to the tune of the old 'Oggie, Oggie, Oggie' chant), and the crowd would respond with the 'Oi, Oi, Oi' part.

Zigger Zagger, Zigger Zagger, (Oi Oi Oi)
Zigger Zagger, Zigger Zagger, (Oi Oi Oi)
Zigger (Oi)
Zigger (Oi)
Zigger Zagger, Zigger Zagger (Oi Oi Oi)

This was often followed by the following words, to the tune of 'When The Saints Go Marching In':

Oh, when the Blues
Go steaming in,
Oh, when the Blues go steaming in,
I wanna be in that number,
When the Blues go steaming in.

Other Shed favourites included:

(To the tune of 'I Was Born Under A Wandrin' Star')
I was born under the Chelsea Shed,
Boots are made for kicking,
Guns are made to shoot,
If you come under the Chelsea Shed,
We'll all stick in the boot.

(To the tune of 'Teddy Bears' Picnic')
If you go down to the Shed today,
You're in for a big surprise,
If you go down to the Shed today,
You'll never believe your eyes,
For Jeremy, the Sugar Puffs Bear,
Has bought some boots and cut his hair,
Today's the day that Jeremy joined the Skinheads!

Of course, one song always associated with Chelsea is Harry J. & The All Stars 'Liquidator', which would be played over the ground tannoy, and the Shed would participate at regular intervals throughout the song with four hand claps and a cry of "Chelsea!" at the end.

Greenaway is often cited as a relative innocent among a more aggressive younger mob. In 1969, Greenaway was already 24. He seemed to leave the organising of the young crowd to Danny 'Eccles' Harkins. Eccles was definitely considered the face of the Chelsea Shed Skinheads at the time. He was featured in a *Man Alive* TV programme filmed at a Newcastle away match, and his name was written on many a wall outside Chelsea Football Ground.

West Ham's main End was always the North Bank, with the South Bank set aside for away fans. But it has to be said that the East Stand, known as the Chicken Run, was just as vocal when it came to singing. The songs were given added emphasis by the sound of heavy boots pounding the corrugated iron that formed the back of the North Bank.

Songs may have included 'Knees Up Mother Brown' or 'We Are The Mighty, The Mighty West Ham', but it would mainly be the tune 'I'm Forever Blowing Bubbles'. This obviously got rewritten by other firms, including Arsenal, as 'I'm Forever Throwing Bottles'.

In early May 1967, West Ham hosted Manchester United at Upton Park. Manchester fans had got into the North Bank and it wasn't long before around 500 West Ham fans decided to take their End back. Bottles and pennies were thrown, newspapers were set alight and thrown. After the game ended, Manchester United winning 6-1, the fighting continued outside on a mass scale, as the Mancs had brought thousands of fans with them.

The following season (1967/'68), lessons had been learnt, and a police tunnel made up of crash barriers was installed on the North Bank. Banners, flags and walking sticks were banned, and the stadium bars took to pouring beer into paper cups, as glass bottles were banned. Other grounds soon followed suit.

Lester Owers (London): "Now going to West Ham, I never wore colours because going from Laindon I bought a return ticket to Upminster, two stops, and did a bung to the ticket collector at East Ham rather than get out at Upton Park where there would be ticket collectors.

"At that time the mob was in the North Bank, but only Man U in '67, that I can recall, took the North Bank, because they got to the ground early. When the West Ham crew arrived, they threw bottles into the rafters in the roof and showered the Man U fans with glass. Carnage! Man U tried to invade the Chicken Run, but the wise, along with the dockers in the stand, retreated.

"I can remember the away match versus Arsenal in '68/'69, I think it was October '68, and the match after, Geoff Hurst scored eight. I was with the Mile End Crew and we all met at West Ham [Manor Road] tube. We changed at Mile End, and while we were travelling to Holborn to change for the Piccadilly line, a few of the lads were swinging on the grab handles and kicking in the roof. Some pulled the grab handles off, as they made a great cosh. When we got to the Arsenal tube, we steamed through the ticket barrier knocking the ticket collector into his hut. Nobody paid and there were no police.

"The match was 0-0, but West Ham took the Arsenal North Bank, there was minor scuffles and the police sent in snatch squads. One of my mates got pulled and they roughed him up before letting him go. After the match the mob went from the ground and up Stroud Green Road; as I used to live in Finsbury Park, I had a lot of local knowledge. They proceeded to do drop kicks on shop windows where the glass wobbled and shattered. Eventually the Bill arrived to break things up, and even some of the locals from a garage came out with large spanners."

Jim Cameron (Glasgow): "My dad took me to London in November 1970 to see Celtic play West Ham in Bobby Moore's testimonial, and I saw my first huge number of Skinheads. I was awestruck and loved the look. I came home, got my hair cut, got a pair of steel toe-capped boots from a friend who was in the Army Cadets, a granddad shirt and braces, I already had a Levis jacket so I was now a 13-year-old Skinhead."

The *Daily Express* picked up on the football story:

Soccer ground thugs were on the receiving end of stiffer-than-usual punishment yesterday.

But Mr Denis Howell, the Minister of Sport, who says "fines are useless" cannot be entirely pleased with the outcome of all of yesterday's court hearings.

While magistrates at two courts – Bristol and Plymouth – sent youths to detention centres, others imposed fines ranging from £5 to £55.

Weapons produced in evidence included steel-capped boots – part of the 'skinhead' uniform, bottles, stones and a spiked ring.
DAILY EXPRESS, OCTOBER 1969

By the early seventies, football hooliganism was seen as a giant threat to society equivalent to the likes of the IRA.

In spring 1972, Manchester United brought down over a thousand fans to Arsenal. Along the way they vandalised cars and shops before getting to the ground, where the Stretford End boys took the North Bank. By the early seventies Manchester United certainly had a reputation for aggro, mainly due to their vast numbers.

John 'Bomber' Wild (London): "As a kid in the sixties before Skinheads came along, it was not unusual to see incidents of violence and trouble at football matches. At Loftus Road, away, supporters' coaches would park in the nearby White City Stadium car park. After matches it was often the case that young kids and teenagers would lie in wait to ambush and stone these coaches in a rampage of wrecking. On several occasions I witnessed this on my way home from games at QPR in the mid-sixties. It became a game for young kids.

"The very rude awakening for me was as an 11-year-old, attending a friendly testimonial game between QPR and Chelsea. This was 1968 on a Monday evening. Some 1,500-strong Chelsea fans rampaged after the game at this local derby. It was the first real outbreak of football violence I saw… On this occasion I was punched in the face by a group of Chelsea lads and my scarf taken. The marauding mob seemed well organised by older kids, it was orchestrated, planned and frightening."

Ian Hingle (London): "I didn't really do football. I mean, I went to Chelsea now and then, but not really. I used go to the Shed, just to watch the fighting and look at the girls, as well as seeing what the blokes were wearing. It was a bit of a fashion parade on Saturday. I mean it's the King's Road. Really, football wasn't really a big thing, not until the World Cup in 1966. Before the World Cup, it was a sort of nerdy thing, old blokes with rattles and a packet of pork scratchings…"

Bill Fordham (London): "In '67 we [Chelsea] went to the Wembley Cup Final, Chelsea versus Spurs. I was with Danny [Eccles], and a load of us didn't have tickets so we stormed the turnstiles. Some got in and everyone was holding the gates back while the rest of us jumped over the turnstiles. There were walls separating each section, and the police were chasing us while we're trying to mix in with the crowd."

Bob Wheeler (Slough): "I was born in Harold Hill, near Romford, so I really should have been a West Ham fan. Gidea Park was all West Ham. There were five of us [in our family], but when it got to six, we managed to get a GLC flat. It could have been Patton or Britwell in Slough. We went down to Britwell, while it was still being built, and there were about ten thousand people on the estate. More than half were west London, and there were a lot from east London too, which is why there was a big Chelsea and West Ham influence on the Britwell Estate.

"When I first went to Chelsea, we played Sunderland and we won 1-0. We used to sit on the benches by the dog track. It was around 1966. As I got older, I started going to away games. Chelsea had a massive following for away games, and basically, we used to tour the country. We went to places I'd never heard of at the time, Oldham, Rotherham, places like that, in Cup matches. Being young, I didn't give a damn what I got up to. I remember at one of the FA Cup games, sitting in the director's box with my feet up, watching the game, thinking, 'This is nice,' until somebody collared you and threw you out. But in them days, you used to get thrown out and you'd get back in again. I remember one game, Man City at Chelsea, I got thrown out about five times during that game. All I used to do was dive back over the turnstiles and get back into the Shed. As you look at the Shed in the top left-hand corner. down about twenty rows there used to be the Slough contingent, with Battersea behind us and Lewisham in front. That's what people tended to do, they used to stay in their groups in the same place every week. As more and more started travelling to away games I remember going to Leeds with 7,000, and to my amazement when we came out of the station you'd actually see washing lines with clothes on going across the streets, that you only ever saw on the telly in programmes like *Coronation Street*."

Bonny Staplehurst (London): "There weren't many of us girls there at the football. The fellas took us for granted. We stood in the middle of the Shed and quite a few times per game we'd fall over, with all the jostling and moving about going on. They just used

The violent face of modern soccer is dramatically reflected in these photographs from the English press

CLOCKWORK ORANGE ON THE PLAYING FIELDS OF BRITAIN

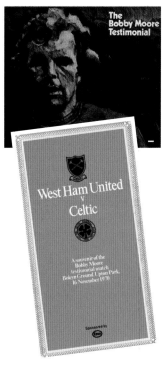

"My dad took me to London in November 1970 to see Celtic play West Ham in Bobby Moore's testimonial, and I saw my first huge number of Skinheads. I was awestruck and loved the look. I came home, got my hair cut, got a pair of steel toe-capped boots… a granddad shirt and braces. I already had a Levis jacket so I was now a 13-year-old Skinhead."
JIM CAMERON

SKINHEAD MEETING, OCTOBER 1969

CARDIFF FC SKINS, 1970

to pull us up. Well, they pulled my sheepskin up, but I'd still be on the floor! Because I was at school in Fulham, I sort of got to know the main Chelsea Shed boys and they kept an eye on us. They would always look after us, even if we went to away games. If there was trouble, we were sort of pushed out of the way. We were never involved in any of that. We saw fights but kept out of the way. I would go on the 'Football Specials', I was only 14 then. I used to babysit my younger brother, Colin, only I'd take him with me instead of staying at home. We'd go to a burger bar called the OK on the corner of Trafalgar Square and Charing Cross, so I sort of got him involved in it too and he was only 9. I think I was a cool babysitter, eh?"

Sharon Williams (London): "I went to Millwall around then, but didn't see any bother with Skinheads involved. I bought my first pair of Levis from Jays on Lower Road. I wore them to a football match, which was against Trinity, and it ended up in a massive fight, all girls."

Clive Knight (London): "I saw plenty of aggro at football. I was Chelsea but when we were playing away, one particular Chelsea mate and me would go to other games around London – QPR, Watford, West Ham and Arsenal. So, no matter if it was QPR versus Millwall or Watford versus Brentford, there was always something 'going on' back then. But… for me it was about clothes and music so when it all went off in the Shed at the Bridge I would be seen edging towards the Bovril entrance. Ha-ha."

Ray Butters (Whitley Bay): "I lived opposite a girl who was a Skinhead. She got talking to me, and introduced me to her boyfriend, who was a Skinhead too. We went down to the fair, and they introduced me to their friends as a Skinhead who had just moved there from Hertfordshire, so I met everybody straight away. There were probably between twelve and eighteen in the Whitley Bay Aggro Boys. All our area supported Newcastle FC, but Whitley Bay is about nine miles away on the coast. So really it was all about territory down there. We used to get squads coming down from inland to the coast. That's where a lot of the aggro took place, on the seafront. So, it was rival Skinheads from areas like Cowgate, Scotswood and different estates in Newcastle. So, there'd be Elswick Aggro, Water Aggro, and they had rivalries with us coastal towns such as Whitley Bay Aggro, North Shields Aggro and Blythe Aggro. If we went to football, people would point us out or we'd point them out, but once we were in the Leazes End, we didn't turn on each other; we were there to fight whoever was playing Newcastle. But come Sunday, all bets were off, and we were back to the status quo. You were always out at weekends and knew who your allies were, and those that weren't. There was very little trouble between the Whitley Bay Aggro Boys and the North Shields, just because everybody knew each other. We always had rows with the London teams. Our mortal enemies were Chelsea but obviously West Ham and Tottenham. Any big cities really, the Scousers, Mancs… it didn't matter. If they weren't from Newcastle, they were your enemy. That was Division One, but there were other teams like Blackpool.

"I can remember going to Cup games as well. We went to one in Walsall, and they put Newcastle out of the Cup. The crush from the crowd was so great, the gates fell over, and we all rushed in as most of us never had tickets. We'd gone down in a minibus, and on the way back we stopped at Sheffield, about half of us got arrested after getting into a fight."

Bill Fordham (London): "I was 17 in the November of '68, but a lot of that time was taken up by football. I did the bank holiday at Margate in '68, but most of it was spent following Chelsea. There would be a group of about twenty to thirty hard core of us going away. There'd be lots just going to the football but I guess we were the ones going for the devilment, the ones looking for trouble. There was a bunch of guys coming up from St Paul's Cray in Kent, and they were absolutely barmy. They cut their hair really short, so they were the first Skinhead types I saw in '68."

Bob Wheeler (Slough): "The biggest punch-up I remember was in 1969. Chelsea away to West Ham. I was in the North Bank with Johnny Falmouth, a big West Ham fan, I can't remember why, we were in there but maybe we couldn't get tickets. Just as the game was about to start, there was a fight that started right in the middle of the South Bank, and the circle was getting wider and wider. I've never seen anything like it because it was from end to end. Then suddenly it went quiet, and everybody wondered what was going on. Then all the blue and white scarves went up all over the South Bank, and by then the North Bank were going mad trying to take it over. It was one of the very few times that Chelsea did well at West Ham. It went on for quite a while and I remember on *The Big Match* Brian Moore saying these were the worst scenes of violence he'd ever seen. It was always dodgy over at Upton Park. We used to drink in the Queens by the market – this was around the time we used to wear the white butchers' coats. There was a geezer called Alan who came down the steps at Upton Park Underground waving a fire extinguisher above his head. I was on the train with Spud Murphy and the Stockwell lot, and he threw it through the doors of the tube train. One of the Stockwell lot caught it and threw it back, and it knocked all his teeth out."

Tony Haddow (London): "When the football came in, and it started going to the Midlands and up north, that's when it all started kicking off. All my mates followed different teams. So, all the lot around Kilburn and Wealdstone were all Chelsea. Around Edgware it was all Arsenal, and still is. I bunked into Wembley when Spurs won the Cup in the sixties. I ended up right at the front, and that day I became a Spurs supporter."

Raymond Potter (London): "All Bang'ole supported Arsenal, so there would be a good forty or fifty of us against the Shed, which was the Palace lot. You'd always notice them, because they were wearing sheepskin coats, and they were known as the Shed men. We'd wait for them after a game by the Bunny Hole, which is a local bridge, and it would kick off."

John 'Bomber' Wild (London): "In 1969, QPR were drawn away in the FA Cup versus Charlton Athletic – it was the first away game I had attended with a friend. The match was memorable for me, as being the first appearance of my newly acquired look. Black Harrington jacket, white Sta-Prest trousers by Westcotteers, Levis still being hard to acquire due to lack of stockists and demand. My Dr Martens boots were the Astro Martins style, a slightly ugly-looking

CHELSEA FANS CHECKED FOR STEEL TOE-CAPS
AT CHELSEA V ARSENAL, SEPTEMBER 1969

> "I remember being there when they started playing 'Liquidator' on the PA system – obviously it was a song sung straight away, predominantly by the Skinheads. I think that's when I realised it was happening everywhere, and that it wasn't just a London phenomenon…"
> TONY ROUNCE

round-toed edition, and named after the recent expeditions by American astronauts to the moon.

"The QPR End was called the Loft; it would be packed with the now emerging Skinhead youths, most being white kids, but we had a fair amount of West Indian kids too. There were people there that seemed to be faces, organisers in advance of any trouble emerging. I distinctly recall two West Indian brothers who never went in for the shorter hair, but sported large Afro-styled hair. Their look was topped off with highly polished Dr Martens and sheepskin coats."

Bob Wheeler (Slough): "Man United had numbers, but they never really had anything other than numbers. Leeds used to play up a lot, as did Millwall obviously, but it was always West Ham from the nine years I went from 1969, possibly '68, to '77 that we never done any good against. Many a time I've been in the Shed and the geezer next to me was wearing a donkey jacket with Dagenham written on the back or something, which is a bit of a giveaway, isn't it? Then suddenly, bang, it would go off, and you're sharing the Shed with West Ham. At their place, it was always dodgy getting back to Upton Park tube. Arsenal had a bit of a firm who were active from around '69 until '73, but I don't think they had anything after that. I don't think we had it with Tottenham."

Tony Rounce (London): "My best mate, Mickey, lived four doors down from me. He was a Chelsea fan, and Millwall played their home games on the different Saturday to Chelsea, so until I started working regularly on Saturdays we'd go over there all the time. I remember being there when they started playing 'Liquidator' on the PA system – obviously it was a song sung straight away, predominantly by the Skinheads. I think that's when I realised it was happening everywhere, and that it wasn't just a London phenomenon, because you'd get visiting firms coming from areas where they had fairly big black populations such as Manchester or Birmingham."

Norman Jay MBE (London): "There weren't that many black faces on the terraces then really. I knew one guy who I used to see at the Hammersmith Palais. I used to go there, but looked too young really, but would go with a group of girls. Anyway, I knew this guy as 'Black Frank', never knew his surname. Millwall fan out of the Elephant. From 1974 to 1980 we were pretty close pals.

"I also knew a fella called Mark, who was a Shed Boy, and a guy called Bab, who used to live half a mile from me and I'd see him at the Palais too, and talk, and you would never think he was a top face. Good as gold. Sharp dresser as well. Properly handy."

Bob Wheeler (Slough): "In 1971 we played Stoke at Wembley and I couldn't get in, because I'd had a drink. So, I climbed up the outside of Wembley on a drainpipe. I was about forty feet up when the coppers turned up. They sent one of their boys after me. I got to the bit where the barbed wire came out, and I tried to get over it. I was kicking the copper in the head, and I looked down, and all I could see was the roof below, so I just jumped down, probably about thirty foot or whatever, and landed on top of these corrugated-roof toilets and it all cracked. These geezers grabbed me. There were three of them from Swiss Cottage hiding up there. I had

practically landed on them, and if I hadn't, I think I would have killed myself. We had to get off the toilets and get through the next set of turnstiles into the ground. I said to them that we couldn't stay there, so when I say jump, we all jump down. The coppers were waiting for us down there too. So, I said now, and they all jumped apart from me, but then I heard this copper shout, 'I know you're up there, son. You might as well come down. How you didn't kill yourself, I don't know. You won't get in now, and I ain't going anywhere.' I thought, fair cop, so I got down, and he was alright, but then the sergeant came along and he was fuming. He got hold of my arms and rammed them up my back. I told him, 'Fair play but you're gonna break my arms. Can you loosen them a bit?' He wouldn't have it, so then I said, 'If you don't let go, I'm gonna hit you.' He didn't, so I managed to get my arms down, turn around and nutted him. I got eighteen months suspended for two years for that. And we got beat 1-0!"

Barry Cain (London): "I wasn't really a football man, but I started to go to the Arsenal 'cos they were local. But I went all over, QPR, and West Ham. You just did back then. One night West Ham was playing Everton, and these guys were just walking round the side and pulling geezers out and walloping them. I couldn't believe it. There was always a bundle at the games."

Jim Cameron (Glasgow): "When Celtic played away, the gang thing was forgotten about, everyone was Celtic. We all got together for the football.

"One story that sums up the youth and exuberance of it all, is that around '71, maybe around a hundred of us, all Skinheads, got a train to Edinburgh, I think it was Hibs or Hearts. We were coming off the train, and there was a large police presence, with their Alsatians. At the time there was an advert on TV for Heinz Beans and the song went 'A million housewives every day, pick up a tin of beans and say, Beanz meanz Heinz.' The whole train of Skinheads, all dressed to kill, started singing that song, but when it got to 'pick up a tin of beans and say' we changed the words to 'you're gonna get your fuckin' heads kicked in!' Even the coppers were laughing, and we were all laughing. We were trying to be hard and tough, but deep down, we were kids.

"We used to sing [to the tune of 'Nick Nack Paddywack']:
B – O – V
V – E – R
Bovver Boys is what we are.
With a knife, and a chisel, and a steel crowbar,
Bovver Boys is what we are!"

Jacky Abramovitch (London): "I didn't really get into the football. I mean I was near the West Ham ground and I went a couple of times, but I wasn't really interested. But Gill was going out with Tom who was a West Ham and they would go occasionally. It was really violent. It was too much. You had to stand then and you got pushed around the North Bank. I didn't like it. Tom was featured on a BBC TV thing about Skinheads and it caused him some trouble at the time. He was just a kid, but he got associated with the bad stuff. We were just naive then. I wasn't really into the really aggressive thing. I think it was partly a response to the scene being taken over by the really violent thing, and it moved away from just being a music and fashion thing. In essence for me, that was what it

was about. It wasn't a political statement at all. We didn't identify it as a tribe or a group. It just wasn't like that for us. For me Skinhead started off as a fashion thing completely and then slipped into being political for some, and when we saw that we started to get out of it."

Bill Fordham (London): "The turning point of my life was 1969, because I went up to Maine Road, Man City away, and got nicked for fighting up there. We were actually getting a pummelling. They charged us down this street, and I picked up this metal sign by the road, and shouted, 'Come on then you fuckers!' I looked around and all my mob had gone, and I'm there on my own. I was getting a battering, and the police steamed in and nicked me. I said I was trying to defend myself, but off I went. They didn't keep me in the cells all night. They eventually threw me out at Moss Side at about ten o'clock at night, and told me to go home. I managed to get home, but had to go back a week later to Salford Magistrates. My solicitor told me to plead guilty, and I'd get a fine. I pleaded guilty and got a two-year suspended sentence. That really put the shit up me. So, I went out the next Saturday night with my mates to the White Lion, Putney Bridge. All hell broke loose down there. Someone I knew got his ear chopped off with a broken beer glass, and I said that's it. I can't go out on Saturday nights any more or I'll end up inside. I started just going out on Thursday nights with my mates down the King's Road, various pubs. I have no idea why we went there but we went to the More Arms at the back of Sloane Square, by St Thomas More's school, and I met Heather there, and eighteen months later we got married, when I was 19. I had still been going to football but steered clear of trouble. Pretty soon after we got married, we moved out of London, and went to live in Somerset to duck out of it. Everything I had done was compressed over three or four years. It was very intense, but I wouldn't give up those memories and experiences for the world."

Bob Wheeler (Slough): "In '73, Slough Town had a big following of kids who were Chelsea supporters as well. We came out of the ground and I saw a little bloke getting a pasting from a big Blyth Spartans fella. So, I went to give him a hand, and got nicked. I got thrown into the back of a police car, and then got handcuffed to the next bloke who got thrown in. Then another fella got thrown in. Then a riot started nearby, so the copper jumped out of the car to intervene. I told the bloke sat in the front that he might as well get out, because he wasn't wearing cuffs. Then after about twenty seconds, I thought hang about, just because I'm handcuffed doesn't mean I'm immobile as such, so I said to the other fella, 'Come on!' and yanked him out with me. We ran up the road, and I saw a Slough supporter, so I asked to borrow his scarf to wrap around the handcuffs. We ran down a side road, which turned out to be a dead end. We could see the police were getting near to the top of the road so we dived over the top of the wall together. We hid there in somebody's garden until it quietened down. It was only then that the other bloke spoke, and I realised he was a Blyth Spartans supporter. So, then we started fighting, handcuffed to each other! Finally, because we were both so knackered, we stopped. We met some mates I knew. They hacksawed the other bloke's cuff off, but when I saw it cut into his arm, I thought no way. I eventually found somebody who got some bolt-cutters. The other bloke wasn't a bad lad actually, and I helped him find his coach to get back home."

YOU'RE COMING WITH US SON, NOVEMBER 1969

YOU'LL GET MORE THAN A BLOODY NOSE, MAY 1971

CHAPTER 12 : AGGRO – SATURDAY NIGHT'S ALRIGHT FOR FIGHTING

Austin Myers (Shipley): "We used to have a lot of rivalry with the Gondola Mob in Bradford, who were pretty much a biker/leather jacket mob. In Shipley, there was Satans Slaves, but we had a bit of an affinity with them, which was strange because under normal circumstances we'd have kicked seven bells of shit out of each other. But because some of them were mates from the past there were even times where we banded together to take on groups from out of town, from local areas like Bingley, Keighley, Otley and Ilkley. I mean there was a lot of rivalry from local market towns in West Yorkshire."

Barry Cain (London): "On a Friday or Saturday, I'd go to the St John of Jerusalem on St John Street, when I was 16, and then all come out of there and get in a minicab and go up to the Birds Nest on Muswell Hill. Because that was THE place, and it was open till 2 a.m. It was heaving in there, heaving. And every single Saturday, there would be a fight; it was like the Wild West. It was unbelievable. You'd be in the toilets, dropping twenty or thirty diet pills and sometimes they'd work and sometimes not. When they worked it was great. Anyway, there was the most vicious fuckers there. A few years ago, I bumped into this woman at a party and she was the barmaid and she remembered that when it went off, she had these steel grilles to pull down because of the bottles flying around. It was a violent era. Football aggro was beginning and it was a very violent time. People were dropping pills, buzzing and getting pissed and anything could set it off."

Jacky Abramovitch (London): "We started getting into Skinhead in 1968, when we were still at school. We didn't go too far from the area, which was East Ham, Manor Park. I mean we go into town for shopping, but not socialising. Latterly there was a big gang called the 'Manor Park' and they were a bit scary. Loads of people coming from everywhere. The leaders were really good-looking boys. They would just fight. It would kick off if you were around that. There were some girls around them, but were just on the fringes of it. It would be Skinhead against Skinhead. It was just like the postcode wars now. People did have knives back then, but they didn't seem to use them like now. It was turf war. If it was anything to do with supplying drugs, well, we really had no idea. I'm totally unaware of that. It was just, 'You're not welcome here, get back on your own…'"

Geoff Deane (London): "I remember a club called the Lorraine Club at the Royal Forest Hotel which was an old Mod thing, and I was on the bus going there and then it got fucking fire-bombed, by the mob from Debden. A Molotov cocktail on the fucking bus! I've never seen anything like it in my life."

Steve Ellison (London): "Skinheads being Skinheads, they didn't mix together that well. I remember going to Southend, the Kursaal, and they'd be running across the Kursaal at each other. They were either Tottenham, West Ham, Chelsea… and they've got all the gear on, and you couldn't really tell who was who, but they knew! It was Skinheads against Skinheads. It wasn't just Skinheads who hated the world. They hated each other too! It was crazy. A very violent time really."

Raymond Potter (London): "There was fighting all the time around here. Even when we were 14 there was a little firm from Streatham called the Lacey Brothers, they came down in cars, armed with shooters. But that soon got sorted out. There was obviously territorial fighting, even with other Skinheads. A lot of the east Londoners moved over to an estate called Ramshaw which was on the Purley Way. A load of them come over our place, the Wadham Club, and it kicked off big time. So, we got a firm together made up of Norwood TOL [Terror Of London], Bang'ole, Leyton Street, Wadham, so we were about a 150-handed. We went over their way to a pub called the Merry-Go-Round and we literally blitzed it. The Old Bill had marched us up the Purley Way and made us sit on the green at the top to try to stop us but they failed. At first you run with the pack, but then you see blokes get their head bust open for nothing. In the end I pulled out of it because it got too nasty, too bloody nasty. Everywhere you went, it was all over football, who you supported and who you didn't support. In our area, there was no racism whatsoever that I noticed. There were a couple of little families who were black, sweet as a nut. Never any problem whatsoever. There was a load of black Skinheads with our mob and they were all top dollar. No animosity, we were side by side, shit or bust. Any rows they'd be there, hundred miles an hour. I remember when we were younger, we'd cut ourselves and join blood. Honest to God, that's how we used to be. Everybody over Wadham had that, girls an' all. That was the sign from where we come from, that was our mark."

Clive Banks (London): "No real violence that I saw. Just young men rutting like young men do. I'm convinced the more the press concentrates on those things, the more copycat it becomes. The Mods and Rockers thing in Brighton was like that. If they had not mentioned it the first time, it would have died down."

Andrew Vaughan (Orrell): "Ah, Slater's Menswear, our shop – our wardrobe for our shenanigans. Looking for love or looking for a fight and finding neither. But we tried. There was never any trouble at the under-18 discos, but every so often though, we'd all be in the Higher End Club when someone would announce that the Dammers were waiting for us on Billinge Hill and we'd all leave the club and yomp up to Billinge Hill to do battle. The Dammers were from the Carr Mill Dam Estate in St Helens and were apparently all Greasers – something us Skins and Suedes detested. I say apparently because of course they were never there.

"We also, on a couple of occasions, walked all the way to Windy Harbour – a couple of miles away – to meet up with Ashton, who of course never turned up. I doubt if there was ever any chance it was going to go off and it's strange that all these fights were about to take place during the summer months and never in the depths of winter. However, to a

> "It was Skinheads against Skinheads. It wasn't just Skinheads who hated the world. They hated each other too! It was crazy. A very violent time really."
>
> STEVE ELLISON

WORK CLOBBER ETHIC, JANUARY 1971

MICK COLVIN AND PHILLIP ELLISDON, BUTLINS, CLACTON, 1968

> "We used to go to the Tottenham Royal and that was the first place I saw real racial fights. Even though there weren't that many black guys there really, and they had the short hair anyway and would be dressed up really sharp. But it would always kick off at some point… I never got involved in any of that. Nah. I was a lover not a fighter. I wasn't even a fucking lover… As I said earlier, it was violent all over."
>
> BARRY CAIN

young teen, it was quite an experience to be with all these older (16-plus) lads walking down the street. In our Rupert trousers, Fair Isle crew necks and Norwegian basketweaves."

Ray Butters (Whitley Bay): "It's funny, we'd use all sorts of weapons: ashtrays, stools and stuff like that, but there were very few bladed weapons in those days. Some people carried them but rarely used them. Looking back now, I'd say it was an act of bravado in many cases, but there was always some nutter who had a reputation. You'd often hear rumours that such and such went to the match with, say, a sickle. But it was probably bullshit, more often than not, you'd never even heard of these people. A group of you might give somebody a good kicking, but usually once somebody was laying on their side with their head covered, you'd run off, and leave them to pick themselves up. We would never think of kicking them in the head or anything like that. It was kind of unsporting."

Tony Haddow (London): "There was a metal aluminium comb with a handle that people would take into engineering or plumbing college, and sharpen them, but I never heard of one person getting stabbed with one of them combs. In a lesson you may mess about manufacturing something maybe, just for a laugh. I don't think anybody used them. The fights were always flashpoints really. Two groups coming together, usually because you were on somebody else's manor. Nobody seemed to get hurt, maybe a split lip here or there, but it was never gratuitous. We went out to have a good time, we never went out for a fight."

Barry Cain (London): "We used to go to the Tottenham Royal and that was the first place I saw real racial fights. Even though there weren't that many black guys there really, and they had the short hair anyway and would be dressed up really sharp. But it would always kick off at some point. This is 1968 going into '69. I never got involved in any of that. Nah. I was a lover not a fighter. I wasn't even a fucking lover… As I said earlier, it was violent all over. At the Manor House, we were leaving, going down the stairs, out to the Seven Sisters Road, and as I'm walking down, there are all these guys standing there, short hair and looking very handy standing there with cut-throat razors. One on every step. So, I'm walking down and get to the bottom and then know they are not after me. I heard outside, that someone tried to pull one of their birds or something. Anyway, the next thing this guy has come running down the stairs and leapt over them all. He goes running out in the street and they all go after him, only he manages to get on a bus and it pulls away into the night. Then another guy in their party tries to do the same

thing, only he gets out and there are no buses. He turns right and they all chase after him. Forty guys. I'm standing outside with my mates and all of a sudden, these guys have come back carrying milk crates and clubs. We've walked round and there was a small group of people standing round this guy who is on his back in the gutter and he didn't look too bad, and we're thinking that he's had a result. Anyway, an ambulance comes along as someone had called one. As they bent down to pick him up, his brains fell out the back of his head. Fucking hell. I looked at my mate and he's passed out. Blood running everywhere. And that was a lesson I learned at only 15/16, you learned something there that you'd never get involved in any of that, because you could end up fucking dead. It made the *Daily Express* on the Monday. They all got nicked years later but whenever someone tried to give evidence, they'd all start singing 'Should auld acquaintance be forgot' in the dock… so no one would give evidence. They still got done though."

Mauro Antoniazzi (Birmingham): "There was fifteen of us riding to Stratford-upon-Avon one day and on that day, I had chosen to wear a mate's World War Two German helmet. When we saw a load of greasy bikers travelling in the opposite direction, of course, we all jeered at them and gave them the two-finger salute! Next thing I saw them coming up behind me in all my mirrors and I was at the rear of our line. Next minute a Triumph was alongside me with a rider and passenger both kicking out at me with their boots. I braked hard and got behind him then accelerated past him on the right. As his passenger spun around in my direction the rider accelerated and his mate on the pillion fell off into the road.

"We all pulled up and put our scooters on the stands or just laid them on the side on the crash bars and there was a big punch-up in the middle of the road. None of my mates were soft and the bikers were soon left battered and bruised! Soon after, the coppers arrived and we explained that we had stopped to help the pillion passenger that had fallen off the motorbike! We got away with it and carried on our way."

Tony Haddow (London): "I certainly won't say that there were never any fights. I remember though being at Liverpool Street station, and walking up the stairs with a mate, and a load of blokes started walking down the stairs, and they took exception to us for some unknown reason. We didn't know each other, but they suddenly rushed us. We really had to put up resistance because they were coming down at us and had us at a right disadvantage. Things like that, flashpoints used to happen here, there and everywhere, but not in the clubs that I remember. The Lyceum, we never had any trouble there, for sure. The Lyceum Ballroom was right at the beginning of it, probably '68. I expect the Tottenham Royal was as well. The Lyceum was different though, you got a lot of soul music, and a lot of Tamla. Again, it was Mods morphing into Skins really."

Barry Cain (London): "Thinking back, we were 16. A big year in your life. We'd go everywhere. We'd go to Kew Bridge, the Boat House, a big dancehall, back in 1968. We found out about them through word of mouth. I remember going there and we were walking over Kew Bridge. There were five of us, but we'd lost three of 'em. Then someone jumped on me from behind, so I shrugged him and run. My mate went one way and me the other. Anyway, I've come to a bus stop. Bear in mind I have no idea what it's about. So, I'm at this bus stop and there are a few people about and I thought, I ain't going to run no more. I mean this is not long after the guy getting his brains kicked out. I'm standing there and suddenly these guys have come over and gone something about my mate. One of our mob was a nuisance, so he's obviously done something and dropped us all in the shit. One guy slapped me in the face, but I'm sweet talking and getting away with it, when suddenly this guy comes over, a proper Skin with proper braces and he's going, 'Let's have him!' Suddenly this bus pulls up, and quick as you like I jump on and do a Seven Sisters Road job and get away. I'm sitting there as it pulls away giving it 'You wankers' and that and praying the bus didn't stop as they all started running at the bus. The following week, we went back twenty-handed, all tooled up. But we didn't find them."

Bob Wheeler (Slough): "We all used a club called ZigZags attached to a pub in the Farnham Road. One night some of the girls met a load of Skinhead lads from Burnt Oak in London. They came down and it all went off. They all had cut-throat razors, every one of them pulled them out. There was an 'ell of a do and a fella called Louis got slashed right across the stomach. It was an open wound, and the only thing that saved him was that he was fat, so it didn't penetrate his organs. We went out and chased them, and the fight went on all the way up the Farnham Road to the Three Tuns Bridge. The police eventually blocked off the road."

Tony Haddow (London): "Kevin Rowland was a bit of a localish boy, and he was always about. But me being from Edgware and his lot from Burnt Oak, there was a lot of friction between the areas, even though it was just one stop on the Underground. It was ridiculous, and my gran lived in Burnt Oak as well, so I used to have to dodge the Burnt Oak boys just to go and visit my gran. I remember that I had a bit of a tear-up one time, and I can't remember how, but I bumped into him and he seemed to know that it had just happened. As he was talking to me he asked me why I was wearing a donkey jacket. As a wisecrack, I just said that it was a 'poor man's sheepskin'. It was strange to see him a few years later on television with his band Dexys [Dexys Midnight Runners], and they were all wearing donkey jackets. Basically though, it was my working jacket, and I usually wore a T-shirt under it, but sometimes a Sherman and a pair of Sta-Prest or some rolled-up jeans and a pair of boots. It was yer working clobber really. I saw him at the Watford Top Rank – we used to go up there a lot. That's where a lot of trouble started happening. I was friends with a lot of guys in Kilburn, Wealdstone, Neasden and all around there. They used to come in en masse on trains straight into Watford. They were a bit of trouble, that lot, but I always got on alright with them. Kevin was there at a Geno Washington gig, and it turned out he was a massive fan. Yeah, he was about, but he's a bit younger than me."

Bernard Jennings (Ruislip): "I remember there was a big crew from south London that called themselves the Ordinary Boys. Because they couldn't afford Squire shop shoes, they didn't wear them but they were aggressive because they wore fairly ordinary clothes. They chased off people who were dressed like us. Thinking back, it may just have been us who called them the Ordinary Boys, but you knew who to steer clear of. In our area the ones to fear were from West Drayton. There was a family there of brothers, there was four of them, all born within a year of each other. They were the hardcore of quite a big group, and you always avoided them. We used to go on holidays to Newquay, which would be around '68 or '69. Everything was quiet for the first week, then on the second week this big mob from West Drayton turned up, and the place was a riot with running battles up and down the streets. That was because West Drayton had arrived. I wasn't really aware of any sort of gang warfare going on but there was always the rivalry between areas. You knew where people came from roughly. I remember going to see Stevie Wonder at Billy Walker's Upper Cut Club in Forest Gate. He did his usual routine of falling off the stage but then he fell off the stage in every performance because it got the girls going. But you realised when you went to that sort of place you were mixing with people from all over London. There was a lot of healthy respect for a lot of those East London guys around there. You didn't go out and dance very much, you stood around and watched.

"Our mob didn't really venture very far normally. If we were going to venture out, we'd go to the Richmond area because we'd probably be there on a Saturday to go to the Ivy shop and there were one or two venues there. Then there was the Watford Top Rank, which was a more 'souly' type place, everybody suited and booted but it didn't stop the fights breaking out. I always found that on a Friday night when people went out earlier in their jeans, it was more relaxed and there was less bother. Go out on a Saturday when everyone is smart and there's probably trouble. I suspect it was just because people drank more. In those days we didn't have a huge amount of money. You went out with ten shillings in your pocket and you knew exactly what that would buy. That might buy you three pints but you had to keep enough money for your fare home. I never smoked and I never took drugs, so that wasn't an outlay I had to worry about."

Bank holiday weekends

TONY ELLIS AND GANG, MARGATE, EASTER 1969

Tony Ellis (London): "I was a bit too young to be involved in the early beach skirmishes but a friend of mine, a few years older than me, said that he'd heard on the local grapevine that there was a battle going to take place at the coast that weekend. Sure enough, it happened. By the time we went a

"Flashpoints used to happen here, there and everywhere, but not in the clubs that I remember. The Lyceum, we never had any trouble there, for sure. The Lyceum Ballroom was right at the beginning of it, probably '68. I expect the Tottenham Royal was as well. The Lyceum was different though, you got a lot of soul music, and a lot of Tamla. Again, it was Mods morphing into Skins really."
TONY HADDOW

BRIGHTON. JULY 1967
INSET: TONY ELLIS AND FRIENDS, MARGATE, EASTER 1969

JOHN AND JANICE, BRIGHTON, JULY 1967

COOLED DRAUGHT BEER
OUR SPECIALITY
THE BEST IN BRIGHTON

Moss Bros

46 47 EAST STREET BRIGHTON

House Hunting?

This hasn't been
Richard's lucky year

FRISKED FOR WEAPONS, AUGUST 1970

These boots are made for socce

FANS going to Saturday's Second Division match at Oxford, where Watford are playing, could find themselves being barred from the United's Manor Ground.

Supporters wearing hobnailed boots, simil... in th...

spread rapidly from train-wrecking to terrace-fighting.

The boots pictured have steel toe caps and metal studs on the soles. Soccer fans who fancy this ty... ...ootwear ...ut nails ...e soles ...more

...retary ...police

them off an... leave and g... wear."

Watford ...litt said: "... it necessary... unsuitable ... age Road."

But he v... spot this ty... police will ...

At Watfo...

Nobbled by their braces

By ROGER MANN

SEASIDE police took most of the sting out of skinhead trouble-makers yesterday – by confiscating their braces.

Police at Southend-on-Sea also took away their belts, and the laces from their 'bovver' boots.

A policeman said: 'We figured they couldn't cause too much "bovver" if they had to concentrate on holding up their trousers and keeping on their boots.'

The police acted when more than 1,500 skinheads converged on the resort from London.

Even so, the police had a busy day. There were scuffles in every amusement arcade along the front, and by the end of the day 50 youths were arrested. Charges include assaults on the police and damage to property.

Woolworth's in Southend High Street closed five hours early after skinheads clutching their trousers rampaged through the store for replacement braces, belts and boot laces.

Shopkeepers had been asked not to sell these goods to skinheads, who then thronged Woolworth's helping themselves to string or anything that would hold up trousers.

Damage

A Woolworth's official said: 'It got nasty when staff tried to stop them. They made for the hardware counter and grabbed hammers and knives. The police came along and the skinheads left. Then it was decided to close at midday and let everyone go home.'

Trouble began in Southend when trains ...skinheads... were met by police. ...railway authorities. ...d seats

Skink...

The pict... that str...

BRIGHTON, Easter Ba... day, 1970. A group of s... traps a man behind a... car. They attack him w... and fists. The man h... them no harm. He wa... walking in the street w... arrived. He is a victim... many others in this ye... law and order is a topi... —of unprovoked aggress...

222

n't —!

...r in socks or ...rnative foot-

...ry Ron Rol- ...ve not found ... anyone for ...ar at Vicar-

..."If we do ...footwear the ...d to act." ...ome match

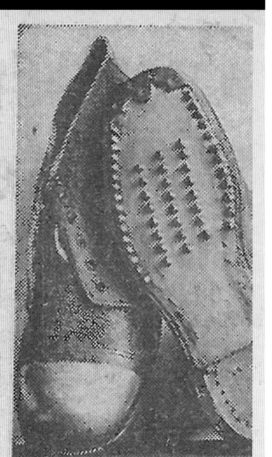

Sept. 1969

Here come the skinheads

IN BRACES, JEANS AND ARMY BOOTS

by Desmond Zwar

HE HAS close-cropped hair, wears jeans suspended two and a half inches above his heavy ex-Army boots, and has his braces on outside a sleeveless pullover.

He is known as a skinhead.

'Our gang turned nasty,' growled one commentator who has seen them in action. 'Comic-paper caricatures no longer funny.'

Skinheads are the latest worry for the police—and for the Rockers and Hippies ('Hairies'), which the skinheads hate.

Chris Hollands, 16, is a skinhead. 'Or "cronhead" on peanut'—a sneering description of the cult directed more at their rattling motor-scooters ('peanuts in a tin') than at their shaven heads.

He lives with his mother and 13-year-old sister near Brighton, will study for O-levels next year and wants to be an actor in the style of Steve McQueen.

NO Flaring

A skinhead is an evolution of the Mod with overtones of the original 'Ted.' His cropped hair ('half of grade one' on the barber's clipper-setting) is an outward and visible sign of his hatred for the Hippie and the Rocker, 'long-haired Greasers in leather jackets and leather pants who love motorbikes.'

Skinheads, dressing to dance to their 'soul,' favour neatness: tailored jackets with an 18-inch split up the back, rounded corners and trousers the same width all the way down; flaring is frowned on.

Their shirts are button-down collared with a button at the back, of heavy cotton and a fine stripe; they are generally from one particular maker who is growing rich with the craze.

At the dance-halls the skinhead is almost aggressively Mod-neat. Only when he is on the way to an 'agro' (aggravation) does he change to the Huckleberry Finn braces, jeans and heavy, sometimes steel-toed boots.

Munching a pizza in an Italian restaurant, Chris explained: 'It's the boredom really. We go down and have a fight and it relieves the monotony.'

THE Greasers

'Last Easter Bank Holiday there were 280 skinheads down at Brighton and we charged this mob of Greasers down on the beach. The holidaymakers ran scattered.

'On the way home in the train eight Greasers came up to three of us sitting in a compartment. One of my mates tipped them and before I knew what was going on the other one was down on the floor getting the boot in my head... first I thought the best thing I do is let the other kettle hit me first. When I boot him in

the face with my forehead, which can break his nose.

'When the chap you're fighting hits the ground you ask him if he wants to carry on. If he does, you kick him in the head. I've heard about not hitting a bloke when he's down, but it's the survival of the fittest, really.

'Girls hang around with the skinheads, they have very short hair, a little longer at the back. I don't like scrubbers, you know—you go up and kiss them and they're yours to do what you want with.'

Richard Mills, 16, a trainee librarian, spent two hours polishing his weighty ex-commando boots on his day off yesterday. Cherry Blossom, spit, a rag and a toothbrush. They cost him 45s. at an army surplus store.

A skinhead, he explained, fingering his thin red braces, is against long-hair, pop, Hippie sit-ins, love-ins and the long-haired cult of non-

violence. 'They are against fighting and you are for it,' he said. 'We are just more manly than they are.'

The disturbing-looking gang of Hell's Angels in German helmets and iron crosses supervising the security of the Rolling Stones' free Hyde Park concert were 'there mainly to keep the skinheads under control, said Richard.

At the Isle of Wight festival the worry was that the skinheads might cause trouble. But they were heavily outnumbered.

'What are we for?' asked Chris Hollands. 'Nothing really. We're just a group of blokes. We're not for anything.'

Skinheads are with us claim hippies

Evening News Reporter

THE ENDELL Street hippies who have pledged themselves to fight for their new home claimed today to have had a meeting with 30 skinhead leaders.

The hippies said their governing council met the skinheads in the disused school they have taken over at Holborn. They claimed: "The skinheads were very sympathetic towards us."

A girl calling herself Denise, who said she has been appointed spokesman for the Endell Street Commune, said the commune would not use violence unless the police tried to force them out... "then we shall use everything we have."

She said the skinheads were interested in taking part in a joint movement of hippies, beats and others against society generally.

Denise, who wears a London School of Economics scarf, refused to answer questions about herself or the eight-man committee she says run the commune. But it is understood that she and at least one other member of the committee were active during the Paris student riots.

...ead attack

...e that shows the violen...
...s at the innocent today

...ne there was someone to ...n record.

...picture was taken by ...Mail photographer Bill ...This is his report of the ...:

...s in Pavilion Gardens, 200 ...om the front, when I saw ...200 skinheads running ...the street shouting ...slogans. They started

off in a sort of jog-trot which became faster and faster. As they increased speed they shouted louder. It was mass hysteria. Two men aged between 20 and 25 were walking through the gardens as the mob ran forward. They were just ordinary chaps, not wearing leather jackets or anything like that. About seven or eight of the

leading skinheads started kicking at them. The two men held out their arms trying to reason with the skinheads who were shouting at the top of their voices. The skinheads took no notice. One of the attacked men ran out of my camera frame and was chased by two skinheads. The rest set about the other chap as he tried to escape behind

a parked car. They kicked and punched him and then ran to catch up the main body. The skinheads broke windows of shops and overturned tables outside restaurants. They held their arms in the air like victorious gladiators. I couldn't help feeling a bit sick watching parents grabbing their children from the gang's path.'

> "One bank holiday loads from Watford went down to Margate. We'd just got down there and went into a pub called the Bali Hai. As soon as we walked in there somebody said something like 'Watford wankers', one of our guys smacked somebody, and that was it, we got chased out of the town. We'd only been there about an hour, and that was it. We had to get back in the car and clear off."
>
> PHILLIP ELLISDON

couple of years later, there would still have been a bit of aggro, but most of it was staged runs across the beach, and maybe finding the occasional Greaser. There's some photos of us in Brighton and me and my mate are wearing this Greaser's hat. We rolled him for it by squirting him with a water pistol and nicking his hat. In the norm though it was just big gatherings and the occasional charges around Dreamland. It seemed to be more staged or put-up jobs than actual bundles. We'd go to Brighton on scooters, but Margate was too far by scooter as somebody nearly always seemed to break down or get killed on the way home. It was always a train to Margate. There were still hundreds of people there but we never went to clubs or anything, it was just hanging around. In the photos we have got short hair and boots but this was going on years before the Skinheads came along. The type of Mods that we were was just part of that evolution. It wasn't like we all just got it cropped one day. The look just evolved. They either went off on the long hair or the short hair route. Our lot went short hair to begin with. We wore commando boots with screw-on soles, and steel toe-caps possibly. Small turn-ups on jeans and the braces that pulled them up short. It wasn't just about copying the Jamaicans with their short trousers. A lot of kids worked on muddy building sites and were labourers, they already had the boots, so they rolled their trousers up rather than have proper turn-ups. I think that kind of gets overlooked."

Phillip Ellisdon (Watford): "When we were going to Butlins one year, there was twelve of us going when one of our blokes pulled out and we had a spare space, and this guy's cousin wanted to come. He wasn't really one of us but filled a gap. Anyway, in those days you used to send your cases to the holiday camp before you got there and then go by train. When you got to the Underground you used to put your hankie out of your top pocket on the handrail, sit on it and slide down it. This guy hadn't put his hankie down, he got down to the bottom of the steps and he'd got this big black stripe up the arse of his Sta-Prest."

Ian Hingle (London): "I remember going down to Margate in the late sixties, '67/'68 or something, and seeing this group of twenty guys all wearing different coloured Harringtons. One guy had his inside out, but the rest were in this great range of colours, all different. Now I reckon they were Sky Jump, because not many were wearing Baracuta back then. There was yellow, pale green, pale blue, bottle green, and I remember thinking, wow, that looks good.

"So gradually I stopped hanging around with them, and I started to get into an American style, a sort of CIA look, though I wasn't conscious of that name then. I used to watch TV programmes like *Bewitched* and I used to love the way that Darrin used to dress, alpaca sweaters and going a bit Ivy League. So, I started to go to Austin's in Shaftesbury Avenue when I was still at school. I used to spend all my money there. I stayed on at school till I was 18 and did A-Levels, but I'd get the money somehow. I used to sell stuff like old toys, clothes and I had a Saturday job, and I'd borrow money off my brother. I had an Austin's suit, which was my pride and joy and I still don't really know what happened to it."

Phillip Ellisdon (Watford): "We all went to Brighton one year. I was 17, just got my driving licence. Some of my mates did not

have scooters and wanted to go to Brighton for the bank holiday. I was a panel beater in them days and people kept giving me their old cars that they could not afford to repair – I had two stuck at the back of our house and one in the car park at work.

"We decided we would take one of the cars to Brighton, but the one we wanted was not taxed and I was on L-plates, so I took a tax disc of a Ford Anglia my uncle gave me and stuck it in the screen of the Vauxhall we was taking. Five of us piled in and set off behind the scooters. When we got there we teamed up with the others and it was not long into the night before a fight broke out and the police started moving everyone on. Every time we tried to park, the police stopped us. We ended up driving down this dark lane, under a bridge onto what seemed like a car park, a result, so we all slept in the car that night.

"We were woken in the morning by aeroplanes taking off. Unbeknown to us, we had parked on the end of the Shoreham airfield runway. Just as we worked out where we were the Old Bill pulled up in front of us and got us all out of the car, searched us and the car. They found the tax disc for the Ford and I was arrested. I had to come back to Brighton to go to court for the offence and was in court with all the others that had been arrested for fighting and other offences. When I got called up for 'fraudulent use of a road tax licence', there was lots of cheers and laughter, embarrassing!"

Jacky Abramovitch (London): "We used to go on trips to Southend in 1968/'69 and we'd follow along all the boys, get on the train at Barking, and when we got off, it was just a sea of Skinheads and Mods."

Bill Fordham (London): "When I went to Margate, you took your bag, and you put it in the left luggage at the station. So, you'd be in your day clothes of boots and jeans. Then at night you'd get changed, and go to Dreamland or the ballrooms. Then you'd try to get to sleep on one of the trains in the sidings at Margate station. There was no trouble there, all the Rockers had long gone. I knew loads of people there, and I remember people drinking phials of methadone poured into orange juice."

Phillip Ellisdon (Watford): "One bank holiday loads from Watford went down to Margate. We'd just got down there and went into a pub called the Bali Hai. As soon as we walked in there somebody said something like 'Watford wankers', one of our guys smacked somebody, and that was it, we got chased out of the town. We'd only been there about an hour, and that was it. We had to get back in the car and clear off."

Michael Holland (London): "The bank holiday fighting at the seaside was also a feature that had carried on from the Mods and Rockers and we wanted to go down there and be part of a bigger Skinhead gang, but being 13 to 14, there was no chance our mums would let us go on the bank holiday. So, a few of us went down to Southend one day in the week during the summer holiday and bowled along the front trying to look hard! Obviously, we were completely ignored. As long as we were home for tea, our parents didn't know."

Phillip Ellisdon (Watford): "There was about twelve of us who went to Butlin's. There were loads of other Skinheads, boys and girls who went there in those days, they came from all over the place but we all got on well. They used to have these dance competitions, and this one was run by the Trojan Records company. Everybody was in on it, there must have been fifty or sixty people in it, but in those days, I was a bit of a dancer, and I won it. I won a lifetime membership to the Trojan Appreciation Society, a big gold Trojan medallion and a certificate. When I came back, I had this guy who worked with me, an up-and-coming proper Skinhead, and after a couple of months I gave it all to him to hang on his wall. I also got entered into a final of the contest that was going to happen somewhere, but I didn't bother going to it."

Paul Weller (Woking): "I'd go down to Selsey on the south coast with my family – there was a caravan site we stayed on and a social club we'd go to in the evenings. There were quite a few kids from London there with much longer hair (like shoulder length), one with a pork pie trilby, so I started growing my hair but not really in any style as such, just long and lank, this was pre-feather cut for guys."

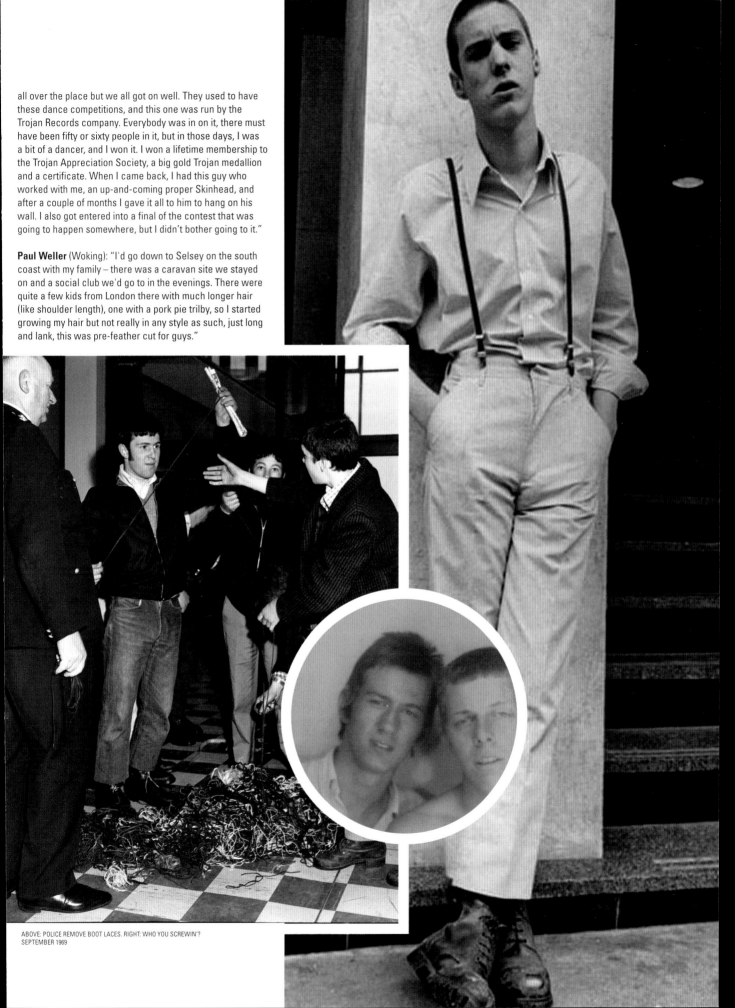

ABOVE: POLICE REMOVE BOOT LACES. RIGHT: WHO YOU SCREWIN'?
SEPTEMBER 1969

Monday March 30th was a damp drizzly affair. While police in London's East End sealed off a caravan site after a tip-off that train robber Ronnie Biggs had been spotted there, the Easter bank holiday still attracted people to the coast. Southend in Essex was no exception, as many people, including Skinheads, descended on the town. This time, though, police had introduced new tactics to uphold the law, as they decided to confiscate shoelaces, belts and braces. This left many people seeking out shops selling string so they could keep their boots on. A police spokesman was quoted as saying, "They wouldn't be much use if they had to fight holding their trousers up. It is more or less the equivalent of debagging them." The youths were met at the train station by welcome posses as soon as they arrived. The officers also built up an impressive armoury of weapons, including iron bars, steel combs, knives and razors.

However, there was trouble during the day as forty-six arrests were made, including charges of assault on police, damaging property and breach of the peace. At the end of the day, long queues formed outside the police headquarters as youths came to collect their belongings. Chief Superintendent Frederick Bonfield said, "Those who tried to terrorise holiday-makers were soon dispersed. I'm extremely happy with the result."

There was also trouble at the seafront in Great Yarmouth in Norfolk, Rhyl in North Wales and Weston-Super-Mare in Somerset. Meanwhile, in Skegness, Lincolnshire, where the Young Liberals were holding their conference, Skinheads were offered biscuits by them in a successful peacemaking effort.

'SKINHEADS HIT A BIT OF BOVVER' screamed the headline of the *Daily Mirror* the day after the spring bank holiday at the end of May. As temperatures hit a warm 69 degrees Fahrenheit (about 20 degrees Celsius), the heat got to some, as many Skinheads met with a line of police at the train station in Southend once again. The youngsters were then lectured about their behaviour, and told to either behave or go home. Many had gone there to claim revenge for their treatment on Easter Monday but were again prevented from causing serious damage.

One incident that made the *Daily Sketch* under the headline 'Hot And Bovvered' told of an off-duty police officer trying to stop a 16-year-old stealing a stick of rock from a Southend seafront shop. Twenty-four-year-old PC Robert Craven had apparently apprehended the youth but was attacked by eight other Skinhead youths. Other police arrived, and the thief was later charged with stealing a stick of rock. Later a train was held up at the nearby Southend Central station and youths were ordered off the train so that the PC could identify his eight attackers.

Meanwhile in Brighton, a train arrived carrying more than a hundred Skinheads who had boarded the train at Redhill, Surrey. They had been seen by British Rail staff and reported to police in Brighton, who had twenty officers with dogs waiting for them. Officers entered the train carriages to find broken bulbs and damaged toilets. They wasted no time in ordering the offenders back onto the train, and under police escort, sent them home less than ten minutes after they had arrived.

There was also trouble involving 400 Skinheads at Skegness in May, with forty-two arrests. Nineteen youths were fined a total of over £200 at a special court, for offences that included theft, violence and disorderly behaviour. One was sent to a detention centre.

Bob Wheeler (Slough): "We used to go away to all these seaside places. You might go to Margate with all the Chelsea mob or Southend with West Ham. I remember West Ham fighting with the Hells Angels at the Kursaal and they were waiting for a load to come down from somewhere else who were called the Blue Angels. There was a really tall fella called Mervin who was about six foot six and West Ham. He'd get about fifteen hundred people following him up the road, all singing 'Mervin is our leader!' all along the Southend front. Then after the fights, they'd all pile back on the train to London around five o'clock. We used to have coaches going from Slough, but once at Southend I was with a lot from the hostel; Ricky was with us, and he was West Ham. We had all the sheepskins on with Chelsea scarves, waiting for the train to pull in from London. When it did, there were about twelve hundred West Ham coming off, so we quickly tucked our scarves underneath our sheepskins and joined them, basically. We made the news once on the telly after fighting with some Hells Angels and smashing up a café."

Tony Haddow (London): "I remember going up to Watford, nobody bought a ticket or paid at the other end. It was like absolute chaos on the train, and we took it over, until we got off for the Top Rank in Watford. We did Margate, Bournemouth and Southend, every bank holiday sleeping under deckchairs on the beach and up in the tropical gardens. There was always trouble everywhere because a crowd of people just attracted trouble. Just like the football crowds, we would get pushed around by the police. It was the same if we went to Brighton, everybody turning up on a bank holiday, and the police decide it's 'clip round the earhole' time. You didn't want to be pushed around, and then people reacted against it. It actually affected people having their weekend break. It sort of ruined it for us, and ruined it for them. It was a new thing, other than the Mods and Rockers, but the police just thought, 'Here we go again', and would ferry us about. People started knocking coppers' helmets off and things like that, which was just high jinks. We didn't even see it as a continuation of the Mods and Rockers thing. It was just a day out at the coast, but people would be coming in from everywhere, and you'd recognise someone from south London or Ealing, and you'd start talking, and the crowd just got bigger and bigger. It was never an arranged thing where we were gonna meet up and cause trouble."

HOLIDAY SNAP, 1970
INSET: READING TOP R

WATFORD AND HARROW SKINHEADS, BUTLINS, CLACTON, 1968

THE RAMJAM CLUB

BRIXTON,   S.W.9   REDpost 3295

SAT, 5th Late Night Session 7.30 p.m. - 3.30 a.m.	**O'HARO'S PLAYBOYS** plus **MAD MOVIES**	7/6 After 9 pm 10/—
SUN, 6th 7.30-11.30	**THE GASS**	5/—

~~~~~~

SAT. 12th Late Night Session 7.30 p.m. - 3.30 a.m.	**THE FERRIS WHEEL** plus **MAD MOVIES**	7/6 After 9 pm 10/—
SUN. 13th 7.30-11.30	**RIK N'BECKERS**	5/—

~~~~~~

SAT. 19th Late Night Session 7.30 p.m. - 3.30 a.m.	**THE SKATALLITES** plus **MAD MOVIES**	7/6 After 9 pm 10/-
SUN. 20th 7.30-11.30	**SHELL SHOCK SHOW**	5/—

~~~~~~

SAT. 26th Late Night Session 7.30 p.m. - 3.30 a.m.	**GENO WASHINGTON** and **THE RAMJAM BAND** plus **MAD MOVIES**	10/— After 9 pm 12/6
SUN. 27th 7.30-11.30	**THE FERRIS WHEEL**	6/—

EVERY FRIDAY 7.30 — 12	**PARTY NIGHT** PLUS LATE NIGHT MOVIE	5/—
EVERY SUNDAY 3-6	**RAMJAM "HOT 100"**	3/—
EVERY MONDAY 7.30-11	**RAMJAM RECORD SHOW**	3/—

THIS PROGRAMME IS SUBJECT TO ALTERATION

MEMBERSHIP 2/6 EXTRA, VALID UNTIL 31st DECEMBER, 1967

CHAPTER 13 : STOMPING GROUNDS

Alan Daly (London): "I started going to the Ram Jam from late 1966 to middle of 1967. I'm as vague on the exact dates as I am on the postal address but it was along the main road through the centre of Brixton. The entrance was between two shops or stores, just a small door with about twenty steps leading up; you paid about six shillings to get in at the top of the stairs; there was then a refreshment area that sold drinks like Coke, milk and orange juice but no alcohol. There were then steps down to the club itself. The business end of the place had a small stage with a couple of rows of cinema seats in front; behind these was a dance floor. Around the dance floor (on three sides, I think) was a terrace of three carpeted steps. Some of the wall was mirrored.

"I recall queuing on the stairs, waiting to get in to see Martha & The Vandellas. I was at the top of the stairs. A guy making a lot of noise pushed past several people and growled at me as he pulled a chisel out. Before I could blink, the bouncers had picked him up and thrown him down the stairs!

"Martha & The Vandellas were a con as they just mimed. I asked for my money back but eased back on the volume as the bouncers arrived. I went to see Solomon Burke and Lee Dorsey there and they both mimed as well. The best live bands for me were Geno Washington & The Ram Jam Band and a little known and less acclaimed Rupert's Rick 'N' Beckers. I didn't mind blues but wouldn't want to waste money on it so you can imagine my disgust when I mistakenly turned up on

nights that featured John Mayall's Bluesbreakers or The Graham Bond Organisation.

"There were nights when I was the only white boy in there. I went to learn some of the moves danced by the Jamaican lads. The race thing never struck me as an issue until one night when a white girl came over to me and said, 'You're my boyfriend, right?' She was followed by a Jamaican guy built like a middle-weight boxer. Posh white girls went to the Ram Jam trying to be dangerous by dancing with black guys. Occasionally, they would realise too late that the attention was uncomfortable. My man confronted me; my stupid gene made me tell him to fuck off. The place was dimly lit but now it was even darker. I was surrounded by a group of rather large black guys and wondered if I'd ever walk again. A guy tapped me on the shoulder and said, 'We takin' care o' bidness, man. You cool.' With that they carted off the would-be Romeo. It seems my regular solo appearances there got me noticed as an OK fella."

Austin Myers (Shipley): "There was the Seven Seas Café which had a history of youth cults many years before Skinheads. It had seen Teddy Boys, Mods, Skinheads, football hooligans and Suedeheads. It was always a central part of Shipley. Its reputation was notorious and many people remember it locally as the place to go. As small as it was, it was a real focal point for gatherings. We used to get people from outside coming in. They would travel four to five miles to meet and feel a part of it. There were pinball machines and the food was real transport café-type stuff such as cup of tea, cup of coffee, burger, chips, beans on toast, the much-loved chip buttie and those types of things. The Rock-Ola jukebox though was packed with stuff like Creedence Clearwater Revival, a lot of The Who, loads and loads of Motown. Bits of reggae such as Jimmy Cliff's 'Wonderful World, Beautiful People'. It had a bit of everything. When the guy used to come to change over the records, we used to tell him what he needed to bring. It was always more reggae, more soul, more Motown. We wanted the stuff on the Ric-Tic or Atlantic labels, and this guy had never heard of it, but it was in his best interest to get this new music. Three records for a shilling, and that jukebox never stopped."

Tony Rounce (London): "We had some good rock clubs in the area such as the Kursaal in Southend and the Roundhouse in Dagenham. It almost felt to me like Stanford-le-Hope was the epicentre of Skinheadism. You didn't have to go too far. Basildon was a new town, and yet I can't remember seeing Skinheads there until much later on, maybe around the time of 'Double Barrel' being released. It was like it suddenly had a great awakening."

Phillip Ellisdon (Watford): "There were lots of clubs locally. We used to go to the Tithe Farm in Harrow, the Queen of Hearts, the Target in Northolt, they were kind of pub clubs around Edgware and Harrow. When you went into London, there was the Underground Club, the Subway in Golders Green. But we only really went into London to buy our pills such as blues and bombers, then head back home again.

> "My man confronted me; my stupid gene made me tell him to fuck off. The place was dimly lit but now it was even darker. I was surrounded by a group of rather large black guys and wondered if I'd ever walk again. A guy tapped me on the shoulder and said, 'We takin' care o' bidness, man. You cool.' With that they carted off the would-be Romeo. It seems my regular solo appearances there got me noticed as an OK fella."
> ALAN DALY

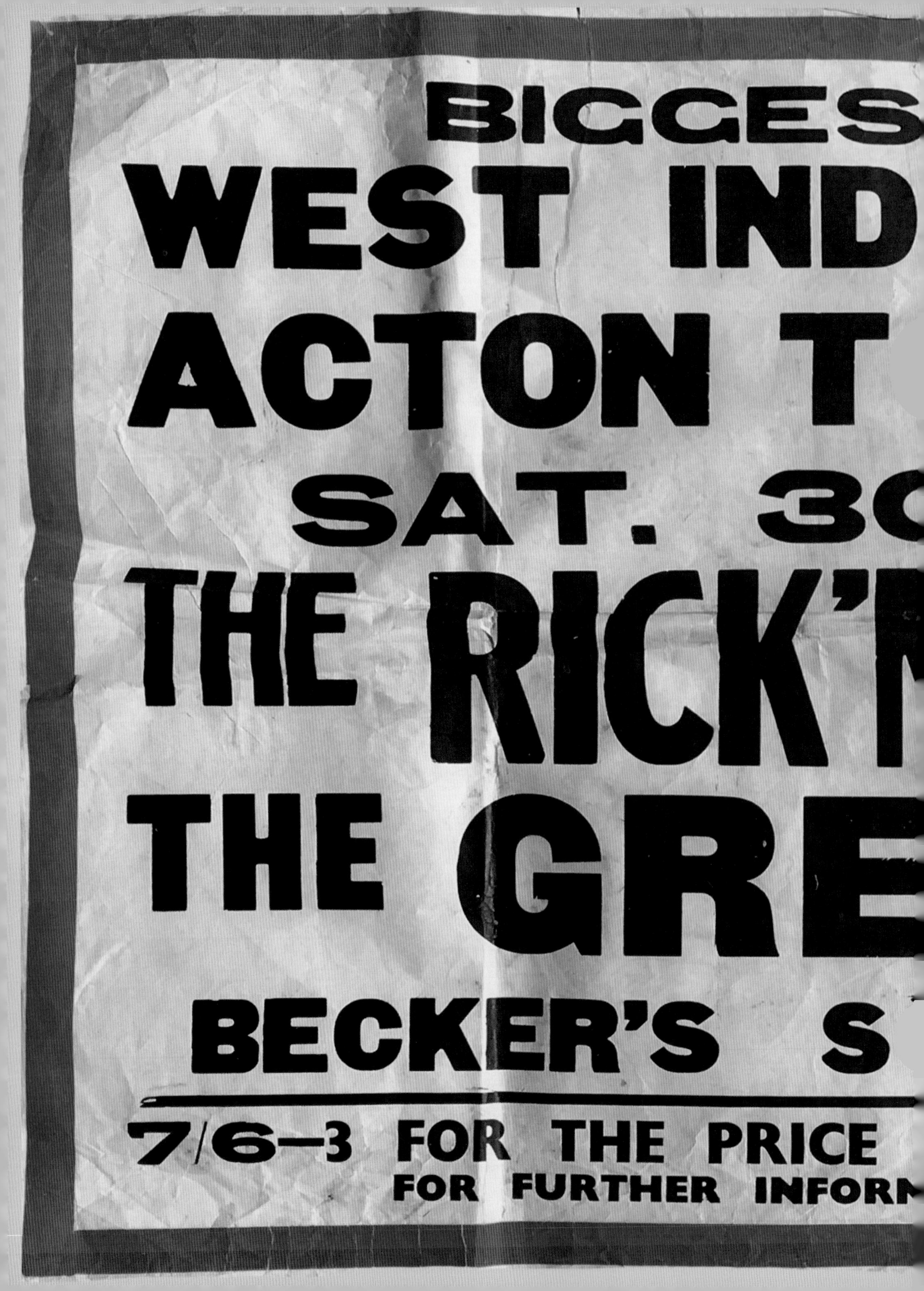

BIGGES

WEST IND

ACTON T

SAT. 30

THE RICK'N

THE GRE

BECKER'S S

7/6-3 FOR THE PRICE

FOR FURTHER INFORM

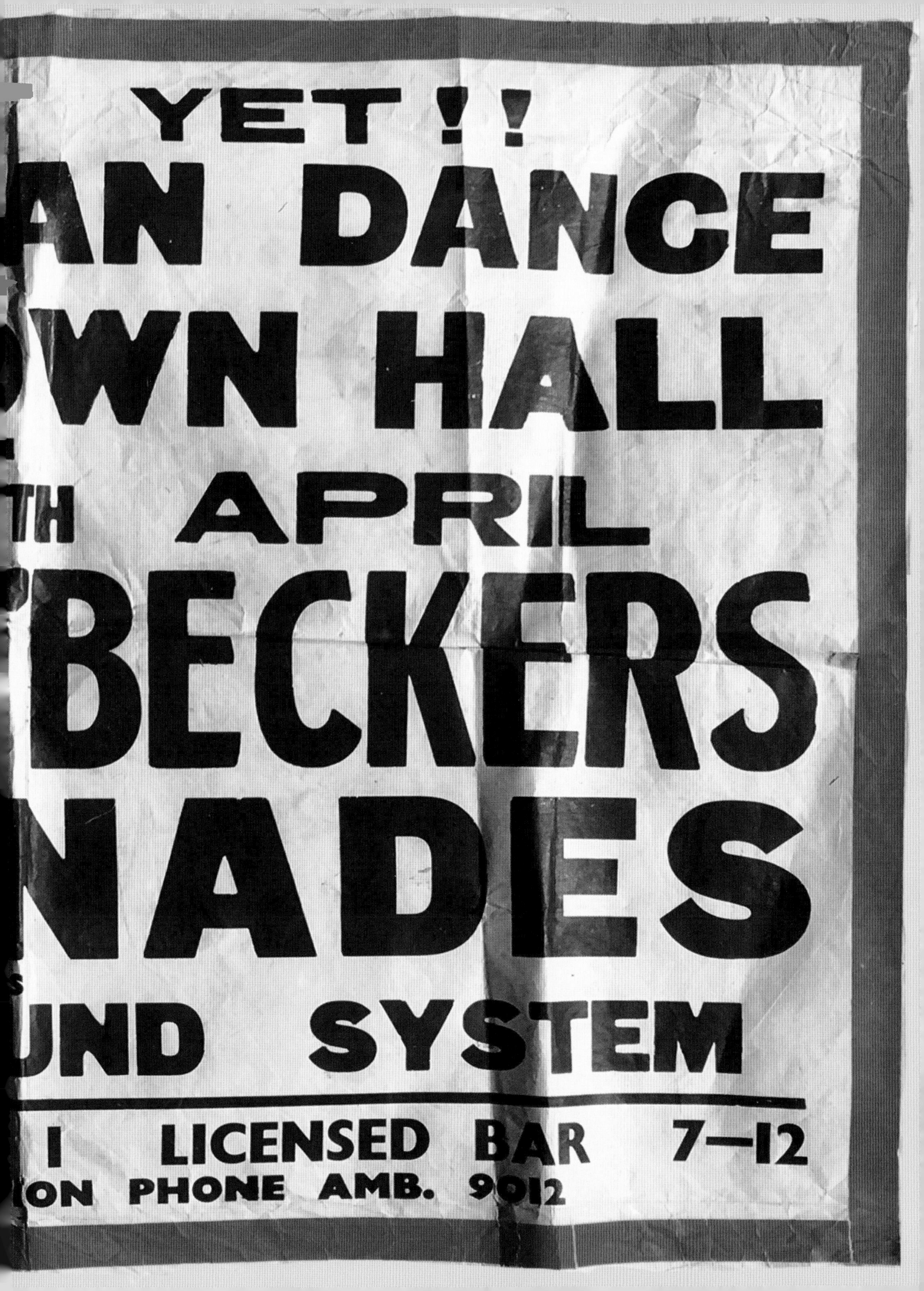

YET!!

AN DANCE

WN HALL

TH APRIL

BECKERS

NADES

UND SYSTEM

I LICENSED BAR 7—12

ON PHONE AMB. 9012

Once I'd won the dance competition, we used to go all over to different clubs and start dancing. You'd soon know that you had upset the locals because you soon started getting beer glasses thrown at you, and things like that."

SAVOY ROOMS CATFORD
HITHER GREEN 8460
DANCING *every* Wed., Fri., Sat. (& Sun. Club Members)
OLD TYME DANCING *every* Tuesday
EVERY WEDNESDAY
TEENAGE
ROCK 'N' RECORD NIGHT

Chris Difford (London): "Trevor Chamber had a hi-fi and a deaf mother, so we played music and danced around a few cans at his house most weekends, or we went to the Savoy in Catford, a very dodgy club full of rival gangs who would come to dance, pick up girls and fight. Tunes ranged from anything Tamla to anything ska. Sometimes The Who.

"I remember dancing at a club and winning a competition with my girlfriend, and we were presented with something by Desmond Dekker; I felt very proud and out of breath. She went off with someone taller than me and we ended up in a fight outside the club. Happy days."

Geraldine Choules (Reading): "Our sister Jackie influenced us in the early days as she was a fully fledged Mod. Her boyfriends were all Mods too so there were always scooters about. But by the time me and my sister Jean were really old enough to get involved it had evolved into Skinheads. That was our era. Around 1968/'69 we started going to the Crescent Club, and Skinheads were really coming into their own. The Crescent Club was in Crescent Road. It was part of Alfred Sutton's boys school, and there was this separate annexe building that was a purpose-built youth club. It was teamed with the Emmer Green youth club. There was a bloke called Brian who ran it. There was a disco and the music was ska, reggae and always soul. Loads of Motown, I guess that was the main music. Stuff like Jimmy Ruffin, The Chi-Lites, The Delfonics, The Elgins, Stevie Wonder and the Isley Brothers. There was also what would have been the first *Tighten Up* album. The boys would turn up, and if truth be told, amongst them were a few troublemakers. The Skinhead boys getting in there didn't really like the boys from Earley because they weren't really Skinheads. I guess they were smarter and I would say there was a little bit of the Mods still in them. They had gone from riding scooters to driving Minis. I would have been around 15 and Jean would have been about 14. We were everywhere when we shouldn't have been because we were too young really. You really needed your ID to get into the Top Rank. But in 1970, we were in the Top Rank on Saturday afternoons, Saturday nights, Tuesday nights…"

Sharon Williams (London): "I would have been going to pubs by then. The Tavern, the Lil', and the Fort. I remember all the boys wore a lovely aftershave called 'Wild Country' which they got off Chrissy Brown's mum who was an Avon lady. There was 'Brut' too of course. I only really liked Skinhead boys if they were blond and had blue eyes! In fact, I probably preferred boys with longer hair."

Raymond Potter (London): "We used to go to the youth club in Gloucester Road, which was practically the only youth club around here. So, because it was filled with Skinheads and Mods, it attracted the motorbike boys from the Salt Box in Addington. There was chaos at times. We used to take our own records down there, which was stuff like Desmond Dekker and Motown, which we bought at Diamonds in West Croydon. There were parties every week, if you weren't invited you'd gatecrash them anyway."

Austin Myers (Shipley): "There was a place in Bradford we used to go to which was cutting-edge at the time. It was called the Continental Coffee Bar, but within that there was a place called 'The Hole In The Wall' and it literally was a hole in the wall. I remember the first time going into this dark, dark place having left what was the average coffee bar of the late sixties. Having to pass this bouncer to get through was hard. If you looked too young, you didn't get in. If you didn't look like you belonged, you didn't get in. The first time I got in there, it was fantastic. All of a sudden you get in and Edwin Starr's 'War' is belting out, followed by 'Needle In A Haystack' and a lot of old soul. It all came alive, and the fact that not everybody got in there made it special. I'd been turned away on a few occasions because they didn't feel I really belonged there, because I didn't look like I belonged there. They started getting fussy later on. They'd let all the Bradford lads in, but if you were from out of town or didn't look quite up to the mark, you'd never make it in. So, then you were stood outside with all the scooter boys or whatever, wanting to be part of it. Then there was a place called the Lakean Ballroom in Shipley. Initially the owners weren't sure they wanted you in the place because it was like an old-fashioned dancehall in the early sixties. Eventually the owners realised they were missing out because punters were going elsewhere to places such as the Mecca in Bradford. So, they suddenly got switched on, and turned it around to the music we wanted to listen to. One of the owners, who I think was called Billy, was the DJ, then they eventually got someone called Barry Shenton. He wasn't that good, and just played any pop records, but we would take in our own records for him to play. They never really got to grips with the soul and reggae stuff we really wanted to hear. There was seldom a Saturday that went by where there wasn't a fight. Not so much the Seven Seas because that was a no-go area, unless you were a Skinhead, Suedehead or part of the Shipley fraternity, without an invite. The Bradford lads used to come through, and there was a lot of them, but they were accepted as being part and parcel of the Shipley mob. But if you had any hair below the collar, forget trying to walk in there. I mean you'd get out… but you'd be sore. The other venues were the same, in that if you weren't a Mod, Skinhead or Suedehead, you're better off not going there because they're not interested in you."

Bill Fordham (London): "From about the summer of '66 until I left, I used to bunk off and hardly went to school. I was a bit of a disappointment to my mum, who thought I would go to university. At the time, though, I'd discovered women and music. So, we used to go round to this girl's flat. In them days you used to get milk and bread delivered to your house. So, the girls used to go and nick bread and milk from some of the flats; we'd pool all our money together to buy a bottle of Camp coffee and as many fags as we could afford. Then we'd sit around with bread and butter, smoke and play records. Then coming up to lunchtime I'd ask to borrow one of their full-length leathers or suede coats, and me and my mate Chris used to head off to the lunchtime sessions at Tiles in Oxford Street. It was called *Beat Club* and German Television used to film it. I was down there when Cliff Bennett & The Rebel Rousers were on."

THIS WEEK AT TILES!
ALL PROGRAMMES SUBJECT TO ALTERATION

Thursday August 11th 7.30 - 11.30 M. 5/- G. 7/6	**THE RICK 'N' BECKERS** PLUS **THE GUESTS**
Friday August 12th 7.30 - 11.30 Members: 10/- Guests: 12/6	**GEORGIE FAME AND THE BLUE FLAMES** Plus **THE WILD UNCERTAINTY**
Saturday August 13th All-night session 7.30 Members: 7/6 Guests: 10/-	**THE PEDLERS ESSEX FIVE — THE PROFILE** Plus DJs CLEM DALTON & MIKE QUINN
Sunday August 14th 7.30 - 11.30 Members 5/- Guests: 7/6	LIVE **HAMILTON AND THE HAMILTON MOVEMENT** Plus **THE ANZACS**
Monday August 15th 7.30 - 11.30 M. 5/- G. 7/6	**THE CREATION** Plus **THE GIBSON SOUND**
Tuesday August 16th 7.30 - 11.30 Members: 3/6 Guests: 4/6	Radio Luxembourg's **READY, STEADY RADIO** The U.K.'s TOP LIVE SHOW with TOP STARS AND D.J.s
Wednesday August 17th 7.30 - 11.30 Members: 3/6 Guests: 4/6	**MID-WEEK R&B SPIN** Presented by CLEM DALTON & MIKE QUINN PLUS LIVE! **JIMMY BROWN SOUND**

EXCLUSIVE REPRESENTATION BY TILES ENTERTAINMENT AGENCY LTD.

Penny Reel (London): "The Tiles night was run by Jeff Dexter on the two times I went down there. The third time I went along to it, it had closed. There were shops in there selling clothes or records. That was an unusual thing, you know. You could buy Mod clothes and listen to the music that was playing next door. They were playing soul, things like 'I Spy For The FBI' by Jamo Thomas, Sam & Dave's 'Hold On I'm Coming', 'Sweet Soul Music' by Arthur Conley, Wilson Pickett's 'Mustang Sally', 'Knock On Wood' by Eddie Floyd, Otis Redding stuff, you know all those classic '67 tunes. At the end of the night, he put on ska. 'Guns Of Navarone' by The Skatalites, 'El Pussycat' by Roland Alphonso, those sort of things. There were about six black guys, and they started dancing, and that was the best dancing I'd ever seen, you know. They danced with white girls, but no white boys danced when they danced. They had a competition, and a black guy won it. That was the first time I'd seen blacks and whites mixing in a club. Tiles attracted a mixed audience. When that ended I started going over to Manor House in Finsbury Park. Ron and Andy used to put on reggae nights there. When I went in, they were playing rocksteady because that sound had taken over from ska. It was a slower, deeper sound, you know. They had a black guy with a sound system playing. I don't know who they were. It could have been Fat Man or Sir Ds or even Count Shelley, but it was a top north London sound operator. I didn't know one sound that night but it would probably be stuff like The Uniques, Techniques, Desmond Dekker. All new tunes, some of them Jamaican, some of them English. I was the only white guy there, except for Ron and Andy who were also white, but much older than anyone else. It's still a reggae club, even to this day – it's run by the black DJ Jesse James."

Clive Banks (London): "We'd go to the Albany on the North Circular Road, which was 100 yards from the Ace Café, and it was a big old pub, with a big old room at the top and we'd go there Friday nights. That was the place that I heard music loud. I was used to hearing it through tiny speakers and on the radio, but never that loud. We were in a place with people you wanted to stare at, because they had all the gear on, standing round the edge, just checking each other out. We'd hear Desmond Dekker and things like that there, Blue Beat records. I never called them Skinheads, that term came later. The girls at that time looked great though, like Julie Driscoll. Feathered fringe, with a mohair coat on, and in my case, I'd have my three-piece green suit on and be absolutely caked in free samples of Brut. Not the Henry Cooper one, because that would come later. We'd go into Swan & Edgar on Piccadilly Circus and they have these tiny bottles and they give you a free sample of it in like spirit bottles. Or Tabac, those were the kind of smells.

"We'd also go to the Crown in Harrow on the Hill on a Sunday night. Seem to remember a lot of Harrow schoolboys in there. Big room at the back of the pub. All of us standing there, checking each other out, seeing what 'you' are wearing."

Brian Wright (London): "It wasn't always the Caxton Club that we frequented. By 1968 we had new faces coming up behind us. Some of us by then had cars so we started going to the Locarno in Streatham on a Monday night, the Bali Hai on Streatham High Road near the ice rink, Sunday nights at the Blue Rooms in the King's Road which was above Sidney Smith's and next door to Peter Jones. If we went further out it would be the Tottenham Royal – we saw James Brown there – Tiffany's in Wimbledon which was part of the Mecca chain, the Lyceum in The Strand, Room At The Top in Ilford. As you got older you just started to go to the pubs where the faces hung out."

Tony Haddow (London): "I met a lot of people in a little club in Barnet called the Cha Club; they played a lot of Tamla and moved on to reggae. There was the Con Club in Finchley, which was the Conservative Club. This was the start of me going out to clubs because these were just local clubs. The Lyceum on The Strand was a big club for me. It was near to where my girlfriend lived. I met her there, and I really enjoyed it – great music, top atmosphere, people from all over London."

Bernard Jennings (Ruislip): "We went to a club in Wembley where there were lots of older West Indian guys who were very, very good dancers. We'd just stand back, amazed at these guys in suits, big overweight fellas who were probably twice our age, dancing very quickly, dropping down and picking up hankies, that kind of thing. We just observed because you

"We went to a club in Wembley where there were lots of older West Indian guys who were very, very good dancers. We'd just stand back, amazed at these guys in suits, big overweight fellas who were probably twice our age, dancing very quickly, dropping down and picking up hankies, that kind of thing. We just observed because you didn't get too involved in places like that…"
BERNARD JENNINGS

LONDON'S TOP U.S & J.A IMPORT SOUNDS
8-11 LIC. BAR
SUNDAY ★ TUESDAY ★ FRIDAY
RAILWAY HOTEL WEALDSTONE
HARROW & WEALDSTONE STN. (B.R. & L.T.E.) BUSES 114 158 182 286 186 H.1. 140

BOOT BOYS, NEWCASTLE, JUNE 1972

TABLE FOOTBALL AND PEPSI, CAXTON CLUB, 1969

didn't get too involved in places like that, because we weren't really welcome, but went to them nonetheless. We'd go to the Roaring Twenties in Carnaby Street and Count Suckle's Cue Club in Paddington. We used to think we were the only white faces in there – there was always lots of white girls but never many white boys. We also frequented the Pink Flamingo in Wardour Street [formerly the Flamingo] but sadly my main memory was having to hand over our cash to these West Indian guys in an alley nearby. This guy asked if I could lend him 2/6d and I said no. Then he asked if I could lend him all my money; then I realised there was another two of them. Luckily, I had a sleeveless pullover on and any notes I had on me were in the top pocket of my shirt, so I just handed him whatever was in my pockets. He seemed OK with that and even said he'd pay me back when he saw me next! I'm fairly sure we were going to see The Amboy Dukes [an English band] but what was more interesting was the records that got played there. We spent a lot of time at the Railway Hotel in Wealdstone. Baron Ray was the DJ there playing great reggae. Later on in time it would be Thursday nights at Ronnie Scott's for a soul night. It was cutting-edge stuff and you realised that the people there were the best-dressed guys and best dancers in London, but this is around '73. But these were all outings and never regular. In the early days it was mainly just whatever the clubs were in the day on our side of London."

Twisted Wheel, but we play better and rarer records than them. It's the Blackpool Mecca. You must come up. Dress smart.' I said, 'What constitutes smart?' He replied, 'Suit or jacket, tie and strides. But you can wear what you want once you actually get in there.' So the first time I went up there was when Dave Godin was at war with Tony Cummins, who later became the editor of *Black Music* magazine and was the editor of *Shout* magazine. Tony was a bit of a purist, while Godin would happily chat about a group such as Martha Reeves & The Vandellas, and Tony found them a bit too pop-orientated. Anyway, the pair had fallen out over what was probably a culmination of a lot of things regarding music. Godin had embraced the northern soul scene while Tony had been quite dismissive of it in print. Tony had never been up to the Mecca, while Godin stated it was like the mid-sixties all over again but with better and rarer records, so Tony organised a coach trip to check it out. Levine had already asked me to go up, so I went on the coach with Tony.

"We got there a bit late and the queue was already forming outside, so we joined that. I saw Ian beckoning me over, but I wanted to go in with the people on the coach. Levine eventually walked up and told me that I must go in with him at the front of the queue. I said no, as I'd been with my mates all day. He said, 'OK, at your own risk!' and wandered off. Anyway, we didn't get in because Dave Godin had phoned up the manager of the Blackpool Mecca to say that there was a coachload of troublemakers coming up from London to mock the scene there and be a nuisance. We were turned away and had to walk around the streets of Blackpool because we'd already sent the coach driver away to come back at 2.15 a.m. Obviously while the pubs were open it was fine, but pubs chucked out by 11.15 back then. There were no late-night burger bars or anything back then. Anyway, it strengthened my resolve and I went up there the following week on my own, and I thought it was the most fantastic thing I'd ever been to. Speeding out of my nut at the Blackpool Mecca listening to all these fantastic records with all these lovely people that liked the same kind of music that I liked. It was heaven on earth to me. I got so obsessed by it that one weekend I didn't go home – I just stayed up there until my money ran out."

Tony Rounce (London): "My first regular clubbing was probably the Blackpool Mecca in that 'living for the weekend'-type clubbing. I'd met Ian Levine in Soul City, and he'd seen our fanzine and was really impressed. Dave Godin pointed us out, as both I and my friend David were in the shop at the time. Ian dragged us off to Euston, where he went to a left-luggage locker and produced this huge box of 45s and took us to this café around the corner. He then started pulling out these records by artists such as J. J. Barnes on Ric-Tic and all these little obscure Detroit labels. He started pulling out Motown records I'd never seen before: Linda Griner, Little Lisa and names that I'd only seen in catalogues. I was impressed, and we became friends. Anyway, Ian's dad had a club up near Lytham, so Ian invited me up to stay at his parents' house. The day before I went, Freda Payne's 'Band Of Gold' had just come in to Record Corner on import. So I took a bunch of records up with me, and I think Ian's dad's club, the Lemon Tree, might have been the first club in the UK to play 'Band Of Gold' as a result of me taking it up there.

"Anyway, I didn't see Ian again for a few months, then all of a sudden, I was in Record Corner at 9.30 in the morning and Ian is standing there. He'd come down for the day looking for records and he started telling me about this fantastic scene that was going on up there. He said, 'It's an outgrowth of the

Barry Quinnell (Eastergate): "After the Birdcage Club closed, it became the Brave New World, then it died a death, so everybody tagged on to the Marina Club. We did sometimes

GROUP SHOT, CAXTON CLUB, 1969

"We'd only have a bottle of ale, because I didn't have much money. I'd walk home from basically Stonebridge Park to the Harrow Road, either because there were no buses running, or more likely because I'd have no money left. We'd get kicked out at 11 p.m., but it would be 12.30 by the time we'd get home. Through Harlesden, Kensal Rise, by the graveyard wall. It was a euphoric walk. You'd have heard and seen great things on your night out."
CLIVE BANKS

go to Kimbell's but you'd always get in a punch-up there. It was lethal, lots of matelots home on leave looking for hassle. The Marina became very popular amongst the all-nighter crowd. I remember at one of the all-nighters at the Marina, some lads from Manchester came down with boxes of records, none of which I had ever heard of before. There were lots of imports on the Mirwood and Ric-Tic labels. That gave me a little motivation to dig deeper. These guys were all talking about the Twisted Wheel club. I only knew one bloke who used to go to the Wheel, called Steve Braggs, who lived in Shoreham-by-Sea. He used to live and work away in Stoke, and he'd get on a coach there that they put on specially to go to the Wheel. He was always saying to me, 'You must come up to the Wheel. It's fantastic!' But in those days I couldn't afford it. That was probably around 1969/'70. That is when I first got to know Steve Braggs. He is still the best dancer I have ever seen. Not only was he super-fit, although he drank and smoked like a trooper, he could do backdrops, cartwheels and spins. He could also run up a wall and flip right over. He had a blazer with a Twisted Wheel badge on the pocket, long before badges were two a penny. He wore it at my wedding in 1973. Sadly he died in 1977 of cancer in St Lukes, Guildford – bloody tragic."

Maggie Brown (Winchester): "My home town is Dundee and two of my older cousins, who still live there, were into the Mod look so I guess I kind of looked up to them as well. There was a massive following from Dundee to Wigan back then. I was influenced by a lot of the fashion that I saw in Dundee in the early seventies – it seemed to me that you could get hold of 'different' clothes that you didn't see down south; this was probably moving more into the Suedehead era.

"I only ever went to Wigan Casino once, as back in the day I was still at school and it was such a long way to go if you only had your pocket money and a Saturday job. Most of us just couldn't afford to keep going there. I would have been around 15 and the place just took my breath away – an experience I will never forget! I can still smell the talc and sweat. And when it came to the dancers… well, what can I say! A coachload of us went up from Winchester. Another club we used to go to was the Rainbow in Farnborough – loads of soul music. We didn't go that often, just a few times, but I remember it so clearly. A lot of people would take speed to keep awake as there was many an all-nighter – it was a thing back then as you probably know! A lot of the older Mods went to the Shoreline Club in Brighton but I was too young to go there."

Tony Ellis (London): "With the gear [drugs] it put you into a different category. There was a bloke called Johnny Lynch, and he wanted to beat me up for years, then he saw us one night coming back from the Palais stoned out of our heads, and he said, 'Fuck me, you're blocked, ain't you.' And he embraced me, and we were OK after that. It was a kind of membership to a club.

"Streatham Locarno was another dancehall we frequented in the late sixties. Hammersmith Palais on a Monday night was great for Motown. 'The Hunter Gets Captured By The Game' was big there. 'Girls Are Out To Get You' when it first came out. The sounds were pretty good there because lots of Mecca places had their dance band. The Croydon Suite was

good too. That was a band, but they had an interval where they played lots of records. The records were good there, the girls were good there, and the bouncers were very violent.

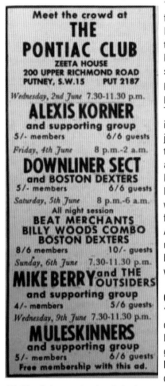

"The Pontiac was the first real club I went to. I remember going up the stairs, there was a big dance floor, a low stage at the front, and pop art Roy Lichtenstein paintings on the walls. That gave it a swinging image, I suppose. We just went there to see the bands really, such as John Mayall's Bluesbreakers, and the Boston Dexters, who were the resident band for quite a while. A record I always remember from there is Freddie Hughes' 'Ooh-wee Baby, I Love You'."

Clive Banks (London): "As for the pills and the drinking, I don't think that was going on so much. Maybe centrally, but only amongst a few. We'd only have a bottle of ale, because I didn't have much money. I'd walk home from basically Stonebridge Park to the Harrow Road, either because there were no buses running, or more likely because I'd have no money left. We'd get kicked out at 11 p.m., but it would be 12.30 by the time we'd get home. Through Harlesden, Kensal Rise, by the graveyard wall. It was a euphoric walk. You'd have heard and seen great things on your night out."

Brian Wright (London): "Ian Hingle was a year above me at school and came from Fulham. He stayed on to the sixth form so we were still both there in '68. One morning I was in the classroom and I looked out of the window that looked onto Palace Street, and I saw Ian Hingle walk around the corner with a soul album under his arm. He's looking immaculate, as ever, his trousers are ankle high to show off his shoes. He's got black shiny patent Smoothies on from a shop in Brick Lane. He's wearing a pair of wraparound sunglasses like Stevie Wonder. As he saw us looking out at him, he looked up to the sky and started shaking his head the way that Stevie Wonder used to do. He always had style. I think we actually met in the Caxton and became really good mates. On Sunday nights we used to go to a pub in Dalston called the Norfolk Arms on the roundabout. That was solid reggae in there. Then we'd go to the Purley Orchid, sometimes the Hammersmith Palais. We went to the Ram Jam Club in Brixton a couple of times but it was a little bit too heavy for us white boys. It was very black. We went Sunday afternoon I think and even then, some geezer said to us, 'If you're coming in here, you better be a good dancer.' Somebody tried to rob me in the

I GET MY KICKS OUT ON THE FLOOR, CAXTON CLUB, 1969

toilets but I had nothing worth nicking."

Clive Knight (London): "We started to hit the clubs: Phonograph at the Refectory pub in Golders Green, the Cavalier Club in Brent (for a very brief time) and the Hammersmith Palais, as well as the glorious and wonderful Tottenham Royal. Other clubs in the area I couldn't get to were the Finchley Conservative Club and the Cha in Barnet, both of which years later I found out that my wife used to go to. Go figure."

Tony Haddow (London): "There were a lot of small clubs like the Railway at Harrow and Wealdstone. The clubs I really remember were the Lyceum Ballroom, which was mental in those days. The Tottenham Royal, which I absolutely loved, a mad club with massive bouncers on the door, but they gave you a reasonable free range, and so there was very little trouble. You'd get everybody stamping with heavy boots on the floor to 'Skinhead Moonstomp'. When 'Spirit In The Sky' came on, everybody went mental to it. You wouldn't think so, but if you listen to it, you can imagine how a load of people could do something to that tune. Other favourites were 'Harlem Shuffle' and 'River Deep, Mountain High' and lots of the reggae."

Phillip Ellisdon (Watford): "The Oldfield Tavern in Greenford was a real Skinhead haunt. Around north London, we used to go to the Tottenham Royal, which was about the furthest we went that way. That was a bit of a haven, because you had the police station right opposite, so if you got in any trouble, you could whip across the road, because there was some serious trouble there sometimes. You really needed to know somebody up there."

Geoff Deane (London): "To me the Tottenham Royal was like Valhalla. It was the best place to me. I genuinely believed then I would spend the rest of my life there, and I would never stop going to this place. It's perfect. Eighteen months later, I wouldn't be seen dead in there, haha."

Barry Quinnell (Eastergate): "I first went to the Roaring Twenties in 1968. I went with a guy called Steve Spencer. It was a rocksteady club, pre-reggae, and it wasn't ska either. Soul boys, in the main, will say that the rocksteady era is Jamaica's finest period because ska was mainly instrumental-based. Suddenly rocksteady provided singers like Alton Ellis, Ken Boothe and Ken Parker singing beautiful

songs recorded originally by soul people such as The Impressions, Jerry Butler. Vocalists like Dobby Dobson were just amazing. Around this time we went to Peyton Place in Bromley. That would be packed with people dancing to mainly Jamaican stuff, and it was all rocksteady. With money being limited you wouldn't go out every week, so you

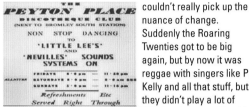

couldn't really pick up the nuance of change. Suddenly the Roaring Twenties got to be big again, but by now it was reggae with singers like Pat Kelly and all that stuff, but they didn't play a lot of novelty reggae. That's what I call Skinhead reggae. No, this was serious reggae. That was when I started getting into Studio One, because I realised that Coxsone was recording Ernest Wilson, Bob Andy and these types of singers."

Barry Cain (London): "At that time, I would go to a place called the Manor House, which is in the corner of where Manor House tube station is. We'd go upstairs there to where there was a club. On a Friday night, and this is at the end of 1967, it was called the Bluesville, and they'd have bands like John Mayall on there and I used to love that kind of music. On a Saturday, it was called the Downbeat Club where they would play stax and soul, and a load of black guys from Tottenham would be there and everyone would be suited. For me, it would be jeans and T-shirt the night before. So, you had this dichotomy, as I loved all the music. Yeah, I had a crop, but there was a problem with the music, because I wanted to see bands like Cream or Ten Years After and with a real severe crop, you'd look completely out of place. So, I sort of had a 'half and half'."

Lester Owers (London): "At the Basildon Mecca, I saw The Equals, Marv Johnson, Johnny Johnson & The Bandwagon, The Upsetters and Max Romeo. We saw Desmond Dekker at the Red Lion in Leytonstone. We'd get a train from Barking, and if you got in the last carriage, you could be out before the bloke got to you to collect the tickets, and then you could go back on the Central Line. Around that time, we're going to the Ilford Palais, Basildon Mecca and the Three Till Two in Southend. The resident band at the Three Till Two was called Sadie's Expression, who just played chart stuff. The policy at places like the Mecca was to have a resident band between the DJ sets, and then you'd get 'dreamtime' when you used to try and do the pulling.

"The further you went towards Southend, the more violent it got. If you went into a pub such as the Tavern In The Town, you felt like there were lasers on the back of your head. It was full of Skinheads, but it was nasty. In Basildon, you'd get punch-ups all the time."

Steve Ellison (London): "I remember going to the Tuns in Beckenham, where Bowie went early in his career, and at the back of that when the Skinheads were in, hearing the proper gear, the proper reggae in there, big time. I also went to the Tiger's Head, which is now a block of flats, in Catford. Also, the Savoy in Catford, the Witch Doctor Club, which was once called Mr Smiths, where Frankie Fraser had a shootout in the sixties. The DJ for the Skinheads was Steve Maxted, ex-stuntman, he was fucking mad, him. He balanced chairs on his face."

Tony Rounce (London): "When I came back from Blackpool a friend of mine called Mike Boothe, who was manager of a record shop in Harrow, said to me that I should go out with him at the weekend in London. He told me about a club called the Subway in Greek Street, and that his friend DJ-ed there playing great soul and reggae records. So, we went down there, and the guy was Brian Peters who had worked at the Scene Club in the sixties. He'd been working at Le Deuce Club on D'Arblay Street and fallen out with them so he started at the Subway. He was playing bits of northern, current funk and lots of reggae to a very mixed crowd – gay, black, kids and older people. This is around the end of '71. It was Saturday night, started at ten and finished at midday on Sunday. If we left early, we would go around to the Flamingo to hear Neville The Musical Enchanter playing records. We'd often be there, and I'd find myself still out at two o'clock the following afternoon after having gone out for ten o'clock the previous night. Brian Peters fell out with the governor at the Subway and went back to work at Le Deuce and I started working at the Subway. I also grew accustomed to going out to other London clubs such as the Roaring Twenties, which was predominantly black and mainly reggae. The DJ Lloydie Coxsone did play a little bit of soul as well. There weren't many Skinheads there by this time though, perhaps one too many requests for 'Monkey Spanner' maybe. I went to the Cue Club a few times. It was only the fact that it was in Paddington that I didn't go much.

"By the time I was DJ-ing at the Subway, I had an arrangement with the owner to have an hour or two break from playing so I could wander over to Carnaby Street and pop in the Roaring Twenties or see Brian at Le Deuce. In fact, that's how I got sacked from the Subway, as I popped over to Le Deuce one night and Jengis, the Subway owner, came in and saw me sitting in playing a couple of records for Brian while he went to the toilet. Obviously Jengis thought I was moonlighting and he actually beat me up. So, I started

working at Le Deuce during the week while Brian did Friday nights and Saturday nights.

"Typical Friday nights would be meeting up with my mate Mike Boothe and Brian Peters and we'd go record shopping because Jamaican reggae record shops stayed open until God knows when, and you could go over to Rita and Benny's at nine o'clock at night and they'd still have a shop full of people if some new tunes had landed. We also went to Junior's Music Spot in Finsbury Park. The guy who ran the shop, Junior Lincoln, had been Jamaican Coxsone's label manager over here since about 1967 so he'd put out all those Blue Coxsone labels and red and white Studio 1 records. It was where Banana and Bamboo Records' headquarters were.

WHERE THE SISTERS ARE! (with apologies to the gang at Frasers)
EVERY FRIDAY 8–11 — Saturday and Sunday
Three hours of solid Funk-Power with — REGGAE with the
★ **BE BE BARON** ★ heavy man in London Town
LADIES! Half-price before 9 p.m. — **NEVILLE** Musical enchanter
Coming in December — THE PIONEERS — DENNIS ALCAPONE
RAILWAY HOTEL - WEALDSTONE Nr. HARROW, HARROW & WEALDSTONE STN. MIDDX. Bus: 114, 182, 186, 286, n

Then to the Railway Hotel on a Friday night to watch B. B. Baron and Chalkie White. B. B. Baron's real name was Ray Peterson; he was a great DJ, and really loved his soul and reggae. It finished at eleven, then we'd go to the Roaring Twenties for a couple of hours and then go to see Brian at Le Deuce and more often than not, end up at the Flamingo at about six in the morning to see Neville for the last couple of hours. That is when it got interesting because Neville would play what they now call 'revive'. It would be rocksteady that had been released a couple of years earlier, and I also remember hearing, for the first time ever, 'My Baby Just Cares For Me' by Nina Simone. He played it off a Jamaican King 78. Neville was a really nice bloke and when he realised we were genuinely interested in Jamaican music, he let us go through his record box, which no other sound man has ever let me do. I remember Gunsmoke, who used to select for Lloydie Coxsone – one night I leant over just to look at the record, and he slapped my hand and said, 'That's close enough!'"

Barry Quinnell (Eastergate): "If I had a fiver for every hour I spent hanging outside the Flamingo Club in Wardour Street, I'd be rich, but we never went in, and I don't really know why. I know that there was a Boots the chemist just around the corner. All the drug addicts could only get their new prescriptions at one minute past midnight because it was a new day and they were pre-dated prescriptions for their heroin. But there were deals going on with speed as well, so we used to hang around for these bloody bad news characters so that we could score blues and bombers. Then we'd find an all-nighter to go to. In the main we used to go to the Subway club in D'Arblay Street, which is quite near the Poland Street car park. If we drove up in a car, we'd always park there, then meet up with a bloke from Basingstoke called Dave, who was a dealer. We'd sit in the back of his Jag and he'd be counting out the pills to us. A nice little story concerning Dave, is that after the Shoreline Club shut, we started going down to Pompey and I got to know some lads from Hayling Island – they had a lovely apartment right on the seafront. Dave was coming down with pills for the Hayling Island boys, somebody got wind of it, and he got busted on the causeway from Havant over to Hayling. Everybody scattered on that one!"

Barry Cain (London): "The Angel was a shithole for pubs. It was useless. When I was 17 I ended up going south

247

"We used to go to the Tottenham Royal and that was the first place I saw real racial fights. Even though there weren't that many black guys there really, and they had the short hair anyway and would be dressed up really sharp. But it would always kick off at some point… I never got involved in any of that. Nah. I was a lover not a fighter. I wasn't even a fucking lover… As I said earlier, it was violent all over."

BARRY CAIN

sometimes. The Apples and Pears, and the Thomas A Becket. Also to the East End, Whitechapel, the Blind Beggar. It was heaving in there. The guys were looking sharp and the girls there… everyone used to think East End girls were easy… like fuck! They were not at all, you know.

"It was great in there. The first time I heard 'I Heard It Through The Grapevine' was in the Blind Beggar. But then that would be followed by 'Where Do You Go To My Lovely'. They were just played over the loudspeaker. I know all the pubs round there. The Hospital Tavern over the road. I used to know every pub in the East End, it was so lively."

Bonny Staplehurst (London): "The clubs I used to go to in 1968/'69 were the Streatham Locarno, the Ilford Palais and the Croydon Queen. Mainly Skinheads in there then, but a mixture of people really. I don't remember going anywhere and it was *just* Skinheads. The music would be varied as well. Bit of Motown and that. Angela would always get served even though only 14 and usually got two Bacardi and Cokes. Then I'd go up for the third and they'd say, 'How old are you?' Always got stopped; in the end I didn't go to the bar. Now, I can't believe I was so young. We always had to get the last train from the Streatham Locarno on a Monday night and it became known as the Last Train To Rainbow City, after the song by The Pyramids."

Barry Cain (London): "When I was 16, we used to go to the Streatham Locarno and it was wall-to-wall Skinheads. Sometimes, they'd have a live band there, playing the hits of the day. They'd have 'dreamtime' when the lights would go down and they play a slower song, and you'd go after a bird and try and snog her, while dancing and getting lacquer up your nose. Only there would be a screen on which would be adverts from local shops, and that was 'dreamtime'. Twice I had to walk home from there, fucking long way that. I used to go via the Temple, because my old man used to do the cab shelter, and he was there for years, cooking for the cab drivers through the night. So, we used to stop off there for a cup of tea and a bacon sarnie, me and my mates, and sit there with all the cab drivers."

Bill Fordham (London): "The big night out was Saturday at the Locarno in Streatham. They had this big dance-band orchestra with three vocalists attempting to perform the latest Motown hits. When they finished their set, the stage revolved and the opening bars of Ben E. King's 'What Is Soul' would be blaring out as the resident DJ started his set. The records being played were almost 100 per cent Atlantic soul and Motown. Things like Sam & Dave's 'Hold On, I'm Coming' and 'You Don't Know Like I Know', The Drifters' 'Baby What I Mean', Joe Tex's 'Show Me' and Rufus Thomas' 'Willy Nilly'."

Barry Quinnell (Eastgate): "I never got to the Cue Club in Paddington or the Ram Jam in Brixton. You see if I went to London, half of my spending money would have gone on the train fare or paying someone's petrol before I got there. In the absence of mobile phones back then I used to meet up with the Gosport lot, and only knew what was going on because I exchanged letters with a girl, Roisin McCarthy, from there. So, I'd go down to her place on a Saturday by hitching a lift, if I could, to save money. I'd go to her house, then all the Gosport lot would come around. We'd all be counting out pills, and seeing who was doing what that night. Some weren't on the scene, while others of us would hitch a lift up to Fareham, and get on the train system. There was a lot of jumping trains in those days. If you could get on a railway station, the world was your oyster.

"Friday nights in Fishbourne, which is about two miles west of Chichester centre, there was a pub called the Bull's Head, and they had a function room out the back, across the car park, and that was called the Sussex Barn. That was a great Friday night session. I'm sure they played ska and bluebeat, but I remember it more for the Motown. It was the first place I ever heard The Marvelettes and Velvelettes. Not sure of the year we went there, but between '67 and '69. Within Chichester itself, there was a café called the El Bolero in South Street. Everybody would meet there downstairs. There was a jukebox with all the great songs of the time. In these little cafés at the time, the underlying script was to score your gear, you know. There was also the Esperanto café in Southsea. I hated risking not being able to get any, not that I ever failed, but there was always that thought in your head. On Friday nights you could go to the Fountain, a pub in Worthing. Robbie May used to DJ and it was very popular, but there would always be somebody dealing in there. It wasn't just music venues though; if you wanted to do something all night you could go somewhere like the King Alfred Bowl in Hove, which was a bowling alley. If you went there on a Saturday morning just for a Coke, there were people in there dealing drugs. I didn't like to leave it until the last minute to score for a Saturday night. I had four rules: I wouldn't go to an all-nighter if I didn't feel I had the right clothes to wear, if I didn't feel the music was going to be good, if I didn't think it was a good venue and if I didn't get any pills. I wouldn't do an all-nighter straight in a million years. I'd always say, 'It's the gear, and it's the gear, it's the venue and it's the music.' If I can't tick all those boxes, I ain't going anywhere. I'd rather hang on to my money."

Bill Fordham (London): "There was also a club in Streatham, Silver Blades ice rink, where they sometimes had live bands performing and I remember seeing Ben E. King give an excellent show. I also turned up to see what was advertised as 'For one night only, the fantastic Temptations'. Before the show started, the management advised that the act performing was The Fantastic Temptations, not the more famous Motown act, and we could have our money back if we wanted."

Barry Quinnell (Eastgate): "The northern soul scene was as bad as it was good. Clubs like the Shoreline Club, the Twisted Wheel and the Marina all played pop records, soul records and Jamaican records. What the northern scene did, in my opinion, was it fucked all that. It made it one-dimensional. It had to be up-tempo soul tracks. I've got a lot to thank the northern soul scene for though because it introduced me to some great music and some wonderful people. What I liked about that scene was that they played something that I remembered before the words 'northern' and 'soul' had ever been uttered in the same sentence, something like Julian Covey's 'A Little Bit Hurt' or Jamo Thomas', 'I Spy For The FBI' or original Motown tracks or whatever – nobody worried. It was more a Modernist scene with good music, it wasn't a soul scene with a load of scruffy bastards, because there's no two ways about it, that's what the northern scene became. Vests and baggies! What's all that about? They wouldn't know how to polish a pair of brogues!"

Tony Haddow (London): "The Tottenham Royal was on a Thursday night, if I remember rightly. I'd been grafting all day at work, and treated like a bleedin' servant by a plumber with 'Do this, do that'. Got covered in shit and dirt, go home, get cleaned up, put on all me gear. Jump on the tube at Edgware station, off at Tottenham. Do the walk down from the station to the Royal. In the queue at the door, and there was always a buzz in that queue. People from all over London, and never any trouble. I mean people left me alone, I could handle myself. I didn't attract trouble and I never, ever started any. Out of our estate was me, Steve Smith and Mickey Timms. The three of us were right at the forefront of it. The venue was a big ballroom that took a lot of people, and it would fill up on a Thursday night. Coming from Edgware, and not being in a big mob but knowing people all around, I just used to do the rounds with people I recognised from other clubs. Having been there from the beginning of the early days gave me that advantage of meeting people who'd been there from the start from different areas. Once it all started expanding, nobody really knew each other."

David Rosen (London): "Our principal club was the Marquee in Wardour Street, the original Marquee. On a Tuesday and Saturday night the club evolved from Mod into Skinhead / Suedehead. One of the DJs I think was 'Whispering' Bob Harris who played great tunes like 'Westbound Number 9', I remember, and soul, like the early days of Al Green."

![marquee club logo] **marquee club**
GERRARD 2375   90, WARDOUR STREET, LONDON W.1.

Top Rank

Jean Brooks (Reading): "We were friendly with the boys from Slough. A lot of the girls went out with army fellas from Aldershot. We didn't mix with them though. This is when we used to go to the Reading Top Rank. Everything revolved around that place during that period. You'd often get visitors from Oxford or Slough there because they never had a Top Rank, but none of them really got on with the Reading lot. I mean, they were all Skinheads but I think the Slough boys were better-looking blokes. The girls would go with them, rather than the Reading ones, and I think they felt a bit threatened by that. But then, if you've gone to school with

somebody, you don't particularly want to go out with them. You don't see them that way, they're just your mates. There would be a lot of trouble at Reading train station, especially outside in the road with fighting. The Reading Skinheads had been banned from the Top Rank, so because they couldn't get in, nobody else would. They'd meet them coming in from the trains from Slough, Hayes or Oxford. These visiting boys would do up these little Ford Anglias, and later the Escorts or Corsairs, and take you out to different towns and nightclubs. Later on, we would go to the Cat Ballou, the Birds Nest and the Blackbird Club in Slough. A lot of what was later referred to as northern soul was played in the Cat Ballou, this would have been around '71/'72."

On August 5th, 1970, around twenty Skinheads, including girls, had a meeting with the Mayor at Reading Town Hall to see if somewhere could be found for them to go, as they'd been banned from the Top Rank in Reading and the youth club they used (Emmer Green youth club) was closed for the summer holidays.

Councillor Bert Williams invited them into his parlour, and offered them cups of tea and cigarettes, as he listened to their problems.

"Well Mr Mayor, we just want somewhere to go in the evenings. A hall or a room or something where we can have records and table tennis or just sit around talking. There is nowhere for us to go in this town. We want a place for just us. We don't want any Greasers, or Hells Angels or hairies or anybody like that. Just us."
Jeff Allamby, aged 17,
READING EVENING POST, AUGUST 6TH, 1970

The Mayor promised to have a word with the manager of the Top Rank to help them.

Geraldine Choules (Reading): "Saturday nights before the Rank was spent in the Boar's Head, the George, the Peacock, the Coopers and sometimes the Captain's Cabin. We didn't go there much though because there was always drug dealing going on downstairs in there. A typical night at the Reading Top Rank would be Dave Anthony DJ-ing – he was the resident DJ – and a resident band [The Ronnie Smith Sound]. You'd be having a good time, and then usually one of the Reading lot would start trouble, and it would really kick off. But then a lot of the time, the bouncers were as much to blame. They could cause as much trouble as they stopped. Often though they were too busy with the girls to worry about what was going on inside. We didn't have anything to do with those at all. It would usually be a little fight on the dance floor, then everyone would run in, and then tables and chairs would come over the balcony onto the dance floor. It got bad – the ambulance men were always coming in and taking people off. There were never any fatalities, but they were lucky there wasn't. It was fist fights and a bit of furniture, but never weapons. A lot of the lads got banned from there, but none of the girls did. They were nice times at the Rank when there wasn't any trouble, because the blokes would dance as much as the girls. In fact, the men were good dancers. If Dave Anthony the DJ was away on holiday or whatever, it was always awful. If they had someone standing in for him, the night was a write-off."

READING TOP RANK, 1970

JEAN BROOKES, GERALDINE CHOULES
AND FRIENDS, READING TOP RANK, 1970

"If you went into Wembley Central station in those days, sprayed in the waiting room was 'Wembley ran from Watford'. You all had your territory, and the Top Rank was a bit of a mecca for people coming in from different areas of London, and it would always kick off somewhere in the Rank."
PHILLIP ELLISDON

Bob Wheeler (Slough): "We used to go to the Birds Nest in Slough and the Top Rank in Reading a lot. There was a club called the Jumping Cat around '64 or '65 at Wexham Drill Hall apparently. Not that I ever went there, but it moved to another place and then it ended up in Slough as the Cat. It was a place we all used to go to. It became known as Cat Ballou when it became an established club. It was basically all reggae and ska, then later Motown. Most of the people in there were dressed Skinhead. We did travel about though. When we went to football in London, we'd go to the Bali Hai in Streatham and Kew Boathouse. We used to alternate between the Reading and Watford Top Ranks. There'd be quite a lot of us from Slough going on the train to Reading. The majority in the main room weren't too bad, but there was an inner place up the stairs, and that was where you used to get a lot of trouble, but I think that was with the older lot. But yes, there were big punch-ups, and sometimes it was just from different estates in Reading, so you might get the Arborfield lot against Tilehurst or whatever. You would come out of the Rank late at night and see hundreds of Reading people outside waiting to beat up people who weren't from Reading. There was always a lot of that going on but it was just part and parcel of the times. On the whole, though, the nights there were good. They did have a ban on boots in there, but boots and braces were what you wore to football. When you went there suited up in your Tonik gear, it didn't really affect you."

Phillip Ellisdon (Watford): "If you went into Wembley Central station in those days, sprayed in the waiting room was 'Wembley ran from Watford'. You all had your territory, and the Top Rank was a bit of a mecca for people coming in from different areas of London, and it would always kick off somewhere in the Rank.

"Watford had its own faces. You had guys like Roy Rumble – if you saw him he was just a little skinny guy, but he was so hard. If you ever saw him dance, it was just like John Travolta did in *Saturday Night Fever*. At the Top Rank, if Roy danced, everybody would stop and watch him. He would dance to all the Motown and reggae stuff, and have crowds staring. He was this real smooth guy, but he could fight as well. He was so quick, he would knock people out before they could even take their coat off. He wasn't a bully though: he was a fight stopper, not a fight starter. He had the right name too, Rumble, if he wanted to have a go.

"There was also a face who was called 'Mad Ralph' because he was a big, hard guy and got his nickname from a comic strip. Watford did have a bit of a reputation in those days, we had lots of faces. Jimmy Jenkins, he was one of the style trendsetters in Watford. It was split up into three main estate areas: South Oxhey, the Meridian and the Holywell. The Rank was the one place they all came together. You'd have your own manors, and you tended to stay away from them, but everyone mixed at the Rank. There were a number of top guys – one was an ex-Mod called Phil Mannell. He was from London originally and quickly became one of the Skinhead faces in Watford. Others followed later – there were lots of others around at the time up for a fight. In they came to the Top Rank looking for trouble. There was a guy from South Oxhey called Shaun Barber; he had a reputation as a hard man. We'd get people coming to the Top Rank from

places like Harrow and Wealdstone, Wembley, Willesden looking for him to pick fights because he was a bit of a hard guy. Everybody wanted to have a go at him, but he could look after himself OK.

"There were many of these guys up the Top Rank and they were sort of the faces in them days, you know. The guys who had all the smooth dressing – guys like Gary Armstrong, Micky Blackburn, Bobby Langdale and Ted Fry had the suits and everything, and you'd wonder what the hell they did for a living to afford such clothes, they were smooth."

As important as pubs and clubs were for socialising, because of the young ages involved many kids just went to community centres, just as they did in the *Paint House* book [*The Paint House: Words From An East End Gang*, edited by Susie Daniel]. Two such clubs were the Lady Gomm and the Caxton Club.

READING SKINHEADS, 1969

The Lady Gomm

Michael Holland (London): "Lady Gomm House backs onto Southwark Park in Hawkstone Road, Rotherhithe, and was built by the Lord of the Manor Sir William Maynard Gomm, for his wife Elizabeth, who bequeathed £5,000 'for the benefit of old men and old women residing in Rotherhithe'. This money built the house as a mission hall and accident hospital in 1885, run by the Sisters of the Church.

"Early mission work included: 'Sunday Schools, breakfast Ragged Schools, classes for older scholars, Bible classes for men and women and mothers' meetings. Their mission in Rotherhithe was combined with an Accident Hospital where men who had suffered injury as a result of accidents in the docks were admitted and treated free of charge. Known also as the Cottage Hospital, there was also a dispensary where those less seriously injured, or suffering from other illnesses, could be treated.' [This was well before the NHS.]

"After repairing World War Two bomb damage, it was used for: 'an LCC Maternity and Welfare Clinic, a Mothers' Club, a Veterans' Club, a Dockers' Club, a Leisure Club for the Disabled, Adult Education Classes and clubs for different age groups of children, from a play group to a youth club for older teenagers', which is where we came in.

"The kids from the adjoining Silwood Estate used the youth club in the sixties and early seventies. The club was mainly based on the ground floor: one room had a telly in; another room had a record player in, just a little Dansette box one that we used to play our records on, mainly singles on the Blue Beat label in the late sixties; another room had the tuck shop in. Of course, we used to slip up the stairs to the out-of-bounds other floors for a laugh and to scare ourselves with ghost stories, and every now and again, we would have a disco on the top floor with one of the youth workers playing the records.

"Because it was just the kids off the estate, we all knew each other so no trouble came from any Skinhead gangs, just us teenagers driving the youth workers mad. The Deptford Gang used to come down, but we knew all of them from school. So we didn't really scare anyone in the club, although I suppose we were quite intimidating when walking along the street in a group. But even then, we never really had money to go anywhere so we would just be a Skinhead gang round the flats where everyone knew us and would frighten us with, 'Oi! Fuck off or I'll tell your muvver!' And as you can see from the photos, only one of our number went for the real short cut. And he was made the Bovver Boy poster boy for youth clubs!

"We did use to go to a youth club in a community hall in Warwick Road, called the Warwick, because they played good reggae, which was still underground then. I suppose there was a little bit of the postcode war going on then, but we used to keep to one side of the hall while our girls danced, and the Camberwell boys stayed over their side.

"Fashion was basically Ben Sherman shirts (sixty-five bob) [65 shillings, or £3.25], which we got from Jay's in Lower Road or Phillips in Tower Bridge Road; or Brutus or Jaytex shirts from the same places. I remember when I bought my first Ben Sherman with my own money, from a paper round on the estate, for twenty-two bob a week and it was great until I got caught thieving the *Superman* comics from the paper shop I worked in. Even though I was paying for the shirt I had to ask my mum if I could buy it. She asked how much and when I said it was sixty-five bob she said: 'You can buy three for that money!'

"Half-inch braces. Levis jeans or cords from Jay's. They used to do seconds in there so you could sometimes get a good bargain. Dr Martens, also 65 shillings from Jay's, or monkey boots, which were cheaper. But I often went over Brick Lane to Blackmans in Cheshire Street as the DMs were a bit cheaper.

"Jackets were windcheaters which I had made in Clothesville in Mare Street and then Squires jackets. We never called them Harringtons because we didn't want to be associated with someone in a soap opera [*Peyton Place*]. You might as well have called them Stan Ogden jackets as far as we were concerned, so we called them after the shop we bought them in. Eventually, Jay's got the cheaper versions.

"Tonik mohair suits and trousers were made to measure in Rosemans in Tower Bridge Road or Jamaica Road, or Nelson's in Deptford high street, and you paid it off weekly or with a provident cheque [shopping vouchers that were also paid off weekly].

"I also used to slip on the old man's trilby when I went out, and put it back on the hook on the way in so he didn't know."

Sharon Williams (London): "I wore the clothes when going to Lady Gomm – quite a few of the girls did and then on a Monday, we'd go to the Rotherhithe Baths disco. My faves were Desmond Dekker and The Supremes. I learnt to dance there really. Certainly, I remember dancing to 'Red, Red Wine' at Lady Gomm with Jane Higgins. I loved the tuck shop and learning to cook there too.

"I had a lovely sheepskin from Petticoat Lane. And a 2-tone skirt and jacket in a green/grey. I teamed that up with white knee-length boots and 'gun metal' tights, all from the 'Lane'."

> **Sallycats**
>
> Calpreta Cotton Dress, superior quality. Attractively trimmed white pique collar and cuffs. This season's winner Cols. Pink, Blue, and Orange. Sizes 36 in. to 40 in. hips.
>
> Washes beautifully. Money back guarantee.
>
> **59/-** + 2/6 P. & P.
>
> Send for our Free Illustrated Brochure.
>
> **Sallycats**
> 8 HEWITT STREET
> MANCHESTER M15 4GB

"Because it was just the kids off the estate, we all knew each other so no trouble came from any Skinhead gangs, just us teenagers driving the youth workers mad… And as you can see from the photos, only one of our number went for the real short cut. And he was made the Bovver Boy poster boy for youth clubs."
MICHAEL HOLLAND

If you don't bov ver, he will.

The Caxton Club

The Caxton Youth Trust was set up in 1948. The youth club's conception was in 1938, although its actual birth was put on hold until after World War Two. By 1948, two Westminster residents, a civil servant and a postman, had the organisation up and running. By the 1960s, 'The Caxton' was a disco based in a youth club situated in the basement of Tintern House on Abbots Manor Estate in Pimlico.

One of Caxton's original youth workers, Roy Hinton MBE, described the youth club in the 1960s: "The club was for local disadvantaged young people and it was a place to meet, dance, socialise and take part in something positive. Tens of thousands of people passed through our doors. The area was working class then, I have seen it grow and change its focus over the years."

Brian Wright (London): "One of the older guys I was hanging around with said that I should go down the Caxton Club. I walked in the door, down the slope, there's a low ceiling, and there's a tune playing, something like Willie Mitchell's 'That Driving Beat' probably or whatever, and that was it, I was taken. It was a revelation. I started going down there in '64 and I bailed out around '69. I went down there every night it was open. Roy Hinton the DJ and I just hit it off straight away. He had a raised counter with a Perspex screen that he sat behind. He had twin decks and they were some of the first twin decks ever made. I went up and asked him to play a record, can't remember what it was, and we had a discussion about it. We seemed to share the same taste in music. I was about 12 going on 13, he was around 18. One Saturday night he said he was going to be late and asked me to help him set up the decks. After that I called for him every night. Roy was an electrician. He'd have been to work and had his tea and while he was getting ready, I would listen to whatever he was playing on his record player, which could be Jimmy Smith, John Mayall or Miles Davis. He played a lot of styles that he may not have played at the club. So, it was an introduction to me of those styles. We'd drive up to the club to get it going. Roy played lots of Hammond organ stuff, Booker T & The MGs, Billy Preston, Jimmy Smith, Wynder K. Frog. The beat was the main thing in that club and the acoustics and the great speakers in there added to it. I only have to hear a record these days such as Eddie Floyd's 'Things Get Better' and I'm back down there. It was that Stax, Atlantic, Bar-Kays, Mar-Keys type of beat. He would play left-field stuff too, such as 'The Letter' by The Box Tops which doesn't fit in with that Mod concept of black music or 'Black Is Black' by Los Bravos, but it has an amazing rhythm.

There would always be slow records played in the middle of the night. In those days a boy and a girl would dance with one leg inside the other one's crotch so during the reggae tunes such as 'Pleasure And Slide' you really got to know about the anatomy of a girl as a teenager. We would watch the black kids dancing and learn from them. There was one great black guy from Brixton, called Kenny, who was a fantastic dancer. Then there were two brothers from Wandsworth Road called Ralph and Malcolm Stanton. They were brilliant, so when you got a tune like 'Billy's Bag' and you get to the middle eight, the floor would clear and they would do this kind of shuffle move that was really quick.

"I ended up cleaning the toilets on a Sunday morning. I just became part of the club, and soon I was playing the records to let Roy have a break. There was another guy called Dennis Conti, and he played the records too. I'd say that everyone passing through the club started in their early teens through to their late teens. It would open at 7 p.m. and shut at 11 on Wednesdays, Fridays and Saturdays. As you walked through the door, there was an unlicensed bar there that sold Pepsi; to the left was the TV room. Laurie Little was employed by Westminster City Council to run it as a kind of youth project so he was responsible for peace and order and was always asking people to leave quietly because it was in the basement of Tintern House, a block of flats. Roy would put on his final record, which was either 'Everybody Go Home' by Eydie Gormé or 'Go Now' by Bessie Banks. You could then see the disappointment in everybody's demeanour. Then the lights would go up and it looked completely different."

Bill Fordham (London): "There was a guy at school called Peter Andon. He was half Cypriot Greek, and he used to bring records into school. This was summer 1966, and a tune I got off of him was 'Baby Do The Philly Dog' by The Olympics. He then told me about the Caxton Club, and I'd never heard of it before. So, we met up and to get there we had to get the bus to Putney, go to Putney station, train to Clapham Junction, on to Victoria. Then we'd walk all around the back of Victoria to get to the estate. Once there, I was just knocked out by the sounds, the atmosphere and the people. It was pitch black, you could hardly see your hand in front of your face, and it was steaming hot. The big tune I remember was 'Rudie Bam Bam' by The Clarendonians. Another big tune was 'Bonanza Ska' by Carlos Malcolm, and all the girls used to do this dance as if riding a horse. They played lots of Tamla stuff too and tunes that stood out were The Ethiopians' 'Train To Skaville', Derrick Morgan's 'Tougher Than Tough', Otis & Carla's 'Tramp', The Mohawks' 'The Champ', Young Rascals' 'Groovin'', The Platters' 'With This Ring'. I went there regularly for about a year."

Brian Wright (London): "We had some great characters down the club. Most of us looked sharp with sharp suits and short hair but there was one guy with a Steve Marriott 'curtains' hairstyle and flamboyant clothes called Tony Murphy. The only way he got away with that was because he was the best fighter in Pimlico. Nobody could criticise him because they'd get a spank. Maxi Justice worked for Dormeuil in Regent Street. He'd nick a suit length for us, three and three-quarter yards, and we'd go to Hymie's the tailor in The Cut at Waterloo, and he'd make it for twenty guineas, which is twenty-one quid, so it was cheap and you looked the business. You only needed two suits probably. One would get old and you would replace it every year or whatever."

Bill Fordham (London): "My brother, and this guy, Mick Humphries, who lived with us, between the two of them their record collection was fantastic. Mick was a friend of my brother, and they were both very much into being Mods, but Mick was always getting into trouble, and his mum kicked him out just before Christmas 1965. So, he came to live with us. Mick was as sharp as a razor, and he had jazz records such as MJQ, Nancy Wilson and Jimmy Smith. My brother had stuff like the Sue records, Tamla, Blue Beat. So, I was hearing all that too. Then I went to the Caxton Club in 1966 and heard rocksteady music that I'd never heard before and to me it was just brilliant. There wasn't that much white music – by '67 there was 'Groovin'' by The Young Rascals and that was a big one, but it was a summer of a lot of Atlantic and Stax stuff with 'Respect' by Aretha Franklin getting a lot of plays down there."

Ian Hingle (London): "I went to the Caxton youth club for a brief period from 1966 to the beginning of 1968. It was the classic thing really why I stopped going, because the kids there were getting younger and I was 17/18, so I was moving on, as you do. It was a youth club, so fair enough. It is quite a big age gap, when you are that age.

"It happened to me when I was 15 and going to the Flamingo and La Discothèque. I thought it was our club, but the older blokes were gone. Anyway, for a while I used to go to the Caxton and it was the most fantastic place. The DJ Roy Hinton, who got an MBE for his youth work, he was a great DJ. He'd play The Mamas & The Papas, The Beach Boys and The Hollies, but he'd also play a ton of Motown. I remember when 'You Can't Hurry Love' came out, he played it six times, which is inconceivable now. 'Beauty Is Only Skin Deep' by The Temptations, he played five times one Friday night. He used to go and buy his records from One Stop in South Molton Street. They used to get all the music there on a Friday and it would be on a Monday elsewhere. I would then get the records I had heard and liked on the Friday/Saturday at the club on the following Monday from my record shop in Fulham.

"I really liked that club and the area of Pimlico in general. It was like Manhattan to me, all tall buildings and really cool, I just found it really exciting after coming from Fulham, which was like a bit of a backwater.

"Those photos of the Caxton that you have were taken one night by a photographer who was doing a feature for some magazine. Even though I was there most nights, funnily enough I'm not in any of them, because the first night he came down, I was suffering from getting properly hammered for the first time. I was only 16 at the time, and I had been at a wedding with my mate. I hardly drank then anyway so I wasn't used to it. Anyway, on that night I am in the signing-in book right at the bottom, as Ian 'The Great' Hingle, written in a drunken scrawl, and that was about eleven o'clock and he'd gone by then."

Bill Fordham (London): "Kids went from everywhere to that club. I went to school in Clapham, so I had an hour's bus ride every morning just to get there, and kids from my school came from all over south London, from our side, Putney,

CAXTON CLUB, 1969

"One of the older guys I was hanging around with said that I should go down the Caxton Club. I walked in the door, down the slope, there's a low ceiling, and there's a tune playing, something like Willie Mitchell's 'That Driving Beat' probably or whatever, and that was it, I was taken. It was a revelation."

BRIAN WRIGHT

south-west London to right over Bermondsey, south-east London. Pete Andon was from Streatham and he went there. I met a girl at the club, Pauline, and she was from Fulham, and went out with another girl called Ellie, and she was from Lambeth. It was mainly south London though. Most of the black guys there were Jamaicans, in that they weren't London-born kids, they had come from Jamaica. It was great, until one night we were leaving the club, when this big group of blokes came up to us blaming us for something we hadn't done, but they gave my mate a spanking, so we got ourselves together and saw a couple of them on their own and chased after them and gave them a good spanking. The Old Bill turned up and I had to go to a juvenile court. After that, because we'd had trouble there, we stopped going to the Caxton altogether. I loved that place, but once trouble starts at a venue, it tends to escalate."

Brian Wright (London): "The club was very white in terms of people in the early days. In the early days it was just kids from the immediate area. As we all got older, going to secondary school, you move out a bit because not everybody goes to school locally. People would bring friends in from other areas. So, you started noticing kids from Church Street, Edgware Road and the estates over there, Vauxhall just over the bridge, Dorset Road, South Lambeth Road, Wandsworth Road, Clapham Junction and so on. Then I'd say, around '67 the word spread about the club because we played such amazing music and we started getting black kids, from Brixton mostly. They came for the music because Roy was playing unbelievable reggae and ska. There was never any trouble in the early days but I guess it started in parallel with the growth of football violence and the whole thing of territorialism. Everybody was getting a bit older and physically stronger and so there was a period of 1967 going into '68 that people started coming down from other areas to take the club and smash it up. The worst was Clapham Junction, and the white kids from Brixton. It just snowballed from there unfortunately. One evening the Clapham Junction turned up mob-handed and they couldn't get in. Laurie had got a tip-off that they were coming and they locked the doors. A bit later everybody thought they had gone, but they had gone back up the slope onto Alderney Street near Ebury Bridge waiting for people to come out.

"There was one guy, Arthur Peck, who was probably one of the best fighters in Westminster, and he had a little firm with him of local boys. It just kicked off into a mass brawl. Arthur got hit over the head with a hammer – it could have killed him but he was fortunate. It put a lot of kids off coming, and it did change after that incident. It always felt a little bit more edgy after that night. To be fair, a lot of the black guys from Brixton and Stockwell helped to defend the club, so there was still no racial tension, which kind of contradicts the popular concept of Skinhead. I was never aware of any kind of tension, even when black guys danced with white girls, nobody gave a toss. Whereas that would be frowned upon and there'd always be a stigma in other certain areas of London about that."

Bonny Staplehurst (London): "We used to go to the Caxton Club in Pimlico, but only a few times. It was a bit lively in there. Sometimes it was terrifying. My sister Janet found it very cliquey. It sort of went from very Moddy to fifty-fifty black

and white and it changed. I guess we were a little bit younger than most. I used to hang around by the phone, that was my spot. You were safe there. Our mate still to this day, whenever he hears 'Phoenix City' he'll duck, 'cos down the Caxton, that would have been a sign for it all to kick off. It was packed in there. No control on the numbers going in really. Gradually people we knew stopped going there. Too heavy."

Brian Wright (London): "By '69, more and more people at the Caxton Club were getting away from the smooth sharp Mod look, and there were a few more jeans and bomber jackets, cropped hair with heavy sideburns and razored partings. Not a lot, but it was noticeable. As the reach of the club spread out further in London, there were a lot more people that we didn't know and the club just didn't feel the same. It gradually felt less and less like a local club, and more just like a venue for people to come to. There was an increase in violence and the music changed to something that really wasn't my bag. Things like the stuff by Judge Dread, 'Skinhead Moonstomp' by Symarip, and 'Monkey Man' by The Maytals weren't my kind of thing at all. Roy just saw it as his vocation to keep kids off the streets, so if he played what they wanted, it helped. Musically, he was very much a purist, but he would have shared an interest, just because he was a generous person. He would never diss or criticise anything, because he knew he was from a different era and background. But on the downside, certain records never got played again, so tunes such as 'Green Door' by Wynder K. Frog or 'You Can't Sit Down' by The Phil Upchurch Combo that had a heritage from Modernism, had no relevance to the new kids coming in, who would assert themselves in a more physical way, rather than a cultural or expressive way. Also, the girls started dressing less in a high-street fashion, that geometric cut disappeared, as it did all over London. They started getting into the two-tone mohair suit, button-down shirts, and miniskirt with white tights. It's the way the look went, so the vibe and atmosphere in the club changed anyway. Apart from being an aural thing, it was a visual thing too. You looked around, you looked for influences, as in, I like his shoes, I wonder where he got them from? Dr Martens don't have the same appeal to me as a pair of wingtip brogues, and never will."

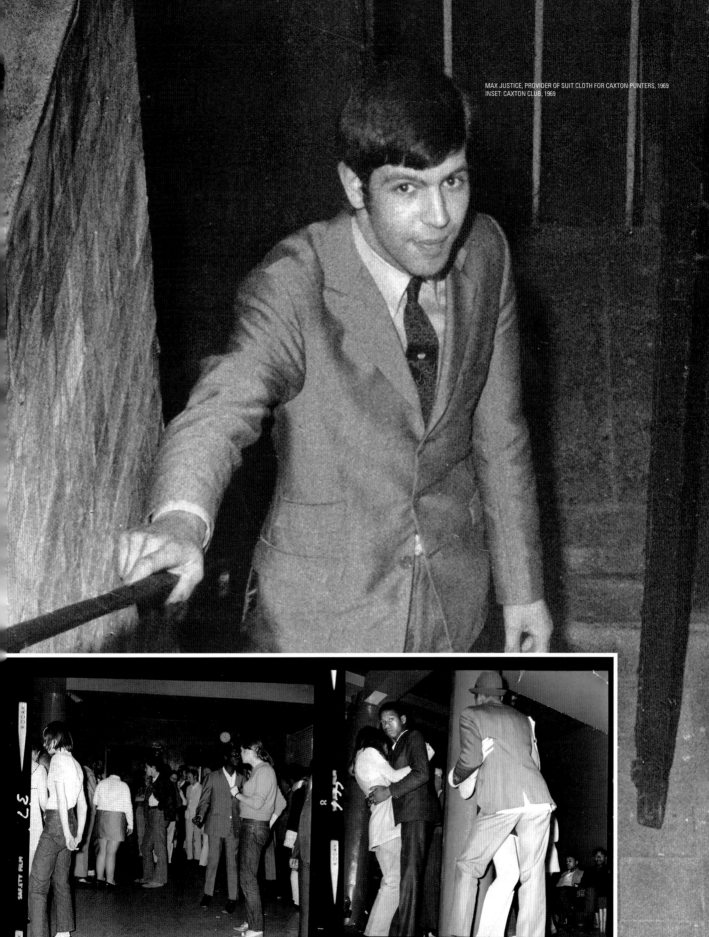

MAX JUSTICE, PROVIDER OF SUIT CLOTH FOR CAXTON PUNTERS, 1969
INSET: CAXTON CLUB, 1969

BRIAN WRIGH[T]

Brian Wright's Caxton favourites

'Guns of Navarone': Skatalites
'Al Capone': Prince Buster
'Take It Easy': Hopeton Lewis
'Feel Like Dancing': Marcia Griffiths
'I'm Still In Love With You Girl': Alton Ellis
'Judge Dread': Prince Buster
'Pressure and Slide': The Tennors
'Phoenix City': Roland Alphonso
'Train To Skaville', 'The Whip': The Ethiopians
'Train Tour To Rainbow City': The Pyramids
'Sweet Soul Music': Arthur Conley
'Land of a Thousand Dances', 'You're Looking Good', 'Stagger Lee', 'Mustang Sally': Wilson Picket
'Satisfaction', 'Respect', 'Hard To Handle', 'Love Man': Otis Redding
'Things Get Better': Eddie Floyd
'Green Onions', 'Hip Hug Her', 'Time Is Tight': Booker T
'The Champion', 'That Driving Beat': Willie Mitchell
'The Champ': The Mohawks
'Tighten Up' parts 1 & 2, 'Here I Go Again': Archie Bell
'In The Midnight Hour', 'Billy's Bag': Billy Preston
'Que Sera Sera', 'Michael': Geno Washington
'The Letter': The Box Tops
'Gimme Little Sign': Brook Benton
'Whole Lot Of Love', '60 Minutes Of Your Time': Homer Banks
'Respect', 'Don't Play That Song For Me', 'Think': Aretha Franklin
'Green Door': Wynder K. Frog
'Private Number': William Bell & Judy Clay
'Last Night': Mar-Keys
'Soulfinger','Sock It To 'Em JB': The Bar-Kays
'You Can't Sit Down': The Phil Upchurch Combo
'The Horse': Cliff Nobles
'Take Me In Your Arms And Love Me', 'Heard It Through The Grapevine': Gladys Knight & The Pips
'Shotgun', 'Shake & Fingerpop': Junior Walker
'Hold On, I'm Coming', 'You Don't Know Like I Know', 'Soul Man': Sam & Dave
'The Duck': Jackie Lee
'Tell Mama': Etta James
'Boogaloo #3': Roy Lee Johnson

LAST RECORDS
'Go Now': Bessie Banks
'Everybody Go Home': Eydie Gorme

ATLANTIC

45 RPM

584083

SWEET SOUL MUSIC
ARTHUR CONLEY

45-2097

THAT DRIVING BEAT
WILLIE MITCHELL

Red Bird
45RPM

BELINDA (LDN)
BC.106-A

BC.106

GO NOW
(Milton Bennett, L. Banks)
BESSIE BANKS
Produced by Leiber-Stoller
A Blue Cat. U.S.A. Recording

INVICTUS

INV 501

GIVE ME JUST A LITTLE MORE TIME
(Dunbar — Wayne)
CHAIRMEN OF THE BOARD

Phil~L.A. OF SOUL

THE HORSE
(Instrumental)
CLIFF NOBLES & CO.
313

GET YA GROOVE ON, CAXTON CLUB, 1969

NEL 2758 NEW ENGLISH LIBRARY

SKINHEAD

The savage
story of Britain's
newest teenage cult
of violence.
By Richard Allen

CHAPTER 14: BOOKS AND FILMS

Not long after 'Skinhead' had gone overground, to the point where it was a look and a name recognised by most people on any high street, a book was being passed around on council estates and in school playgrounds. Someone would be telling you, "You've gotta read this, it's written by a geezer called Richard Allen."

The young and impressionable were then told tales of the sex and violence that lay within its pages, as well as bang up-to-date information on what you should be wearing. "Telling you, this Joe Hawkins, mate, only 16, but already the leader of his gang…"

Who could resist that?

The first book, *Skinhead*, which was published by the New English Library in June 1970, can now be judged as cashing in on the scene. But at the time, the glorification of the general delinquency and aggro at football matches described in the book ensured it quickly gained a cult status.

It later transpired that in reality the author 'Richard Allen' was one of many pseudonyms for a writer called James Moffat. He was born in 1922 and was Canadian. He studied law at Queen's University in Canada, but soon dropped out to travel the world. He ended up in the UK in the 1960s. He was a hack writer, who it is said worked under at least forty-five different names, as basically a gun for hire, churning out something like 290 books on demand. Children's books, pulp fiction novels, ghost-written sports books, all came from the pen of Moffat.

He was 48 at the time of Skinhead and he was called in to write the book, as he was considered the fastest 'hack' that the New English Library team knew of. Which was handy, as he was given a deadline to complete the book of just a week. His research comprised driving over to east London and having a drink with a group of Skinheads in a pub. They were resistant at first, but as the beer flowed, so did the stories and 'Richard Allen' absorbed as much of it as he could. The book was out within weeks with a Skinhead, who had been photographed in Croydon, staring defiantly at the reader on the cover. Its tagline, printed in white text on the bottom left-hand corner, promised the reader "The savage story of Britain's newest teenage cult of violence."

Of course, a generation of little 'erberts knew nothing of Allen/Moffat's back story then, nor would we have cared much. We just wanted to get our grubby paws on the books. When we did, we discovered what we had been told about: loads of random gang and football violence, illicit and unlawful sex and overt and over-the-top racism. The language used to describe a lot of what takes place in the Allen books would simply not be tolerated in today's more enlightened world, but back then it was in everyday use. Despite, or maybe because of that, depending on what side of the fence you were on, this book and the seventeen others that were to follow over the next ten years sold in massive numbers. Indeed, the first one, *Skinhead*, became a million-seller. Richard Allen was even described as the 'Dickens of the Skinhead movement'.

The hero of those early books, Joe Hawkins, as mentioned earlier, was described by his creator as "semi-educated, enjoying the charade of being a decent citizen even as he battered some innocent's skull to pulp." In *Skinhead,* Joe is a member of an east London gang, Plaistow to be precise, but he is soon branching out and looking for richer pickings by moving 'up West' in the follow-up, *Suedehead*. He remains, however, a nasty piece of work.

James Moffat responded when charged with being a racist, that he and his books were only reflecting society. Moffat, described as an 'alcoholic chain-smoker', died in November 1993.

The eighteen books in the series are as follows. Original copies, in excellent condition, are now highly collectable.

Skinhead (June 1970)
Suedehead (1971)
Demo (1971)
Boot Boys (1972)
Skinhead Escapes (1972)
Skinhead Girls (1972)
Glam (1973)
Smoothies (1973)
Sorts (1973)
Teeny Bopper Idol (1973)
Top Gear Skin (1973)
Trouble For Skinhead (1973)
Skinhead Farewell (1974)
Dragon Skins (1975)
Terrace Terrors (1975)
Knuckle Girls (1977)
Punk Rock (1977)
Mod Rule (1980)

Norman Jay MBE (London): "My bible was *Skinhead* by Richard Allen. That and *Suedehead* where the two boys are on the cover in Crombies. I've got the whole set of them as first editions. My Jane got them for me as a birthday present. I loved all of them. *Skinhead* was the first book I remember reading. I used to be able to quote whole passages of those books.

"Joe Hawkins became a fucking icon for us. Even though he was a fictional character, round our way, Joe Hawkins was the fucking Don. You know, sticking the boot in… Richard Allen referenced certain places in west London and Acton and I'd think, how the fuck does this guy know that? His research must have been really good. I found out later that Richard Allen wasn't even his real name and in reality he was an active fascist!"

Jim Cameron (Glasgow): "In Glasgow, we had very little Afro-Caribbean influence. Until we saw the Richard Allen books,

> "My bible was *Skinhead* by Richard Allen. That and *Suedehead* where the two boys are on the cover in Crombies. I've got the whole set of them as first editions. My Jane got them for me as a birthday present. I loved all them. *Skinhead* was the first book I remember reading. I used to be able to quote whole passages of those books."
>
> NORMAN JAY MBE

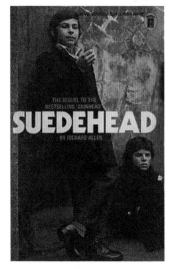

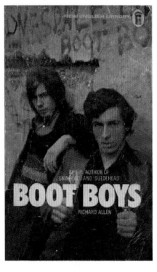

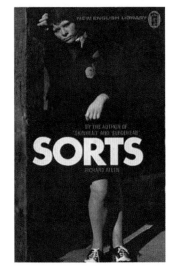

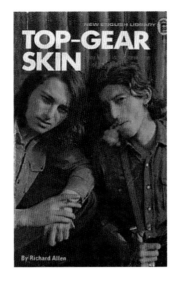

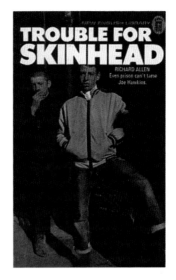

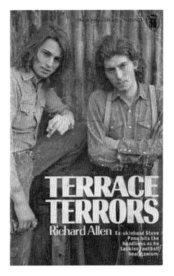

we'd never even heard the term 'Paki-bashing'. That wasn't a Glasgow term, but then some of the Skinheads in Glasgow started using the term. On the whole I never saw a lot of the racist thing in Glasgow, with the Skinheads. I honestly didn't. But in reality, the Richard Allen book wasn't that great. It was cheap pulp."

Clive Knight (London): "I never rated the Richard Allen books. They came out at the back end of my time as a Skin. I did see them in the bookshops and did gloss through them but they never seemed real to me, and certainly, when scanning the books, I did not recognise what he was writing as what I had lived."

Jim Cameron (Glasgow): "When the Richard Allen books became popular in Glasgow, some kids in Glasgow started wearing West Ham scarves because Joe Hawkins was a West Ham fan. I mean the racist thing was nonsense, but we all looked up to Joe Hawkins books. My best friend Mitch, who lives in London now, funnily enough, his mum was a sales rep who went down to London every week. I remember him saying to his mum, 'Next time you're in London get me a West Ham scarf.' He used to wear it on his wrist, going to the Celtic games. And then we started seeing a few West Ham scarves in the Jungle [North End terracing]. It was the Joe Hawkins thing. As a football fan, I loved West Ham. Clyde Best, Bobby Moore, Geoff Hurst, Martin Peters and their manager Ron Greenwood. The West Ham manager was quite close to Jock Stein, our great manager."

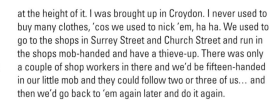

at the height of it. I was brought up in Croydon. I never used to buy many clothes, 'cos we used to nick 'em, ha ha. We used to go to the shops in Surrey Street and Church Street and run in the shops mob-handed and have a thieve-up. There was only a couple of shop workers in there and we'd be fifteen-handed in our little mob and they could follow two or three of us… and then we'd go back to 'em again later and do it again.

"We'd grab Sta-Prest and Toniks, Ben Shermans, always a Ben, not Brutus. I had a Harrington away and a Crombie. I bought my sheepskin off an old Jewish guy down in Petticoat Lane. He wanted £35 for it and, if I remember right, I offered £30 but he insisted on £31.

"My first crop was from the barbers near Surrey Street, a geezer, 'Italian Tony', and my dad took me. He made me have it. Told me it would last a long time – ha ha.

"Even though I was only 14 in '68/'69, I was drinking in pubs like the Forum in Croydon, the Red Deer and clubs, Sinatra's and the Orchid. They used to have dos for the younger ones on Saturday afternoons in Sinatra's and Mondays at the Orchid. Still used to have a beer in there too…

"Music-wise, I remember T. Rex and 'Ride A White Swan', which was a big Skinhead tune when I was 15, Slade when they were Skinheads, 'Spirit In The Sky', Norman Greenbaum, The Chi-Lites and of course, Desmond Dekker,

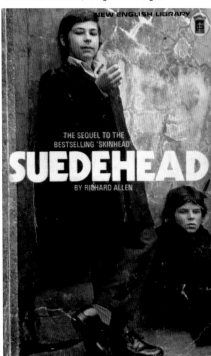

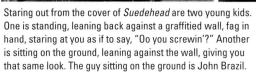

LEFT: STEVE COURTMAN AND JOHN BRAZIL ON THE COVER OF *SUEDEHEAD* (TAKEN AT SCARSBROOK RD, SALEM PLACE, CROYDON)
RIGHT: EITHER SIDE OF DEAN COUBROUGH, 2017

Staring out from the cover of *Suedehead* are two young kids. One is standing, leaning back against a graffitied wall, fag in hand, staring at you as if to say, "Oo you screwin'?" Another is sitting on the ground, leaning against the wall, giving you that same look. The guy sitting on the ground is John Brazil.

John Brazil (London): "I was born in 1956 and I first noticed the Skinhead fashions when I was about 11, so I was 13/14

'The Israelites' and 'Young, Gifted and Black' and all that. Also loved 'Band Of Gold', Freda Payne, 'Pick A Rose For My Rose', Marv Johnson, and 'Stoned Love', Diana Ross and The Supremes. My fave tune would be 'Boom Shaka Laka' by Hopeton Lewis, from 1970.

"Used to be a big store in Croydon called Kennards and it had a big mall, a sort of arcade-type thing, going from

Church Street to North End, up into the high street, and it had a couple of bridges going over that mall and that used to be our little haunt and we used to hang about there, with our gangs, and have a tear-up. Also used to go to football, up the Palace now and then, and there was always a punch-up there. I was always at it.

"Around the Croydon area, there was about five or six little mobs and we used to mix it with the older ones. Most of my mob, I used to go to school with. We'd be about twenty-handed. On a Saturday, we'd meet at 10 a.m. or 11 a.m. in a café called the Lunchbox. I'd be up early, 'cos I used to do a paper round, 'cos like my mum and dad didn't have no money, so I used to have to get my own money. I also used to work on the market, selling a bit of fruit and veg, you know.

"Anyway, we'd meet up at the Lunchbox, have a bit of breakfast and then, when we were team-handed, have a walk down to Kennards and have another cup of tea and see what was about. Actually, that's how I got involved with the book. This chap came along and said to us, 'Do you fancy being on the cover of a book?' and then I said, 'Yeah alright then mate, whatever.'

"There was five of us with him originally and he asked where was the best place to have the photo taken. So, we took him to a few places in Croydon, where we'd hang about and that, and we ended up in an alley by the swimming baths and he took his photos. In the end, he just put me and my mate Steve Courtman on the book. He mentioned he'd give us a drink for doing it, but we got knocked for it, never got a penny from 'em. I'm wearing my nicked Crombie in that. A couple of my other mates were on *Boot Boys* I think. The same geezer came round again and photographed more of our gang. He promised us the earth, but gave us nothing.

"The geezer on the cover of the first book, *Skinhead*, was called Les Kent and he got a good kicking when that came out and everyone was saying to us, 'Cor, you gonna get a good kicking when that comes out,' but we got nothing. They loved us. Well, Steve's old man gave him a good hiding 'cos he had

a fag in his hand! When I went to see Steve not long after, his old man said, 'Little bastard, just kicked the fuck out of him…'

"All the Suedeheads used to go down to Brighton and have a couple of little ding-dongs with the Rockers. That was when it went from brogues to loafers. Mohair strides and the shirt tucked in. I also used to wear Dealer boots and Dr Martens. Used to get them in West Croydon, shop called Hollidges, or from a traveller fella called George, he used to serve us.

"I had a suit made when I went to Tavistock school. The tailor used to make them for the footballers. He was close to the school and a café we used to use. 'Cos I was still at school, I managed to talk him round and my first suit was £24. It was a blue and gold Tonik, which was lovely, with a three-button jacket.

"Our youth club was the Old Town Boys Club, which is still going. We'd all go up there and thought we were Jack the Lads. But this club leader we had, Tony, you just couldn't beat him whatever happened. I never forget we went rock climbing one day and were on the way back. We were messing about at the back of the coach. We're only 13/14.

Anyway, my mate Tommy Short was sticking his two fingers up and gets caught. 'Tommy, pack that in,' says Tony. 'I ain't doing nothing, Tone,' Tommy says. Anyway, five minutes later he does it again. He gets warned again and again pleads his innocence. Five minutes later, he does it again. 'Right Tommy, I did warn you,' and he pulls the coach over, open the doors and says, 'Right, out you get.' Tommy says, 'I don't know where I am!' and Tony says, 'You'll find your way home,' and drives off! Left him there.

"Another time, we were having a sparring competition at the club. All got our gloves on and that, and it was good fun. Tony says to put the gloves away, and I said OK, but carried on boxing. 'Right,' he says, 'put the gloves away, you've had a warning.' I just carried on. 'Right, that's it, you're banned for a week.' So, I stuck one on him! Give him an upper cut, and he says, 'You're banned for a month.' It didn't mean nothing to

"Anyway, we'd meet up at the Lunchbox, have a bit of breakfast and then, when we were team-handed, have a walk down to Kennards and have another cup of tea and see what was about. Actually, that's how I got involved with the book. This chap came along and said to us, 'Do you fancy being on the cover of a book?' and then I said, 'Yeah alright then mate, whatever.'"

JOHN BRAZIL

THE SCOTSWOOD AGGRO BOYS,
JULY 1972

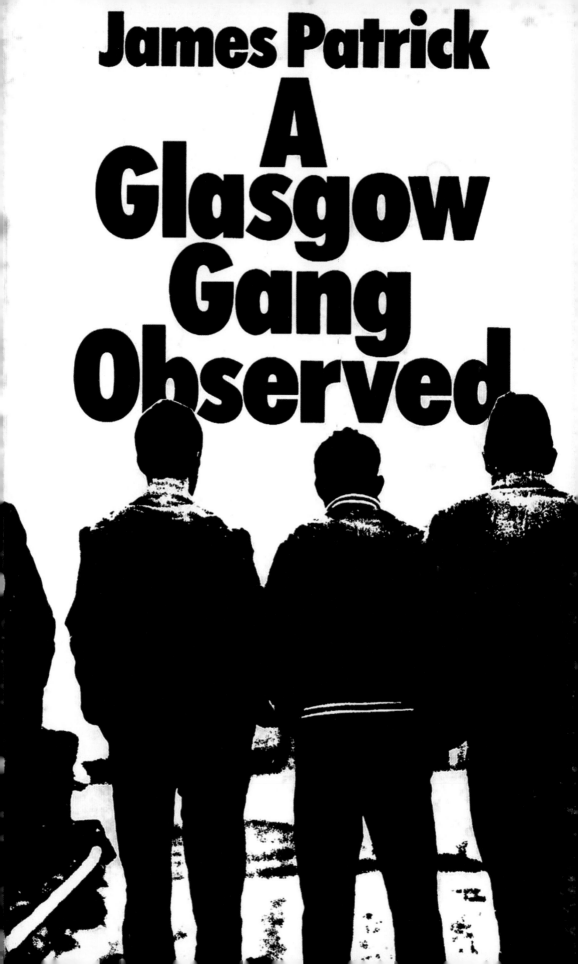

James Patrick
A Glasgow Gang Observed

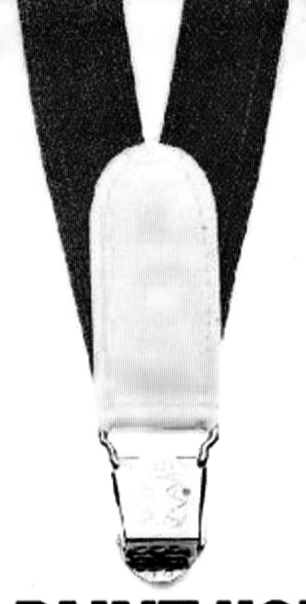

THE PAINT HOUSE

WORDS FROM AN EAST END GANG

PENGUIN EDUCATION SPECIALS

"And our gang was 'The Shamrock', and 'The Shamrock' came from an area right next to us, known as the Gam Gad, that was original 'Shamrock' but when the high-rise opened, we became part of their gang scene. The gang goes back to the thirties. We fought with the Posso gangs and the Springburn gangs. Gangs that bordered your area. During the Skinhead days, I was about 14 to 15, arguably the best days of my life. It wasn't all violence and bleak. We had some great laughs."
JIM CAMERON

me, so I went in the next night and apologised, told him I didn't mean it. He accepted the apology but said, 'You're still banned for a month, and if you do anything else, it'll be two.' Well, I swear that was the longest two months of my life. All my mates were in there every night and letting me have it 'cos I couldn't go. That club leader taught everyone there really. You didn't mess with him. He taught you the rights and wrongs.

"For me, it all moved on when I got my first car, though we'd still meet up for a game of football and then go for a Wimpy, and then bump into the pictures, but gradually we just moved. I nicked my football boots from this geezer who worked in a sports shop in Church Street. He said, 'I'm watching you, looks like you're about to nick something,' and I said, 'I'm having them, mate,' looking at the boots. Anyway, we ended up having a thing going. I'd walk in, give him the signal, and get two pairs. One would be for me and I'd sell the others and give him his bit from them. Nice little scam. We all came off of council estates, my brother was in a wheelchair and my mum and dad couldn't drive and they had their hands full, if you know what I mean. If you wanted something, you had to get it.

"My old mob still meet up, last Friday of every month for a beer. Down to about ten of us now. I let it all go as I got older and got the car, but since you got in touch to ask about doing this, I've just bought a Harrington, ha ha!"

Two other books that cover the culture from a factual basis rather than fiction are *The Paint House: Words From An East End Gang* and *A Glasgow Gang Observed*.

The Paint House is written by several people who come from Stepney and Bethnal Green and linked to a specific gang known as the Collinwood. First published in 1972, it follows the members of a community centre known as the Paint House. It makes for depressing reading, and concentrates on the more racist and violent aspects of the gang.

A Glasgow Gang Observed by James Patrick is an observation study of a juvenile gang called the Young Team, between October 1966 and January 1967. Slightly pre-Skinhead, again, it follows violence, mainly territorial, but it does have some nice clothing details. The Scottish slang can sometimes make for hard reading.

The 'gallous gear' then was: a dark suit with a middle vent of twelve to fourteen inches in the jacket (two vents were 'played oot'); two to three inch flaps over the pockets (a ticket-pocket was de rigueur); tight trousers with one-inch turn-ups (the season for two inches was to come before my four months were over and the fashion of no turn-ups at all was already passed); ties had to be spotted with a matching handkerchief 'fur the toap pocket' (by January the white polka dot was out, and 'college ties', bought or preferably stolen from Forsyth's, Rowan's or Carswell's were all the rage); shoes, otherwise known as 'yir manoeuvres', were ridiculed unless they were London toes (this later changed to brogues, which like 'college ties' are more middle-class items of dress). Tim advised me when ordering a suit to ask for 'a finger-tip jacket', i.e. one which stretches to the end of the boy's middle finger when his

arm is at his side. Alternatives were reefer or denim jackets and suits ('Eddie's got a right cracker'), patch pockets, pleats for vents, hipsters (really 'on their way oot', but still acceptable if cherry-red and split over the bridge of the foot), and, for those with more exotic tastes, leather and suede and mohair coats and suits. The whole effect was summed up in the phrase 'aw geared up'.
JAMES PATRICK, A GLASGOW GANG OBSERVED

Jim Cameron (Glasgow): "That *Glasgow Gang Observed* book is set before the Skinhead scene came to Glasgow. In later life I got to know a couple of guys that were in it. It's a very bleak book. We've had a gang culture in Glasgow since the thirties. It's very violent, and there are parts of Glasgow I don't like. I mean I love my city to bits, and I couldn't live anywhere else, but like every other big city, we've got a lot of bad things, and the violence in the Glasgow gang scene, even in the Skinhead days, created a lot of bleakness. That book portrayed it quite well. It's quite depressing at times.

"The territorial trouble was part of our lives. We were brought up in huge tower blocks. It was around '67 when they had just opened. I think I'm right in saying this, but Sighthill was the biggest high-rise estate in Europe. There were about twenty high-rise blocks. And our gang was the Shamrock, and the Shamrock came from an area right next to us, known as the Gam Gad, that was original Shamrock but when the high-rise opened, we became part of their gang scene. The gang goes back to the thirties. We fought with the Posso gangs and the Springburn gangs. Gangs that bordered your area. During the Skinhead days, I was about 14 to 15, arguably the best days of my life. It wasn't all violence and bleak. We had some great laughs."

The one film that depicts the Skinhead/Suedehead era head-on, and indeed in some respects shows the transition between the two, is *Bronco Bullfrog*. Shot on the streets of London's East End in 1969, it was released in London in October 1970. Its cast was made up, not of actors, but of local east London residents, who were for the most part attending local drama classes run by the 'mother of modern theatre', Joan Littlewood.

When the film opened, the critics loved it. They celebrated its neorealist filmmaking style, with the *Evening Standard* describing it as a "smashing and pretty sobering cockney film". It even went on to win an award at Cannes. Despite all that, many who saw it didn't rate it at all, finding it 'amateurish' and 'poorly acted'.

It closed eighteen days after its release at the Cameo Poly in Oxford Circus in the West End of London. The film's distributor, in truth, didn't know what to do with it. They even considered a name change for the film, with *Around Angel Lane* considered. In the end, it was pretty much shelved for thirty-odd years.

The film that replaced it at the Cameo was *Three Sisters*, directed by Sir Laurence Olivier. Its premiere was attended by Princess Anne. As she walked up the red carpet, she was met by a protest and a few stray rotten tomatoes thrown by the Beaumont Youth Club of Leyton demanding that the Bronco film be reinstated. "Princess Anne Met by Skinhead Mob at Film Premiere" thundered the *Daily Telegraph*, reporting the incident the next day.

Princess Anne, instead of being too bothered by it, instead accepted an invitation to see *Bronco Bullfrog* the following week, and this she duly did at the Mile End ABC, finding herself sitting next to Sam Shepherd, who played the part of 'Bronco Bullfrog'. Shepherd bent down to kiss Princess Anne's hand, only to be later dragged away by the police, and issued with a severe warning about his behaviour.

The director of *Bronco Bullfrog* was 25-year-old Barney Platts-Mills, whose father, John Platts-Mills QC, had defended Reg and Ron Kray and the Great Train Robbers earlier in the decade. Barney Platts-Mills picked up early film work at Shepperton Studios and contributed in a minor way to films such as *Spartacus* and *A Kind Of Loving*. He eventually moved in the world of Free Cinema, liking the idea of 'accessible, free, working-class cinema'.

He then met Joan Littlewood. Platts-Mills made a half-hour short film called *Everybody's An Actor, Shakespeare Said* using Littlewood's 'boys' who attended her drama workshops at the Play Barn. One of the boys, Del Walker, made quite an impression on Platts-Mills. He decided to use Del as the figurehead in a film he was planning, which went on to be *Bronco*. The storyline followed him and his best mate Roy, as well as a group of their mates, as they roamed the streets of Stratford and its surrounding environs in east London, looking for easy money and cheap thrills through petty crime.

Its plot was concocted by the workshop students and pretty much based on their own lives at the time. To secure the actors for the roles, Platts-Mills got them time off work and doubled their wages while they worked on the film.
We see the gang break in at a local café, and run into their old pal Jo Saville, known to them as 'Bronco Bullfrog'. Jo is fresh out of borstal and already planning new skulduggery. Before the next planned robbery, Del meets Irene, played by Anne Gooding, and they strike up a relationship. Facing dissenting parental pressure however, they begin planning to escape from the dead-end life that is mapped out for them. The climax of the film finds Del, Irene and Jo on the run from the authorities.

The fascinating thing in the film for most, though, is the clothes worn by the boys. Very much Skinhead/Suedehead in style, the crossover away from the crew-cut look to a longer-haired look is clearly evident.

The rough-and-ready approach to the film, with its use of untrained actors, either spoils the film, or actually makes it more enjoyable, depending on your viewpoint. But what is undeniable is that for many with an eye on the clobber, it is the details and hairstyles on show that keep them watching.

After the end of filming, none of the cast acted again. Sam Shepherd moved from running pubs and working in clubs, to ending up working on Spitalfields market. Del went back to plumbing and eventually moved to the Isle of Wight. Sadly Anne Gooding, who played Irene, died at the age of 50.

It is said it is an honest film," Shepherd once said. "An honest film with dodgy acting, dodgy actors. We were

"*Bronco*" Sam Shepherd . . . He organised the demo—but it was "nothing personal"

all like that in those days. Turn your back and we'd have nicked the camera."

During the years of its disappearance, *Bronco Bullfrog* was spoken about in hushed tones as being a 'lost classic' of British cinema. We were also aware of dodgy VHS copies of it that were doing the rounds in the late nineties, and these were highly sought after. Then, the original negatives of the film were discovered in a skip. They were rescued and returned to Platts-Mills, who set about re-releasing it with all the bells and whistles available in 2003.

The film continues to divide opinion. Some love it, some hate it, others don't get it at all.

A bit like the world of Skinheads and Suedeheads when you think about it.

BRONCO B

Del Walker   Anne G

ULLFROG

ing Sam Shepherd

CAXTON
DISCOTHEQUE

834 1883

R. HINTON
834 3640

L.S. LITTLE
733 4829

CHAPTER 15: SUEDEHEAD ERA

So, who knows why or when the Skinheads got tagged Suedeheads. Well, as stated earlier, the *Daily Mirror* had mentioned the name way back in early February 1970, but the clothing dealer John Simons has yet another take.

John Simons (London): "Some of our early customers around then, well to us, we called them 'Suedeheads'. They had a clean-cut, collegiate look with a hard London edge. I would suggest that I didn't hear of a major movement because they were thin on the ground, those guys, they were the kind of elite. I would also suggest that 'our' Suedeheads pre-dated the Skinheads, but only at the Ivy shop in Richmond. Absolutely!

"I'm not saying [they were] all over, and you have to remember the geography of this, but they were around in '64, '65, '66… they wouldn't have that name in the mainstream then, of course, but it was a certain look, a harder look than Carnaby Street at the time. Sharper. Yeah, yeah, yeah… They wore chinos, short in the leg, 15-inch bottoms, brogues, with an Ivy-style blazer, with an Atkinson's Irish poplin tie, not a knitted tie, they did not wear knitted ties. They wore the military stripe. Really nice stripes… If the name had existed in the mainstream, our customers at the Ivy shop would have been nominated as Suedeheads. People might challenge that, but you can't make this shit up! I was there on a daily basis. Front line. I doubt I used that expression – Suedeheads – more than twenty times in those days.

"It was a great look and there wasn't any difference from the standard Ivy League look really. Later at the Squire shop in Brewer Street, after the Skinheads had appeared and gone overground, we had what I call sophisticated Skinheads.

"Another look that I remember was the 'California' look. Long blond hair, but wearing the Ivy clothing. Like the early seventies surfers. Never see anyone mention that though…

"Nowadays, there is a sin of misinformation… There is too much of a big black line from when The Beatles started. Everything before that has been disregarded. The fifties weren't in black and white. The photos were in black and white, but my life wasn't!"

Brian Wright (London): "Our natural hinterland was the King's Road, Chelsea, as well as the West End, so we naturally got into going down the King's Road. The Birds Nest was probably the place to go, certainly on a Friday and a Saturday night. This is around '68 onwards. They started getting into funk, so they'd be playing James Brown, and it was very good for funk for about two years. Then you got T. Rex, Rod Stewart & The Faces, but they still played a mixture. My mates were going the full way with the flares, and all that with their feathered haircuts. I just kept my style with sharp suits, button-down shirts if I could find them, brogues, short hair with a side parting, college-boy cut, basically. There would be nights when there might be five of us, and there's five birds from Chelsea or Clapham Junction or wherever, so we'd get chatting, but the birds couldn't

work me out. Because I looked so different to my mates, they thought I'd just come out of prison. The girl would look me up and down in my suit, my short hair and my Mod gear, and she might be a few years younger than us, therefore she'd have no concept of Mod. If she'd only just become a teenager in 1970, by '72 we are still going down the Birds Nest, the Trafalgar, the Chelsea Drugstore and places like that. They'd have no concept of what had gone before, so I looked like their dad. I just loved how I looked.

"I had a Saturday job, as well as my job as a printer's apprentice, on a market fruit stall. I was earning more on the stall than I was as an apprentice. I knew this bloke who worked in Moss Brothers in Covent Garden, who used to fancy me and Brian, the bloke I worked for. He used to come up to the stall and give us a carrier bag of gear that he'd nicked out of the shop, and we'd give him a carrier bag of fruit in exchange. I'm about 21, and had cashmere roll-necks worn inside my suit or a cashmere cardigan worn with a button-down shirt. Because I knew it was good gear, it gave me confidence. I didn't care about brown velvet suits, I just thought I looked the nuts in a jacket and a sky-blue cashmere roll-neck. Every so often you'd meet a chick that did get what you were into."

Andrew Vaughan (Orrell): "I was there at the Royal British Legion under-18 night. Me and my mates were in our two-tone tonic trousers, Ben Sherman shirts and highly polished brogues. Right little Suedeheads we were – acting hard, watching the girls and older boys dance. Shuffling our feet to the rocksteady beat of Jamaica via Trojan Records of London. For reggae was the music of the time and we loved it as much as you could love anything at 12 years of age. In fact, what wasn't there to love about this great dance music that was all wrapped up in the culture of our times? Smart music for smart young boys and then…

"Some of our early customers around then, well to us, we called them 'Suedeheads.' They had a clean-cut, collegiate look with a hard London edge. I would suggest that I didn't hear of a major movement because they were thin on the ground, those guys, they were the kind of elite. I would also suggest that 'our' Suedeheads pre-dated the Skinheads, but only at the Ivy shop in Richmond. Absolutely!"

JOHN SIMONS

"One Friday night in March 1971 something happened. In the spot where the DJ played a half-hour of pop music – and just after an airing of 'My Sweet Lord' by George Harrison and 'Resurrection Shuffle' by Ashton, Gardner & Dyke – a song came blasting out of the sound system that was so different, so wonderful that nothing would ever be the same again.

"The song was 'Hot Love' by T. Rex. It was brilliant then and while it's still brilliant now it was never as good as that night in Orrell, near Wigan, West Lancashire, when 150 teenagers sang the 'na, na, na, na, na, na, naaa' refrain in unison.

"We eagerly awaited next week's *Top Of The Pops* and we weren't to be disappointed. The appearance of T. Rex was to go down as one of the classic *Top Of The Pops* performances as the lead singer, Marc Bolan, in his satin, velvet and lace with a dab of glitter under each eye, slayed the nation. It is generally considered to be the moment that glam rock was born: in a BBC studio in west London. However, some of us know it all happened a week earlier, 200 miles north.

"We also knew that nothing would be the same again…"

Chris Difford (London): "I followed my passion, which was music, and slowly being in a band dragged me away from the streets and the gangs, which by then had begun to drift. Prison took some away, and drugs the rest. I was lucky to escape when I did. It did get very dark towards the end."

Paul Weller (Woking): "Two of the top boys in Woking were a black fella called Abe Milan and a white fella called Ricky Vince, both hard nuts and both brilliant dressers. I knew Ricky a little as his mum and mine were friends. I remember seeing him walking down Walton Road near Stanley Road where I lived, dressed in a petrol blue suit jacket, red gingham shirt, faded Levis jeans, red socks and oxblood Smooths. He just looked like the coolest person I'd ever seen. If I think about it now, I'd probably still think the same thing. I don't think that style can be bettered."

Norman Jay MBE (London): "In September 1969, I start in my secondary school and I go from short trousers to long trousers. The monitors there, all from the fourth year, were all Skinheads and they were terrifying. A lot of them wore hobnails. One of them filed back the leather to reveal the steel toe-cap. They then died away and by my second and third year, it had become smart. Suedehead really.

"There was a kid called Rudy Weller and he wore clothes six months before the rest of us did. Don't ask me where he got the money from. He was like a walking mannequin. Because we saw him every day, you saw what the fashions were going to be in advance.

"Rudy and Seamus, the older brother of my classmate Dermot, were buying from the Ivy shop in Richmond. The brogues and the plains. My school was only five stops from Richmond, so we went down there by train. Without Rudy, who was a couple of years older than us, we wouldn't have known of these styles for another year. He went on to be a famous sculptor and his work includes *The Horses of Helios* sculpture on Haymarket in the West End.

"Rudy was the first to wear monkey boots. 'Got to get them,' we said. The black boys loved the monkey boots. Funnily enough a lot of the white kids wore only leather-soled shoes, with a Blakey on them. They had to have that 'click'.

"Dermot then grew his hair a bit longer and was the first Suedehead I knew. I was a bit fearful of the Skinheads, but the Suedehead thing was big in our school. The Suedehead thing didn't last that long though. I was just aware of it being a schoolboy of 13 going on 14. I was a schoolboy 'wannabe' really. A lot of black kids weren't on it, but because I went to football, home and away with Tottenham, I just knew of it."

Geoff Deane (London): "As I remember it, it wasn't like a definite thing going from Skinhead to Suedehead. It was sort of what we are now, we are now something else. It was every fucking month, it changed a little bit. Suddenly you were looking at what you were doing six months ago and it had changed subtly.

"When it went up north, and then the Manc mugs came down with their bleached Levis, my natural instinct was to position myself as far away from that as possible. Then it started to get in the newspapers and at first you're really excited and then you're more like [groan]), and so the hair started getting grown and it became more about the suits and the blazers. Polaroid sunglasses, plain and tassel loafers, Gibson's.

"So, if you were going out in a pair of Prince of Wales trousers, loafers, a blazer with a shirt and a college tie, with a tie pin, you ain't really a Skinhead any more. Your hair is a bit longer, yeah that is kind of Suedehead. It was organic. It just moved on."

Andrew Vaughan (Orrell): "The music was still ace; the football was fun for all the right/wrong reasons but the fashion was about to go all over the place. Little did we know we had – for the last fifteen months or so – been the smartest dressed we had ever been, or would ever be! Somewhere, that period would stick with us. We were moments late for Skinhead but we celebrated our 11th and 12th birthdays with our heads easily Suede."

Paul Weller (Woking): "Funfairs were also a good place to see what new styles kids were wearing. Knitwear was popular, crew-necks (I liked Brutus crews), sleeveless jumpers (claret, dark blue and red were popular), cardies, some 'chunky' like an old man's cardy with chunky buttons and some regular knit. I had a sleeveless red cardigan, which I loved. I'd wear it with a gingham checked Brutus. Ben Shermans were a pound more than Brutus, so I'd say Brutus were more popular with kids for that reason alone. I bought my first Ben Sherman after I'd saved and bothered me mum for the rest to get it. It was a long-sleeve, lemon colour."

David Rosen (London): "The whole Suedehead thing started when the hair just got longer. It was more of a 'brush cut'. The significant moment for me was being upstairs on the bus with my mates and we're going into the West End, to the Marquee, and you feel like a million dollars because you've got your brogues on, your Ben Sherman, your Harrington, or your suit jacket, and all of a sudden, some older boys get on in the most beautiful two-tone Tonik suits from the tailor Sam Arkus, proper loafers, Fred Perry, nothing aggressive other than their energy. The aesthetic was basically Dexter Gordon on the album *One Flight Up*, when you look at his suit, or the Modern Jazz Quartet."

Bernard Jennings (Ruislip): "I don't remember the term Suedehead at the time. 'Brush cuts' is what we had, that's what we used to call them, but I think that was just an American term for something longer than a crew cut. You always wanted your hair long enough to have a parting in it. If we ever called ourselves anything in our mob, it was 'Yanko'. I'd been on holiday in Spain, I'd bought a pair of loafers out there, and the make was Yanko. So, we thought of ourselves like that. We weren't real Americans, we were Yankos. It was a particular name our little bunch used at times."

Brian Wright (London): "I identified with the Mod look, but I never identified myself with the Skinhead thing at all. When the Suedehead thing came out I let my hair grow slightly longer, for sure. I wasn't so sharp, but there were still classic things. Because of the football violence, and later the political association attached to the Skinhead look, I come from a family of lefties originally anyway, so that wouldn't have been considered appropriate. I certainly remember the term 'Suedehead' being used. There were definitely people who identified themselves as Suedeheads if they chose to, and people, in turn, would be identified by that term by others if they could see certain characteristics in their image during that very short period of time. It was a subgroup anyway, it never became a mass group."

Paul Weller (Woking): "Levis Sta-Prest were the bollocks, such great colours. I loved the white ones, bottle green, black and petrol blue, and my favourite were the ice blue colour. I even wore these to school for a bit, with white basketball boots – this must have been '71 – until I was spotted!"

Lester Owers (London): "I never got involved with the Suedehead thing, as I only had a crop once in '69, and I was more in the Ivy style, shopping almost exclusively at Austin's and the Squire shop. My last bespoke suit was 1970, a three-piece three-ply mohair with a herringbone stripe in the weave; it was blue but changed to a sort of petrol blue-green. I had all the trimmings: cash pocket, flaps on both back pockets, zip, adjustable sides, four pleats, ticket pocket handstitched. Four pockets on the waistcoat, £46.

"By the end of '71 it was moving from Squire shop/Ivy clothes to the Village Gate with the French cut, in Old Compton Street. The locals were in the old mohair, and there was me in a three-piece French-cut suit, with hair like one of The Faces [Rod Stewart's band]. The locals were the dinosaurs. It was still the divide from buying one's clothes from shops around the Soho area. I never shopped in Carnaby Street, so you always had the edge over the high street uniform types.

"As for Suedehead, I never really got involved – that is for the younger types who were stuck in a rut playing catch-up. They were still wearing the same gear, but with longer hair. The trouble was the clothes became a uniform, such as the Crombie, etc., until the early seventies, when the split came, and some got into rock and became head-bangers, Bowie fans and such. But that was down south, and not the northern soul boys.

"At the peak of Skinhead in '69 , it was *Tighten Up*, but only the diehards stuck to reggae afterwards. I was doing jazz and soul."

David Rosen (London): "I noticed a shift in '72, '73 when glam rock came in. Marc Bolan and all that, though for me the most important thing that came about was The Faces, when they stopped being The Small Faces. Everybody gradually got into a looser look, grew their hair long, but it was still 'Hippy geezers', wasn't it?"

Michael Holland (London): "The Skinhead thing didn't last long. Probably '68 to '70 when we all discovered Led Zeppelin and had to be Hippies! Unfortunately for me I had just had my hair cropped with a razor-cut parting on the day that we found out we had to grow our hair long, so it took me a bit longer than my mates! I also sold all my reggae 45s for 50 bob [£2.50], because as a kid you went for the fashion full on, no half-and-half measures – the reggae had to go. I still shed a tear over them records now!"

John 'Bomber' Wild (London): "By 1971 the term 'Suedehead' was being used. I do not really recall it being a widely used description in my area… we were using the term 'Smooth', because that's how quickly the whole Skinhead, Suedehead, Smooth youth style moved. You could be something in Manchester for example and something completely different in London, which really seemed to be setting the pace with the changes in dress code and hairstyling."

Bryan Duffy (Royton): "At the same time as people were using the term 'Suedehead', we also used the word 'Smoothie' or 'Smoovie' – both were used. A Smoothie was a lad with all the up-to-date Skinhead styles whose hair was longer – usually collar length. The hair, however, was styled, cut short at the

> "At the same time as people were using the term 'Suedehead', we also used the word 'Smoothie' or 'Smoovie' – both were used. A Smoothie was a lad with all the up-to-date Skinhead styles whose hair was longer – usually collar length. The hair, however, was styled, cut short at the front and top. It indicated a smooth dresser and had nothing to do with the style of shoes. I'm pretty sure we were using the term 'Smoothie' before the word 'Suedehead'."
> BRYAN DUFFY

287

REGGAE
REGGAE
VOL
TWO

MAIN IMAGE: ON THE STREETS, SEPTEMBER 1972
INSET LEFT: MAURO ANTONIAZZI, 1972
INSET RIGHT: MAURO ANTONIAZZI, 1972
INSET TOP: EVO, DES O'CONNOR, JOCK, TINY AND HILTON, BARRY ISLAND,
AUGUST 1970

CHANGING FASHIONS. RAY BUTTERS (SECOND FROM RIGHT IN LEFT-HAND PHOTO) AT SPANISH CITY THROUGHOUT THE YEARS

front and top. It indicated a smooth dresser and had nothing to do with the style of shoes. I'm pretty sure we were using the term 'Smoothie' before the word 'Suedehead'. Incidentally, I put the popularity of 'Saturday Night At The Movies' by The Drifters down to the fact that from early 1971, when it was played, people, mostly the girls, would sing 'Saturday night with the Smoovies'. The thing with the Drifters lyrics reminded me of another song corruption from earlier on: 'Hey Girl Don't Bother Me' by The Tams: 'Grebos [Greasers], don't bother me, Grebos, don't bother me... I'm a Skin, you'll get your head kicked in, don't bother me!'"

In 1972, Dave Collins released a 45 on the Rhino label called 'Smooths And Sorts' dedicated to these kids, 'Sorts' being the name for the girls.

Ray Butters (Whitley Bay): "We were always one beat behind the south. Whatever happened in London and the outskirts eventually travelled up north. Crombies, Ben Shermans, small turn-ups on your jeans, and little things like changing the buttons on shirts to match. Although there was a basic uniform, in every area you always had your own idiosyncrasies. North Shields was red socks.

"I think my favourite of all the styles was when we all wore suits. I couldn't buy stuff off the peg because I was so tall. I used to go to a little tailor in Blyth to get my suits made. I had my Crombie made by a tailor in Newcastle. We used to go to a cobbler in Shields who put segs in everybody's shoes. If you bought shoes, you'd immediately get segs put in, because you had to hear them when you were walking.

"All the styles constantly changed, but they all seemed to blend seamlessly. I don't know who made the decision or where it came from, but one day somebody would turn up with something like a star jumper on, and the next day we would all have star jumpers. We would buy Sabre jumpers in very bright colours. I loved them, they just looked so good. They were quite expensive, 100 per cent wool."

Andrew Vaughan (Orrell): "Winter, however, was when we came into our own as it gave us a chance to wear that magnificent Crombie overcoat that we all owned. Now Crombie is an old English tailoring firm and to buy a proper Crombie overcoat would today cost you something like £800. Needless to say, ours cost much, much less, and were bought like all our clothes from Slater's menswear shop in the Makinson Arcade. The Crombie we had was a black or navy woollen overcoat, single-breasted, that rested on the knee. The buttons were concealed, the pockets slanted and the breast pocket would often be adorned with a red handkerchief to match the lining. In Wigan we also would sew a Lancashire red rose badge onto the breast pocket."

Paul Weller (Woking): "I can remember going up to Petticoat Lane with my folks on a Sunday. That's where I got a Crombie, not a real one, but a snide one, and a pair of Prince of Wales trousers, which I loved. Most people were wearing loafers by now, though they were hard to find in Woking. Then I heard about Dazzles, which was a little semi-detached house just near the station. There was a side door you went in, and inside were boxes and boxes of shoes, and some clothes. That's where I got my Frank Wright loafers; you paid a few bob a

week until it was paid off. On a Saturday morning it was fucking heaving with kids all after the same shoes! I never really liked the clumpy look of Frank Wright loafers. I'd seen older lads wearing loafers and they were much more streamlined but I never knew where to get them, Royals maybe. I remember following this older kid around school 'cos I'd spotted his fringe and buckle loafers. Oh my God! I wanted those shoes! I couldn't ask where he got them 'cos he would have fucked me off, probably a slap or two, nasty cunt he was."

Austin Myers (Shipley): "It was more comfortable when the Suedehead era came along. A lot of the guys thought that they'd done the Skinhead thing and were moving on. So, they decided to grow their hair a little bit and stop the shaved parting business. Then the Crombie-style coats came in. People were walking around in these coats around Bradford and that area. It was unheard-of to see former street urchins become as well dressed as the men that were running the businesses in the city. Everything kind of sharpened up and there were retail outlets getting a lot wiser too in the Bradford and Leeds areas.

"There was a main shop in Shipley, the town where I came from, called Henry Smith's in Commercial Street. We told him what he needed to start selling. He went and got Brutus, Jaytex and Ben Sherman shirts. He got the Levi Tonik parallels as opposed to the tapered two-tone Sta-Prest. He realised he was on to a winner, because the Skinhead look, going on to the Suedehead look, had started to grow in a town with a population of around 25,000 at the time. It became one of the main outlets for our look. Then there was Kirkgate market in Bradford where you could buy Harringtons and Peter Brunskill's where we bought our sheepskin coats. You could buy all the types of footwear from Industrial Footwear in Thornton Road, where they also did loafers, Dr Martens boots, Royal and plain-cap brogues. Fantastic places that we had access to, to get good clobber. It was amazing because we were behind London and bigger cities but we weren't that far behind because we had guys who were following Leeds United, Chelsea and West Ham United who regularly went backwards and forwards from the north to the south, which, back in the day, was quite unusual. So, we were seeing everyday fashion in London when we visited the likes of Chelsea, West Ham or Tottenham. There was a similar thing with Newcastle United, even though we were arch-rivals – the town I lived in had an affinity with both Leeds and Newcastle. We had good friends in both camps. So, the Suedehead thing got very popular. We weren't sneered at and seen as problems. We were seen as smart guys. It still wasn't very well received, because it was another uniform, but it was a uniform that people were more prepared to accept after the Skinhead look. To me, the perfect look was a pork pie-style hat, a good-quality Ben Sherman shirt or an Arnold Palmer, a genuine Crombie overcoat, a stud holding what we would call 'a wipe' in the pocket, two-tone petrol blue Sta-Prest, red socks and plain-cap Royals."

Clive Knight (London): "It all started to peter out for me in 1971. I left an all-boys secondary modern school in north London to do A-levels at a co-ed college in Harrow. Girls! Enough said. Yes, going to college was a bit of a watershed. Loads of Hippy types there so I started being exposed to their music. Interestingly enough, hindsight has shown that the music of theirs that I liked had its origins in R&B.

"It was after we moved away from the Skinhead scene that we came across the term Suedehead. However, even though we wore our hair longer than most of the lads, we still considered ourselves Skins. I loved that period of time. For sure, there was always a bit of aggro waiting round the corner but if you stayed in the areas you knew, or you at least knew lads from that area, you were pretty safe. And knife crime was virtually non-existent."

Norman Jay MBE (London): "By 1970/'71 we were all wearing knock-off Crombies, as no one I knew could afford the real ones. Market Crombies they were. We bought our DMs in Blackmans in Cheshire Street. We would be shit scared of going there though, because those areas would be so territorial back then. We only ever had any racial trouble when we went off our manor. If we went somewhere like Harrow, a couple of black boys on our own… we'd get legged by every white kid we saw.

"All my mates were Chelsea and I was Tottenham, so there was no way we were going into a West Ham area, no fucking way! It took us weeks to muster up the courage. We'd get on the train at Acton, the old Broad Street station, and get off at Liverpool Street. We used to stay away from all the pubs, you know on a Sunday morning, because every now and then you'd see a little firm. In truth, they weren't going to do anything to us, because we were little kids, but you know, you're fearful. Anyway, we braved it to go down there and I got my first DMs in 1970."

Phillip Ellisdon (Watford): "We went into London in 1970 and saw all these guys from West Ham with long hair, large wool checked suits, paisley shirts with long collars. They wore moon shoes, a Dr Martens-type shoe, and flares! It was not long before we all followed suit. The Skinhead era was dying and the East End was again setting the trend. It was not long before everyone started to grow their hair long and wear different clothes, and the Suedehead era was emerging.

"We never identified with Suedeheads like we did Skinheads, we never called ourselves that, we were still Skinheads but with long hair. Even now we are all still Skinheads in our minds – it was a great period, that was our era."

GIRLS DANCING, LADY GOMM 1970

John 'Bomber' Wild (London): "I recall at football matches the changing and different styles of clothing being worn. I stood on the Loft terrace at QPR once, chatting to a lad from Sunderland, who was stood the other side of the dividing railings. He proudly remarked on his Prince of Wales check Harrington jacket that he was wearing, and I was sporting a new Crombie-style overcoat. 'Harrington's are out now down here mate, it's Crombies,' I recall saying. It was all interesting and friendly banter. Even in the earlier days of '69/'70 when clubs from up north visited London, while we were wearing full-on Skinhead clobber, a lot of these older northern fans still had longer Hippy hairstyles and double denim."

Norman Jay MBE (London): "I would do a paper round and save most of my dinner money, and starve all week, just so I could afford to go to football [Tottenham]. I remember going up to West Brom for my first away game, December 12th, 1970, and we lost 3-1, with Tony 'Bomber' Brown getting a hat-trick, and at half time they were played the fucking 'Liquidator'.

"Three years later I go up to Wolves, first time I'd been to Wolves. It was the first leg of what was then the UEFA cup, a Thursday-night game. We won 2-1 up there, took thousands, got to be 20,000 up there, we all bunked off school, everyone went, it was the most unbelievable day.

"I got the hiding of my life when I got back though. We didn't get back till three o'clock in the morning. Again, half-time, they played 'Liquidator'. All their lot were Skinheads and all our lot just weren't any more. Yeah, we had boots, but also jungle greens, and, because a lot of our mob were working for the council, donkey jackets."

Lorraine Le-Bas (Southampton): "I went through the Skinhead, going into Suedehead look, then grew my hair before getting a feather cut again. We used to wear all the clothes, and me and my mates used to go to the Top Rank in Banister Road on a Tuesday, to go dancing to reggae and soul.

"There were two boutiques in Southampton at the time. One was Tammy Girl, which you only went into if you were broke, really, because the clothes were crap. The other one was across the road, and called Snob. When that opened up it was a bit more upmarket. I thought I've really got to have a Crombie now, so I went in and had a look. They had the cheaper range Crombies, and I thought, well I can afford them, but I ended up looking at the dearer ones. I thought that the only way I am going to get one of these is if I can get around my mum. She was brilliant with a needle, and she used to make a lot of my clothes anyway. I'd get the patterns for these dresses, and she'd say, 'Oh my God, is that all you want darlin'? I can make them.' So, she used to save me an awful lot of money. Anyway, I took her into Snob, and luckily Christmas was on the way, so she agreed. I brought the coat out of the changing room, and had my fingers crossed that she wouldn't look at the price tag. She said, 'I don't bloody believe it! If I took you to a shop and told you that's the coat you've got to have, you'd have said, "Never in a mad fit am I going to wear that, Mum, it's bloody awful!" For once, you've actually chosen a sensible coat!' It was hilarious, she didn't even look at the price tag. She had a good look over it and didn't think it was badly made."

"The headmistress at the time allowed us to wear our Crombies to school – uniform was very strict back then – as she thought they looked very smart. You would also find a copy of *Skinhead* by Richard Allen in many a satchel!"
MAGGIE BROWN

CROMBIE

Something to get excited about

Anna from 26 gns.

seal of SUEDECRAFT quality

LORI AND JANE WITH FRIENDS, LLORET DE MAR, 1972

Paul Weller: "Woking Football Club was amazing! Not 'cos it was cutting edge or trendy but because for me it helped open up a whole world of sounds and clothes, style and friendships. Most of those things have endured too. It was my first awakening to real style."

1. I'M GONNA RUN AWAY FROM YOU
Tami Lynn - (Atlantic) 1965

2. 54-46 WAS MY NUMBER
Toots & The Maytals - (Trojan) 1970

3. GIVE ME JUST A LITTLE MORE TIME
Chairmen of The Board - (Invictus) 1970

4. THE LIQUIDATOR
Harry J. All Stars - (Harry J) 1969

5. DOUBLE BARREL
Dave & Ansil Collins - (Maxi Trojan) 1970

6. GET UP, I FEEL LIKE BEING A SEX MACHINE
James Brown - (Polydor) 1970

7. SIGNED, SEALED, DELIVERED I'M YOURS
Stevie Wonder - (Tamla Motown) 1970

8. I HEARD IT THROUGH THE GRAPEVINE
Marvin Gaye - (Tamla Motown) 1969

9. BAD WEATHER
The Supremes - (Tamla Motown) 1973

10. I'M STILL WAITING
Diana Ross - (Tamla Motown) 1971

11. CHAIRMEN OF THE BOARD
Chairmen Of The Board - (Invictus) 1971

12. BIG FIVE
Prince Buster - (Prince Buster) 1970

13. WET DREAM
Max Romeo - (Unity) 1968

14. BAND OF GOLD
Freda Payne - (Invictus) 1970

15. THE HARDER THEY COME
Jimmy Cliff - (Island) 1972

1   2   3

4   5   6

7   8   9

10   11   12

13   14   15

G FOOTBALL CLUB DISCO FAVES '69-'73

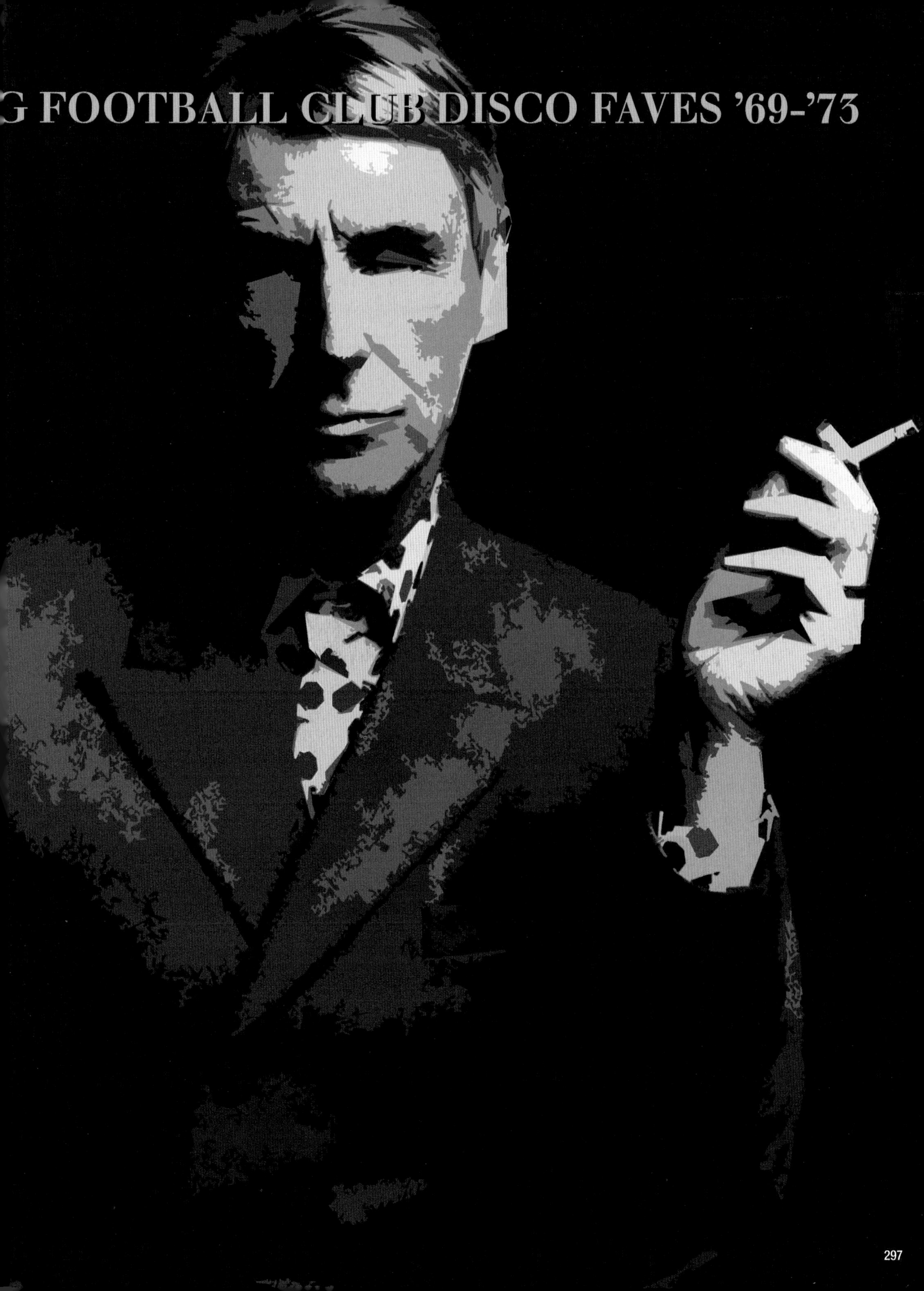

> "We were called 'Tasty Geezers' but it was just Smoothies when we started wearing two-tone suits, Sabre jumpers and loafers. After a while it became all about trying to look good, and impressing the girls. We kind of outgrew the violent aggro side of it and it became more about let's see how good we can look. We need to look better than you."
>
> RAY BUTTERS

Shoes by
TOPPER
BRITISH AND CONTINENTAL
SHOE AND SUEDE SPECIALISTS

57 SHAFTESBURY AVENUE, LONDON, W.1   GERRARD 2329
34 COVENTRY STREET, LONDON, W.1   GERRARD 2329
60 QUEENSWAY, LONDON, W.2   BAYSWATER 2615

Maggie Brown (Winchester): "A lot of the girls at my school, Danemark School for Girls in Winchester, started dressing in Tonik suits, Crombies with a silk hanky and a tie tack in the top pocket, you know, the usual… Ben Shermans, Brutus, Jaytex shirts, Fred Perry. Tonik dresses were a favourite, especially the 'keyhole' dress… so smart! I bought mine from Snob in Southampton – green and brown Tonik. I remember thinking I was the bee's knees as I hadn't seen anyone else in Winchester wearing one. There was a club in Winchester called the Copacabana where all the teenagers went. I remember wearing it that night and a mate of mine called Sharon had also bought one that very same day in blue and gold Tonik, champagne Tonik, I think they called it. We both thought we were the very first one in Winchester to wear this style of dress on that Saturday night way back in the early seventies, but we just found it amusing and complimented each other on our excellent taste!

"The headmistress at the time allowed us to wear our Crombies to school – uniform was very strict back then – as she thought they looked very smart. You would also find a copy of *Skinhead* by Richard Allen in many a satchel!

"Other favourites were Trevira coat-dresses, also worn with a silk hanky and a tie tack in the top pocket, or Tonik skirts. Coat-dresses were great as you could wear them as a dress or over the top of a Tonik skirt and shirt as a coat. Trevira and Tonik pinafore dresses were also popular with the girls and we would wear a Ben Sherman or checked shirt underneath them or a Fred Perry.

"There was a shop in Winchester called Posner. It was a bit old-fashioned but they always had a very good selection of Trevira coats, dresses and skirts, some Tonik and some just plain – petrol blue was a favourite colour with a lot of girls as I recall. Prince of Wales check and dogtooth check was another popular look, as was the velvet-collared Crombie. We also wore long knee-length cardigans which usually had a cable pattern at the front and pockets. Long knee-length waistcoats were also popular with the girls.

"I also remember diamante star brooches and little bunches of fruit brooches being worn by girls, who pinned them to their Crombie collar, both of which I had and wish I had kept! Shoes were usually loafers or a similar loafer style; I also remember having a pair of low-heeled black patent lace-up shoes with squared toes – I loved them! A lot of the girls' shopping would probably be done at Snob or Chelsea Girl and Dolcis, Manfield or Freeman, Hardy & Willis for shoes (Ravel if you could afford it back then) to name but a few. Everyone wore Brut, the original small glass bottle which came in a light brown box. Both boys and girls wore it. The fragrance was different to the later Brut [33] that came on the market; I swear it smelled much sweeter, from what I can remember."

Paul Weller (Woking): "I loved the way the girls dressed, a very sexy look. I never saw any girls wearing DM boots. They would wear Levis jeans but with clumpy-heeled shoes mainly from Ravels, I think. Their make-up was stunning too, very pale lips and heavy make-up and long lashes. Feather cuts were big, cut fairly short on top (but not cropped) and longer sides and back. The white Holy Cow tights with

Trevira suits were fab too. Keyhole dresses, sleeveless and above the knee with a matching long jacket – petrol blue and green were popular colours. Girls would also wear Crombies. Tight cropped sweaters were very cool too. I think some were in Angora wool, kinda fluffy. Later on, smock dresses came in again, a great look. Everyone wore Brut perfume, girls and boys."

Ian Hingle (London): "I grew my hair and became a Suedehead. It wasn't called that then, though to be fair it wasn't that long after. You'd get blokes like me wearing mohair trousers with two pleats, and a narrow bottom and always too short. And wingtips and an American shirt, never a Ben Sherman. Suedeheads were just better dressed, really. Shoes and trousers as opposed to jeans and boots. Skinheads would have worn what you would call basically work wear, and they were up for a punch-up. You didn't really want to have a ruck with a suit on.

"I was fascinated with the roll of a collar, so soft, and we'd wear a tie undone, like Frank Sinatra, well that was the idea."

Sharon Williams (London): "I suppose I went Suedehead at 15 – well, I certainly wore a lot of suede! Shoes, skirts and a lovely suede coat. Never seen without my Holy Cow tights back then, white they were with holes down the side. I also had a pair of oxblood shoes, which had yellow laces, which I adored. I shopped mainly in East Lane or Petticoat Lane, though I also loved Ravels on Tower Bridge Road and I would have got my camel suede shoes from there."

Bryan Duffy (Royton): "In reality a number of people started to grow their hair as 1971 went by, and by that summer it was possible to see gangs of lads with this style, a sort of college-boy, Skinhead crops just growing out and collar-length hair. This was certainly the case in Royton at that time. So, Skinheads, Suedeheads and Smoothies together, all wearing the same types of clothes, only the hair styles different. What happened was, during 1971 most people started to grow their hair and the true 'Skinhead' look faded out – a crop was not a common sight by that autumn. It was not unusual for someone to have been a Skinhead in January 1971, to be Suedehead by that autumn and a Smoothie by Christmas! Late summer/early autumn, first red socks then Crombie overcoats started to be worn. They became very popular and indicated a slight change in style to Suedehead. The novel *Suedehead* was familiar to us all by this stage, and the clothes worn pretty accurate – our hair, though, generally was a bit shorter at that time."

Ray Butters (Whitley Bay): "We were called 'Tasty Geezers' but it was just Smoothies when we started wearing two-tone suits, Sabre jumpers and loafers. After a while it became all about trying to look good, and impressing the girls. We kind of outgrew the violent aggro side of it and it became more about let's see how good we can look. We need to look better than you."

Jacky Abramovitch (London): "Suedeheads to me were more like the Mods who didn't go the whole way as a Skinhead, so sort of jumped from Mod to Suedehead and missed out being a Skinhead. Maybe they were slightly softer and not associated with any of the racist stuff.

I remember the Union Jack appearing a lot around that. Back then we would all say, without realising it was remotely rude or offensive, 'Let's get it at the Paki shop.' I mean our little group didn't do Paki-bashing; I don't remember any of that. Actually, we had a friend Glen who was Indian. Where we lived at the time in East Ham, there wasn't anybody there who wasn't working-class white. Then we started seeing all the press reports in the papers on the Paki-bashing and my parents were pretty horrified, because they thought I was going to get in trouble. I think that is when it really broke up. It just wasn't political."

Bonny Staplehurst (London): "I started work at 15, so I started to let the Skinhead thing go, and never really got involved in the Suedehead thing. Once I let it go, I stopped wearing the Skinhead clothes and got into this French look. That was the influence really of my sister Janet. My mum took us to the cinema every Tuesday and Audrey Hepburn was a favourite, so we picked up on that sort of classic look and that filtered in. We used to wear a kilt, Shetland sweaters from Lafayette down Regent Street. You used to have to have a navy jumper, a cardigan. That was the ultimate. We also liked Biba and I loved Bus Stop, for the shoes. Our mum used to take us abroad. We'd go to Italy, and we did really well with shoes in Trieste. We'd try and get loafers. We also got some leather jackets and I had to wear three at the same time to get through customs. Whenever we'd go abroad, we'd take a box of singles and our Dansette with us. Always.

"Over here, we used to go to Ravels, though we knew it as Studios. We loved brogues and loafers. Because we are tall, we always liked lower shoes, you know, flat shoes. Russell & Bromley were good too. We loved shopping, always liked clothes, fashion, style. Our mum would always get us a new outfit for Easter, Christmas and that, so most of our clothes came from that. I thought we were quite boring, because we never really changed styles too much, but other people call it classic, so more style than fashion. My dad had a paper stall, so we would get every magazine going at home and when we was really young, we'd be reading those. We'd also get a load of knock-off stuff coming through the flat. Dad would get a suitcase, a sort of lucky dip 'cos you didn't know what was in there. He'd give a tenner for it, and most times it would be full of clothes. Funnily enough, a lot of French clothes, Daniel Hechter sweaters and that. Sometimes there might be nothing in it. Once we got a parcel full of shoes, lovely stuff, but none of them fitted us. Very *Fools And Horses*."

John 'Bomber' Wild (London): "From 1971 to 1973 I was still in the last knockings of school. Entertainment was the local dance held in a community centre, youth clubs and the occasional attempt to gain access to a local discotheque called the Birds Nest, a chain of clubs around west London and on the outskirts. The Birds Nest had a very space-age interior, all silver chrome and purple, and the dance floor was made of steel. There were seating booths around the club, plush leather, and the tables adorned with telephones to dial other tables to chat up the opposite sex. On the occasions I dodged the doorman as an underage punter, the phones never seemed to work. But just gaining entrance was good enough for me.

"The music was usually what I would class as club/chart soul, lot of Motown and Stax. Al Green, Donnie Elbert were popular too. A lot of these places had a dress-code policy, always a shirt, sometimes with a tie. Most lads would always carry a spare neck tie just in case.

"Most of our access to dances at this time would be the local community-centre dances where a mobile disco would set up a regular club night; there were quite a few in Slough where I was now living after a move out of London… my favourite was called Jessica's. Jessica's was run in a village-type hall, a high-beamed ceiling and a stage at one end where the DJ set up his rig. They would project lighting around the walls which was usually moving bubbles, it was all very psychedelic-looking. Then, they would run old movies on the walls, any old crap really, a fifties Western, or a dodgy kung fu film, but it was all very effective.

"It was a time to adopt your best Smoothie clobber, tonic trousers, topped with a window-pane check Jaytex shirt. A crew-neck Shetland sweater by Sabre finished the look

"I would say the music was far less serious at these nights; a selection of chart soul and reggae, and glam rock. Our estate was plagued with druggies at the time, a lot of them were teenagers, and occasionally they would turn up and cause trouble and all hell would break loose. On one occasion a guy turned up with a horsewhip and proceeded to belt people with it. A mass brawl followed.

"The pinnacle at this time would be to gain access to Hammersmith Palais De Dance, a large ballroom in Hammersmith that ran a disco night on a Thursday. The Palais was the place where people dressed well, and were right on the button with their clobber and knew a few new dances. To gain access, me and a friend, Terry, convinced his older cousin and her friend to accompany us, just so we could get past the doormen to gain entrance, as it was always easier to get in as a couple. The bonus was the fact that these girls were about two years older than us, and were previously two of the coolest and smartest Skinhead girls on our estate, and they had a car, a Mini."

Norman Jay MBE (London): "*Clockwork Orange* came out during the Suede era. I saw bowler hats on the terraces. Firms also started to spray their boots. I sprayed my boots silver. I remember going up to Sheffield United that year and they were all red and the Sheffield Wednesday skins were all blue. Northerners had it all wrong though. A lot them were still Rockers and northern soulers, but most of the white kids I knew then, and I'm talking 1970/'71, were getting into Bowie, starting to grow their hair and get into the early glam thing."

Ian Hingle (London): "Someone who really captured that look then was Alan Hudson, the Chelsea footballer. Him and Charlie George, Steve Kember. I mean George was a scruffy fucker really, but I still loved the way he looked, he looked fantastic. A sort of Chelsea look. Wide-lapel jackets and penny round collars.

"The early seventies was a funny time then, as I was 23 and a little bit old for all that really, if you can believe it. I mean that sounds strange saying that, when here I am nearly 70 and still going out dancing, but anyway, back then we'd go to the Birds Nest on a Thursday and a Sunday. On the Thursday, he'd play The Faces, Gary Glitter, even though you can't mention *him* any more, James Brown, a real mixture. It didn't matter what genre back then. We'd used to go to the Wheatsheaf beforehand back then on a Thursday, and I had longish hair. Now my hair was pretty curly, so I used to have to straighten it and then I'd walk in a place wearing a Shetland crew-neck, with no air con, and within ten seconds, I'd look like Jimi Hendrix!"

Maggie Brown (Winchester): "As time went on the look for girls became a little more feminine. Little smock dresses worn over hot pants – well, more like little shorts than the tighter hot pants that a lot of girls wore back in the seventies – was quite a good look which was classier, in my eyes. Little mini ribbed cardigans and jumpers, checked A-line miniskirts, full-sleeved crêpe de chine blouses and more feminine shoes. The whole look became a bit 'softer' when Suedeheads came in but there was still that element of smartness there and you could tell that it evolved from the Skinhead era. Boys started growing their hair a bit more and shirt collars became more rounded – penny collars I think they called them. Tank tops and more brightly coloured shirts came into fashion. Crombies were still being worn with Tonik trousers by the boys. They all seemed to carry black brollies around with them, to complete the 'look' I suppose. I would say by the mid-seventies a lot of it began to fade when glam rock came along! Even the boys started wearing platform shoes."

Paul Weller (Woking): "After the Brutus checks and ginghams, and the Ben Shermans, shirts started to change. The penny round and beagle collar shirts came in, some plain, some patterned. I had a dark blue beagle collar made by Brutus, I don't remember Ben Sherman getting into this style? One of these shirts with a Fair Isle sleeveless jumper looked great and later on the knitted tank tops which looked great too. I had a black one with a red star on it. Crombies still held sway but I think a sheepskin would have been the ultimate Skin/Suede coat, well out of the younger kids' reach though. I also loved the fly front, dark blue rain macs too, probably Aquascutum though I never had one at the time.

"Then came roll-neck jumpers and Budgie jackets; a certain softening of the styles, less rigid I guess. Feather cuts, trousers got bigger and in mad checks, shoes got clumpier and platform sole shoes, probably where I bowed out. I got seriously into music and went the more trendy route with Oxford bags and clogs! Which fucking crippled my feet trying to get them to stay on! A few of my mates carried on and became, I suppose, 'Soul Boys'. They lived for dancing and the music, Philly, early disco, etc., and clothes still. By now I was wearing cheesecloth shirts and had a pair of red tartan loons and swapped my Brutus for patchouli oil and smoked dope."

Geoff Deane (London): "I went to Rimini with my mate Neil around then, and we saw these shoes and they had big built-up toes with stitching down the middle and a side buckle.

And there was nothing like 'em in Ravels, or England! And we're both like 'Fuck it' and we spent all our holiday money on these shoes. Toppers in the UK eventually brought them over.

"We came back to wearing Fair Isles, and the shirts had a butterfly collar, patchwork shirts from CCS, even trousers with a slight flare from a shop called Carvil, which was a little bit the Squire shop and it's something completely different again and you are starting to morph into the whole Budgie thing, late '71/'72, and then into The Faces, Rod and them… Another shop I really rated was Take Six, great for your working-class boys and it wasn't mentally dear – it really was our bread and butter. It never really finished for me though, the clothes buying.

"You know you can't explain what it was like back then. Today, there are no secrets any more; it's impossible to have a secret. Any shop, any musician, anything art-based. It's out there on social media or in a newspaper or Sunday supplement. It wasn't like that then. So, it grew and you had to sneak about."

Norman Jay MBE (London): "I personally didn't get any clothes made until I left school and got my first job in 1974, and by then all the black guys would get high-waister trousers, with a different colour waistband. We used to wear them with Toppers shoes. The tailor was out of Shepherd's Bush market. The cuts were ready in a week and he was as good as any East End Jewish tailor, let me tell you. All the black guys I knew would go there. By then I was a serious clubber, a wannabe football hooligan and a hustler. I did everything to get money to feed my clothes habit, my record-buying habit and my football."

Bryan Duffy (Royton): "As we got into 1972 hair was getting longer and by that summer the whole thing was pretty much over as people started to wear penny round beagle collars, tank tops, stack-heeled shoes, bags, glam rock-inspired clothes, particularly Slade – stuff all sorts of kids wore. In 1970 we all had pretty much the same hairstyle and were easily identifiable as Skinheads by that and our clothes. This could not be said by mid '72 as all sorts of people wore all sorts of clothes.

"Funny thing is, Suedehead should have been the pinnacle for me. I was 17, had the clothes, the whole look and could get out and about more than that 15-year-old Skinhead. Suedehead was a great look for school – you could wear the whole lot! There were certainly some advantages to this – for a start I appeared to be more attractive to a certain type of girl. 'Get out with Barbara, you. You know she fancies you,' and, from one of the West Indian girls I sat next to in one class, 'Hey, Bryan, my sister got her eye on you, she tink you a reel tasty geeza' – these things never happened to me as a young Skinhead! The truth was, though, Suedehead never quite had the edge to it that I had enjoyed as a Skinhead. There was something about it, you felt part of something. By the Suedehead era, I had realised it was all just an ever-changing fashion."

Clive Knight (London): "We had to rely on public transport, the tube, to get about. When the first car came on the scene, around 1972, we spread our wings north to Hemel Hempstead and Watford and south to Croydon and Purley. By then most had dropped reggae and ska and were playing soul from the Dramatics or The Delphonics and the Motown stable, plus American imports from Contempo Records just off Oxford Street.

"And last but not least, the ubiquitous Birds Nests [Chelsea, West Kensington, Waterloo, Muswell Hill, South Harrow and West Hampstead]. I met my wife at the Muswell Hill Birds Nest!

"That period 1971 to 1973 was a real shift in music tastes and fashion styles – remember Ziggy Stardust, and Roxy Music's first album came on the scene in 1972."

Geoff Deane (London): "You'd be walking around and always see one bloke and think, 'What's he wearing?' There was one bloke called Queenie who was always *just* on point, and ahead of what you were doing. In fact, he was still way ahead when I was doing the Bowie thing. I remember seeing him at Bowie at the Rainbow and he walked in and looked fucking better than Bowie did. 'How the fuck have you done that?' He definitely came from the same Skinhead background, so he had followed the same trail as I had. He was leading it all really. Every time you saw him, the barnet was different. A different colour, a different length… what the fuck… we were always that one step behind."

People had moved on musically too. In the main, reggae music was the domain of black people. At the height of the Skinhead movement white kids would happily brave the rather menacing environments of places such as the Ram Jam Club or the A Train. They happily spoke in mimicked phrases, using Jamaican patois such as 'rass', 'pum pum' and 'pussy clot'.

The alienation came when reggae music started to move away from the 'Skinhead reggae' fascination of guns and girls, and became more directed at the Rastafarian culture.

'Babylon' and 'Zion' didn't relate to any white kids living on a council estate. Biblical references and praising Jamaican heroes brought blank looks, and the kids who had smirked while dancing to Max Romeo's 'Wet Dream' found themselves standing at the side of the dance floor. 'Skinhead Train' by Laurel Aitken had been an anthem to sing along to, but they certainly didn't join in when he sang, "Emperor Haile Selassie, the conquering lion of Judah".

Suedehead would fade too, and the terraces and youth clubs would attract a far rougher and readier breed, that lacked style, but kept the basics: 'Boot Boys'. They would have to find a new soundtrack, and it was predominantly white music.

In the late sixties there'd been a band called Neat Change that played around Hounslow doing heavy Motown numbers. They'd started off as Mods but adopted a much more Skinhead look.

But the best known white band were Slade from Wolverhampton. They'd appeared on the cover of *Disc And Music Echo* magazine on October 11th, 1969 with the line 'Skinheads launched on record!' but the music, 'Wild Winds Are Blowing', was hardly dance music. They'd gone through various name changes, such as The In Betweens and Ambrose Slade, before settling on just Slade. Of course, the image didn't last long and they would soon find fame and stardom through their 'glam' phase. Other bands that had flirted with the look were The Hammersmith Gorillas and The Jook.

Noddy Holder's single concession to Slade's bygone 'Skinhead' image are his boots. Gone is the rest of the uniform – the super-crewcut 'barnet', regulation braces, the aggressive attitude; replaced in turn by shoulder-length locks, red velvet jacket and a softly-spoken, almost apologetic air.

But he still sports the infamous 'bovver' boots. Though now they are more fashionable than functional. A deep red in colour, wet-look in style, and highly polished to make a regimental sergeant-major's heart proud.

This aside, Slade are certainly 'Skinhead' no more.
DISC AND MUSIC ECHO, NOVEMBER 13TH, 1971.

"Everyone made an effort to dress up then – it was an amazing style and more varied than what its popular image has become. I never saw any bare heads, skin-tight jeans and high-leg DMs; it wasn't like that at all! It was extremely smart and had no politics or philosophy beyond great clothes and great music."
PAUL WELLER

By 1973, the Boot Boys were more likely to be dancing and singing along to Elton John's 'Saturday Night's Alright For Fighting', which contained the line "My sister looks cute in her braces and boots", than they were skanking to 'Stir It Up' by Bob Marley & The Wailers.

Ian Hingle (London): "Looking back on it, though Skinhead was very popular, there was probably no more than a few hundred really smart dressers. Most people then were just wearing the clothes of the day really, but the best ones were different. They just looked different."

Pete Schaffert (Kent): "In the early seventies, reggae was almost non-existent on the radio apart from the hits, invariably with overdubbed strings for the UK market. Still, I do recall being on a school trip and getting the coach driver to 'crank it up' when 'Pied Piper' by Bob & Marcia came on the radio. So, it would be the youth clubs and funfairs that would play the stuff you really wanted to hear. I-Roy's 'Hot Bomb' and Greyhound's 'Sky High' were *big* tunes in the clubs in '72. Dreamland in Margate was a great place to go to hear tunes played at a seriously loud volume."

Penny Reel (London): "I bought records in Portobello Road from a guy selling second-hand stuff. He had a million Island label records. I got them for ten pence each. Mint Wailers tunes, you know, that now sell for £1,000. That's where I got most of my music from. Me and Steve Barrow went to this shop, and virtually cleared it out. I mean, we left a load behind, but we bought thousands of records there. By the time we bought most of them, they'd gone down to five pence each. There was Island, Blue Beat, Rio, Doctor Bird, Treasure Isle, Blue Cat, R&B, Ska Beat… they were all there.

"In 1972, Tesco's bought up all the old Pama stock, so Tesco shops throughout the country were selling them for three pence each. They'd bought a million records from Pama to distribute amongst their shops, and this included all the stuff that Pama released such as Camel and Bullet labels. I never went there though. Later on, in '77, Keith from Daddy Kool bought a million records from Pama, so I eventually got them from him. I used to sort out his stock, and get them boxed up, and he'd give me free records and said, 'Take what you want.'

"In 1975, I got all my Prince Buster stuff such as 'Barrister, Pardon', 'Ten Commandments Of Man' on Blue Beat, plus his FAB and Prince Buster label stuff from a shop a couple of doors down from Dub Vendor. They were all a penny each. They had all these Blue Beat singles and originally sold them for three shillings each. They must have made a profit, but had loads more to sell. In the end, you could buy 100 for a quid. I walked to Clapham from Notting Hill, and spent two quid there to get 200 records. Nobody else was buying them at the time!"

Pete Schaffert (Kent): "When I moved to Newbury in about 1972, I met three or four fellow reggae fanatics and went to more clubs and gigs. My first gig was Desmond Dekker live in Thatcham, 1973 I reckon, and meeting him after the gig and getting a signed photo was the icing on the cake. I had a couple of jobs while at school at this time, so had a fair amount of spare cash. This meant I was able to buy more 45s as well as the LPs… Most people had stopped wearing

the clothing by this time, but I still wore Ben Shermans, Fred Perrys and Levis, and still do to this day."

Paul Weller (Woking): "Everyone made an effort to dress up then – it was an amazing style and more varied than what its popular image has become. I never saw any bare heads, skin-tight jeans and high-leg DMs; it wasn't like that at all! It was extremely smart and had no politics or philosophy beyond great clothes and great music."

Andrew Vaughan (Orrell): "So how long did this Suedehead thing last? I can't really remember as the clothes all got a bit daft as the button-downs gave way to penny round, pear-shaped collar shirts, the Toniks turned electric and petrol blue while everyone slowly began growing their hair into feather cuts and the Skinners white jeans and Flemings jeans we were all sporting got wider and wider. It was, however, great while it lasted – two years, maybe three. But of course, it didn't last only that long. It kept going and it's still going and that why Slater's Menswear in the late sixties/early seventies was as important and influential to me, to us, as was Woodhouse in the late seventies/early eighties and how important John Simons is to us now we are old men."

Clive Knight (London): "Today, if you were to see me walking down the road, and you knew what you were looking for, you would see more than a little whiff of Skinhead about me. I still wear Fred Perrys, and button-downs shirts, but have put on a bit of timber over the years so find the American brands of Gant, Orvis and Ralph Lauren offer good checked button-downs that fit the fuller man.

"I still have a pair of oxblood American Royal brogues; the Americans call them long wings. I also have oxblood Smoothies by Church's, which some used to call plain-caps. Four years ago I was in Baltimore and managed to pick up two pairs of Bass Weejun fringe and tassel loafers, black and – yes! – oxblood. I wear Tootal scarves. I have a Duffers top coat modelled on the Crombie and wear a ridiculously extortionate Baracuta G9 jacket. I also bought a bunch of Banana Republic chinos on a previous visit to the States, which are my Sta-Prest substitutes.

"Is my mission finished?

"No. I still hanker for a pair of Gibsons similar to those that I bought from the Squire shop. They are the shoes I am wearing in the photos you've got of me. I honestly cannot remember how much I paid for them but I do recall my dad having a fit when I told him. I think I spent more on those shoes than he earned in a week. He mumbled something about 'The lad's got more money than sense' and walked out of the room!"

David Rosen (London): "For me, if I had to describe Suedehead to someone who has never heard of it, I'd say it was a less aggressive part of Skinhead. It was even more about the birds, the clothes, the music, a real nice style, rather than kicking someone's head in.

"In truth, it all goes back to a Mod spirit."

TOP: DAVE ROSEN, LONDON 1970
MIDDLE: STEVE SMITH, TONY HADDOW AND GIRLS,
SPRING 1969
BOTTOM: PHIL ELLISDON AND HIS FORD ANGLIA WITH
ROSTYLE WHEELS AND BLACK WINDOWS, 1972

Thanks to all those mentioned in the Acknowledgements for the photos throughout.

Other credits:

Bruce Fleming: 22–3
Gered Mankowitz © Bowstir Ltd 2021/Mankowitz.com: 36
Hulton-Deutsch Collection/CORBIS/Corbis via Getty: 166
Mirrorpix: 14, 17–9, 32, 84–6, 119–21, 133, 144, 147–9, 168–71, 175, 177, 190–2, 194, 198–201, 203, 206, 208, 210, 220, 225, 236, 275, 288
Neil Kenlock: 104, 117
Phil Dias: 108–9, 112–3
Red Saunders: 98
Reg Lancaster/Express/Hulton Archive/Getty: 152
Sheila Rock/Shutterstock: 6
Tony Othen www.bedehouse.org: 94, 225, 256–7
TV Times/Future Publishing Ltd: 2–5, 180–5
Endpapers pictures from the scrapbook collection of
Bob Wheeler and Coleen Wheeler, 1969 - 74

SAVE THE LAST DANCE FOR ME, CAXTON CLUB 1969